Lady Underground's Gift

Liberating The Soul Within Us

by
Eileen H. Simon, D.Min.

CHIRON PUBLICATIONS • ASHEVILLE, NORTH CAROLINA

www.ChironPublications.com

Interior and cover design by Danijela Mijailovic

Cover Image by Nyochi from Pixabay

Printed primarily in the United States of America.

ISBN 978-1-63051-780-9 paperback

ISBN 978-1-63051-781-6 hardcover

ISBN 978-1-63051-782-3 electronic

ISBN 978-1-63051-783-0 limited edition paperback

Library of Congress Cataloging-in-Publication Data Pending

In Gratitude To ~

Charles and Kathleen Simon,
Richard, James, Thomas, William, and Robert Simon, and Diane Simon Kersey, Mary Jane, Sharon, Alayne, Linda, and Michelle Simon, and Randal Kersey,

Nelda Chafitelli, Jane Catherine Lauer, Joy Belluzzi, Carole Fisher, Salve Kai, Helen DeVanna, Mary Helow, Patrice Vincent, Diane Ghioto, Mary Cherry, Ryan Kersey, Diana Heritage, Barbara DeVanna, Maureen Sullivan, Judy Haas, April Barrett, Kathleen Padden, Callistus Welch, Joanne Padilla, Jerry Parr, Linda Griggs, Deborah Troy, Elinor Chafitelli, Larry Noto, Barbara Baber, Michael Montague, Eleanor Moore, James Bacik, Debra Crawford,

and to those I have been privileged to companion on the journey for manifesting soulful aspects of Lady Underground's energy in the

Emerging New Paradigm

~

Table of Contents

INTRODUCTION TO LADY UNDERGROUND'S GIFT

Throughout the journey of ensoulment, we meet ourselves in various disguises on the road of life. On our travels and adventures, in our heroes and heroines, in our dreams and imaginings, in our desires and loves, in our joys and sorrows, in our work and celebrations, in our solitude and service, in our sufferings and sacrifices, in our losses and deaths, we are being met and summoned by images. They invite us to reflect on our lives, to experience and discover greater depth and meaning, and to allow our souls to be birthed and to become embodied consciously. Transformative images stir our depths, move our hearts, and engage our consciousness; at times they alter it, sometimes rather surprisingly and significantly. Dream images, for example, may remain and impact us for some time as they continue to cause wonderment, to stir emotions, arouse desires, inspire reflection, prompt inner work, and even influence and quicken soulful decisions. At times, a sculpture, symphony, play, dance, poem, film, book, relationship, or contemplative experience might have the same effect, for they can awaken our imagination, touch our hearts, move us deeply, and open us to expanded vision, regardless how or in what way this may transpire.

The famous poet Rainer Maria Rilke wrote in *Letters to a Young Poet* that we must give birth to the images that captivate our imagination, suggesting that the process is going by a way of knowing-by-not-knowing, with a spirit of humility and patience, remembering that *everything* is gestation, and then birthing the images that engage us. He gives further guidance about this soul work in his poem "Turning Point," noting that the "work of the eyes is done, now go and do heart-work on all the images imprisoned within you." Rilke's wisdom suggests that we can grow in awareness through attending to the images that speak to us and deeply affect us. One such renowned, perceptive observer of images and the landscape of human interiority was C.G. Jung. As the father of depth psychology, Jung was a pioneer and explorer of images in the unchartered depths of mystery that is the human soul. Jung honored his psyche by tending the images of his inner terrain. Throughout his midlife years of inner probing, he detailed and illustrated in *The Red Book* the images that engaged him. Both for Jung and Rilke, working with significant images was a portal to awareness.

Images that affect us can be recorded, dialogued and played with, painted, contemplated, processed using neuroscience techniques and body-energy therapies, metabolized, and integrated into our continuous emerging true nature. Moreover, transformative images that stir our imaginations and engage our depths are inviting us to awaken to our soul's essence and to the deep instinctual, ecological, and illuminative wisdom within our inner wells for the furthering of consciousness for ourselves, culture, global community, and the Earth herself within the unfolding 14 billion-year-old Universe Story. One such image that has summoned me in my life process is the image of Our Lady of the Underground, the Black Madonna of Chartres, France. She is one image of the Dark Feminine, the "other side" of the Great Mother Goddess. On the continuum of the archetypal energy of the Great Mother, the Dark Goddess is the earthy, immensely powerful "Other," more shadowy, hidden, unknown, sublime, and mysterious dimension of the Goddess. Mother, virgin, and conduit of wisdom are aspects of her potential universal patterns of energy for development. This is as true for men as for women. We all possess the universal patterns of archetypal energy within our inner pantheon; the archetypal structuring being woven in the interactive field of all life. Also, the real meaning of motherhood is not limited solely to women who have given birth; it is a fundamental pattern of energy inherent in both men and women. In general, the Western world has experienced gradually more of the emergence of the feminine principle in the process of recovering, reclaiming, and befriending this foundational energy (the masculine principle being the other foundational energy). However, it simply is shallow and insufficient to speak about an overarching global aspect of the Great Mother's energy that has emerged more notably in the latter half of the 20th century and in the unfolding 21st century without recognizing and speaking specifically about the Dark Feminine. Thus, the focus of this book is the rich archetypal image of Lady Underground, the Black Madonna of Chartres, Notre-Dame de Sous-Terre, and the exploration and challenge of what it means psychologically and spiritually to embody the Dark Goddess's energy (or another image of the Dark Feminine). She is reemerging at this historical time to summon, guide, and empower humanity through this unprecedented evolutionary stage as we live into a greater complexification of consciousness within the overarching context of the unfolding Universe Story.

What is the story behind the image of Lady Underground, and how did this image come to capture my attention and to engage my depths? Well, a phrase that has long captivated my attention is Nietzsche's statement, "The tree that would grow to heaven must first send its roots to hell." While I did wonder about this statement, that is where the intrigue ended! Then, about 17 years ago, after reflecting on Nietzsche's words, I dreamt about the very image of Lady Underground that resides in the crypt at the Chartres Cathedral; in that dream, the keys to *this* cathedral and to *this* Black Madonna were in my pocket. At the time of the dream, I did not know about her or the cathedral, but just three days later, I was given a sculpture of Lady Underground and a book about her and the Chartres Cathedral; the person who gave me these also told me the story of this Black Madonna. I was shocked as I realized that the gift that was being given to me was the image of the Black Madonna in my dream. At that time, I didn't pay much attention to the image; I simply put the figurine and the book on my library shelf. Two years later, however, by way of another dream, my depths summoned me to a journey to Chartres. Nietzsche's words then came back to haunt me! Little did I realize that a journey to Chartres, France, would augment my being plunged into a deeper dark-night descent/ascent in my ongoing process toward consciously befriending my roots and embodying my soul.

The longest journey is the journey inward. Lady Underground's dark night of initiation in the Dark Feminine is an inner descent in the movement toward conscious embodiment of her archetypal energy, which is never in and for oneself alone. The very dynamic of the regressive process is also a progressive summons back into the human circle enriched with greater consciousness, responsibility, and humble service. Lady Underground's gift of love is paradoxically an unsentimental radical summons into a progressive dark night of initiation in the Dark Feminine. This process of seemingly infinite duration of psychospiritual dismemberment, endurance, sacrifice, surrender, death, and rebirth involves the demagnetization of shadow and affectively charged inner-self parts and images that are embedded in archaic psychic structures; this is one stage of the process of separating, extracting, and metabolizing the swamplands of the psyche. Lady Underground activates a progressive confrontation and a positive disintegration of our distorted dichotomized thinking and charged emotions, which keeps us imprisoned in states of arrested development, alienation, and meaninglessness. Her presence beckons us to befriend and to embody all the ridiculed, judged, shamed, abandoned, repressed, and dissociated parts of our own nature as women and men. Her initiation affects the whole of a person, both soma and psyche. Her medicine of initiation catalyzes our depths, not outside the context of our body, nor just from our neck up, but her initiation is in and through the whole of who we are, including our body. In her dark-night initiation, the alchemical cooking opens a soul potentially to a more expanded embodiment of awakened-passionate heart and compassionate presence in the ordinary of everyday life in all of its dimensions. For example, intimations of Lady Underground's emerging energy from dark-night initiation are reflected in such experiences as embodied instinctual wisdom, awakened-passionate heart, compassionate presence, strengthened potential to hold the tension of the opposites, keen discriminating ability, joyous passion, erotic bliss, enlarged capacity for Eros and creativity, embodied inner authority, respect for "otherness," trust in the way of knowing-by-not-knowing, and attentiveness to the inner guiding principle. These noted examples can be characteristic of growth in individuation, but also, they suggest signs of everyday lived virgin and conduit of wisdom energy in the now of life. Also, for Lady Underground, the body is not will-directed matter; the body is accepted and respected as the sacred container and manifestation of the soul. Her energy reflects the intersection of a passionate sexuality and an interiorized spirituality, of soma and psyche. Furthermore, her energy ushers in a grounded awareness of an interconnectedness and relatedness with our inner cosmos and the earth of our body, along with our outer body, the Earth herself.

There are many ways to describe and to amplify the dynamic of embodying the archetypal energy of Lady Underground; dark night of initiation in the Dark Feminine is *one* template that is useful in attempting to clarify the process and mystery that a soul experiences in humanizing and consciously embodying Black Maria's archetypal energy. One such progressive dark night of initiation began some years ago in the larger overview of my life. Noting this reality gives further context to my experience of the image of Lady Underground. The rite of initiation intensified for me when I was asked to participate in a panel on the Divine Feminine at a large interdisciplinary conference in Topeka, Kansas. Everything rational in me wanted to say no to this request, and yet at a bodily, instinctual level, I experienced an intuitive, felt knowing that somehow I needed to say yes, as it had something to do with the vocation of my life. The nine-month period prior to the participation in the Kansas event, the process of my *propaedeuticum* exams, thesis, and final case exams of the Inter-Regional Society of Jungian Analysts (IRSJA), and more specifically, the arduous dark night of initiation, augmented in the summons to intentional solitude at the Chartres Cathedral in Chartres, France, have been the regressive-progressive dynamics that have continued to form my soul and my vocational path.

On July 20, 2001, I was standing in solitude in the center of the labyrinth of the Chartres Cathedral. After passing my written and oral *propaedeuticum* exams for IRSJA, I experienced a large dream that was the catalyst that propelled me to Chartres to spend two weeks in intentional solitude in the lower crypt of the famous cathedral that houses the Black Madonna, Lady Underground. While in a contemplative stance within the labyrinth's center, I was aware of a felt sense of energy behind me, and then I heard this energetic, light-hearted young female voice, "Ma-Ma! Ma-Ma!" A spontaneous smile came over my face. I opened my eyes and turned around to see a beautiful child about 5 years old standing behind me. Her pose was one of outstretched arms, facial expression of awe, and sparkling eyes cast upward toward the large stained-glass window of the Virgin on her throne.

My heart opened, and as I turned back around to face the window, I heard within me, "Come down into the crypt of my heart and be still." At the time, I felt drawn to return to the lower crypt of the cathedral to be in solitude. The numinous encounter with Lady Underground in the upper body of the church and more so in the lower crypt of the cathedral moved me profoundly and activated a huge rite of initiation in the Dark Feminine.

In retrospect, this religious and archetypal experience awakened a realization of a vocational summons that will continue to shape and inform the rest of my life. The experience of Chartres drew me, allured me into depth, and thrust me into a deeper psychospiritual descent of entering the gate of blackness to face and befriend my inner terrain at a level not previously known. The numinous encounter in the upper church and in the lower crypt activated dream images of dark black piles of garbage with horrific stench in the swamplands of my soul that I could not ignore in my inner soul work. Both personally and theoretically, Jung held that numinous experiences were essential for individuation. He noted in *Memories, Dreams, Reflections* that the years when he pursued his inner images were the most important in his life—that in them everything essential was decided and that the core elements were the *prima materia* for a lifetime's work. While a numinous experience can be a source of consolation, compensation, affirmation, healing, and grace, it also can be an indication that there is an underside of larger affectively charged energies in the psyche that are distinct from the ego and that must be worked with and embodied consciously. For anyone of us, taking seriously the wisdom of Jung and Rilke by attending to the images that deeply affect us can render embodied awareness that can be generative for us and for others. Thus, while my two numinous experiences in Chartres were a summons, grace, and soulfully significant, they were not a sign of maturation or a final realization; rather, the event activated Lady Underground's intense dark night of initiation in the Dark Feminine and revealed core material for my further growth and development in the lifelong journey of individuation. The Chartres experience offered me the sobering and grounding opportunity to realize a bit more the meaning of Nietzsche's words that the tree that would grow to heaven must first send its roots to hell!

Jung indicates, in *Mysterium Coniunctionis*, that when you realize that your matter is going black, rejoice, as this is the beginning of the work! Oh, happy day!, or as St. John of the Cross notes, "Oh happy night!" For most, myself included, it is a not so humorous or a happy reality when dark night is imposed by life, either from within or from without, because as Jung further wrote in *Mysterium*, the experience of the Self is always a defeat for the ego. This horrific night of initiation moves one through the eternal cycle of sacrifice and relinquishment, and the inner journey motif of death and rebirth experiences. There is no dawn of embodied consciousness without the twilight and midnight of dark night. This progressive life-death-rebirth process continues to form me anew in the journey to embody consciously the archetypal energy of Lady Underground.

My hope is that this text raises awareness of a more enlarged perspective of the primordial, archetypal, depth dimensions of Lady Underground's potential energy (mother, virgin, conduit of wisdom) for enlivening holistic psychospiritual growth and embodied consciousness. As we unearth buried and hidden energies, we begin to discover the wisdom of the body, the felt sense of being authentically in our skin, and the inner strength, love, and generativity of being ensouled consciously while making a contribution in outer life. Moreover, my wish is to help us to see this reemerging vital foundational energy within a broader evolutionary frame, if we are to patiently contribute to furthering the birth of the dawn of new horizons and frontiers in humanity's journey toward greater complexification of consciousness at this historical time. The value and need for this Dark Feminine energy for balanced, integrated development is significant for humankind and the planet in this 21st century. She summons us to a new paradigm: conscious ensoulment. Our American culture, Western society as a whole, and the global world are gripped by extreme polarization and a whirlwind of chaos, especially with the United States's 2016 preelection, postelection, and current political times. Dark night is upon us and liminality surrounds us. Turbulence, anxiety, ambiguity, anger, fear, disillusionment, and protests mark this time. This is a hallmark sign of a "weather forecast" of intimations of the Dark Goddess, and more specifically symptomatic of Lady Underground's twilight of dark-night initiation in the Dark Feminine at both a personal and cultural level. In a quantum evolutionary world, polarization is unavoidable. Symbolically, the eruption of chaos, struggle, and positive disintegration is part of the darkness of the night sea journey, of Gethsemane, and of Calvary that precedes the emergence of the transcendent function and the resurrection. Moreover, it is symptomatic of a deeper reality of humanity's depths wanting to be heard and integrated individually, collectively, and in our evolving cosmos. The inner and outer turbulence in America and globally are intimations of the stirrings of the Dark Feminine. More than ever, at this accelerated unprecedented time, humanity is in need of Lady Underground, especially her deeper generative dimensions of the virgin and conduit of wisdom energy. The Dark Feminine's primordial, universal pattern provides meaning and guidance for potential growth and development. As an archetype, it gives emphasis to presence in the now, to process, and to allowing all life forms to develop according to their natural dynamism and to paradox in letting the opposites coexist creatively. These qualities, enacted in the journey of ensoulment, are essential if we are to move forward with hope in birthing a greater unity and complexification of consciousness in this startling and challenging time, which demands a deeper exploration of our common priorities and identity as a country within the web of all life.

Thus, psychospiritual growth issues mark this time on both a personal and collective level. We are experiencing and navigating one of the great in-between periods in human history, a tumultuous time of transition. Humanity's spiritual narrative is ancient in comparison to the existence of formal religions (referring to any of the official religious institutions that have certain doctrine, dogma, structures, rituals, and beliefs, and whose function for the human psyche is to offer authentic containment for primordial experience). At times, formal religions may function to control or block certain levels of experience in the psyche by restricting various experiences or by authoritatively issuing a protected containment of certain aspects of primordial experience mediated to consciousness. Spirit is not constrained by formal religion. Spirit animates and energizes all creation. We are oriented toward mystery/Mystery. Spirituality is a broad concept that includes both existential, lived experience and the academic discipline of spirituality. As such, spirituality concerns an ancient and primal meaning, connectedness, interdependence, and interrelatedness inherent in humanity and an evolving creation itself. Furthermore, spirituality is a portal to nurturing the dialogue and communion with the transcendent manifested in the already/always present Other, both within and without.

Today, many individuals pursue the spiritual journey without any explicit relationship to organized religion. Others can be unaware of the potential wisdom that a certain tradition may offer. Whatever our religious background and affiliation may or may not be, depth psychology, a 20th-century phenomenon, opens a new portal into the spiritual life for us today in our holistic, integrated, psychospiritual quest. Neither Analytical Psychology nor spirituality as a discipline has a monopoly on the truth of embodied consciousness and the implications of such an adventure in human interiority. Also, depth psychology is not a substitute for spirituality. Yet, unlike spirituality, especially mystical traditions such as the Carmelite, as reflected by John of the Cross, Jung's theory provides ways for dealing with psychic content that lacks integration. Though there are recognizable parallels between depth psychology and spirituality, their intent and goal are not the same. However, being open to a healthy pluralistic view offers an attempt to dialogue, envision, and circumambulate the ebb-and-flow journey home, while always remembering that the experience is greater than any particular attempt to understand and represent it.

The great Jesuit theologian Karl Rahner viewed the revelatory process as a coming to greater self-awareness in the ordinary human experience of life. For Rahner, the genuine experience of self is precisely the experience of the Mystery. Depth psychology furthers the possibility for an embodied awareness of this encounter by giving us ways to connect to the vitality of meaning in our symbols. To include in our consideration of our spiritual quest the reality of the unconscious and how it shapes, forms, and influences our relationship to self, others, Other, culture, the global community, and the Earth herself impacts our soul's process.

The *unknown* is within us. It manifests in numerous ways, such as an arousing desire, a love that captivates us, a frightening dream that troubles us, an alluring image that engages us, a fantasy that seduces us, an infantile attitude and behavior that runs us, an unsettling chaotic fear that grips us, a great loss that plunges us into a dark wood and the way unknown, or some physical symptom that addresses and plagues us. The unconscious is not the Divine, but it is another valuable source, accessed by the Holy, to touch, heal, guide, and empower us. We do not encounter the Other in a vacuum. The mystery/Mystery is experienced in and through our human psyches, our bodies. Thus, if we are open, Analytical Psychology has a vital contribution to offer people who desire a more holistic embodied spirituality, or a deeper meaning, purpose, and identity. If we lack openness to depth psychology as a rich resource for development, our spirituality, or our human interiority may run the risk, potentially, of being too one-sided. A prospective, creative complementarity emerges in considering the distinct but mutually enriching insights of both disciplines. This book notably addresses what Analytical Psychology offers people in search of a more holistic, embodied, psychospiritual consciousness that includes the Dark Feminine.

As we enter further into the 21st century, the value and need for an incarnational awareness seems essential for our time. The present historical era in our culture and global community demands a new paradigm of an embodied consciousness. Patriarchal rigidity and domination are increasingly being challenged in America and throughout the world, including within religious institutions and governments. During the last 60 years, the resurgence of the feminine archetype has been manifesting in our individual, societal, and global lives. The challenge today is to coparticipate in the discovery, recovery, integration, and conscious balance of all of our soul's essence, including the dark and light dimensions of the feminine archetype. Being ensouled in the deeper dimensions of the Dark Feminine energy is vital if we are to live through and metabolize the growth opportunity in the dark night looming over our democracy, society, and worldwide web of life. Only through integrating the gift of dark-night initiation will we, as a culture and world community, find a collaborative way forward in birthing the dawn of a greater complexification of consciousness.

Feminine energy is part of our humanity and is present in both men and women, as is masculine energy. In embodying consciousness, *both* genders need a well-differentiated masculine and a well-differentiated feminine. The Dark Feminine is one aspect of the feminine foundational principle in both men and women. This energy in its depth of richness is a portal to mystery/Mystery, instinctual body wisdom, and hidden, unknown, lush, rejected, dissociated, dormant aspects of oneself that are potential generative resources for life. The encounter with the Dark Goddess can deepen the meaning and mystery of one's existence. The person who endures a descent of the dark night of initiation in the Dark Feminine can grow in integration and become more whole in the process of developing a well-differentiated feminine and masculine energy in which neither is inferior to the other, but equal. Lady Underground's dark night is like going through the rollers of an old Maytag washing machine: She wrings us out dry and draws from us our essence—our authentic soul. The reality is that going through the wringers of the Maytag might seem quick, and Lady Underground's initiation seems forever from the ego's view! The unfolding journey into the depths evokes the question: Are these depths, is this center at the heart of being, trustworthy? Is the center, for me, sustaining and life-giving? Seemingly, only darkness, emptiness, and dead silence are evident. Often depression and despair loom heavy with the sense that one has been duped. It causes one to wonder *Is there a God*? Is there a God who cares, or as one analysand exclaims, "Is there a God or a Whatever who even gives a damn for me?" If there is a God, how could such a Being allow this dark night? At its darkest point, the rite causes one to question the very center. And yet, here in the heart of our *matter*, often our *matter* that is most despised, judged, repressed, and dissociated, is Lady Underground. She is for our wholeness. Her night of initiation is an encounter and a summons into healing, into wholeness, and into a psychospiritual maturity that strips and wrings away attachment to infantile baggage and sentimentality. Psychologically, the Dark Feminine holds the connection to creativity and to growth in conscious ensoulment. Out of chaos, emotional upheaval, and the process of demagnetizing affectively charged archaic self-parts, with which the ego is often unconsciously overidentified, can come creativity and vision that usher in new life.

With all archetypes, there are two poles. As an image of the "other side" of the Great Goddess, Lady Underground's way is not the way of naive innocence and sentimentality. She is an image of the Great Goddess who both gives and takes life. Death is part of life. In Lady Underground's dark-night initiation, death is in service to growth and life. The Dark Mother's call to conscious ensoulment seems radical for some. As one successful businessman put it, "I would have to sacrifice too much in my outer world, which I have worked ambitiously to achieve in life. I don't like what is coming up in my dreams. I find it depressing. I want to have pleasant and affirming dreams. In my universe, I like to have everything just stay consistent. I am conservative, and I don't know why this Black Madonna is in my dream, but I want a different dream." The "other" side of the Dark Goddess can be devouring, depressing, and chaotic to the ego that is out of touch with one's darkness, naïve to the mystery of the dark and light sides of life; oblivion to change is the one constant in life. Some people will honor and embody the archetypal energy and grow in their potential; others will do so in various degrees; and some will never take responsibility for their life so that the archetypal energy will remain dormant, and psychospiritually they will remain eternal adolescents. However, if one can endure the initiation, one can mature and discover an enlarged perspective while remembering that there is no one way that the mystery/Mystery can draw a soul. And so, even the Unknown Dark *She* offers the journeyer a depth of vital energy in liberating the generative soul within us. Who is any one of us to question how the mystery/Mystery draws us? Conscious feminine and masculine adult development is accepting of the darkness within us. Thus, the terms *feminine* and *masculine* in this book are not to be associated with biological gender. Whether we refer to these distinct energies as *masculine/feminine*, *yang/yin* (Chinese), Shiva/Shakti (Hindu), and/or Bridegroom/Bride (Mystical Theology), we are each responsible in the journey of individuation to embody these energies consciously. What does predominate in the North American culture is a more rational mentality that is grounded in 2,000 years of embodied practice of and credence in a patriarchy (power) that wounds and imprisons men and women.

Rational, logical, linear, solar consciousness has dominated our culture, even though the archetypal roots of the Dark Feminine existed and were honored for ages by American Indian ancestors in attitude, custom, and ritual. Feminine lunar consciousness tends to be more diffuse. The Dark Goddess is intimated in an instinctual, felt, body sense; an attentiveness to the here and now, to process, and to allowing the opposites to coexist naturally; a knowing by way of not knowing; and a grounded paradoxical trust that the wisdom of the creative relational way often is in the mysterious still-black nothingness and in the unclear, unsettling, absurd, dark chaos.

While there has been a reemergence of the feminine foundational principle in the Western world in the last 60 years, there has been a real lag toward the awareness and integration of the dark side of the feminine energy. This aspect of the feminine has by and large remained exiled into the unconscious. Few realize that this deeper, earthy, immensely powerful, shadowy "other," hidden, unknown, sublime, and mysterious dimension of the archetype is a rich resource for living a more holistic balanced psychospiritual life that is vitally needed if our nation, world, and planet are to thrive in these extreme times. In North America, for instance, there is little consciousness of the experience and appreciation of the Dark Feminine. We have not been educated in the value of darkness and the significance of the Dark Goddess's energy, especially the deeper dimensions of virgin and wisdom, and thus tend to have an eclipsed view. As a culture, we are more invested, driven, and informed by materialism. In North America, Lady Guadalupe in Mexico is one image of the Dark Feminine archetype. However, in the wider horizon of human history, many faces of the Dark Goddess have surfaced in mythology, fairy tales, sacred texts, poetry, art, film, music, and dreams, in cultures around the world. Some representatives of the Dark Feminine reappearing in various writings in the last 30 years are Isis, Lilith, Inanna, Sheba, Kali, Tara, Kuan Yin, Mary Magdalene, Old Woman at the bottom of the riverbed, Grandmother Earth, Lady of the Valley, Sister, and the Black Madonna. One particular mirror of the Dark Feminine among the multiplicity of Black Madonnas is Lady Underground, the Black Madonna of Chartres, France. She is *one* image of the energy that appears to be reemerging as a wellspring of possibility for our personal and collective lives. She ushers in an energy that emphasizes a conscious, body-felt, sensory experience, an instinctual wisdom, a bodily connectedness and relatedness, and a more realized interior oneness that manifests as awakened-passionate heart and compassion presence in the marketplace of the ordinary of everyday life. Our body is an intimate and familiar dimension of our existence as human beings. Conscious ensoulment occurs in and through psyche and soma.

We can no longer individually and collectively live estranged from our instinctual roots, which are a vital lifeline in conscious, holistic living. As we embody consciousness through the process of befriending the Dark Feminine archetypal image, we do so with a return to the outer circle of life with a greater awareness, reverence, and responsibility to the humanization of the body of humanity and its own primary and natural source, namely the *Earth* herself. This conscious vision is birthed from our intimate relationship with the Dark Feminine and embodying her deeper dimensions of virgin and conduit of wisdom energy. The value, need, summons, and process of this dynamic perspective is explored in this book.

Whether we speak in the language of Jung's depth psychology of the Self, or in the language of spirituality of the Mystery, there are similarities in the alchemical process of holistic embodied psychospiritual growth. Jung's Analytical Psychology is a creative complementarity to spirituality, which together offer a broader, more integrative view to help and to inspire us to live a more conscious embodied life. With the return and call of Lady Underground, the original source of the ancient past is transformed into the present and becomes a promise for the future for our path toward an interiorized wholeness. Furthermore, the time has dawned for us in our evolutionary development as a people to adopt a more expansive perspective based on cooperation rather than on patriarchal supremacy and planetary domination. Holistic consciousness, engaging the imagination of increasing numbers of people, summons us to new ways of being in the world, not in oppositional isolation or confrontation, but in collaborative networking that births new frontiers of wholeness, hope, and possibility. In this time of a paradigm shift, it is an essential part of the evolution of our consciousness to plumb our depths, to find, and to embody a deeper human interiority both individually and collectively as a society and global family. The dislocations that exist in the outer arena with the horrific chaos and shadow that looms over our country and world are making it imperative for us to turn inward to locate ourselves in a more grounded awareness. Given the evolutionary trajectory, the current American culture, and the international community, it seems essential to hearken to the call of the

Dark Feminine, to recognize the symptoms of destruction and deadlock polarization, indicating an imbalance of the masculine and feminine and the need to honor and to integrate the lost Dark Feminine.

Throughout this text, it is essential to remember and to understand that when Jung uses religious language of his heritage, he is using terms symbolically and psychologically, not theologically. This book is intended to be a source of inspiration, empowerment, and guidance for a wide range of people serious about embodying consciously deeper dimensions of holistic psychospiritual growth and development that makes a difference in both the inner and outer worlds. In this text, the expression "mystery/Mystery" or "spirit/Spirit" is used at various times. Some reading this book will do so through the lens of spirituality and their contemplative religious experience and/or to some degree via the filter of their religious tradition and spiritual practice. For these readers, a numinous religious encounter may be discerned through their contemplative practice as an experience of the intimation of the transcendent Ground of Being and their sense of reference is Mystery with a capital "M." For readership from a depth psychology outlook, an archetypal numinous religious experience is essential in the healing path of reconciliation and unity of psyche's inherent polarities in the progressive process of embodied consciousness in individuation. The latter is an interior psychological dynamic in which the god-image/goddess-image is generated from the psychological agent, the archetype. Because this concerns a psychological process and does not refer theologically to the nature of God, mystery is with a lower-case letter "m." Jung's psychological framework aids us in understanding and facilitating the context for healing the psyche in the journey toward wholeness—conscious ensoulment. Contemporary spirituality, especially mystical traditions of spirituality, broaden our horizons of authentic human possibilities in envisioning a new consciousness that embraces deeper dimensions of human interiority in and through transformation in the Divine. I invite you to read, question, wonder, and allow the material to stir and engage your depths, while maintaining an openness to consider a more expansive holistic integrative psychospiritual healing perspective in its multidimensions of the *one* journey toward the center.

In this book, the archetypal image of Lady Underground, the Black Madonna of Chartres, is explored as a gift of the primordial Dark Feminine. She awakens and enriches our personal and collective lives with depth in our path of ensoulment within the relational web of all creation. Analytical Psychology offers tools and a language to help disclose this archetypal energy deep within our lives, societal psyche, and the universe, which holds generative promise for our renewal and for the cosmos, especially in navigating this paradigm shift in evolution at this historical time. The text will attempt to make her energy more discernible and her challenge more imperative. Clinical work, mythology, fairy tales, sacred writings, poetry, history, theater, film, dance, art, and sculpture will be accessed to amplify and enrich the subject matter. Reflective quotes related to the chapter material are noted at the beginning of each chapter for your consideration, dialogue, and contemplation. Every chapter will offer a section on inner work opportunities as possibilities for assisting in unearthing, metabolizing, and integrating the material. The writing will illuminate the process of incarnating Lady Underground's energy through her dark night of initiation in the Dark Feminine. Moreover, the book opens us to the realization that the way of the Dark Feminine is an ancient path for today's psychospiritual journeyer. Hopefully, we will recognize her when we see her, welcome her among us and are even more open to befriending and embodying consciously her essential energy.

CHAPTER ONE
LADY UNDERGROUND

Called or not called, the god [goddess]will be present.
~The Delphic Temple Oracles

You, sent out beyond your recall, go to the limits of your longing. Embody me. Flare up like flame and make big shadows I can move in. Let everything happen to you: beauty and terror. Just keep going. No feeling is final. Don't let yourself lose me.
~Rainer Maria Rilke

Anyone with a vocation hears the inner voice...
the voice of a fuller life, of a wider, more comprehensive consciousness.
~C.G. Jung

Introduction to Our Lady of the Underground

Who is she? Who is the mysterious unknown she, *who is*? Who is the Dark Goddess as manifested in the archetypal image of Our Lady of the Underground, the Black Madonna in the lower crypt of Chartres, *Virgini Pariturae*? Who is this dark, unfamiliar emerging feminine image/figure who is in the dreams, art, petroglyphs, literature, plays, film, contemporary ballet, literature, and song lyrics of modern men and women? Who is this Dark Feminine presence who sometimes is encountered in numinous religious experience, meditation, contemplation, or active imagination? Within our human interiority, is the encounter and relationship with goddess any different from god? Is the accompaniment of goddess distinct from god for the voyager of the darker night sea depths as the soul's heart opens to an inexhaustible and incomprehensible mystery/Mystery that is ineffable? One reads contemporary titles like *The Unknown She*, *She Who Is*, *Goddess: Mother of Living Nature*, or *Women, Earth, and Creator Spirit*. Is this just a superficial passing trend in our culture in an effort for inclusive language? Or is this feminine presence part of the resurgence in the great global unparalleled shift in consciousness that is needed and addressed by the late Thomas Berry, cultural historian and major contributor to cosmological spirituality, or contemporary, international scientists like Bruce Lipton, M.D., the pioneer research cell biologist, and Edgar Mitchell, D.S., astronaut and pilot of Apollo 14 and founder of the Institute of Noetic Sciences? What causes this feminine presence to reemerge now in human history in so many diverse cultures, traditions, and disciplines, including theology and spirituality? What are Lady Underground's attributes? How do we maintain consciousness of her and relate to her in a grounded way in everyday life and not become identified with her? Does she make a difference to the common person, and is her energy accessible to them? If we are drawn by her love, and say yes to the experience of her summons, how will our everyday life be altered as we live and function in the world? Does the numinous experience of Lady Underground influence our spirituality in our inner depths and our outer praxis? What is her earthy, darker, more shadowy, immensely powerful, "other" energy that longs to give birth to new life and to bring balance to the masculine and feminine energies in both men and women, as well as to the Earth herself?

Furthermore, what is the new conscious wedding to which Lady Underground beckons us and asks us to embody in this 21st century?[i] Back in the Bronze Age, a union of the mythic images of feminine and masculine principles was symbolized in the sacred marriage of the goddess and the god, a ritual that was thought to assist the regeneration of nature. With the greater consciousness of 4,000 years, is it possible for the human imagination to recreate consciously the sacred marriage with the same purpose: the renewal and revitalization of generative life? With a quantum cosmic-planetary

---

[i] The opening reflective questions in Chapter One are intended for imaginal wonderment, reflection, and discussion. Chapters Three and Four will unfold a deeper exploration.

worldview, what would the modern text and presentation of this ancient myth be like? With the restoration of the differentiated conscious feminine and differentiated conscious masculine to a conscious relationship of equality, mutuality, and respect, might there then be the possibility of a new emerging mythology of the universe? Furthermore, might we dare to imagine embracing a new mythology marked by a conscious worldview of the interdependency and interconnectedness of all of creation, or what Hildegard of Bingen refers to as "the web of all life," and what modern creative thinkers speak about in quantum theology and ecospirituality? A key question then becomes: How does the Dark Goddess's archetypal image, such as Lady Underground, the Black Madonna of Chartres, enable us to access our deeper depths, "drink deeply," and generatively bring forth to the light of consciousness personally and collectively a more awakened-passionate heart awareness and compassionate presence as we are about our daily service to the mystery/Mystery within the everyday, unfolding, evolving Universe Story? How can we come to an awareness and embodiment of our ancient future, which is the eternal now for our Western world and global community, especially given the present darkening that looms over our nation and the international community with such realities as climate change, racism, bigotry, misogyny, global terrorism, oppressive and annihilating dictatorships, cyber warfare, lack of social-political-religious inclusivity and tolerance, gun violence, income inequality, human trafficking, war on drugs, deadlock polarization, and threat of nuclear warfare?

Dark Feminine

In our present era, the feminine principle is emerging more, and with it comes a resurgence and a renewed interest in the Dark Feminine, an aspect of the feminine energy. The feminine principle is one of the two great archetypal foundational energies of our evolving cosmos, with the other being the masculine principle. Throughout history, there are several feminine archetypal images that have arisen of goddess figures that symbolize various aspects of cosmic nature in the web of all life. The Great Mother Goddess endures as one of the primary goddess images in human interiority. Her archetypal energy has various gradations within the continuum of potential energy that is available for growth and development. Some core dimensions of the goddess energy include mother, virgin, and conduit of wisdom. Lady Underground as a primordial image of the Dark Feminine is a deeper, earthy, immensely powerful "Other," shadowy and often hidden, unknown, sublime, and mysterious aspect of the Great Mother Goddess. In general, the Western world has experienced gradually more of the emergence of the feminine principle in the process of recovering, reclaiming, and befriending this foundational energy. However, it simply is shallow and insufficient to speak about an overarching global aspect of the Great Goddess's energy, which has emerged more notably in the latter half of the 20th century and in the emerging 21st century, without recognizing and speaking specifically about the Dark Goddess. A key sign of her resurgence is chaos and turbulence experienced personally, societally, and within various cultures. In an era of the reappearance of the Dark Feminine, liminality marks the present, unparalleled, evolutionary development (to be addressed thoroughly in the Chapter Five section: "Implications For Culture and World Soul"). In all times, this darker aspect of the feminine has been both feared and sought after, criticized and tolerated, hated and admired, banished and welcomed, annihilated and celebrated. This potentially rich aspect of the feminine is often sentimentalized and thus remains unintegrated, and/or misjudged, misunderstood, despised, condemned, repressed, and dissociated from our human experience.

Dark, earthy, and immensely powerful, the primordial feminine has been a significant influence in human history. She has manifested in images as diverse as the Mesopotamian Goddess Inanna/Ishtar (the Sumerian Goddess Inanna is she whom the Babylonians called Ishtar), the Hindu Goddess Kali, the Egyptian Goddess Isis, and the Tibetan Buddhist Goddess Tara. Another revelation includes Lilith described in the Talmudic legend as created simultaneously with Adam and as his first wife, the Black Goddess of both wisdom and the fire of sexuality. Also, there is Sheba (in Islam she is known as Bilqis, the Lady of Wisdom), the black Shulamite of Hebrew scripture known to Solomon—that sensuous maiden from the biblical Song of Songs, who is dark, beautiful, and depicts the erotic face of Sophia, and Mary of Magdala of the New Testament. Moreover, the primordial feminine is reflected in Sister as portrayed in the Native American fairy tale, Grandmother Earth of indigenous peoples, Our Lady of Guadalupe in North America, and the Black Madonnas of medieval Europe, including the Black Madonna of Chartres. The Dark Feminine allows the opposites to coexist naturally and creatively. Thus, the Dark Feminine incorporates the energies of chaos and creativity, death and rebirth, peril and promise, annihilation and fresh possibility, malevolence and goodness, sorrow and joy, extinction and transformation.

Characteristic of the Dark Feminine is allowing paradox, attending to process, and focusing and being attuned in the present. Images that are reflective of the Dark Feminine principle have been noticeably absent in the Western world for centuries, until the last 30 years, when the Dark Goddess began reemerging in realms of dreams, art, poetry, music, dance, film, theater, spirituality and the rediscovery of the petroglyphs. With the resurfacing of the Dark Feminine energy within the evolutionary frame has come a growing interest in understanding, honoring, befriending, and integrating this archetypal energy.

Sir Laurens Van Der Post, a good friend of Carl Gustav Jung, once noted that history, as a record of the past, has been told primarily in terms of its outer eventfulness, which in a sense is the least of history. However, history progresses on two levels, a profound one and a manifest one that is not fully expressed. This second level makes itself known through the ways in which we shape our lives in our quantum evolutionary world as well as through the failures, disasters, and atrocities brought about because its hidden, inner eventfulness is not fully consciously recognized and given its due in the human spirit and in societies. There is no dimension of history in which this is more true than the way with which the feminine has been subordinated by patriarchal societies. Until the last 60 years, the feminine has been inadequately acknowledged in our cultures and civilizations.[1] The result of this colossal neglect, which is with us still, is seen in the decay and erosion of the feeling and caring values of life. Instead, we perceive the driven pursuit of rationalism in the establishments of our Apollonian, achievement-orientated culture, supported by patriarchal structures and driven by ubiquitous consumerism. The loss of the feminine, especially the deeper "other" dimensions of the Dark Feminine energy, has led to a magnitude of undeniable manifestations of shadowy symptoms in our time, which indicates that we have become overly one-sided or neurotic.

An example of this reality is the sharp polarization, in this country and in others, on many levels, politically, racially, ethnically, and religiously, manifested in the Women's March on January 21, 2017, the rallies against the Paris Agreement withdrawal, the protests ahead of and during the G-20 Summit in Hamburg, Germany, on July 7, 2017, and the Charlottesville, Virginia, protest, on August 12, 2017, which was preceded by a surprise, organized, white-nationalist and -supremacist march in torchlight procession—a symbolic rally with regretful hate chants meant to evoke similar marches of Hitler Youth and other ultra-right-nationalist groups. Further examples are the abuses of power that have infiltrated our world and are operative in authoritarian leaders and dictators, terrorists, some police, and in human relationships, including our relationship to the Earth herself. Furthermore, while we are unable to know the archetypal energy of the Dark Feminine directly, intimations of this energy have been reflected through the lens of the creative by contemporary artists, poets, composers, filmmakers, theologians, and contemplatives. Their perspective can stir our imaginations and awaken us, individually and as a culture, to a more expanded vision of the energy that is manifesting in our time. Long before the collective is aware, the visionaries and the creative artists who are in touch with the unfolding depths reveal the emerging energy to us through their many various art forms. Some artists reflecting the Dark Feminine include Frank Howell, Michael O'Neill McGrath, and Y.G. Srimati, especially in his 1990 watercolor of Kali—"Mother India: The Goddess in Indian Painting" in his exhibition at the Metropolitan Museum of Art in July 2011. A few authors from various disciplines who have enlightened our horizons of the Dark Goddess include Marion Woodman, Matthew Fox, Andrew Harvey, Diarmuid O'Murchu, Sir Laurens van der Post, Clarissa Pinkola Estes, Fred Gustafson, Esther Harding, Betty DeShong Meador, Maya Angelou, David Whyte, and Helen Luke. Dancers such as the Contemporary Dancers of Pilobolus performing at The Joyce Theater in New York express symbolically the unfolding interactive energy patterns of the ever-present Ancient One. Thus, we realize that both the rising chaotic and the creative energetic echoes of the Dark Goddess's reemergence in our time suggests a summons toward a shift in an entirely new level of consciousness. The returning goddess calls for a shattering of rigid categories, for a loosening of attachments and identifications with archaic structures and their contents, a willingness to hold opposites without opposition, and a readiness to embrace an Earth-centered norm of reality and value. She calls us to engage in cooperation, to wed reason and order to creativity, and to embrace the chaos and unknown in the darkness that can ultimately lead to embodied wisdom and transformation on personal and global levels.

Our personal and collective story as a society and civilization can develop, and we can grow in conscious interiority through the images that deeply affect us in our lives. They can be processed, metabolized, contemplated, integrated, and embodied into our evolving story. In our dreams, in our aspirations, in our work, in our yearnings, in our loves, in our sufferings, in our solitude, on our travels, we are being met by and addressed by images. They are inviting us to a deeper interiority, to allow our stories to unfold and our souls to be birthed and to be embodied. This is true not only for individuals but also for the world soul of humanity. Transformative images stir our depths, engage our consciousness and, at least temporarily, change it, sometimes surprisingly and significantly. Dream images, for example, may affect us for days and continue to trigger emotions, arouse desires, kinesthetically stimulate our inner sensory receptors, stir fantasies, cause wonderment, and enliven imagination and vision. At times, a play, an opera, a sculpture, a film, a symphony, a person, or a meditation might have the same effect. The major symbolic experiences of this kind we call religious.

If these powerful archetypal images are strong enough, they can impact a person's life and can give it shape and direction. They provide profound underlying structural support and meaning. Cultures and religions are repositories of transformative images from the past. The cultures of humankind housed and treasured the primordial images of the collective unconscious and have made them available to people in their religious rituals. When a person experiences one of these images deeply, it has a significant effect upon consciousness. The activation of an archetype releases patterning dynamics that can restructure the energy field both in the psyche and in the outer world. Lady Underground (or any image of the Dark Feminine) is one such archetypal image that has the capacity to influence us to greater levels of consciousness in human growth and development, personally and globally.

How is this understood through the lens of Analytical Psychology? Depth psychologist Carl Jung envisioned the human psyche as consisting of three strata: the conscious portion of the psyche with the ego as its center; the personal unconscious, which relates solely to the individual's experience; and the collective unconscious, which is common to us all and whose contents are universal and hereditary. The contents of the collective unconscious manifest in the forms of symbolic images, or archetypes, representing the primordial events that shaped human history. These archetypal images, which include such symbols as the father and mother, the sun and moon, hero and heroine, birth and death, are common to all people, whatever their personal or cultural experience and inheritance. The archetypes are given life and expression in the world's mythologies and cosmogonies in an attempt to explain what is behind the creation and the future direction of both the cosmos and humanity.

Given the inherent ability of the human collective and the personal unconscious to communicate with the conscious portion of the psyche by means of such archetypal images, it is natural that symbols of all kinds can evoke profound responses in us. The Black Madonna of Chartres is an example of this. By tapping into the legacy of the collective human experience, symbols like Lady Underground speak to our instincts as well as to our psyche. Thus, symbolism can be a truly international form of communication, bypassing the barriers of language, race, and culture, speaking directly to each level of the human psyche; but most meaningfully, symbolism speaks to the collective unconscious. Symbols are the language of the collective unconscious.

Black Madonna of Chartres

In the small old French town of Chartres, about 40 miles outside of Paris, is the dwelling of the Black Madonna. In the cavelike crypt of the magnificent

Gothic Cathedral of Chartres, the "Acropolis of France" (Rodin), is the statue of Our Lady of the Underground; also, a 12th-century mural of her is painted on the wall in the sanctuary area of the crypt. Sometimes referred to as Lady Wisdom, Wisdom on the Throne, Seat of Wisdom, Virgin about to give birth, and Black Madonna of Chartres, all are she to whom I refer sometimes as Black Maria.

Chartres attracted pilgrims at an early date, first of all to Our Lady of the Underground Grotto, then to the cathedral that Bishop Fulbert built in the 11th century. One enters the crypt on the north side of the cathedral to visit the grotto underneath the church. The underground structure is one of the largest of any cathedral in France. Descending into the cavelike structure, one has the sense of entering the dark womb of this immense cathedral. Just before entering the sanctuary where Lady Underground is located, one passes an ancient hundred-foot-deep well. There, walking into the rather dark, earthy, simple sanctuary, one beholds the Dark Lady. On the front of her throne is inscribed *Virgini Pariturae*, meaning the Virgin about to give birth, even though she is holding the divine child on her lap. *Notre-Dame de Sous-Terre*, meaning "Our Lady of the Underground," is etched on the side of her throne. Even though the painted mural on the wall is an early original of Our Lady, the first Black Madonna statue was destroyed in a night fire on June 10, 1194, which did severe damage to the cathedral and the town. However, within 50 years, the cathedral was rebuilt in its present glory by the people of Chartres. Today, this majestic cathedral still draws many pilgrims far off across the endless cornfield of the Beauce.

Historical Perspective

During the 12th century, the pilgrims of the Christian era had a flourishing devotion to Mary, the mother of Christ, in France and in other parts of medieval Europe. Among the many Black Virgin statues that are found throughout Europe, including some 170 in France, Chartres was perhaps the most sought-after site for pilgrims of that era and remains so today. People come from around the world to visit and to experience Mary's energy in this sacred space.

What is it about Chartres that draws so many people to this medieval sacred *temenos*? What attracts people to Chartres is the architecture, sacred geometry, theology, spirituality, and psychology of the cathedral, manifested in the beauty and in the mystery that the cathedral, itself, is the vessel of the Virgin Wisdom, decorated majestically with images and symbols of her teachings. The magnificence of the structure is especially reflected in the famous north rose window of the cathedral, where the Dark Virgin and her child are the focal point of this mosaic glass in the upper church; just as in the lower crypt, the dark, earthy, immensely powerful archetypal images of the statue and the mural are central. These characteristics, along with the fact that Chartres was the first cathedral in which Mary appeared on the church's front design, reflect the intention of the feminine principle in Western culture. The cathedral was constructed during an era when the feminine was revered as worthy of respect and service. While this deep appreciation of the feminine has long been devalued because of the dominance of patriarchy, today this dark, immensely powerful and rich archetypal image of Lady Underground has wisdom for us as we endeavor to live consciously through this tumultuous unprecedented time in this 21st century.

To further appreciate the richness of this image of Lady Underground, and if we are to open its deeper layers of symbolic and analytical meaning, it is essential to understand its historical origins. This Black Madonna is not an isolated entity. She exhibits her own uniqueness yet is related to the larger world of mythology and religion. Her archetypal nature necessitates her belonging to many expressions of the feminine archetype throughout the world, though more specifically to the dark side. This relatedness does not negate her psychospiritual value and power; rather, it connects her to the natural principles of energy that govern the human psyche and express themselves in various mythologies and religions of this quantum world.[2]

The noted authority and medieval historian Malcolm Miller, who has dedicated his life to studying and lecturing on the history, architecture, theology, and spirituality of the Chartres Cathedral, gives no credence to the theory that the origins of Chartres are pre-Christian. He holds that the origins of Chartres are lost in the mists of time, where legend and history are interwoven and have been further confused by the imagination of later centuries that mingled a Druidic tradition with a pre-Christian virgin cult.[3] However, from the ongoing historical scientific research of ancient and mediaeval times, several sources indicate that there were, in fact, pre-Christian origins, especially regarding the crypt.[4 5 6 7 8]

Some scholars suggest that the Crusaders brought the Black Virgins back from the East or that the statues may have originated in Byzantium and were brought to Western Europe by admirers escaping iconoclastic disputes. Current research indicates that the Black Virgins, so esteemed in certain French Cathedrals, Chartres being one of them, as well as in Spain, Switzerland, and Poland, are chiefly the basalt statues of the Egyptian goddess Isis. The confusion between the Black Madonna and Isis is easily understood, since the materials with which many of the statues are composed are black basalt stone or black ebony wood.[9] As Christianity asserted itself, many statues of the pre-Christian deities were destroyed, and yet others, at the time of the Crusades, were brought from the East and absorbed into the generalized worship of the great goddess by virtue of only a change of names. Hence, the Black Virgins in Europe came to be a survival and continuation, under a new name and in a new religion, of goddesses from the classical world, particularly Isis.[10 11]

Therefore, really to appreciate the richness of the symbolism of an enthroned Black Madonna holding the Divine Child (Lady Underground) as an archetypal image, it seems important to review briefly the cultural context, mythology, and symbolism of her Egyptian prototype, an enthroned Isis holding Horus. To encounter this ancient Egyptian milieu is to discover a rich template for understanding the symbolism and analytical meaning of Lady Underground. In this process, it is important to remember that we cannot fully understand the Goddess Isis and what she means in her connections to Black Maria of Chartres. An archetype cannot be reduced to a specific interpretation or meaning. Because of its invisible aspect, it remains incomprehensible and a mystery, and even though its numinosity can be experienced, we will never fully integrate and embody the archetypes. Nevertheless, we can, to a certain extent, circumambulate the archetypes by showing their different aspects and functions in the psyche.[12]

Relationship to Isis

For the last 200 years, ancient Egypt has captured the imagination of scholars and laymen alike, resulting in a deluge of books describing this most mysterious of civilizations. In researching ancient Egypt, we come to understand that this culture had a deep religious perspective that influenced the cosmology of this ancient civilization. At the heart of the Egyptian worldview is a fundamental backdrop that reveals a culture that is primarily religious and symbolic. The world of the Egyptians was religious, first and foremost. Their perspectives regarding the feminine principle in the creation myths, the roles of the gods and goddesses, the function of the Nile in their lives, the principles of balance and order in daily life, the view of and belief in the afterlife, and the sense of a transient state resulting in constant change and detachment — all are dynamic, natural parts of the milieu of the ancient land. Questions that concerned Egyptians were: How did creation come to be? How do we exist? What is the purpose of our life? How do we keep the natural order and balance of life flowing? Who are we in relationship to the bigger picture of life and the afterlife? The Egyptians's world was mythological, as their civilization existed before the birth of philosophy. Unlike the Greek and Roman cultures that were dominated by static, fixed, and logical thinking and language that was discriminating, the Egyptian milieu was characterized by associational and symbolic thinking and language.

In Egyptian mythology, Isis is considered the most illustrious of all the ancient goddesses. For over 3,000 years, from before 3000 BCE to the second century CE, Isis was revered in Egypt as the Great Mother Goddess of the Universe. The earliest representations reveal her with a special crown and a throne. Her very name says much about who she is as a goddess: in Egyptian her name was really Auset (Isis is a Hellenized version), which means throne. The hieroglyph that represents Isis is the throne, and this image shows her as literally the power of the earth, of which the royal seat is but a representation.

As the lap of Isis provides a seat for Horus, and as every Egyptian king is an incarnation of Horus, that place whereupon he sits, namely the throne, may be considered to be Isis herself. To take this interpretation a step further, the throne as a high place, usually set upon a dais, is therefore reminiscent of what is called the Primeval Mound, the first point that arose from the waters of chaos and the point from which all subsequent creation would take place. Isis as the throne is analogous to the Primeval Mound. For the Egyptians, land means the emergence of the Primeval Mound, the First Place, or the Primeval Throne, and with it, the establishment of order and direction.[13] It is from this association that Isis acquires her significance as the World-Mother, the point from which all life emanates.

From the earliest times, Isis was identified with a number of other goddesses. This process, called *syncretism*, increased over time with Isis eventually eclipsing all other goddesses, Egyptian or foreign, and their characteristics. *The Book of the Dead* refers to Isis by all her names. Marie-Louise von Franz speaks of her as a symbol of psychic wholeness, the Self, in a feminine form.[14]

By means of Greek mercenaries and merchants, as well as the successors of Alexander the Great, who ruled Egypt, Isis worship was exported to the classical world, where she is identified with Athena, Artemis, Aphrodite, and virtually every other goddess. Temples of Isis are found all over the Mediterranean basin: in Athens, in Rome, and as far away as the British Isles. People of every nationality, race, and class honored Isis, endowing her with all the qualities of their native goddesses. Exactly why Isis was able to absorb all these other goddesses is hard to say. In addition to Isis as representative of Divine Wisdom, perhaps more than any other, she symbolized the devoted wife of Osiris and mother of Horus.

The cult of Isis became so intense in Rome that, at times, it was prohibited by law, then restored once again. The last stronghold of the Isis tradition was at her temple on the Island of Philae, where pilgrims from all over the Mediterranean flocked until 537 CE. Subsequently, the temple was closed by Justinian and thereafter converted into a Christian church. From the foundation of Alexandria until the official acceptance of Christianity as the state religion of the Roman Empire by Constantine, ancient polytheism strove hard to survive by re-adaptation. Under the influence of Isis, it experienced a remarkable transformation.

Although finally eclipsed by the triumph of Christianity, Isis survived in the forms of the Black Madonnas and the Blessed Virgin Mary. They follow and parallel the ancient Egyptian statues of Isis as the Throne holding her son

Horus on her lap and portray Mary as the Throne of Wisdom with the infant Jesus on her lap. The religious group of Isis declined only in name, for the potency of her rituals flowed into the sects of the Black Madonnas and the Blessed Virgin Mary, to whom the same qualities, divine works of mercy and love, are attributed. Like the fertile waters of the Nile that brought life to Egyptian people, then as now, the goddess herself returns by another name to enliven her people.[15] [16] The form and name are second to the *essence* and *experience* of her energy. The Black Madonna/Mary holding the infant Jesus on her lap is often portrayed in a manner quite similar to representations of Isis and Horus. Lady Underground exemplifies this reality *par excellence*. What is said of Isis can be said of Lady Underground.

Having crossed over to the rich, ancient culture of Egypt to examine the context of the Isis image, the Egyptian prototype of Lady Underground, we come back more informed to consider her symbolic and analytical meaning. Whereas Isis and other older goddesses were the Mothers of Life, in Christian belief, the Virgin Mary is the Mother of God as incarnated in Christ. Like Isis, her prototype, the Black Virgin, and specifically Lady Underground symbolize and reflect the same overall vision of the whole of creation. But although the Black Virgin is linked to Mary as the Seat of Wisdom, there is a clear distinction implicit in the two images. Within the Christian perspective, particularly the Catholic tradition, distorted attitudes toward instinct, especially as related to sexuality, have sometimes split off nature from spirit. Historically, there has been more emphasis on spirit and less appreciation and value on nature or the body. Because of this, the image of Mary lacks the deeper dimension of instinct that belongs to the older goddesses such as Inanna (Sumerian Goddess of heaven and earth) and Isis. Instinct is cast with a cloud over it because it is associated with the body, temptation, and the sin of Eve. Mary's immaculate conception and the virgin birth of her son cast her outside nature. The dualistic perspective and tendency to split nature and spirit have been issues in Christianity, especially in Roman Catholicism. How to experience, appreciate, and honor the realm of the whole person within the fuller psychic spectrum of energy has been a struggle for many traditions. The image of the Black Virgin, and specifically Lady Underground, does not carry this split, as does the image of the Blessed Virgin Mary. The idea that wisdom, once intrinsic to Isis as the Mother of Life, comes from within nature, and is part of the life process itself, which is within the totality of the Divine, is not easily experienced in relation to the image of Mary.[17] The Black Virgins of the West are true continuators of the ancient Black Goddess tradition in ways that the orthodox rituals and devotions to Mary generally are not.[18] The Black Goddess Isis is personified in the Black Virgins. The Black Maria of Chartres is a primary example.

A protégé of Jung, Gilles Quispel, historian of religion at Utrecht University, lectured at the Jung Institute in San Francisco on the Black Madonna. Quispel had a key role in the international effort of scholars and researchers in the acquisition, translation, and publication of Christian Gnostic Gospels such as the Gospel of Thomas. These early texts, which were leather-bound papyrus manuscripts, were found preserved in an earthenware jar at Nag Hammadi in Upper Egypt in 1945. For Quispel, the Black Madonnas, Chartres being one, have a crucial psychic role in our befriending and embodying consciousness as men and women. For him, unless we become conscious of this primeval image of the Black Madonna and befriend the energy of this archetypal image within ourselves, humankind will be unable to resolve the issues that face our polarized contemporary world. Quispel perceives the Black Madonna as the only living symbol left in Christianity. He has related her to the early Christian Gnostic tradition in which the Mother was called Wisdom, Earth, Holy Spirit, Jerusalem, and even Lord. For the early Christians, the Holy Spirit was personified as the Mother and prayed to because She was considered God. In the Gospel according to the Hebrews, Jesus called the Holy Spirit his Mother.[19]

Thus, we can begin to see the ancient influence of Isis along with the realization that the power of the feminine voice was still manifest in some of the very early historical manuscripts. The inclusion of the feminine is seen also in the second-century work titled *Metamorphosis* or *The Golden Ass*, in which the author, Apuleius,[ii] describes the travail of Lucius, who was accidentally transformed into a donkey. In a beautiful sequence from the story, Lucius, who is at the end of his rope, prays to Isis as the Queen of Heaven for help in his broken life, for rest and peace from his tribulations, and for restoration of his person. Isis, who is moved by Lucius's prayer, responds to him conveying that she is the mother of all life, overseer of the elements, honored all over the earth under many forms, varying rites, and changing names. Isis addresses Lucius: *Behold, I come to you in your calamity. I come with solace and aid. . . .*[20] Lucius's life is touched and transformed by Isis, and further in his story he expresses a prayer to Isis of gratitude, humility, and a deep sense of ineffableness about his experience and relationship with Isis.[21]

Lucius's prayer of the second century is the invocation of many people's prayers in the first and second centuries, many in the ancient manuscripts found at Nag Hammadi, as well as many today in the night sea journey of life, whether we call the feminine energy by the name of Isis, Lady Underground, or another title. Among some of the early texts discovered at Nag Hammadi is a poem, "Thunder, Perfect Mind," lost to the desert silence, where it lay buried for over 2,000 years. The poem is uttered by a strong feminine power, as reflected in some of the lines.

> For I am the first and the last.
> I am the honored one and the scorned one.
> I am the whore and the holy one.
> I am the wife and the virgin. . . .
> I am the bride and the bridegroom. . .
> I am the silence that is incomprehensible... (p. xvi) [22]

By the time Rome took control of the Church, this rich, powerful, feminine voice, reflected in the poem and in Lucius's prayer, was lost to the dominance of an undisputedly patriarchal, masculine voice that referred, in prayer and liturgical ritual, to the Holy Spirit as masculine. The voice and power of the image of the Black Goddess was squelched and forced into the recesses of the underground.

The ancient worldview regarded the Earth as a living body, a living being, who from the beginning of time had been addressed as Earth Mother. The

---

[ii]Apuleius was a Roman writer from North Africa who, after his conversion to the cult of Isis, became one of her priests. Noted from: *Wise Women*, edited by Susan Cahill (W.W. Norton and Company, New York, 1966), p. 6.

power of life did not stem from a transcendent outside energy but was rather an imminent power contained within the field of Nature. Christianity considered this as heresy, and the Protestant Reformation was determined to break from goddess views of the past. God as the creator was seen solely as existing outside of nature and, specifically, outside the body of the goddess. Unlike the perception of today of seeing nature from a quantum cosmic evolutionary view of diversity-in-unity, a dualistic outlook emerged with often harsh value judgments and condemnation made about various diverse aspects of reality and foundational principles of energy. The oneness of all creation was denied, and dualism arose, splitting distinct dimensions of nature, for example, matter and spirit, feminine and masculine, life and death, light and dark, and good and evil.[23]

Symbolic Meaning of Lady Underground

With this background, we now turn to consider more deeply the rich archetypal symbolism of Lady Underground of Chartres. It is important to realize that symbolically she is a testimony to the enduring ancient memory of the *prima materia*. Lady Underground represents and expresses an echo of the rites of Black Isis. Thus, it is no accident that Black Maria is within a grotto, in an underground cavelike dwelling, and near an ancient well where priests and priestesses gathered in prayer to be initiated in the ways of wisdom. Symbolically, Lady Underground represents the potential blessing to be experienced or manifested in the harvest of the crops from the fertile black earth; pregnancy and childbirth; the lush, earthy, ecstatic, pleasures of sexuality and the body; and the joy and passion in love making and all cocreating in the life-death-life cycle. Lady Underground is a powerful symbol of the Black Virgin as the waiting, fertile Earth or the deepest recesses of a womblike cave/crypt. Symbolically, she holds the terrors and beauties of the underworld of our depths as we go through the tenebrous ways of healing and initiation in the ongoing process of our soul about to be born (*Virgo Paritura*). To be held on the lap of the Black Maria is symbolically and paradoxically to have her summon us to more enlivened, soulful conscious life through her dark night of initiation, of disorientation, loss of meaning, confusion, emptiness, darkness, suffering, sacrifice, surrender and death in the alchemical opus of *metanoia*. She is the bridge between our unconscious depths and conscious self, and as such, can open us to befriending the deeper dimensions of our blacker-than-black underground earth, especially our most despised, scorned, rejected, repressed, and dissociated parts of nature as men and women.

Lady Underground sits on a throne, a Primeval Mound, and as with Isis, the experience of her catalyzes a new creation coming forth from this place. As the throne, for the Egyptians, is reminiscent of Primeval Mound, so too, for those whom the Black Madonna summons, the throne of inner, grounding authority emerges gradually, through a dark-night initiation in the descent into the chaotic depths of the unconscious in the process of befriending our darkest self-parts and issues. The Egyptian word for the great flood, the primeval flood, is a feminine word, *mehet weret*. The great flood seems to indicate that the earliest conception of the primeval waters is the feminine. The Mound comes forth out of the chaotic waters. Since the Egyptians saw the feminine principle as the life-giving, creative force bringing forth this Primeval Mound out of the water, so too, Lady Underground emanates the new life, the emergence of expanded meaning, vision, creativity, and the conscious embodiment, born out of the chaotic depths of doing one's inner soul work.

Like the Hindu Goddess Kali, whose name means black, the Lady of the Underground is black. What is the meaning of her blackness? Perhaps the meaning is related to the idea that she is the Earth Goddess and the blackest earth is the richest, the most fertile. Perhaps she is black because, like Kali, she values the dark, the night, the unknown, the rejected, repressed, dissociated, and death aspects of life that Western culture attempts to deny, transcend, or shies away from as part of reality.[24] She is dark as the matrix and dark as the vortex from which all creation comes and to which it returns. Black Maria's depth of underground blackness represents a richness, as seen in Kali. Kali is the personification of death, death in service to life and growth. Arduous and painful as this reality can be, she opens us to new generative life as she confronts and clears us of all that is phony, sentimental, irrelevant, and infantile. She is tough love! She calls us to authenticity! Lady Underground, like Kali, is not only the creator, mother, and nurturer of all, but is also the devouring destroyer and goddess of death. The dark side of life and death are an integral part of nature, manifested in the web of all life. Overall, we are not educated about rites of initiation, darkness, suffering, sacrifice, surrender, and death, so it is no accident that Lady Underground is black. Black is dark and obscure, envelops and swallows, is cavern and abyss, night, despair, and death. Suffering through the many doses of the alchemical cooking process in the annihilating experience of metabolizing Black Maria's archetypal energy is the portal to the mysterious, still light of dark and is, as well, the germinating seed of expanded vision, meaning, and wisdom.

So, in reflecting from a deeper context, what is the meaning of this Madonna's blackness? In the continuum of her deep-reaching dimensions (virgin and conduit of wisdom), she opens the inner eye in the dark of depth to realize gradually that her concealed aspect is a night that heals, a silence that speaks, an unfamiliar and unknown presence that companions, guides, and empowers, a love that illumines, and yet paradoxically, forever remains mysterious and lies beyond our grasp. Furthermore, the dark night of initiation in the Dark Feminine of her energy mirrors and resonates with the blackness of nothingness and the experience of incomprehensible mystery/Mystery, as noted by contemplatives of various traditions, and theologians such as Karl Rahner, S.J., who see the experience of Mystery as forever unknowable, unfathomable, hidden, mysterious, ineffable, the nameless one, or what John of the Cross calls, *silent music*, and *sounding solitude*, what Therese of Lisieux identifies as *a concert*, what Moses de Leon notes as *Hidden of all Hidden!*, what Rumi expresses as *Love, the Supreme Musician*, and what Julian of Norwich refers to as *touchings*. There is more to Lady Underground than what meets the outer physical eye!

Analytical Meaning of Lady Underground

In considering the symbolic meaning of Lady Underground, it is important to also have an awareness of her psychological meaning as well. The magnetic-like power of the energy field behind an archetype can both destroy and create, weaken and restore. The realization of this power psychologically is vital, especially in embodying consciously the potential energy patterns for growth, as we need to recognize the difference between archetypal and personal energy.

Lady Underground, as an archetypal image, holds creative energy for us, so long as we are not identified with it, which would be destructive. The key seems to be to recognize how we relate to the archetypal image in everyday life. The issue is not the feminine *per se*, but how to relate to the dark side of the feminine in a conscious, grounded way. If the containing ego is not strong enough (which only gets developed through good-enough mother energy that is mirrored and mediated, and through befriending, metabolizing, and integrating the shadow, along with the ability to endure holding the tension of the opposites until something new arises from the depths) to relate to the numinous power of Lady Underground without identifying with her, destruction lies ahead. To identify with her is to act as if one *is* she, the Black Goddess, without the rooted feminine ground of awareness that she is who she is and we are who we are in our humanity with all its boundaries. To *identify* with her is hubris, involving an inflated attitude, flawed judgment, or distorted, arrogant, grandiose behavior; in any case, there are destructive consequences. To *relate* to Lady Underground is to be conscious that the ego is the medium through which the divine energy flows but that, most importantly, the ego is *not* the divine energy or the source of that energy.[25] For example, Maya Angelou related to and respected the mystery/Mystery and was a conduit of the divine/Divine energy when she held a soulful poetry reading with all her oozing sensuality, and when she was finished with that, she was about her ordinary life in a down-to-earth enjoyable way, like sharing with others a home-cooked meal! Cellist Yo-Yo Ma was a conduit of the mystery/Mystery in his respective part at the funeral Mass for Senator Edward Kennedy, and when he exited the Basilica, he was simply himself among the many, mingling and being present to those gathered for the service. At John McCain's funeral, Renée Fleming was also a powerful conduit of the divine/Divine energy through her solo, and afterward she joined the congregation.

Marion Woodman, in *Dancing in the Flames: The Dark Goddess in the Transformation of Consciousness*, notes that in the initial development of learning to relate to archetypal energy, we often think of the archetypal as having two opposing sides. For example, we can tolerate thinking of the good-enough mother as providing security, nurturing, cherishing, mirroring, and being the protective feminine, but we in the West tend to split off and dissociate the qualities of the fierce and terrible devouring death goddess.[26] To live a life so split would constellate such rigidity, repression, and devaluation of the dark shadow side of psychic life and would diminish the capacity to discover and to appreciate the gift in the psyche of relating to the archetype in its deeper levels (virgin and conduit of wisdom). In the West, we are not educated for darkness and conscious suffering. People vary in their ability to patiently and willingly persevere with darkness, the unknown, or painful experiences; the natural human tendency is to run from such energy. If one can refrain from manic flight, one can descend into the dark aspects of the unconscious, stay with the alchemical cooking and suffering, and gradually find one's unique way in appropriating and honoring the energy. Paradoxically, one begins to realize that Lady Underground energy is both destructive and creative and, in fact, are one and the same process. As Marion Woodman points out, within a broader view, the words positive and negative ultimately do not apply, as they are judgmental. The goddess who bestows life is the goddess who takes life away. "She is the flux of life in which creation gives place to destruction, destruction in service to life gives place to creation" (p. 7).[27] Without Kali and the same principle that is manifested in Black Maria, the psyche would not be stirred to its depth, or as Jung once noted, "One does not become enlightened by imagining figures of light, but by making the darkness conscious" (*CW 13*, par. 335). Without Lady Underground, there would be no motivation and challenge toward a balanced, differentiated, embodied consciousness, and the gift and the appreciation of the rich, dark, black underground-earth shadow parts of the psyche would remain unintegrated and split off from consciousness. Furthermore, without her, the capacity to experience the deeper, hidden, more sublime dimension of the restorative aspects of the dark black of Lady Underground's dark night of initiation, that is, drinking deeply from the inner well, being empowered for care of both our body and the body of the planet, having a greater ability for relationship, compassion, and wisdom would remain untapped in the unconscious.

Lady Underground's pregnant, recreative nature draws us into the descent, into black darkness, where alchemically our virgin (true) nature is refined in the heat of the progressive, transformative dark night of the descent/ascent journey in the Dark Feminine. This process is no romantic sentimental collective trend. Metabolizing and integrating Lady Underground's energy is the experience of the alchemical operations in all the stages of alchemy, with the *nigredo* being the beginning of the alchemical *opus*. This is not a joy ride for the ego! Psychologically, this process is the night sea journey of individuation. It is a process that involves the cycle of sacrifice and surrender to the life-death-rebirth experience, and the quest from innocence and naiveté to embodied consciousness. (This arduous venture will be developed in Chapters Three and Four through the exploration of the stages of twilight, midnight, and dawn of dark night initiation in the Dark Feminine. The symbolic and psychological aspects will be studied in depth.) For the soul, it is as if Lady Underground holds with benevolence the undeveloped parts and the abandoned, betrayed, despised, condemned, dissociated, and killed-off parts of the psyche that have been forced into the underground of our souls. It is only through the descent into the dark aspects of the unconscious, staying with the suffering as one struggles with the shadow in the *nigredo*, that there is then the possibility that eventually the split-off and undeveloped parts can be integrated into consciousness. The *prima materia* is found in our shadow within our underground, and this is what the Black Maria holds in such reverence. She receives us as we are naturally in our undifferentiated energy and draws us into the cauldron that holds us in the alchemical process of our transformation. In this way, the virgin truth of who we are is born. Again, it needs to be emphasized that, for the ego, this purification process is not experienced as a sweet *aha* moment!

Thus, psychologically, through dark-night initiation, the Dark Feminine, as imaged by Lady Underground, draws us gradually to die to our narrow, one-sided, neurotic, ego knowing; to have the patience and courage to descend into our dark, unknown, chaotic matter; and to discover and to bring forth the richness of the fertile, dark, black earth of who we are as persons. Jung once stated, "The greater the light, the darker the shadow" (*CW 18*, par. 10). Lady Underground challenges us to take off the artificial, cosmetic, one-sided identification with goodness, purity, innocence, naiveté, perfection, roles, accomplishments, control, and "lily-white, light" persona that is cut off from dark shadow, including instincts, and subsequently leaves us ungrounded in reality and far from the simplicity of our truth. Her homeopathic remedy is the restorative necessity, value, and gift of black darkness. Her corrective medicine is through the experience of the alchemical process and several doses of mortification, aridity, darkness, and emptiness. The ego's experience of this homeopathic prescription is not initially one of feeling better, rather, the ego often feels as if dying is the ego's profession! The medicine the ego is summoned to swallow is not always easy to accept. As Jung wrote in *Mysterium Coniunctionis*, "The experience of the Self is always a defeat for the ego" (par. 778).[28] Lady Underground's medicine is captured well by the poet Wendell Berry: "To go in the dark with a light is to know the light. To know the dark, go dark. Go without sight, and find that the dark, too, blooms and sings, and is traveled by dark feet and dark wings" (p. 254).[29] Lady Underground faces us with our blacker than black, with our greatest, horrific fear buried, imprisoned, or frozen in our subtle body and, by drawing us into her alchemical night of initiation, she gradually shows us the treasure hidden away within, and opens us to expanded vision, deeper meaning, purpose, and wisdom. If dark-night initiation in the Dark Feminine can be tolerated, so that the soul experiences the depth of the more sublime dimension of the restorative aspects of Lady Underground, then there is the possibility of being drawn interiorly to an experience of love and of drinking deeply from the inner well. Love brings our infirmities, our wounds of origin within our dark, underground matter into the light of consciousness. Love is the antithesis of fear. Love melts fear. It expands where fear constricts and paralyzes. Love receives and embraces where fear repels and rejects. Love, the mystery/Mystery, heals.

Psychologically, awakening to this Dark Feminine energy imaged through Lady Underground may occur in a variety of ways. Some examples in which the psyche may reveal itself are a dream, a *temenos*, a sculpture piece, an opera, a relationship, a fairy tale, nature, loss, illness, suffering from some aspect of life including trauma, and/or solitude. What is important analytically is that the experience of this Dark Feminine energy in its many, various manifestations needs to be worked with until the energy is unearthed, mediated, metabolized, finds its humanized form, and is consciously embodied within us. Of course, we remember, the energy is never fully embodied, and as finite beings, the energy will always remain beyond all our knowing and our grasp. This process may occur for individuals in different ways. One way that the energy becomes mediated and metabolized is through the analytical relationship. Chapter Four will illustrate how persons can be assisted in humanizing and grounding the Dark Feminine energy through the analytical relationship. This particular relationship holds the potential to be an important, spacious, nonjudgmental container in the analysand's need for mirroring, and for addressing and processing unmetabolized dark shadow, including the soul's attempt to be heard through the body, primitive affect, and infantile neediness, as well as numinous experiences and undeveloped parts, especially in Lady Underground's dark-night initiation rite.

The unconscious depths are an important aspect of our humanity and may be related to and accessed by women and men in various ways according to their needs and inclinations. The alchemical process of metabolizing the Dark Feminine energy can bring about a gradual movement of ensoulment in the transformation of energy from hard and rigid to soft and fluid, from frozen and stiff to open, receptive, and pliable, from distant and absent to present, related, and compassionate, from undifferentiated unconsciousness to differentiated consciousness, and from a constricted, low-vibration energy field to a more sustained, expansive energy field. This renewal is within the relational web of all life. The Black Madonna, as imaged in Lady Underground, calls us not to abort the rich dark earth of who we are, that is, our body, especially our subtle body, with its personal and archetypal cellular memory within the neuropaths of our energetic self, but rather to befriend and to embody the full nature of who we are as men and women. Her message is one that asks us to relate to the goddess as nature and nature as feminine.[30]

While there are many, diverse ways, and there is no one way, the viewpoint described previously arises from my personal and professional experience. My professional background as a Jungian analyst, spiritual director, educator, body-energy practitioner, and as a workshop leader has included 25 years of formal training and experience in body-energy work in many forms. As an analyst, this has been part of my analytical way of working in a more integrative, holistic, and embodied manner in my consulting room. My experience has sensitized me to listening and holding space for the soul with a particular attentiveness and attunement to the body, including the subtle body and the human energy field. When I process a dream, I consider many aspects, while remembering always that the psyche is not experienced in a vacuum, but in and through the body. Thus, I allow myself to wonder what, if anything, does this dream say about the body, where is the energy stuck, and where is the energy attempting to be heard, moved, and integrated in this dream? Regardless of what templates analysts, therapists, or spiritual directors access, what is essential is that the analysand, client, or directee is received and respected in the unique way the mystery/Mystery draws a particular soul in the unfolding analytic, therapeutic, or direction process.

Particular to the Jungian modality of inner work is active imagination, the term Jung used to refer to his work with his inner images. Simply understood, active imagination is a process of engaging one's images for a greater awareness of their meaning. Active imagination is one generative way to objectify the unconscious in order to make it conscious. The technique can be a portal to enhancing one's life, and one's relationships, and to opening to a larger purpose. Jung's experience with active imagination was manifested in different forms. For example, Jung drew and painted his images in journals and in *The Red Book* to give expression to his depths. He entered into dialogue with various inner figures to allow and to honor parts of himself a voice and development in his life. Jung worked with stone, carving images and inscriptions of importance and meaning to him. While Jung had his ways of attending to his inner images, today there are many other ways of doing active imagination that can be accessed, including various forms of body-energy work, which help to facilitate an integrative embodied consciousness. Some other modalities of active imagination are left-hand /right-hand technique, different types of artwork, movement, sand tray, poetry, creative writing, music, ancient or contemporary meditation practice, contemplation, Eye Movement Desensitization and Reprocessing (EMDR), and Emotional Freedom Technique (EFT).[iii] While there is no one way, accessing forms of body-energy work within the scope of various active-imagination exercises adds depth and a more integrated holistic dimension to analytical work. Contemporary science reveals that the adult brain remains open to change throughout the lifespan. Various active-imagination practices are one way to activate the brain in shaping and in promoting integrative well-being, which subsequently widens our capacity for generativity into the interconnected world in which we live. Archetypal energy needs to be unearthed, metabolized, humanized, socialized, and embodied, or otherwise the energy remains unintegrated, and archaic patterns of beliefs, attitudes, emotions, and behaviors continue to be reenacted in life. Remember Nietzsche's wisdom, that if a tree is to grow to heaven, it will need to first send its roots to hell.

[iii]EMDR: Eye-Movement Desensitization and Reprocessing is a form of psychotherapy originated and developed by Francine Shapiro, Ph.D. The therapeutic modality helps to liberate a client/individual into the present by resolving charged psychic realities derived from earlier life experiences that have set in motion a continued pattern of affect, behavior, cognitions, and subsequent identity structures and self-object parts. The therapeutic process uses a bilateral stimulation (eye movement, tones, tapping), in order to reduce the influence of the aforementioned and to allow the development of more adaptive coping mechanisms. EMDR aids in building skills for managing charged affect, which may arise with processing distressing memories. From a Jungian context, it assists in demagnetizing a complex. Also, the technique aids in containment and in being more grounded. This modality can help to build ego strength, manage affect, improve awareness of triggers, and open the active-imagination process and dialogue with self-object parts and the wisdom of the psyche.
EFT: In the late 1990s, Gary Craig originated the therapeutic tool known as Emotional Freedom Technique. EFT is the simplest and most common form of meridian tapping. EFT is a tool that aids a person in demagnetizing physical and psychological issues through the use of meridian tapping while processing content being addressed by the individual. Also, EFT is a way to open the active-imagination process and to dialogue with self-object parts and the deeper layers of the psyche, including wisdom figures. While a person can do the technique alone, as in any form of body-energy work, analytical work, therapeutic work, or spiritual direction, the practitioner, analyst, therapist, or spiritual director serves the other as a valuable witness as the psyche of a soul expresses itself in the journey of ensoulment.

One clinical example is Ann, an analysand who does a session of body-energy work in conjunction with her weekly analytical session. Ann is a 46-year-old single Caucasian schoolteacher who came to analysis because she was depressed. Three years ago, Ann had a numinous dream of an unknown, earthy, black woman that she refers to as Earth Woman. Ann felt both touched and frightened by this image. She drew the figure of the black woman who was underground and brought it to our session to process her feelings and thoughts about the image. Ann wanted to work with the image in her dream through bodywork. Ann's way of bodywork is through her breath, sound, and movement; these modalities are a direct form of active imagination. The conscious focus is on the imaginal as it expresses itself through the breath, sound, and/or movement. The body is the medium; the breath, sound, and movement are the message. Images manifest in the process. In this particular form of work, the active-imagination dynamic and dialogue that arise within the analysand is a felt physical and emotional engagement through the medium of the body. Just as the witness value is key in the analytical relationship, so too, in the psychotherapeutic body-energy work, the role of witnessing seems essential as the psyche expresses itself through the body. Through holding the space consciously and through my presence as a witness, I reverence, support, and contain the unconscious material as it manifests in the analysand. Ann's body-energy work took this form for a few years. As she worked with her dream images by sensing where these images were in her body, she was able then to breathe into these areas through her active imagination. In the process, the images often began to change, cellular memory emerged, and eventually blocked energy gave way to sound being released from her body as some primitive affect; rage or grief was released. Some of the other forms of body-energy work that Ann has initiated in her analytical experience have been EMDR and EFT. The EMDR has been a helpful form of inner work that has assisted Ann in demagnetizing some of her self-limiting beliefs, such as "I'm not good enough," and "I'm not smart enough," as well as some of her various charged emotions, such as anger and resentment. When Ann has been stuck and paralyzed by her fear, or in some form of a fusion complex (she wants to change and simultaneously doesn't want to change), it has been EFT that has been the modality of active imagination and energy work that has been the helpful avenue of shifting her seemingly locked energy grid that is manifested in her tight, constricted body stance. Ann has grown in her somatic awareness through her inner work with her dream images and through various modalities of body-energy work within the analytic frame. Ann's bodywork is one way that she attempts to listen and to honor the deeper layers of her psyche and especially the energy of Earth Woman, as she journeys toward embodied consciousness.

In ancient Egyptian cosmology, the cosmos was likened to a magnified pregnant woman who brings forth life. To experience Lady Underground is to be pregnant symbolically as a small cosmos, that is, a microcosm of the Egyptian cosmos. In Egyptian mythology, the body of Nut swallows the Sun in the evening, regenerates it, and gives birth to it again in the morning. So, the sun's daytime path starts from her pubis and goes to her mouth. Symbolically, to be taken into the dark womb-like heart of Lady Underground is to be regenerated in her womb from the patriarchal way of ego control and will-directed power to a more expanded awareness and embodiment of our true nature. This dark night of initiation in the Dark Feminine is a letting go in the cycle of sacrifice, surrender, and a death to our way, including *our* innocence and naiveté in the "day of development" to be reborn anew in the "afternoon of our life" in a way that respects and relates to the Dark Goddess and that integrates and reflects more of our soul's authentic essence. It is a gradual process of a more expanded conscious embodiment of who we are as men and women within the web of all life in the unfolding Universe Story. It is the night sea journey of progressively befriending and embodying consciously what Hildegard calls "the greening power" or the "moistness" of the spirit/Spirit deep in the human soul and the body of the Earth herself. And, it is the arduous summons of what Paul Tillich, theologian of culture, describes as the challenge to find the heights of the Mystery by delving into the depths of human experience in order to discover the inner well that lies hidden within all of life.

Hence, old wineskins cannot hold new wine. Through alchemical transformation, our old, rigid psychological structures (our adaptive coping and protective defense structures that we developed to sustain ourselves despite family systems, neighborhoods, schools, organizations, churches, etc.) loosen and dissolve through befriending the unknown, chaotic, ambiguous, dark, inner landscapes. It is going by a way of "knowing-by-not-knowing." It is dying to control and will-directedness. Lady Underground demands trust and surrender to the process, and that means entering the obscure darkness. Only through this descent, which seems never-ending and yet necessary, does one progressively come to know one's restorative principle of Eros and wisdom in the arduous path toward consciousness within our evolutionary cosmic-planetary life. It is the journey of Lilith, Inanna, Psyche, and the Black Nubian Woman. This is the life-death-rebirth cycle, the Paschal Mystery, the Mass, the divine feminine alchemical process of slowly being cleansed, cooked, reshaped, and reborn to be returned in dawn of dark-night initiation in the Dark Feminine with a more awakened-passionate heart, compassionate presence, and embodied consciousness within the unfolding Universe Story.

Conclusion

We realize that the old container cannot hold the new energy. The gift of the primordial Dark Feminine energy of Lady Underground is an ancient energy for today's journeyer. This Dark Feminine energy needs to be mediated and personalized if we are to live a conscious, grounded life within the evolving Cosmos Story. We next turn to the following chapter, New Paradigm, to explore the reason and need for this process of interiorization.

In summary, Lady Underground is an archetypal image of the Dark Feminine. On the continuum of the archetypal energy of the Great Mother, the Dark Goddess is the deeper, earthy, immensely powerful "Other," more shadowy, and often hidden, unknown, mysterious, and sublime dimension of the Goddess. The various aspects of potential energy for development in the continuum of her universal patterns are mother, virgin, and conduit of wisdom. Characteristic of the Dark Feminine is allowing paradox, attending to process, and focusing on and being attuned to the present. She emerges at this unprecedented time to challenge our one-sidedness and lack of balance, our human-centered norm of reality and value, and to beckon us to reverse our destructiveness to the Earth and to all forms of life. As we befriend the process of the personalization of the Dark Feminine, we do so with a return to the outer circle of life with a greater awareness and responsibility to the humanization of the body of humanity and its own primary and natural source, namely the Earth herself. Thus, she summons us to new frontiers of embodying a deeper conscious identity both personally and collectively, for in a quantum interconnected and interdependent relational web of life, what happens to one, including the body of the Earth herself, happens to and affects us all. Intimations of her energy reemerge at this turbulent time to awaken us to embody the depth dimensions (virgin and wisdom energy) that we will need if we are to meet the current environmental crisis and to discover our deeper identity as a country and who we are as a part of the global community. Through Lady Underground we (individually, collectively as a culture, and globally as a community) may begin to discover and recover more of our soul's balance and essence within the fuller energy spectrum of life experience, including both light and dark, life and death, creation and destruction, feminine and masculine, joy and sorrow, sexuality and spirituality, fullness and nothingness, all to be consciously honored. Through her we may awaken to the realization that we can live responsibly with meaning, purpose, and direction while responding to the contemporary challenges of our planet. To be drawn by Lady Underground and to surrender to the descent into our interiority through the dark, alchemical excavation process is to open to a renewed birth in embodied consciousness, responsibility, and humble service. With a greater sense of ensoulment, we can break forth in ecstatic dance and in the exaltation of the restorative powers of the Dark Feminine, which is expressed beautifully in the Tao te Ching:

> The Valley Spirit never dies.
> It is named the Mysterious Feminine.
> It is there within us all the while
> And the doorway of the Mysterious Feminine
> Is the base from which heaven and earth sprang.
> Draw upon it as you will, it never runs dry. (p. 31) [31]

INNER WORK

The beauty of the Way is that there is no "way."
~Loy Ching-Yuen

Naturalness is called the Way.
~*The Secret of the Golden Flower*

The way is not in the sky. The way is in the heart.
~Gautama Buddha

I give you news of the way of this man, but not of your own way.
My path is not your path…The way is within us, . . .[W]ho should live your
own life if not yourself? So live yourselves. The signposts have fallen,
unblazed trails lie before us. Do you not know that you yourselves
are the fertile acre which bears everything that avails you?
~C.G. Jung, The Red Book

The right way to wholeness is made up of fateful detours and wrong turnings.
It is…not straight but snakelike, a path that unites the opposites,
. . .a path whose labyrinthine twists and turns are not lacking in terrors.
~C.G. Jung, Psychology and Alchemy

Don't be satisfied with stories,
how things have gone for others.
Unfold your own myth.
~Rumi

While there is no *one* way, the following modalities are offered for exploration and assistance in honoring, unearthing, metabolizing, integrating, and embodying material that engages the reader's depths. These various forms of active imagination and inner work are intended as possible ways to open to deeper levels of meaning in the quest toward consciousness. These subsequent offerings in no way exhaust the many viable means of doing inner work, nor is the noted material meant as a substitute for listening attentively to the intimations of the mystery/Mystery, to one's own creative depths, and/or to the clues and the guidance that can arise from the psyche in soul's process of growth. Inner work sections will follow each chapter.

~Reflection, Discussion, and Journaling Questions

- There are many images of the Dark Feminine. Who is the Dark Feminine for you, and how have you experienced her in your life?
- What is your understanding of the Dark Goddess as manifested in the archetypal image of Our Lady of the Underground?
- What intrigues you about Lady Underground?
- In celebrating and integrating the ever-ancient, ever-new energy of Lady Underground, name and describe how you metabolize and embody her energy in your life.
- In what way does Lady Underground challenge you to grow?
- Realizing that Isis is a prototype of Lady Underground, how does Isis and all that she symbolizes relate to what matters most for you?
- What aspects of the cultural milieu of ancient Egypt are rich resources for our contemporary culture?
- In what way does the mythology of ancient Egypt speak to the contemporary psychospiritual seeker?
- Befriending and embodying the archetypal energy of Lady Underground requires embracing the recurrent energy of the growth cycle of sacrifice in the life-death-rebirth process, along with the developmental challenges of the quest motif in our life. Where do you perceive the signs of death, chaos, and/or the eruption of diehard

archaic patterns of energy in your life and in the global community that are calling for a conscious shift?

- How have you perpetuated or colluded in the repression of the feminine and especially the Dark Feminine? Where is the repression of the feminine operative in our institutions, our country, our world, our planet?

~Process Exercises

- After reading Chapter One, consider the image that captures and engages your attention. Find a comfortable posture that enables you to be in silence. Close your eyes, bring your attention to your breathing and take a few long, deep-belly breaths while allowing the belly muscles to relax. Then, begin to exhale slowly as you allow your body to relax, release, and let go as you open and enter into the silence. Stay with the relaxing, deep-belly breaths until you are present to yourself in your body. When you feel attuned to yourself, begin to call to your awareness the image that caught your attention in Chapter One as you continue to breathe naturally. Then, take another deep-belly breath and, as you exhale, focus in and notice what is arising within your body as you are present to yourself. Maintain this process of deep-belly breathing, of exhaling slowly, followed by focusing in and paying attention to what is manifesting in your body as you are present to yourself. Consider doing this exercise for about 20 minutes. Next, take another deep-belly breath, and as you exhale slowly, focus in and be attentive to what you notice as you are present to yourself. When you are ready, begin to open your eyes as you reorient yourself to your outer dwelling. Take some time to recall your experience. You may want to record it as a way to respect and to objectify further your depths. Some possible reflection questions to consider might be:
    - If your image could speak, what would the image express to you?
    - What was it like for you to experience your image?
    - Did the image change in any way during the process?

- What is the psyche attempting to engineer as you are attentive to this image?
- If you were to speak to your image, what might you want to communicate?
- What have you learned from the experience?
- Finally, as you focus again on your breath, acknowledge yourself and your depths for your inner work as you bring closure to your process.

- Jung observed the tendency of the human psyche to use a circle or a sphere to convey wholeness. He called these psychic images mandalas, a Sanskrit word meaning circle. The mandala is a universal symbol of the Self that expresses the psyche's fundamental orientation toward wholeness. Jung often sketched mandalas in his notebook as a way to be attentive to his soul in his search for meaning and development. Draw a mandala of the image that engaged your attention in Chapter One. Or consider what you most question, wonder about, or struggle with as you reflect on the material in Chapter One. If your "wonderment," "question," or "struggle" had a color or an image, what would it be? Draw a circle, be mindful that there is a center to the circle and then allow yourself to express your color or image in the form of a mandala. Give yourself permission to spontaneously allow what emerges and unfolds within you and then express it in your mandala. When you are finished, notice and record the feelings, thoughts, or sensations that you experienced while drawing your mandala and after completing your mandala. What awareness have you discovered through this exercise?
- Reflect on what moves, inspires, intrigues, concerns, and/or disturbs you in Chapter One. Consider allowing yourself to enter into an active-imagination exercise with this part of yourself. An active-imagination exercise is a dialogical process between the conscious and the unconscious in an attempt to assimilate unconscious contents through some form of self-expression. This type of exercise gives a voice to parts of the personality that are usually not heard. While

there are many ways of doing active imagination, this particular process exercise invites you to consider doing a right-hand /left-hand active-imagination experience. Find a quiet place that is conducive to self-reflection and allow 20 to 30 minutes of uninterrupted time to do the exercise. You will need a ballpoint, a felt pen, or a pencil and some paper or a personal journal. Remember your dominant hand represents your conscious voice and your nondominant hand in this exercise represents the part of you that is "moved," "inspired," "intrigued," "bothered," or some unconscious part of the personality with which you would like to work. Begin with your dominant hand and allow to arise what comes forth, as you start to write what is emerging within you. Then switch to your other hand, your nondominant hand, and allow this hand, which represents some part of your unconscious, to express freely whatever is emerging as you respond to the conscious part of you (represented by the dominant hand). As the dialogue unfolds, continue to switch the pen/pencil from one hand to the other, as you allow the respective parts to be expressed. When your process feels complete, bring closure to your process and acknowledge yourself for your inner work. This is a powerful way to do an active-imagination exercise in working with your dream images, and inner parts of your personality that are longing to be heard, befriended, and integrated into consciousness. Of what have you become conscious through your active-imagination exercise?

~Body-Energy Work

- After reading Chapter One, consider what reality is stirred in your depths that is challenging you to a more enlarged self-awareness. Regarding this reality, what (if any) are the discounting beliefs, attitudes, or charged feelings that you have about yourself that are gripping you and driving you in your present life? Record your self-limiting beliefs, attitudes, or charged feelings, and consider doing an EMDR exercise with a trained EMDR practitioner as one possible way to demagnetize the discounting beliefs and possible charged feeling-toned response and cellular memory surrounding the reality that is challenging you. This process is a creative way to access the active imagination in the experience of healing and integration.

- Meridian tapping, of which Emotional Freedom Technique is the simplest and most common form, is an effective tool that can assist in the process of demagnetizing self-limiting beliefs, shadow material, complexes, or the struggle with the tension of opposites. Gary Craig is the originator of EFT. The modality uses tapping on key acupuncture points while calling to awareness self-limiting beliefs, charged emotions, or some issue of concern. Extensive scientific research reveals that EFT is an effective tool in addressing physical and psychological issues, including anxiety, depression, and post-traumatic stress. This technique can be a vital tool in demagnetizing a charged complex, an intrusive self-defeating thought, or a gripping emotion in the everyday journey of life.

Reflect on the recorded list from the previous exercise. Given the reading and what was activated within you, ask yourself: In this present moment, what captures your attention the most that is longing to be heard, metabolized, and integrated in embodied consciousness? Conscious of your self-limiting beliefs and charged emotions, consider doing an EFT session with a qualified EFT practitioner. Doing an EFT sequence is a way to engage your depths and to objectify what is attempting to be integrated into consciousness. The tapping is a modality of body-energy work that touches into the active-imagination process and potentially offers a more integrative approach in the process of inner soul work. After your EFT session, consider recording your experience in a journal. The following reflective questions may assist you in objectifying and integrating further your EFT body-energy experience:

- What did you learn about yourself through your EFT experience?
- How was your active imagination opened in this experience?

    - As you focus on your inner life right now, what is arising within you as you are present to yourself?
    - In reflecting on your inner work and your present outlook, what do you perceive the psyche is attempting to engineer?
    - What is the summons of your soul at this time in your life?
    - How are you willing to honor your soul's summons in your everyday life?
    - Take some time to acknowledge yourself and the inner work you have done.
- What image speaks to you the most from Chapter One? As you bring your awareness to your breath and scan your body, where do you sense the energy of this image within your body? Consider finding a quiet and safe setting where you might have space to move and not be interrupted in any way. Allow yourself to take a deep breath and focus on whatever image is emerging in you right now that most captures your attention. Again, where do you sense the energy of this image in your body. In this exercise of soulful arising movement, your breath, sound, and movement are a direct form of active imagination. The conscious focus is on the imaginal as it expresses itself through the breath, sound, and/or movement. In this process, the body is the medium; the breath, sound, and movement are the message. In this particular form of tracking your image within the experience of your body, the active-imagination dialogue is a felt physical and emotional engagement through the medium of the body. Allow yourself to move freely in your soulful arising body movement, and when your experience feels complete, take a deep breath as you find your way to bring closure to your process. When you are finished you might want to record your experience as another way of objectifying and befriending your depths. This body-movement exercise can also be done with two others: One person holds consciously the space for the individual who is the body mover; and the other is the observer. The exercise can allow 10 or 15 minutes for the movement component and then time for processing the exercise. Again, if you do this body-

movement exercise alone, or if you do it in the presence of two others, remember before you finish to take time within yourself to acknowledge yourself for your inner work.

CHAPTER TWO
NEW PARADIGM

Sooner or later, nuclear physics and the psychology of the unconscious will draw closer together, as both of them independently of one another and from opposite directions, push forward into transcendental territory.
~C.G. Jung

The day is not far distant when humanity will realize that biologically it is faced with a choice between suicide and adoration.
~Pierre Teilhard de Chardin

Why are we able to master great technology, but do not yet
understand our own hearts? . . .the nature of love?
And why are we willing to make endless outer journeys but are
loath to make the significant one: the journey within.
The inward journey may frighten us, yet it. . .holds the real treasure.
There...spirit waits to reveal. . .the secrets of
what is holy, and the encounters with truth that change everything.
It is the journey that opens the eye of the heart...
~Paula D'Arcy

Enter by the narrow gate. The gate is wide and the road easy
that leads to destruction and many choose to travel it.
Narrow is the gate and difficult the road that leads to life, and few find it.
~Matthew 7: 13-14.

Introduction to the New Paradigm

Presently, in this historical time, our country, global community, and planet are undergoing a major evolutionary shift, and this development cries out for and summons us to a new paradigm of an embodied consciousness. An overshadowing turbulent dark night looms for humanity and all planetary spheres of life, beckoning us forth and obliging us to embrace transformation in adapting to a new way of being and a new worldview of an embodied consciousness more radical than most people want to consider and/or can imagine. The famous Indian mystic and scholar Aurobindo Ghosh noted at the end of his life that if there was to be a future for humanity, it will wear the crown of feminine design. Richard Tarnas, philosopher and cultural historian, postulates in his famous book *The Passion of the Western Mind* that there is a tremendous need for the emergence of the feminine, and in particular a new mode of perception in our culture that heralds the end of the old paradigm and the protracted era of fundamentally patriarchal dominance and control of the "Western mind."[32] Andrew Harvey, the internationally acclaimed poet, novelist, mystical scholar and teacher, and author of more than 30 books, stresses that awakening to the sacred feminine is a crucial part of surviving the next era of humanity. Harvey is ardent about this reality: Unless we know consciously "what the sacred feminine really is—its subtlety and flexibility, but also its extraordinarily ruthless, radical power of dissolving all structures and dogmas, all prisons in which we have sought . . .to imprison ourselves—we will be taken in by patriarchal projections of it" (p. 1).[33] Without question, our cosmic world is in a major transition and a crossroad, an era that is both perilous and promising. At this significant time, depth psychology keenly serves humanity by raising our awareness of recognizable archetypal patterns that form, shape, and guide the emerging, evolving, and unfolding planetary story of continuity, change, and meaning. We know within Jungian psychology that the Dark Feminine archetypal energy allows energies of difference and/or opposites to coexist creatively. For example, the Dark Feminine seeks to empower both feminine and masculine energies in a mutual interaction of equals in which neither is subordinated or sacrificed to the other. As the regime of patriarchy in all cultures, in its many dark, complex, oppressive, and deep-seated manifestations, begins and continues to crumble and disintegrate around the world, the summons, desire, and search for a more expanded horizon of an embodied consciousness demands our perduring, discriminating, and discerning attention. Unending courage and trust in the process is heroically needed. The ongoing difficulty and daunting task, as we attempt to move toward this challenge, is the awareness that doing so calls for both an embodied conscious personalization of the feminine archetypal energy (both the dark and light aspects) based on the language of Analytical Psychology and a well-grounded interiorized religious development based on the language of contemporary integrative spirituality.

An aspect of the Dark Feminine, especially the image of Lady Underground, is the emphasis on the essential role of the body in bringing the energy inherent in the archetypal symbol into life. As noted above, it is the nature of the Dark Feminine to empower energies such as the feminine and masculine to coexist creatively within the flow of life. When we are in proper relationship to the Dark Feminine, we have a greater capacity for the creative holding and balancing of the mutual interplay of the energies within the container of the body, rather than splitting, demonizing, and banishing one side or dimension of the different energies into the unconscious. For example, the Dark Feminine's gift and summons for conscious sojourners is to honor, balance, and integrate with discrimination both the feminine and masculine energies. The creative dynamism of this archetypal energy of the Dark Feminine is an integrative "both/and" rather than a dualistic "either/or" vision.

Subsequently, this chapter will address the present historical need for an embodied humanization of the archetypal energy of the Dark Feminine. The theory and language of Analytical Psychology offers a window to understand this particular archetype. Furthermore, the theory and practice of Analytical Psychology is a rich resource in contributing and assisting the culture's shift in this direction. The paradigm shift that is called for in this 21st century is supported by the scientific underpinnings of quantum physics, which is a creative complementarity to Analytical Psychology. We now turn to explore the call and need for the change.

Characteristic of the old, dying paradigm, historically, are polytheism and monotheism as we have often experienced them, both of which involve a projection "out there" onto Mother (Nature) or Father (Sun) or their surrogates.[34] For example, in all religious traditions there is the tendency to project outward the god or goddess energy onto outer "carriers" within a particular tradition. Some fervent believers, such as devotees or zealous disciples, can have an inordinate attachment and a clinging attitude to these "carriers" manifested in some concretized way or within the tradition. As noted in Chapter One, the issue is not the archetype *per se*, but rather the difficulty is how to relate to the archetype in a conscious way in everyday life without identifying with the archetype or being attached to a representation of the archetype, such as Lady Underground. To relate to the archetypal energy is to be conscious in a grounded way that the ego is the instrument through which the divine energy flows and that the ego is not the divine energy or the source of that energy. To be excessively attached and cling to any various religious rituals, practices, sacred places, statues, texts, "religious" articles, authority figures, or a particular institution such as "Mother Church" is to keep the energy somewhat projected outward. Such clinging and strong attachments are risky because the tendency is toward illusionary thinking and magically believing that the god and goddess are "out there" or within the concretized makeup of the "carriers" of our projections. Perhaps to our surprise and shock, in reality, in attachments and projections it may be understood that our gods and goddesses are all "outside." Jung warned against this tendency and challenged especially the Christian tradition to offer resources that would assist the believer to experience potentially the kingdom within:

> Too few people have experienced the divine image as the innermost possession of their own souls. Christ only meets them from without, never from within the soul. So long as religion is only faith and outward form, and the religious function is not experienced in our own souls, nothing of any importance has happened. It has yet to be understood that the *mysterium magnum* is not only an actuality but is first and foremost rooted in the human psyche (par. 12-13).[35]

Probably, most of us would deny consciously the tendency to keep the energy of such attachments projected outward in our everyday lives, especially in the practice of our spirituality until, as Jung noted, our attachments, that is, our one-sidedness or our neuroses, are challenged, especially in the second half of life when we are confronted with our false selves, idols, and false gods/goddesses.[36] [37] Jung described this time in life as a call to shift from an outer orientation to an inner orientation. In his view, this shift marked the major turning point between the first and second halves of life.[38]

The mystic St. John of the Cross, in his classical writings on *The Dark Night*, insisted, "*nada, nada*," in other words, don't make anything (drugs, money, sex, power) your god or goddess.[39] In the classic *The Interior Castle*, Teresa of Avila states that the problem in life is that we do not know ourselves because of our outer numerous preoccupations; hence, we have a certain level of understanding but, fundamentally, we do not grasp our reality.[40] We roam outside the castle of our lives, preoccupied with many things, in each of which we long or search for something more. Teresa acknowledges that in her own life she wandered for 18 years, torn among numerous preoccupations, business affairs, for example, family, friends, possessions (each potentially good in itself), and the call to a deeper living.[41] Meandering ungrounded outside the castle or "crypt" of our lives, thrusting the energy of the gods/goddesses outward and /or concretizing the energy in certain forms within any one religious practice or tradition or reality in life leaves us unconnected to our real depths and to our capacity for embodied awareness. The more we are driven and at the cause and effect of the "outside," the less free we are to be attentive to the intimations of the mystery/Mystery and the summons of our soul. To continuously cling, subtle though it may be, to "the right one" or "the perfect one," or "the way" or "the truth" and/or to concretize the archetypal energy of the god or goddess is to project the energy outward onto a "carrier." As indicated earlier, one who does so runs the risk of becoming one-sided or neurotic, of aborting the challenge to incarnate, humanize, personalize, and embody the archetypal energy, and of never discovering and personally experiencing the kingdom within one's nature. Matthew Fox, a contemporary creation theologian, in his book *One River, Many Wells: Wisdom Springing from Global Faiths*, reminds us of an important truth in the process of this night sea journey of befriending and embodying the archetype of the god or goddess. Fox begins his observation with a quote from the Christian mystic Meister Eckhart:

> 'Divinity is an Underground river that no one can stop and no one can dam up.' There is one underground river—but there are many wells into that river: an African well, a Taoist well, a Buddhist well, a Jewish well, a Muslim well, a Goddess well, a Christian well, and aboriginal wells. . . .To go down a well is to practice a tradition, but we would make a grave mistake (an idolatrous one) if we confused the well itself with the flowing waters of the underground river. Many wells, one river. (pp. 4-5)[42]

The divine mystery has relied, and continues to rely, on the evolution of human consciousness for an ongoing embodied revelation, that is, an embodied personalization of the archetypal energy. As noted in Chapter One, this energy is manifested through mediatorial images/symbols, which are the language of the unconscious. For Jung, a symbol is the best possible expression of something relatively unknown. It does not define or explain; rather, it points beyond itself to a meaning that cannot be sufficiently expressed in the familiar words of our language.[43] The precise image is the bridge or the transformer that carries the energy between unconscious and conscious, self and other, and self and the web of all life. Our reverence is for the mystery/Mystery and our service is to the mystery/Mystery, not to the bridge or the transformer.[44] While the image initially appears from the unconscious as "numinous," and while the temptation to become attached to this felt sensory aspect can be strong, over time there is a gradual fading of the numinous energy through a symbol.[iv] [45] Remembering Ignatius Loyola's wisdom on discernment in his *The Spiritual Exercises of St. Ignatius* (Jung both valued and lectured on the *SE* in 20 lectures from June 16, 1939, to March 8, 1940) is helpful about this reality. Ignatius states his guidance in the form of a probing reflective question: "Are you more attached to the consolations of God, or the God of consolations?" We are in service to the mystery/Mystery not to the bridges or the transformers. That is *nada, nada.*

[iv] The experience of the "numinous" will be discussed in detail in Chapter Three.

When Gods/Goddesses Die

When an image in any mythic-poetic system, religious tradition, or institution no longer points beyond itself to the mystery/Mystery, then it is empty and dead for us. It is devoid of meaning and of the numinous for us. When this occurs, for whatever reason, then the bridge as a vital and meaningful source of divine energy in the psyche dies for us. Attempts at trying to crank up the energy in our control driver, and/or in our magical thinking, as if we are the master of it, is an illusion. To continue to give credence to these images in some form of ritual or worship in an attempt to derive meaning, satisfaction, or consolation is to be in service to false gods/goddesses.[46]

Furthermore, psychologically speaking, a false god/goddess is a lesser god/goddess, meaning a more constricted, rigid psyche and subsequently a tendency to be less grounded within one's human development.[47] The more one is on the outside, the less one is related to the depths within one's soul. To be attached or to be "wedded" to a false god/goddess is to concretize the energy into an idol, which is inconsistent with the actual nature of mystery. When the energy becomes fixated or literalized in a belief, an image, a ritual, a spiritual practice, or a certain stance in life that is no longer generative, it tends toward rigidity and fundamentalism. This literalizing of the energy is an act of hubris or of blasphemy, as it is an endeavor to control the autonomy of mystery/Mystery by fixing the image. As James Hollis notes in *Tracking the Gods: The Place of Myth in Modern Life*, the fixation of image is literalism, and literalism is idolatry.[48] Idolatry is not the outcome of people's obstinately choosing that which is positively insidious. Idolatry is generally the result of something good being revered beyond its value. It is a good upheld to an extreme and thereby distorted. It is a good become a "god." Anything to which we have overly intense, invested energy can become a "god." Some of the leading, enslaving gods of our age are power, money, sex, drugs, relationships, possessions, internet, and political and scientific certitude. Often these gods/goddesses are worshipped not out of conscious authentic love, but out of compensation for an unconscious, inordinate need for control and order, security and power, and/or to anesthetize emotional pain, such as self-hatred manifesting as coldness, lack of feeling, and/or obsessiveness. Regardless of the form of attachment and idol worship, it tends to be self-validating, self-perpetuating, self-protective, resistant to change and dialogue, and consequently deaf to the call of psyche's path or to psychospiritual, embodied awareness.

Thus, to continue to give credence, to cling, and to be wedded to our attitudes toward images and behavior that are stagnant is to worship false gods/goddesses and to limit the autonomy of divine energy to what can be experienced and contained. This perpetual attachment to this "clutch" approach in life may lower anxiety somewhat and may provide a false suit of armorlike clothes to a personal illusory security and to an overidentified religious persona. However, as Hollis states in *Tracking The Gods*, the truly religious attitude toward life obliges us to suffer ambiguity, to endure the unknown, to discern the movement of mystery as it changes and disappears, and to await patiently the mystery's new emerging manifestation..[49]

Attending Mystery

Throughout time, keen observers of the depths such as poets, artists, musicians, and mystics have been attentive to the intimations of mystery/Mystery. In the same way for all of us, the development of the human personality, through the individuation process, summons us to a perduring attentiveness to subtlety in words, images, emotions, and the resonance of energy with courage, openness, trust, patience, and discernment for the direction of the soul's energies. Respecting and surrendering to this emerging, evolving, and unfolding reality is not always easy! The ego is often unattuned and unaware of the deeper archetypal stirrings within the psyche, including the somatic unconscious. These universal patterns of energy are attempting to form, shape, and guide the soul's summons to authenticity, meaning, homecoming, and service. Honoring this dynamic is also true for the development and growth of any institution, culture, or global community. As an individual, institution, culture, or global community matures, a greater tolerance of ambiguity and chaos is necessary, both for growth and for reverence for the mystery/Mystery, especially in an unfolding evolutionary universe! This growth process of a perduring attentiveness to mystery/Mystery is within the energy structure of the planet. Energy underlies all life. Energy flows in certain patterns, along specific paths, interacting and interrelating, affecting and connecting matter and consciousness alike. Both our inner and outer landscapes are paradoxically characterized by the dynamics of the opposites of chaos and creativity, threat and promise, destruction and innovation, extinction and transformation. The principle of equilibrium or entropy specifies that the distribution of energy in the psyche strives toward a balance. As Jung stated:

> The psyche is a self-regulating system that maintains itself in equilibrium as the body does. Every process that goes too far immediately and inevitably calls forth a compensatory activity. Without such adjustments a normal metabolism would not exist, nor would the normal psyche. (par. 159) [50]

Although the energy represented in polarities seeks stability, such a state is never fully realized. The polarity of energy is indispensable for the life of the psyche, the growth of the soul, and the evolution of the world soul. If there were no exchange of energy, the psyche would cease to function. This dynamic is operative in all of nature. The awareness of this reality is key to understanding the overall underpinnings of this chapter. The exploration of quantum physics and Analytical Psychology will hopefully provide even more clarity.

Quantum Physics and Analytical Psychology

In 1932, Jung and Wolfgang Pauli, the world-renowned physicist and 1945 Nobel Prize winner, began their long friendship in the dialogue of Analytical Psychology and quantum physics. Through the association of these two pioneer thinkers, developments in physics profoundly influenced the evolution of Jungian psychology. Conversely, many of Jung's abiding themes shaped how Pauli understood the physical world. These thinkers shared a sensibility both with theorists at the frontier and the alchemists of old.[51]

What is quantum theory? In essence, quantum theory states that the whole is greater than the sum of its parts. This principle underpins all reality. What we sense and experience is a great deal more than the initial, external impression that we may glean. We experience life, not in isolated segments, but in *wholes* (quanta). Regardless of what our physical eye may observe, the constellation of energy in form is not inert, lifeless pieces of matter, but living energies. Moreover, our naming of the living reality we experience will be less than what its real essence is: an essence best understood by interacting with it experientially rather than attempting to conceptualize the reality.[52] [53]

At a perceptual level, quantum theory evokes a new creative way of viewing and understanding the world. Rather than seeing the world from a classical lens of solid objects, governed by deterministic laws of nature, the quantum view sees the world as dynamic and alive. The nature of reality at the microscopic, subatomic level is seen as connecting, interacting, and interrelating. Jung's view of the archetype as an energy continuum of infrared to ultraviolet frequencies coincides with the quantum idea of patterns of energy that touch our lives not as an inert, lifeless reality, but as a living, vibrational energy. When an alive pattern of energy, such as the archetypal image of Lady Underground, breaks through to consciousness, the energy modifies conscious understanding and meaning. The structure of our belief system, once held as truth, is altered not by will-directedness, but from the surging energy arising deep within our psyche, moving and weaving the story of our soul as we birth more of our essence and embrace a more expanded sense of our soul's path and call. This emerging energy beckons us forth to claim and embody consciously a deeper interiority, which allows for more of the depth of our true nature. In this process, we need to remember that from the view of quantum theory and Analytical Psychology, an archetypal image (Lady Underground) is more than our perceptions and experience of it and more than any attempt to name the living reality we experience.

Jung used the image of a spectrum in describing the energy flow and balance between instinct and spirit in the psyche. (Remember, when Jung is talking about instinct and spirit, Jung is speaking from the context of the interplay and flow of energy within a continuous range of an energetic field. Jung, in his evolutionary quantum view, perceived humanity from a holistic perspective and not from a dualistic mindset. In discussing instinct and spirit, he is describing different aspects of the energy flow within a continuum of the psychoid spectrum of the interactive energy field. Jung is not conversing theologically, as some contemporary theologians tend to contend and, thus, misunderstand and misinterpret him.) The dynamism of instinct, in which all bodily instinctual energies originate, is at the infrared frequency end. At the ultraviolet frequency end is the dynamism of the archetype in which images and dreams originate. The archetype is *psychoid*, meaning that its energy can be experienced through both body and psyche. Again, Jung is not speaking dualistically, for the body is the manifestation of the psyche. The key is honoring, holding, and balancing the energy in a grounded, conscious way, versus tending toward only one dimension or being overidentified with one end of the spectrum. At this historical time, with the emerging pattern of the Dark Feminine energy, as exemplified in the symbol of Lady Underground or some other image of the Dark Feminine, it is vital to humanize and to embody this energy from a quantum physics view, if our world is to embrace the new paradigm and a greater complexification of consciousness. Lady Underground is one image of the Dark Feminine energy. To embody her energy is to unleash the often stymied and repressed Dark Goddess energy from the unconscious earth of our bodies, which causes our being energetically to vibrate in a resonance that is known and felt consciously. Furthermore, it is to open to the deeper dimensions of her energy, the virgin and conduit of wisdom energy, which is so needed now in our culture and global community. The tension of the opposites must be held consciously, within the body, until the energy has a chance to transform into the ultraviolet side of the archetype and until the emergence of the creative new energy, a gradual process that is one long dark night of the soul. The body vibrating with new energy resonance is the same as the vibration in sound waves in the quantum sense. A soul that is vibrating embodied higher resonance stands to connect, interact, and interrelate in deeper and richer realms and causes a rippling effect around it in the ordinary of everyday life.

To ground this theory, I tell the story of my tribal drum, which was given to me as a gift from the Tonga people and Koka, a medicine man, out in the bush of Zimbabwe in southern Africa. I was invited to visit the Tongas and to teach Reiki. On my journey I had made arrangements with my guide and translator to meet and dialogue with a medicine man out in the bush. This experience was a real highlight of my adventure to Africa. An example of the quantum vision is my drum. It is currently used in workshops, in group settings of people gathered for solitude, and in symbolic rituals. Externally, the drum seems to be a dead, inert, material object that I could dismantle into its various parts. But if I take any fragment of the drum and place it under a powerful microscope, I will discover moving particles. In the quantum context, I am invited to view my drum as something that is alive. It is made from the wood of a tree in the bush and the skin of a bull that was slaughtered by the Tongas for a community celebration.

Koka, the medicine man, insisted that the drum's skin be made from a freshly slaughtered bull and not from an old skin, as the drum was to go to America for a "new healing energy work." The skin was placed in the river and covered with mud for three days in order to strip the hair from the skin and to soften it to be fired and stretched for the cover of the drum. The design painted on the drum came from a dream of the medicine man, and the paint used came from the sap of the tree. The "life" is crystallized in the skin and in the timber, which are composed of the same particles that make up my body and everything else in the universe. I witnessed the alchemical process of the slaughter, sweat, toil, love, joy, and creativity of the Tongas, which gave my drum its essential nature and which is having an effect on my feelings and thinking as I write these words.

The drum was heated over the campfire and played at a ritual celebration, followed by a feast, and then used for the dance that took place around the campfire before it was presented to me as a gift. This drum traveled all over the world for six months via the mail before arriving at Dulles International Airport. My drum is a constellation of living energy, which at subtle, energetic levels affects my psyche, just as I am affecting my drum when I play it.

Another practical, everyday example of the quantum model is turning on a light switch. From objective watching, the action of flipping on the light may be described as cause and effect. Quantum thought calls and challenges us to the awareness that such an "effect" is only viable in an electromagnetic universe. Lifting your hand to activate the light is also affected by the law of gravity. Hence, there is more to turning on the light than mere cause and effect, which has to do with the "part" that can only be fully comprehended within the wider universal "whole."[54]

What is the interplay of depth psychology and quantum physics? The continuing evolution of cultural and global consciousness is dependent on holistic conscious participation in the individuation process—not as isolated beings, but as cocreative, conscious participators in an alive, pulsating universe where everything connects, interacts, and interrelates. We are not the masters of creation; we are collaborators in a dynamic process that is much greater than we. Moreover, we need to stop experiencing the world as a purely physical entity, separate and distinct from ourselves, and relate to it as a flow of energy that by its nature includes us. We are all interconnected in this electromagnetic evolving universe. Our capacity to influence global and planetary consciousness will emerge through cooperative interaction rather than competitive discord. Furthermore, our interrelationship with the web of all life is a learning of respectful interdependence and not that of domination, exploitation, terrorism, combat, and warfare — dangerous and lethal dynamics that can lead to ultimate self-destruction. September 11 is a horrific manifestation of this deadly reality.

Jung and Pauli, in addition to the famous paleontologist Pierre Teilhard de Chardin, S.J., were forerunners regarding the realization that consciousness is a property of all living systems. In a quantum context, this realization becomes the basis of not merely the awareness, but more importantly for relationships, an innate potential for mutual cooperation within the one relational web of all beings and systems in creation. Within this model there is a shift from dualistic independent identities to interconnected and interdependent relationships within the one quantum universe. For example, this might be manifested in the consciousness of an analyst and analysand in a felt new level of the analytical relationship experienced in the interactive field in the consulting room. Another realm of appearance might be the emerging awareness of a newly felt bond of oneness with the universe itself, as in an experience of a sunrise or a sunset.[55]

There is on the horizon a growing paradigm shift, and this change is being informed by a shift in the quality of human and planetary consciousness. In 1971, Dr. David Bohm, a physicist at London University who had worked with Einstein, proposed that the universe itself is a hologram. He was inspired to create a model of the universe that could incorporate the many paradoxes of quantum physics.[56] [57] Bohm claimed that the cosmos is not a dualistic universe. The holographic model states that every piece is an exact representation of the whole and can be used to reconstruct the entire hologram. An individual and society are by nature a whole that appears as a dynamic web of inseparable energy patterns. The emphasis is on process, movement, and energy. In the creative current, past, present, and future are indistinguishable. Every creation of matter, influenced as it is by consciousness, is a recapitulation of all past creation and holds an inherent propensity to become something more than it is at any present moment. For Bohm and modern physicists, reality is an unbroken, coherent whole that is involved in an unending process of change called holomovement.[58]

Thus, if the paradigm shift that is occurring is to be furthered, and if this creative holographic movement of consciousness is to proceed at personal and societal levels, detachment from our idols, as noted previously, is necessary. In our evolutionary quantum universe, soul is summoning us to a broader conscious interiority that beckons us to greater responsibility and generative service in our cosmic development. The time has dawned for us to adopt a broader perspective based on cooperation rather than on patriarchal supremacy and planetary domination. Holistic consciousness, engaging the imagination of increasing numbers of people, calls us to new ways of being in the world, not in oppositional isolation or confrontation, but in collaborative networking that births new frontiers of wholeness, hope, and possibility.[59]

In this time of paradigm shift, and from the perspective of Analytical Psychology, it is an essential step in the evolution of our consciousness to withdraw our projections and to begin the arduous, painful process of discovering the mystery/Mystery within. In the quantum context, this alchemical work leads to the discovery and embodiment of our essential nature. In other words, this alchemical work brings about the death of the false gods/goddesses. This alchemical process is another way of describing the experience of Lady Underground's dark night of initiation in the Dark Feminine, which will be addressed in the next chapter. The divine is experienced in and through our human psyche in the very earthy body that is ours in this world. The biblical author of Luke/Acts wrote that Christ informed the Pharisees that the kingdom of God does not come through observation, nor it is "here," or "there"; rather, he wrote "the kingdom of God is within you" (p. 1718).[60] Some mystics, such as Teresa of Avila and John of the Cross, were pioneers of human consciousness whose lives reflect an interiorized spirituality and wellspring of creative activity. Jung, as a scientist, was an explorer and frontiersman of the depths of the unconscious, and as such, he was a beacon of light illuminating what is possible in human growth and development in the journey of homecoming, especially in the second half of life. While life at all levels is obviously complex, interactive, and open-ended, as it is influenced, guided, and lured forth by larger universal sustaining life energies, the summons to be voyagers of the night sea journey and to embody our psychospiritual depths remains an imperative challenge for humanity in this 21st century if we are to emerge, evolve, and unfold in a generative way—all in service to larger life.

Today we are collectively venturing into a greater complexification of consciousness as we are ushered into the summons of a new paradigm in this 21st century. We are being called to plumb our depths, to find and to embody a deeper human interiority, our interior castle. The dislocations that exist in the outer sphere, with the horrific shadow of *dark night* that looms over our country and global community, are summoning us to face our reality with courage and to turn inward to locate ourselves in what Paul Tillich refers to as the "ground of our being" (p. 124).[61]

Patriarchy on all levels of life is no longer plausible, as it is ungrounded in human instincts. The unconscious compensation manifests with the discharge of dammed-up energy in the instincts and encoded in psychosomatic symptoms. A new paradigm of consciousness is emerging and is challenging us to live in a balance of equals from the ground of our being where the tension of the opposites is held in a creative interplay: chaos and creativity; peril and promise; life and death. Many men and women who are attempting to do their inner work toward embodying the new model are discovering an image of that balance of equals through the Dark Goddess (who allows the opposites to coexist creatively) who emerges from the unconscious to enliven us anew. Lady Underground is "one" image of this balance; it is obviously not the only image, nor is it "the" image.

Conclusion

Because an overshadowing, chaotic dark night looms for the inhabitants of this planet and the Earth herself, the present historical time of transition in our country and global community yearns for and demands a new paradigm of an embodied spirit/Spirit consciousness. From the perspective of Analytical Psychology and contemporary holistic spirituality, it is an essential step in the evolution of our consciousness to withdraw our projections and to begin the arduous process of discovering the mystery/ Mystery within and of embodying our essential nature as men and women. The task of the second half of life summons us to be voyagers of the night sea journey and to probe and to embody consciously a deeper human interiority.

The new emerging paradigm calls us to engage relationally and cocreatively with an Earth-centered norm of reality and value, along with an honest desire to live in a balance of equals from the ground of our being where the tension of opposites is creatively held. For some people who are attempting to integrate the new paradigm, the Dark Feminine has meaning because it recognizes and honors a balance of equals. The Dark Feminine allows for differences and the opposites to coexist creatively within the natural flow of the web of all life. "One" image of the Dark Feminine that reflects this value is Lady Underground.

In summary, this chapter reflects "one" way of viewing: the major evolutionary shift of our historical time; the need for the lost feminine, especially the Dark Feminine; the importance of a conscious psychospiritual embodied interiority; and the value of Lady Underground's energy. No one viewpoint has the corner on truth. From a quantum lens we are relational by our nature, and as such, the need for ongoing openness and dialogue remains a dynamic part of the process in the progressive challenge to consciously embody spirit/Spirit. We are in service to the mystery/Mystery, not to "bridges," theory, or any other realm—that is *nada, nada.*

The next chapter will explore the image of *dark night* as a symbol and a rite of initiation in the process of embodying consciously the deeper dimensions of the Dark Goddess energy represented by Lady Underground. Embodying consciously a deeper psychospiritual human interiority is a call and challenge for all of us in today's unprecedented shift in evolution. *Dark night* is an image for our time. Hopefully, in examining this rich, paradoxical symbol, we will discover that the daunting experience of dark night is a rite of initiation and one way to view grounding the new emerging paradigm. As such, dark night summons us to bring forth the gold of the unconscious as we undergo a major evolutionary shift in consciousness, both individually and collectively. T.S. Eliot notes that as we age, so too the world, and it will become stranger and more complicated as it evolves. Regardless, he invokes us to remember:

> We must be still and still moving into another intensity
> for a further union, a deeper communion. . . (pp.189-190) [62]

INNER WORK

The beauty of the Way is that there is no "way."
~Loy Ching-Yuen

Naturalness is called the Way.
~The Secret of the Golden Flower

The way is not in the sky. The way is in the heart.
~Gautama Buddha

I give you news of the way of this man, but not of your own way.
My path is not your path. . . .The way is within us,
. . .[W]ho should live your own life if not yourself? So live yourselves.
The signposts have fallen, unblazed trails lie before us. Do you not know that you
yourselves are the fertile acre which bears everything that avails you?
~C.G. Jung, *The Red Book*

The right way to wholeness is made up of fateful detours and wrong turnings.
It is. . .not straight but snakelike, a path that unites the opposites
. . .a path whose labyrinthine twists and turns are not lacking in terrors.
~C.G. Jung, *Psychology and Alchemy*

Don't be satisfied with stories,
How things have gone for others.
Unfold your own myth.
~Rumi

~Reflection, Discussion, and Journaling Questions

- Realizing that projection is inevitable and that this dynamic catalyzes us into life, how have you projected outward the god or goddess energy onto outer "carriers?" How do you imagine yourself befriending and taking responsibility for this energy in your life?
- What self-parts of you remain in an undeveloped protracted childhood and/or adolescence, using your little-boy and little-girl games to seduce, manipulate, and attempt to control others to mother and/or father you—to take care of you, versus assuming responsibility for yourself, doing your inner work, and finally growing up?
- What are your numerous preoccupations that serve as an avoidance for you taking responsibility for the call to a deeper conscious living?
- Where do you perceive the dynamics of polarization operating in your life, major institutions, the country, and the global community?
- What are the psychological and spiritual payoffs you receive by continuing to cling and to give credence to false gods and/or goddesses in your life?
- Where do you encounter your shadow the most, and what is your attitude and feeling about this part of you? How do you imagine that you might befriend this aspect of yourself, that it might actually become an asset for you?
- What are the dangers for individuals, for governments, for religious institutions, and for the future of our planet when the shadow is denied, unmetabolized, and unintegrated?
- Dualisms undermine the tension of the opposites, the holism, and mystery of life. They tend to demonize and project the shadow onto an external scapegoat and subsequently discourage the integration of our personal, social, religious, political, and cultural shadows. What do you perceive as the primary either/or dualisms that continue to be operative today?
- What is your understanding of the importance of a deeper conscious interiority? How do you experience your soul summoning you to a deeper conscious interiority?

- What image describes your quest in life, and where do you see yourself developmentally at this time in your journey?
- What is your understanding of the value of the Dark Feminine's emerging energy at this historical time for our global community?

~Process Exercises

- After reading Chapter Two, consider the image that captures and engages your attention. Find a comfortable posture that enables you to be in silence. Close your eyes. Bring your attention to your breathing and as you do so, take a few long, deep-belly breaths while allowing the belly muscles to relax. Then, begin to exhale slowly as you allow your body to relax, release, and let go as you begin to open and enter into the silence. Stay with the relaxing deep-belly breaths until you are present to yourself in your body. When you feel attuned to yourself, begin to call to your awareness the image that caught your attention in Chapter Two as you continue to breathe naturally. Then, take another deep belly-breath and, as you exhale, focus in and notice what is arising within your body as you are present to yourself. Allow to arise what surfaces within you and, just as two persons might enter into dialogue, give yourself permission to enter into participating actively in an imaginative experience and/or dialogue with "a part of yourself" that has emerged from your depths. Remember there is no right or wrong way to experience this exercise; how you enter the experience and engage in the process is just fine. Trust yourself as you continue to breathe in and out in what is natural for you. Maintain this process of deep-belly breathing, of exhaling slowly, followed by focusing in and paying attention to what is manifesting in your body as you are present to yourself. Consider doing this exercise for about 20 minutes. Next, take another deep-belly breath and, as you exhale slowly, focus in and be attentive to what you notice as you are present to yourself. When you are ready, begin to open your eyes as you reorient yourself to your outer dwelling. Take some time to recall your experience. You may want to record it as a way to honor and to objectify further your depths. Some possible reflection questions to consider might be:

- If your image could speak, what would the image express to you?
- What was it like for you to experience your image?
- Did the image change in any way during your process?
- What did you discover about your body as you encountered your image?
- If your body could convey your awareness, how might you honor and express your body's awakening?
- When you do not listen to the intimations of your dreams or the images of life that are engaging you, how does the unmetabolized energy manifest in your body?
- What is psyche attempting to engineer as you are attentive to your image in this process?
- If you were to speak to your image, what would you want to communicate?
- What have you become aware of through your experience?

If you like, you can express your awareness in a poem or a drawing as another way to objectify what arises from your depths. Finally, as you focus again on your breath, acknowledge yourself for your inner work, as you bring closure to your process.

- Draw a mandala of the image that engaged your attention in Chapter Two. Or consider what do you most question, wonder about, or struggle with as you reflect on the material in Chapter Two. If your "wonderment," "question," or "struggle" had a color or an image, what would it be? Allow yourself to express this color or image in the form of a mandala. When you are finished, notice and record the feelings, thoughts, or sensations you experienced while drawing your mandala and after completing your mandala. Some possible reflection questions to consider might be:
  - What awareness have you discovered through your mandala exercise?
  - What title would you give to your mandala?

    - In completing your mandala, describe your experience of your energy in your body?

  Remember, this is *your* inner work, and there is no right or wrong way to do this exercise. What is most important is to follow your inner guidance and instinctual wisdom as you engage in your process through this exercise.

- Reflect on what inspires, intrigues, concerns, and/or disturbs you the most in Chapter Two. Allow yourself to enter into an active-imagination exercise. While there are many ways of doing active imagination, this exercise invites you to consider doing a right-hand/left-hand active-imagination experience. Remember, your dominant hand represents your conscious voice, and your nondominant hand in this exercise represents the part of you that is "inspired," "intrigued," or "bothered." Also, you need a pen or pencil and paper to do this exercise. Begin with your dominant hand and allow to arise what comes forth from within you as you start to write what is emerging within you to the part of you represented by your nondominant hand. Then change hands and hold your pen or pencil in your nondominant hand as you allow to arise what comes forth from within you in response to the communication from your conscious voice. Allow the dialogue to flow and to continue until it naturally feels complete for you. What have you become conscious of through your active-imagination experience? Again, remember to take time to acknowledge yourself for being attentive to your inner work.
- Reflect on your understanding of the new paradigm. If you were to visit an art museum, what painting or sculpture captures for you the energy of the new paradigm?
- There are many different styles of music. Allow your imagination to wonder and to consider what type and what piece symbolically expresses for you the energy of the new paradigm? Allow yourself to listen to this piece of music. What about this music moves your heart and soul? How do you experience your body as you listen soulfully

to this piece of music? You may want to record your perceptions as a way to further honor, to objectify, and to integrate your awareness.

- Perhaps you have had the opportunity to attend a theater and to experience a creation by masterful choreographers and performed by talented dancers. Is there a performance that stirs your imagination, that moves your heart, and that captures for you symbolically the energy of the new paradigm? If you were to write about this performance and the new paradigm, what might you express in your writing?
- What passages from the sacred texts of the world religions speak to you of the new paradigm?
- Who are the contemporary theologians, spiritual leaders, scientists, artists, poets, musicians, dancers, and culture leaders who are giving voice and challenging others about the vision and embodiment of the new paradigm? Write about how each inspires you.
- Contemplate what in nature speaks to you about the emerging new paradigm?

~Body-Energy Work

- After reading Chapter Two, consider what reality is moving your depths and is challenging you to a more enlarged self-awareness. In regard to this reality, record what, if any, are the discounting beliefs, attitudes, or charged feelings that you have about yourself that are gripping you and driving you in your present life? Also, note to what degree are lethargy and fear paralyzing you in embodying a more expansive consciousness? Consider doing an EMDR exercise with a trained EMDR practitioner as one possible way to demagnetize the discounting beliefs, attitudes, charged feelings, and cellular memory surrounding the reality that is challenging you. This process is a creative way to access the active imagination in the experience of healing and integration.
- Meridian tapping, of which Emotional Freedom Technique is the simplest and most common form, is an effective tool that can assist in the process of demagnetizing self-limiting beliefs, shadow material,

complexes, or the struggle with the tension of opposites. Reflect on the recorded list from the previous exercise. Given the reading and what was activated within you, ask yourself, in this present moment, what captures your attention the most that is longing to be heard, metabolized, and integrated in embodied consciousness? Find an EFT practitioner and do an EFT sequence as a way to honor your depths and objectify what is attempting to be integrated into consciousness. The tapping is a modality of body-energy work that touches into the active-imagination process and potentially offers a more integrative approach in the process of inner soul work.

- What image speaks to you the most from Chapter Two? As you bring your awareness to your breath and scan your body, where do you sense the energy of this image within your body? Consider finding a quiet and safe setting where you might have space to move and not be interrupted in any way. Allow yourself to take a deep breath and focus on whatever image is capturing your attention the most from Chapter Two. Again, sense where the energy of this image is in your body. In this exercise of soulful, arising movement, your breath, sound, and movement are a direct form of active imagination. The conscious focus is on the imaginal as it expresses itself through the breath, sound, and/or movement. In this process, the body is the medium; the breath, sound, and movement are the message. In this particular form of work of tracking your image within the experience of your body, the active-imagination dialogue is a felt sensing physical and emotional engagement through the medium of the body. Allow yourself to move freely in your soulful, arising body movement, and when your experience feels complete, take a deep breath as you find your way to bring closure to your process. When you are finished you might want to record your experience as another way of objectifying and befriending your depths. This body-movement exercise can also be done with two others, where one person holds consciously the space for the individual who is the body mover and the other is the observer. The exercise can allow 10 or 15 minutes for the movement component, and then time for processing the exercise. Again, if you do this body-movement exercise alone, or if you do it in the presence of two others, remember, before you finish, to take time to acknowledge yourself for your inner work.

CHAPTER THREE
DARK NIGHT OF INITIATION

The tree that would grow to heave must send its roots to hell.
~Nietzsche

Abandon hope, all ye who enter here!
~Dante

Die and Become! Until thou hast learnt this,
Thou art but a dull guest on this dark planet.
~Goethe

. . .to arrive at what *you do not know*
. . .go by a way which is the way of ignorance.
. . .to arrive at what you are not
. . .go through the way in which you are not.
~T.S. Eliot

What hurts the soul? To live without tasting the water of its own essence. . . .
Use night to wake your clarity. Darkness and living water are lovers.
Let them stay up together. . .
~Rumi

The brighter the light, the more the owl is blinded.
~St. John of the Cross

The dread and resistance which every natural human being experiences
when it comes to delving too deeply into himself [herself] is, at bottom,
the fear of the journey to Hades.
~C.G. Jung, *C.W.* 12, par. 439

But man's [one's] task is. . .to become conscious of the contents that press upward from the unconscious. Neither should he [one] persist in his [one's] unconsciousness, nor remain identical with the unconscious elements of his [one's]being, thus evading his [one's] destiny, . . .to create more and more consciousness.
~C.G. Jung, *Memories, Dreams, Reflections*

The substance that harbours the divine secret is everywhere, including the human body. . . .and can be found anywhere, even in the most loathsome filth.
~C.G. Jung, *C.W.* 12, par. 421

I myself know a few individuals who have had personal experience of this phenomenon. . .which, as Hildegard [of Bingen] implies, brings into awareness areas of psychic happenings ordinarily covered in darkness. . . .Its effect is astonishing in that it almost always brings about a solution of psychic complications and frees the inner personality from emotional and intellectual entanglements, thus creating a unity of being which is universally felt as "liberation."
~C.G. Jung, *C.W.* 13, pars. 42-43

Introduction to Dark Night

The mystery/Mystery calls to us in a thousand ways. When we are holding the miracle of a newborn infant the mystery/Mystery seems to be somewhat more real and tangible. It can be there when we experience a marvelous performance of a ballet, the rapturous movement of sensual intensity in a tango, or the soundless sound of a felt resonance in the heart and in the whole body at the end of a symphony. Sometimes we behold the mystery/Mystery in the view of an expansive lake, a splendid sunrise or a brilliant sunset, or a moment's stillness in the beauty and uniqueness of the changing seasons. The sound of a loved one's voice or of a spontaneous free-spirited child can evoke a sense of the mystery/Mystery, as well as the fragrance of a rose, the warm touch of an embrace, or erotic love making. Occasionally, the mystery/Mystery manifests in the depths of silent solitude. At times, a dream image, a sculpture, painting, play, poem, opera, or book might have the same effect, for they can stir our imagination, move us deeply, and open us to mystery/Mystery. While many of us can resonate with at least a few of these examples, most of us do not recognize readily the awakening call of being summoned in a *dark night.*

What is a *dark night* and what activates this dynamic in the human personality? What takes us out of the "day" of development and into a *dark night*? What mobilizes our move from a luminous world of knowing to a dark region of knowing by a way of not knowing? What energies are stirred in the psyche by the symbol of Lady Underground's *dark-night* initiation in the Dark Feminine and experienced in and through the body during the process of the rite? What is the alchemical cooking that is catalyzed in the traveler's arduous path in black night of initiation?

In this book, *dark night* will be referred to and discussed as a metaphor to designate the alchemical, transformative, initiatory journey of descent/ascent into the Dark Goddess energy, imaged in Lady Underground. Furthermore, *dark-night initiation,* as defined and developed in this text, is one way (template) to view the very process a soul goes through in unearthing, metabolizing, personalizing, and embodying consciously the archetypal energy of Lady Underground. Without *dark night* the archetypal image of Lady Underground remains skeletal. Traversing through the night is the initiatory path of humanizing, socializing, and embodying consciously the archetypal energy.

Dark night is a symbol. For Jung, a symbol is not an allegory or a sign. He considered a symbol to be the best possible expression of something that is basically unknown. "A symbol does not define or explain; it points beyond itself to a meaning that is darkly divined, yet still beyond our grasp, and cannot be adequately expressed in the familiar words of our language" (par. 644).[63] A symbol is a bridge to an unseen shore. Hopefully, in considering various dimensions of dark night, we may gain an appreciation of its symbolic and psychological significance in relationship to the archetypal image of Lady Underground. Moreover, the value of this study is to explore how the experience of the energy of Lady Underground (or another image of the Dark Feminine) through dark night is a rite of initiation for some individuals in the "night sea journey," which is Jung's image for the second half of life in which psyche is engineering an adaptation to the inner world.[64]

Symbolically and psychologically, all of life is a dark-night journey. The beginning, middle, and end of the journey are dark, from the ego's finite perspective, and contained within the realm of mystery that remains throughout a lifetime. This is a global view and the broadest way to interpret *dark night*. From this perspective, there is only one night. The more specific view is that there are pivotal times when energy begins to emerge, as certain dynamics of one's psyche intensify in adult development. In this book, *dark night* will be interpreted as consisting of three stages analogous to a normal night: "twilight," "midnight," and "dawn." There are some characteristics or predictable patterns to these stages.

Furthermore, in this book, dark night will be explored symbolically and analytically in the context of Lady Underground's rite of initiation into the Dark Feminine archetypal energy. A rite of initiation suggests an induction or a portal into another realm or domain of awareness, something new, something unknown, unfamiliar, or mysterious. Mircea Eliade, in *Rites and Symbols of Initiation*, describes the archetypal pattern of initiation manifested in many cultures as having four main characteristics: separation, ordeal, encounter with the divine, and return. "Separation" involves something's ceasing in order to begin life in a different or new way from what was previously known or familiar. "Ordeal" entails a death to archaic patterns and structures of the ego and the personality that no longer serve psyche and are no longer generative ways of being in our everyday life. When there is death, then life emerges, as death and life are different chapters in a cyclical story, a cosmic pattern of truth manifested in the very seasons of nature. Death is a prelude to life and life is a prelude to death. It is a very scary ordeal to separate, detach, surrender, and let go of infantile patterns of behavior and defenses that have protected and yet constricted our humanity, and moreover, to die finally to an identity defined by self-limiting beliefs and old wounds that no longer serve us in living generative, meaningful lives. For many we suffer from a bankruptcy of imagination. We are unable to conceive life in a more expansive way. Soulful conscious development is not in a vacuum. Going through the ordeal phase puts us in touch with neglected parts of our unconscious. Integrating authentic growth in this stage involves befriending the unconscious figures and the distressing, fear, chaos, anxiety, and ambiguity that need to be honored and metabolized for each soul, if new life is to be embodied. Hard as it may be to remember and to appreciate Jung's words, at the ordeal stage, it is of value to recall again, "one does not become enlightened by imagining figures of light, but by making the darkness conscious." The only way out of "ordeal" is through it. A further part of the rite of initiation is the experience of the mystery/Mystery, or what T.S. Eliot describes as the "intersection of the timeless moment," and what Julian of Norwich refers to as "touchings." Paul Tillich says it well: "Accept the fact that you are accepted, despite the fact that you are unacceptable" (p. 162).[65] In some way, there is an "encounter with the numinous," whether the mystery/Mystery is named or not named. And finally, there is a "return" to the human circle enriched by greater consciousness, responsibility, and humble service.[66] These archetypal, energetic patterns of initiation draw and summon us to a depth encounter, to a deeper interiority.

Lady Underground's overarching rite of initiation in the Dark Feminine will be viewed in this book through the lens of the progressive journey of night from twilight until dawn. We will discover that the emergence of Lady Underground's dark-night initiation stages of separation and ordeal will be experienced primarily through twilight and midnight. Dawn of Lady Underground's dark night of initiation will be explored primarily in the stages of encounter with the holy/mystery and the return, which are developed in Chapter Four. Whether we clearly know the language, stages, and patterns of initiation through dark night is not as important as acknowledging, sacrificing, surrendering, and befriending the inevitable turmoil, struggles, conscious suffering, and challenges of our soul in our everyday life. Some of these real, unavoidable life realities include: relationship strain and conflicts, warring desires, traumas, painful detachments, illness, losses, spiritual crises, natural disasters, and difficult crossroads. Only through persevering and metabolizing suffering are we able to grow and to emerge from life's inescapable challenges with a more grounded, integrated self-awareness, meaning, and direction in life. Through initiation we birth our essential nature. The process matures us—liberates us! We open to releasing the potentials of the generative power of our soul and our path in life. We become consciously responsible for the energy we bring into any relationship and the web of all life. However daunting initiation stories may be, the unknown dark territory of a rite of passage will open before us only to the extent that we surrender courageously to the quest, maintain a humble attitude and a perduring attentiveness to the journey, and that we consciously sacrifice what is needed to make the quest. When we muster the courage to face the unknown and the realities that drain and diminish our energy field such as fear, lethargy, naiveté, attachment hungers, trauma, destructive and self-limiting attitudes and patterns of living, then we begin to birth a greater depth of who we are and a grounded trust in a fuller spectrum of our purpose in life.

Now the challenge comes! One can't just talk the talk; one needs to walk the walk, to actually make the journey! Each soul in hearing the summons of the depths must venture wherever the road leads. This means honoring the call, in spite of the intrusive inner critical voice, the unsettling fear in our body, the sweating in our palms, the shaking in our boots, and the collective opinions and criticism of others. Being drawn into a rite of initiation is not an invitation to the candy shop! When we surrender and enter the path of initiation, we find ourselves face to face with the naked, stark truth of life *as it is*, not the illusionary, romanticized, or Hollywood version. Suffering quickens consciousness and tends to loosen and lessen the supreme-court judge in most of us. We begin to become more sensitive, respectful, and tolerant of others. Gradually, we open to understanding the growth opportunity in initiation, while also recognizing that many mask, anesthetize, or dissociate the struggle, fear, pain, terror, and suffering of this natural dynamic in life. Thus, if we are a perceptive soul, we grasp that most people's lives are composed of a series of separations, ordeals, encounters with the mystery, and returns, and furthermore, that initiation represents one of the most ordinary, significant, and universal psychological and spiritual phenomena in the history of humanity.[67]

In order to set the context for the discussion of the experience of Lady Underground, through the stages of dark-night initiation, a brief review of Jung's view of the day of development or outer journey, which precedes the inner journey, is being presented in the following section. Having an overview of all of life as a dark night helps us to comprehend the framework and importance of the day of development and its relationship to twilight, midnight, and dawn. Schopenhauer said, "The first forty years of life furnish the text, while the remaining thirty supply the commentary; without the commentary we are unable to understand aright the true sense and coherence of the text together with the moral it contains" (p. 16).[68]

Journey into Consciousness: Day of Development

Central to Jung's psychology is the development of a person over a lifetime. It is a growth process from undifferentiated to differentiated energy, from unconsciousness to embodied consciousness. Jung's theory for viewing the human personality is very comprehensive; it is essentially a psychological view of human development characterized by a journey motif. Although development is continuous throughout a person's lifetime, there are significant crossroads that can be referred to as "stages of life." There are four in Jung's view: childhood, youth and young adulthood, middle age, and old age.

For Jung, the psyche refers to the totality of the personality, which includes all psychic processes, conscious as well as unconscious.[69] The psyche is like a spaceless space, an inner cosmos with an inherent wholeness that has to be consciously birthed and developed. The psyche functions through energy, or libido. The movement of energy in the psyche is fundamental to the life of the psyche. Because of the flow of energy, the psychic life is an energetic process, as opposed to a static one. The principle of opposites is the basic process by which life energies are created and kept in motion. With the presence of opposites, tension exists within the psyche. Because all of life is energy, life depends on forces held in opposition. Jung refers to this in *Two Essays On Analytical Psychology* when he says, "Life is born only by the spark of opposites" (par. 54).[70] This reality is true in the outer cosmos as well as in the inner cosmos of the psyche.

The dynamics of the psyche are an energetic, self-regulating system that brings about the journey. These dynamics are the fundamental horizon that allows the journey and the process of healing to take place for the person. The very dynamics of the psyche are a catalyst for transitions, passages, and critical thresholds in the path to wholeness. For Jung, the fundamental ground and the horizon of experience for this journey over a life-time is mysterious.

The goal of development is to become individuated, or what the noted Jungian analyst James Hollis refers to as *homecoming*. By individuation, Jung means the process of becoming differentiated and of developing one's personality fully.[71] He sees this journey of individuation as having two phases that more-or-less correspond to the first and second halves of life. The first half of life includes the stages of childhood, and youth and young adulthood; the second half of life includes the stages of middle age and old age. The first half of life is characterized by adaptation and conformity to the outer world; the development of the person during this period is primarily ego development. The second half of life is characterized by adaptation to the inner world; in this phase one is summoned into the depths of the personal and collective layers of the unconscious. Having a healthy ego structure and being grounded in consciousness are necessary in order to make the descent, to return more aware and able to live the symbolic life, and to make a conscious contribution in ordinary reality.

This journey into embodied consciousness demands more than an intellectual understanding of Jungian theory. Coming home in the second half of life means to befriend and to embody consciously who we are through a proper relationship with the Self, the archetype of wholeness that is both the regulating center and the unifying principle of the psyche. This journey involves integrating unknown, rejected, repressed, and dissociated parts of the soul, as well as discovering and embracing our soul's emerging vocation. When we embrace our depths with humility and integrity, we emerge in a healthier and more authentic relationship to the mystery/Mystery, our self, others, and all of life. In recovering the lost, split-off parts of ourselves that have been banished in the underground dark caverns of our soul, we unleash a greater depth and breadth of our natural way of being. In befriending our darker, shadowy parts, we open to an expanded inner spaciousness, and subsequently, generosity can emerge and tend to flow from a more grounded, genuine consciousness, rather than to derive from unconscious infantile neediness. With a greater conscious containment, our ability to choose and to maintain healthy boundaries and to claim and to speak our voice, our reality, our inner authority can occur, since we can distinguish more freely and clearly between our truth and another's truth, realizing in integrity that we can only live the summons of *our* path.

Jung observed that the personality begins in an unconscious state; Erich Neumann referred to this stage as the "uroboric state" (p. 10).[72] The uroborus is a primal Egyptian deity symbol in the form of a circular snake swallowing its tail. This circular image represents the state of the psyche of a newborn infant. For Jung, the psyche is a self-regulating energy system. At this level of development, all is unconscious, and the polarities of the personality exist together in an undifferentiated state of primal unity, or described symbolically, all is in a Garden of Eden state. Psyche at this phase is a symbol of the primordial night; that vast realm of darkness out of which consciousness gradually emerges as an individual personality begins to grow.

Later, in the adult years of the second half of life, psyche will summon an individual to reenter this dark in order to experience and bring forth the hidden treasure from the wellspring of the unconscious. This stage symbolically and psychologically is a dark night *par excellence*. The archetypal descent into the unconscious is paralleled in the "night sea journey" of the sun in Egyptian mythology, wherein the sun is born every morning and dies every evening. In the darkness of the underworld, the sun is transformed, recharged, and then reborn in the morning. The interplay between life and death is a particular dynamic in Egyptian mythology, wherein life is regenerated in darkness and in death; the perspective is that in the darkness of the ground the seed that is planted is regerminated and new life emerges. So, too, Jung held that through the self-regulating system of the psyche, energy recedes from the light of consciousness (regression) into the dark of the unconscious in the archetypal descent as psyche's attempt to heal, balance, and bring into consciousness renewed life for the whole of the energetic system.

Early development was not a major focus for Jung's studies. He postulated that the ego does not emerge into its full existence until about the age of 3 to 4.[73] Today, with the knowledge and awareness of Object Relations theory, infant observation, and contemporary scientific research on the brain and human development, a wider view is held, that an element of perceptual organization is present at birth. Before the end of the first year of life, a unique human process of the psychic unfolding of an ego structure is in operation.[74]

Puberty is a pivotal time of transition in the human life span. This stage ushers in a growth period that catalyzes a gradual separation from the parent figures. Jung held the view that the growing child is not fully born until psychic birth has occurred at puberty. This milestone in development is normally a time of differentiating from the parents. In general, at adolescence the youth begins to test limits and pull away from the protective parental atmosphere into the reality of greater independence, self-expression, and exploration, as well as into the reality of a challenging world of tensions, conflicts, and uncertainties that are experienced both in the inner and outer worlds. This developmental period of youth, along with young adulthood, normally spans from the time of puberty until middle age, which begins approximately between the 35th and 40th year of life. By and large, this phase of growth encompasses both maturing and widening the circle and horizons of life. Nonetheless, there also are parts of the psyche that, for one reason or another, remain dormant and/or are not integrated into consciousness, and these psychic parts are transferred to the unconscious. As young adulthood emerges in a world of diversity and complexity, consciousness intensifies the further activation of the dynamics of the opposites and the struggle with their tensions. At this stage of growth, homecoming is not about returning and remaining a perpetual resident in the unconscious state of Eden, living eternally Peter Pan's theme, "I don't want to grow up!" Instead, the developmental juncture in the pathway of growth is leaving Eden (symbolic and psychological separation of child from mother's womb) and embracing the process of reconciliation of opposites in the quest toward embodied consciousness.

In concluding this overview of the day of development, it is important to remember that Jung considered the first half of life a necessarily one-sided journey. One cannot develop both sides of the psychic polarities simultaneously. One side is cultivated in consciousness, while its opposite in the unconscious lies dormant, yet to be awakened and realized in consciousness. For example, after 20 years of 12-hour workdays, Ken, a 47-year-old male research scientist was anxiety ridden from the pressures of work, his thinking function having been highly exercised in his demanding profession. Attending a class at the Smithsonian Institution germinated his interest in Oriental gardening, which became for him an avenue of befriending his inferior feeling function. In the second half of life, when the Self[v] is calling to be heard and integrated into consciousness, it is often through the inferior function that, according to Von Franz, the unconscious can come in and so enlarge consciousness and bring forth a new attitude.[75]

Dimming the Light of Consciousness

Bernadine, a 40-year-old married woman and nurse at a local hospital, dreamed that it was early evening when she realized that she had lost her purse. She searched frantically for it in her house when, suddenly, all the lights in the house started going out, one after another. As Bernadine goes about her everyday life, she often finds herself wondering if she had married the right man, if she had taken the wrong path, and if she was missing her life. She questioned the very meaning of her life.

Dwight, a 42-year-old CEO of an advertising agency, described himself as someone who likes to look good, sound impressive, work hard, and win at the game of golf. He reported that the last three months had been difficult at work, as he had to push himself to manage all the strategic planning for the company. Dwight felt as if all his creative juices had disappeared, and his worst fear was that others at work or in his golf league might realize this, and for Dwight this would be really embarrassing. Twice he dreamt that it is dusk, and he is teeing off at the ninth hole when his golf shoes somehow mysteriously go off his feet and disappear into the ground. Dwight is baffled by these dreams and wants them "stopped or fixed right" before they impact his golf game.

---

[v] While Jung would eventually come to describe the Self as the totality or wholeness of the psyche, inclusive of both consciousness and unconsciousness, he initially used the word *Self* as we use it every day, to indicate personage. He developed his thinking about the Self as a distinct psychological term over time. The Self has come to mean the center—a unifying and organizing principle of the psyche. The Self is the totality of the psyche, including the pool of all archetypes.

Both Bernadine and Dwight seem to be experiencing the onset of some of the stirring and dimming of the light of consciousness. While their dreams are disturbing to them, they do not realize or appreciate yet that, as dusk begins to occur in their day of development, also within this dynamic process is the other or "under" side, the potential growth for renewed life and generativity within each of their psyches.

Dark Night

In the cycle of human development, as the stirring and fading of the light of consciousness begin, often a person experiences the conscious attitude as no longer sufficient to provide meaning and energy for the journey. We don't know all the reasons that propel us into a dark night, and that is partly what makes it dark! The black of night extinguishes our light of knowing and understanding in our perceptual world. Night negates the light.

Evelyn Underhill, noted English poet, novelist, and writer on mysticism, held that one does not choose the dark night, the night chooses us.[76] One may choose to resist and/or abort the gift of dark night, but one is not the author of one's night from the ego standpoint. Jungian analyst James Hillman, wrote that the black of night dissolves meaning and the hope of meaning; thus, one is benighted.[77] And Jung, speaking of the night sea journey in the second half of life, noted that if one realized ahead of time what the experience would be, one would never make the journey.

The events or experiences that activate a dark night at personal, archetypal, and societal levels can vary from one person to another and from one culture to another. What takes us out of the day of development and into the twilight and midnight of dark night can be a combination of realities. Some of the possibilities that plunge us into a night are: betrayal, abandonment, illness, death, failure, depression, divorce, a crisis, a certain stage of spiritual practice, global tragedy, retirement, post-trauma from war, social injustices, geographical relocation, and environmental catastrophes. A thousand gates open to night. Regardless of the precipitating outer circumstances, psyche is engineering some movement at personal and collective levels. Descent is built into the human psyche. Descent is an archetypal pattern that none of us can avoid. Dark night ushers in a dimming of the light of consciousness as the energy recedes into the dark of the unconscious, and twilight of dark night is activated in the human person.

Twilight of Dark Night of Initiation: Symbolic Significance

What does the onset of twilight of dark night mean symbolically in relationship to the archetypal image of Lady Underground? Twilight of dark night initiation in the Dark Feminine is a unique unfolding for each person in and through the matter of an individual's life, with all its ambiguity. There is no one portal. For example, Harry a 44-year-old married father of three and an engineer reported that he had lost his job and felt like a failure, as if the electric power was out in his inner home. Barb, a 38-year-old single businesswoman, described herself as an "A" personality type, stated that she had gone to sleep feeling fine and woke up crying and out of sorts after having dreamt that she had lost her purse and her GPS, that her iPhone had had a major glitch, and that her bank account had been emptied. Barb has suffered a loss of meaning and purpose in her life, as if her being had been unraveling for the six weeks since she'd been in a major car accident. Harry indicated he had financial security on account of his family's trust fund, yet, despite that financial security, he'd felt lost and lethargic for the last two dismal months: "Yes, I lost my job, but I have financial security, and yet, it is as if all the meaning in my life has evaporated. Where did I go wrong? What is wrong with me?" Symbolically (and also psychologically) speaking, the dimming of daylight consciousness was befalling the souls of Harry and Barb. Both are suffering a loss of meaning in life. Jung's definition of neurosis is the "suffering of a soul that has not discovered its meaning" (par. 497).[78] The midlife storm of the hero/heroine mythic journey of initiation in the quest for meaning has begun for both. While this symbolic mythological pattern is operative normally in midlife development, what, if anything, is different for the individual who has in his or her inner psychic landscape the archetypal image of Lady Underground or another "face" of the Dark Feminine? Although there is no one way, and each soul's path is unique, generally speaking, as the light of consciousness fades for a person who has the archetypal image of Lady

Underground, or another "face" of the Dark Feminine constellated in their psychic makeup, there will be not only the midlife mythic pattern of growth activated, but gradually in the turbulent process of the inner journey, there is some experience with the Dark Feminine and a summons toward a deeper descent in human interiority in the path of humanizing and embodying the Dark Feminine archetypal energy. Through our humanity, we all have the Great Mother foundational principle within us, and thus we all share in the Dark Feminine's energy that is woven throughout the web of all life.

For example, Marietta experienced the Dark Feminine in the form of Our Lady of the Valley, an image of the coastal region of Venezuela. For one month, as she did her inner soul work, she felt a persistent stirring in her abdomen and heard from within, "Come down into the darkness." As this was processed, Marietta indicated that she did not address this in previous analytical sessions because she didn't like what she was hearing and didn't want to know what it meant. Moreover, she thought that if she didn't report it in analysis, then perhaps she could prevent whatever was occurring and subsequently avoid doing any more shadow work! Marietta, who initially had been deeply moved by a numinous experience of the Dark Feminine through an encounter with Lady of the Valley, and who had an ongoing dialogical relationship with her, now found herself determined to put the brakes on the Dark Feminine! In Marietta's words, "No way am I going down. I don't want to hear about down, darkness, or anymore shadow work. I want you (Eileen) to know that I am integrated!" I had been silent during this time as Marietta clearly and emphatically expressed herself. She continued as she leaned forward in her chair, dramatically staring at me with determination while saying, "I have had enough about down! I don't want to hear 'Come down' or anything more to do with descent and shadow!" For Marietta and for all of us, it is difficult to accept and to embrace genuinely that the dynamic and reality of descent and shadow are part of life. For every one of us, it takes humility to be open to accepting our shadow and to having a perduring attentiveness to doing the inner work, to metabolizing the energy, and to integrating the shadow. Only the well-armored, the naïve, or the slippery, justifying, rational one would deny shadow and put a spin of good and light around it as a defense to avoid dealing with it, as we all have at one time or another. As my friend Jerry Parr, the former director of the Secret Service, once reflected to me, "There is a thin line between the saint and the sinner, the protector and the killer. We all need to be consciously responsible for our shadows." Marietta and all of us who resist the experience of the inner descent and shadow work, choosing instead continuous flight and displacement of our energies, in one form or another, in the outer world of life, could benefit by remembering the wisdom of Goethe:

> . . .so long as you haven't experienced this: to die and so
> to grow, you are only a troubled guest on the dark earth. (p. 100) [79]

Oh, what a paradoxical "gift" Lady Underground brings in her twilight of dark-night initiation! What we resist will persist. The Self, the organizing principal of the psyche, which includes the Dark Feminine, wants growth for us and will ask us to sacrifice our likes, dislikes, comfort, vigilance, naiveness, sentimentalism, magical thinking, and will-directed schemes to achieve it. No matter how lofty our illusionary, controlling mindset and protective defenses might be for us, the nature of the Self and what this Dark Feminine archetypal energy is engineering is of greater depth and breadth than the ego, with its narrow confines, can grasp. Opening and surrendering to the mystery of the unknown is frightening, so the capacity to let go and to proceed will vary for each of us. The mystery/Mystery is the author of the process. In some unknown and often mysterious way, the soul has an encounter with the Dark Feminine either in a dream, some art form, nature, active-imagination exercise, a meditation, or in some existential human experience. In the mystery of the process, the soul is seduced, stirred, awakened, and/or touched by the energy of the Dark Feminine through some initial numinous experience. Then, very gradually over time, the alchemical cooking in the pot of transformation begins to occur as the dynamics in the process intensifies in twilight. Through Lady Underground (or another image of the Dark Goddess), a soul is drawn into initiation in the Dark Feminine. In twilight, the very energy of Lady Underground is about "seducing" one away from an insecure, false, adapted identity and an attachment to the collective; she slowly liberates, empowers, educates, loves, guides, and inspires one toward one's naturalness and the embodiment of one's unique essence, truth, voice, and path.

What is meant by being seduced by Lady Underground in twilight? Ronald Schenk notes in his article, "Mining/Fishing/Analysis: Seduction as Alchemical *Extractio*," that what many call seduction, the alchemists term "chemistry"; James Hillman labels it "strip mining." The etymology of the word *seduction* comes from two Latin components, *se*, meaning away, apart and *duc*, meaning to lead, guide, direct, and draw; so to *seduce* means to lead away, to direct, guide, or draw away, as well as to lead astray, to move away, or to draw apart or separate from family /society, or to divert from allegiance.

The association of seduction with sexual intercourse did not occur until 16th-century puritanism. The initial meaning of *seduction* has fundamental themes that allude to the same motifs as the Jungian notion of individuation: for example, moving away from the beaten path or the herd, eschewing obedience to a collective or ego-centered standpoint, and following a unique, peculiar, or solitary way. Also, *duc* is part of the etymology of the word *educate*, meaning to *lead out*, and implies, as Jungian psychology does, that there is something to be learned from the suffering of separation. Furthermore, from the perspective of alchemy, the operations in the process of *seduction* are *separatio* and, more particularly, *extractio*. Through the extraction process, the pure is separated from the impure. Schenk emphasizes that extraction brings forth "essence," the authentic aspects or qualities of the Self. Through the spiral process of extraction, more of our authentic person, our true nature, our "essence," the Self, emerges and becomes consciously embodied. Jung connects extraction with the Self:

> In the unconscious are hidden those sparks of light, *scintillae*, the archetypes, from which a higher meaning can be "extracted." The "magnet" that attracts the hidden thing is the self. . .or the symbol representing it (par. 700).[80]

Hence, symbolically, twilight of Lady Underground's dark-night initiation is the rite of being drawn, seduced toward one's soul "essence" through the alchemical extraction process.[81]

For some there can seem to be a tendency toward romanticized overtones concerning the idea of having a Black Madonna numinous encounter; this can be true especially if one remains stuck at the initial stage of the numinous encounter and resists doing the inner work. For example, there are some people who have numinous Dark Feminine experiences of a Black Madonna, Tara, Sheba, Grandmother Earth, Lilith, Mary Magdalene, Lady Guadalupe, etc., and who tend to manifest a hubris attitude, a perceived specialness because of this experience, and yet they are rather resistant and defended about doing their shadow work. It is not enough to experience, talk, or write about an archetypal experience of the Dark Feminine. The energy of the Dark Feminine needs to be unearthed, metabolized, humanized, socialized, and embodied consciously. As noted in the introduction, while a numinous experience can be a source of consolation, compensation, affirmation, healing, and grace, it also can be an indication that there is an underside of larger affectively charged energies in the psyche that are distinct from the ego, and that must be worked with and embodied consciously. Having a numinous encounter with the Black Madonna, or with any other image of the Dark Feminine, is not necessarily a sign of virtue, maturity, and/or psychic integration. The rite of initiation in twilight, of being drawn or seduced by Lady Underground, is not necessarily a felt awesome amazing reality! The actual experience of a soul in twilight feels anything but wonderful. The experience can trigger vigilant control, paralyzing fear, anxiety, and ambivalence, as in the above-noted experience of Marietta. Unlike the physical world, where one is sometimes seduced by the natural beauty of a sunset, paradoxically, in the psychic world at dusk, one is often resistant, confused, bewildered, and upset by the loss of direction as one is drawn into an inner, unrecognizable landscape. There is no inner GPS or app. The soul is disoriented in twilight. It is the onset of the alchemical night process of being stripped in the mining excavation for the soul's essence. Thus, Lady Underground's dark-night initiation is about bringing in a different sense of Eros than that which is guided by the preconceptions of puritanism and which provides the base of our conventional understanding of seduction.[82]

To initially descend into the "crypt" of one's earth is to be unsettled by the wave of anxiety, ambiguity, chaos, and darkness. The journey to embody our soul essence is nothing short of experiencing suffering and death from the ego's perspective. In fact, for some souls at twilight, physical death would seem like a welcome relief, rather than having to go through the purgation of the *nigredo* state. The latter inner war of the tension of the opposites was described in earthy terms by one 45-year-old man named John, who connected with the Black Madonna in an active-imagination exercise during his daily walk outdoors. In session, John noted, "Well, the dung is hitting the fan, and quite frankly, literally checking out seems like a real viable option, even though I know I won't check out. I'm just telling you about the inner war in me. I liked life the way it was for me. I like things *my* way. I don't like the ambiguity in my life right now. I'm angry about it. It is hard and it is depressing." Another analysand, Mary, put it this way: "I go to the lake, and part of me really wants to dive in and not come back." While these overwhelming anxiety, end-it-all moments are as real for these individuals as they are for any one of us who experiences this energy, John and Mary also noted other brief moments of being nurtured by the Madonna; both reported the felt "visit" from the Dark Feminine as a welcomed consolation that temporarily strengthened each of their souls.

John described silent tears rolling down his face and feeling depressed as he reflected on the loss of his health while walking and contemplating the sorrowful mysteries of the Madonna. When he got to the particular mystery of the Madonna beholding her dead son, John explained that he felt an undeniable body sensation of peace come over him. For John, it was as if the Black Madonna was present personally to him in his loss and that it was as if she was holding *his* dead self. The numinous visit did not change John's health; however, the felt reality that he "was held" enabled John to hold and to carry with an acceptance what previously had seemed impossible to him. This moving and touching experience of felt kindness caused John to cry and to sit down on the ground in the park as he experienced this energy. Paradoxically, the very energy of Black Madonna that brings a death of structures and patterns of the ego, also brings consolation in our suffering and eventually new life. Mary brought to session a drawing that she made after an active-imagination experience of the Black Madonna like a tree holding her, which gave her a strengthening and grounding sense in her body. Mary continues to come back to this image as she does her inner work with shadow material.

What John and Mary describe, along with other souls who touch into the reality of twilight for a shorter or longer period of time, is the suffering of holding and containing the tension of the opposites until something new arises from the unconscious (the transcendent function). Both John and Mary wrestle with the temptation to abort the energy and shortcut the pregnant possibilities that can arise in the process from their depths. They, like most of us, have the wishful and illusionary thinking that all the inner work is done on demand, according to the ego's plan and quick-fix time! If the process depended on our ego's direction, most of us would be opting for a shortcut modality and the fast track of dark-night initiation! Like pursuing a Black Friday super deal, the ego, especially a strong, will-directed ego, will look to cut a deal any day of the week with its magical thinking. There are no shortcuts or maverick deals in dark-night initiation. The reality is one can struggle for a very long time with a powerful energy pull from an overidentification with one side of the pole of an archetype. For example, one can be overidentified with the inner, critical, terrible mother, demanding tyrant father, responsible and dutiful son or daughter, or controlling power drive. Lethargy, fear, or inner-attacking, self-limiting beliefs can cause one to succumb to the pull of the tension at one end of the pole, as manifested in the temptation "to check out," or to "dive in and not come back." The exhausting struggle of this tension is real. To cave, to go down the slippery slope, and to go along with one's convenient rationalizations seems like a real, welcome, and viable option when one is afraid, tired, and weary from the intrusive spinning of self-defeating thoughts, anxiety, ambiguity, aridity, and darkness, rather than enduring and holding the tension of the energy.

Also, we live in a quick-fix culture that promotes taking a drug and a pill for just about anything. It takes an enormous amount of energy to struggle to choose to contain and to hold consciously the opposites until something new emerges within the person! From the ego's narrow perspective, seemingly no good could possibly come from Lady Underground's twilight of dark-night initiation. A television commercial during prime time on the value of the Black Madonna's twilight of dark-night initiation would be a hard sell to our ego-gratification, collective mindset, and an even more impossible sell as a prime-time ad about the growth opportunities in midnight of dark-night initiation! Moreover, even a commercial with an earthy ooh-la-la Black Madonna offering a guaranteed "hot deal" for growth in our core essence would not make the cut for prime-time commercials, even for the Super Bowl! The collective would be more attuned to the comic relief of a Papageno mentality in Wolfgang Amadeus Mozart's *The Magic Flute*! And yet, the Self, the archetype of wholeness, and the archetypal energy of Lady Underground is engineering something far more than the ego can imagine or the collective can appreciate. There is a definite tension that arises within a person as an individual experiences the energetic pull from the other end of the pole. Psychic growth occurs through the ongoing conscious intent to bear the tension, struggle, sacrifice, and surrender to the process until sensing an opening to the strength and empowerment of the emerging new energy, as noted by John and Mary. Their task of consciously holding and enduring the intense energy, each in their unique way, is the same pattern found in Psyche's life in the account of Psyche and Eros. This is a myth within a Latin text from the second century A.D. about Lucius of Patrai and his transformation. As with any myth, there are multiple dimensions of meaning and understanding. The story has been interpreted by some to reflect the psychic development in a woman's soul, and some see the tale as manifesting the maturing process of a man's anima in his journey of psychic integration. The latter perspective is held primarily because the myth is told in the larger context of the adventures of Lucius, the hero. Whatever your view may be, let us be open to what the story stirs in our depths and what we can learn about the dynamics of dark-night initiation.

In Greek mythology, Psyche is a king's beautiful daughter who aroused the jealousy of Aphrodite, the Greek goddess of love and beauty. Aphrodite condemns Psyche to death in order to eliminate any competition between them. Aphrodite's manipulative plan to have Psyche go to a lonely cliff to await her "marriage of death" to the supposed monster-god goes awry because her son Eros, who is the Greek god of love, falls in love with Psyche and takes her to a hidden place where they live in nuptial bliss. Eros visits Psyche every night, though he insists that she neither ask him to tell her his name nor demand to see him. Eros has a dominating, controlling power stance toward Psyche in order to keep her in the "dark" (unconscious) as a manipulative way to ensure his deception to his mother. Respect, mutuality, and equality are not characteristic of the relating dynamics. Psyche's sisters induce her to defy Eros's controlling rule regarding "the cover of night." Psyche does, and almost instantly, she loses Eros. After his tantrum, he retreats to mother to sulk for almost the rest of the story. Then, the god Pan instructs Psyche to pray to the god of love. Finally, Psyche realizes she must go to Aphrodite, who in her tyrannical attitude assigns Psyche four of the lowest tasks as a condition for her deliverance from the state of nothing to which Aphrodite has reduced her as a mortal.

In Psyche's devastation at having been abandoned by Eros, she immediately wants to drown herself in a river. Not being connected to and grounded in her own instincts, inner value, and depths, she is vulnerable and susceptible to being at the cause and effect of others and life's events. She is prone to accommodating and being pulled into the energy and drama of others. Psyche lacks grounded inner self-esteem, healthy boundaries, an inner authority and voice, and conscious embodiment. At each difficult point, Psyche wants to quit, end the journey, and kill herself. At this stage, she tends toward all-or-nothing thinking. She experiences intrusive, destructive thoughts just as any one of us might while making the journey, or just as John and Mary did in the previously noted examples. Eventually, Psyche encounters Pan at the river's edge, where he dissuades Psyche from drowning herself. He then invites Psyche to connect with matter, the very earth and instinct of her being, in an appropriate way, not in a suicidal way. Pan does this by challenging Psyche to be open, to be alone with herself, and to consider sitting, waiting, and listening attentively to her depths for a solution as she sits by the river-bank. The summons here is the challenge to bear one's loneliness, to endure one's psychic ache and wounds, to persevere alchemically through the black darkness, and to suffer the tension of the opposites. In doing so, one opens to a greater spaciousness within and to the capacity to develop an effective relationship to the Self. In the words of Jung, "The patient must be alone if he [she] is to find out what it is that supports him [her] when he [she] can no longer support himself [herself]" (par. 32).[83]

Thus, the invitation is to hold the tension of the energy, letting go into the body of felt experience; being with what is, and allowing the process to arise and unfold while waiting patiently for the unique life-meaning and direction of the emerging instinctual wisdom of the inner depths. For Psyche and for all of us, this is a gradual learning process. This expanded growth is not a reality that the ego delights in and finds energizing! A real challenge for the ego is letting go of the controlling mind and its effort to analyze, judge, and manipulate everything. Even more difficult, is the challenge to relinquish accepting what others say or don't say, and/or how others respond or don't respond personally. Like Psyche, the ego is summoned to die to the infantile, destructive stance of assuming it is the cause and effect of what others think, say, do, or do not think, say, or do. Psyche had to let go of worrying about what Eros thought, said, did, or any magical thinking about Eros. Psyche had no control over Eros. She could only surrender and be present to what was arising within her in the *now.*

At times, we all have slipped into the pull from destructive energy and acted out the tension through self-sabotaging thoughts, destructive behavior, or end-it-all thinking and/or action. For any one of us who is interested in the quest for embodied consciousness, enduring the alchemical cooking process is a stretch in inner growth and maturity. Some of the vital dynamics of the Dark Feminine include challenging the sojourner to live consciously related to one's depths. Moreover, the task is to live in support of a balance of equals, from the ground of one's being, where the opposites are allowed to coexist and the tension is held in a creative interplay (e.g., chaos and creativity, death and rebirth, sorrow and joy, terror and wonder). Psyche honors this vital dynamic in the way she responds to Pan's suggestion to consider the potential of another option. The Dark Feminine way is a process of being present in the here and now, patiently waiting in the unknown, chaotic, and ungluing darkness that is anxiety producing, until something within emerges to offer the means, the way, the strength, and the courage for whatever is next. Subsequently, for Psyche, that challenge would be the horrific process of completing the four tasks assigned by Aphrodite. In reality, this was Psyche's twilight and midnight of her dark-night initiation. The entire journey was her alchemical extraction operation to bring forth her soul essence through the process. Rather than looking on the outside, the path is a movement toward an inner process with a perduring attentiveness to the mystery/Mystery within, which is the only trustworthy source, despite all the ambiguity, chaos, and anxiety that arise in the experience.

The energy of the Dark Feminine principle, as manifested in Psyche's story, evolves through the process of remaining alert to the inner center and riding the heightened waves of anxiety every time something happens to stir the psyche. This is a creative and a liberating act. This process enlarges the soul. Psyche needed to separate herself from an unconscious identification with Eros. She needed to wait, listen, work with, and discover her emerging unique soul essence. As she endured the difficulties of her four assigned tasks, she progressively and consciously embodied more aspects of her true nature, subsequently opening to a greater interior freedom and relational capacity with Eros. For any one of us who can choose to bear a patient attentiveness to the inner arising darkness, one will discover in this challenging frontier aspects of one's soul essence, if one can separate, differentiate, and take responsibility for the parts of one's self that one has unconsciously projected onto another (Eros) and desired or expected the other to "carry." Within the process, one can unearth undeveloped gifts that are part of one's natural being. In this interior alchemical process, the container for Psyche's depths is being developed and strengthened in a conscious, grounded, instinctual way through her experience of holding the tension of the opposites in a creative interaction.

Moreover, some of the energetic patterns revealed in Psyche's myth are the very energy of Lady Underground of Chartres; namely, befriending, metabolizing, and embodying the emerging, challenging energy manifested in the dynamic patterns of death and rebirth, chaos and creativity, and darkness and illuminative wisdom. This is a natural growth dynamic, whether personal or planetary. We witness this reality in the changing of the seasons. As difficult as it is for any one of us to face and to let go of old ways, Lady Underground and all aspects of the unifying principle of the psyche seek for us to reconnect with the primordial inspiration and wisdom within us. This reality is not just for the sake of regressive, dreadful suffering, but to liberate our generative natural soul essence for a more conscious expanded life. The chaos, the darkness, the destruction, and the death are a precondition for a more enlarged conscious life.

Being consciously attentive to the dark silence within the center, and receptively (not passively) waiting is a sacrifice. Psyche makes the sacrifice that takes her further in her development, although intrusive, despairing thoughts continue to afflict her at later stages. The sacrifice that is required of Psych, as well as of Mary, John, or any one of us, is not a choice made only once. Sacrificing and the death/rebirth experience are key dynamics in the whole humanizing process of the quest toward individuation. This reality is also core to Lady Underground's dark-night initiation. Old, defended ways of being need to be sacrificed in order to open to an inner spaciousness for the new emerging life that is attempting to be embodied consciously. Inner depth work is not a party! The charged critical inner thoughts of Psyche or the intrusive self-limiting and self-defeating killer thoughts that any one of us may experience, suggest and symbolize that the regressive pull tempts at each new stage of growth. Some examples of self-sabotaging thoughts are: I didn't please or satisfy the other; I'm not good enough, smart enough, valuable, worthy, loveable, talented, coordinated, articulate, experienced, beautiful, or handsome. Some instances of the contrary, defensive thinking of superiority that are equally destructive include: I have it all; I am the best; I am right; what I think is what is; and I am better than another. Besides this reality, some persons can have an unconscious masterful part that is vigilant, will-directed, and unwavering in the service to avoid feeling and vulnerability, as a protective shield against judgment, shame, abandonment, hurt, and/or trauma. This defended unconscious imprisoned part can drive a person and create havoc in interpersonal relationships. Relinquishing old constrictive ways of being requires deep focused inner work if a soul is to know a more enlarged soulful consciousness. Different degrees of these noted aspects of the psyche and the destructive dimensions of the ego will be confronted in the purification in descent of twilight and will intensify in midnight of Lady Underground's dark-night initiation.

Two persons who have done a great deal of inner work with these unconscious psychic imprisoned parts are Meredith and Frank. Meredith, a

61-year-old bright, contemplative, married woman is a successful artist, an empathic psychologist, and a trauma specialist in private practice. Frank, a 52-year-old single man is well educated and enjoys friends, classical music, theater, tennis, and traveling. He's also a successful, well-respected, published author. Both Meredith and Frank are highly functional, professional individuals, and yet both realize how their vigilant, imprisoned self-part impairs their lives. As Meredith became aware of this psychic part, she referred to it as Nono, and Frank called his inner alienated, respective part, Retard. Meredith, in an earlier phase of her work, had brought to a session a copy of Edward Munch's famous painting, "The Scream." For Meredith, the image portrayed a sense of her helpless, impoverished, abandoned, abused, and dissociated part. When Meredith was a toddler, her mother had been deaf to Meredith's howling as she and a nurse had subjected Meredith to traumatizing enemas that were physically damaging. Her mother died of cancer when she was 5, and her father remarried when she was 7. During Meredith's childhood and adolescence, her stepmother had shamed, mocked, and abandoned her. The family milieu gave sole credence to intellect, and expressed emotion was never tolerated. As she gradually became more aware of Nono, her split-off unconscious part, Meredith was shocked at how much power this scorned and rejected self-part had in her outer life. Frank, an exceptionally talented man with two doctorates, sat silently with his head down for five minutes before looking up and confessing that even if he had had a third doctorate, he still would not be smart enough. Frank's mother often called him "Retard" as a toddler and as a youth because gum infections caused him to drool. Given Frank's theater training and his well-developed reaction-formation mask, most people would be shocked to know that he suffers daily from sabotaging, intrusive thoughts of *you don't know* and *you are not smart enough.*

If the core essence, the creative energy, and the more expanded natural soul are ever to be liberated from the utter aridity and darkness of twilight initiation and the rejected, impoverished part of Meredith, Frank, or of any one of us, then gradually, the once-needed, coping, protective, defended way, which now strongly resists growth toward embodied fullness, will need to be heard and befriended. Furthermore, the dark medicine in twilight is the darkness of aridity, the loss of meaning and satisfaction in what was once valued and prized in life. The soul needs to be supported patiently through the positive disintegration in this anguishing alchemical cooking process. Lady Underground's dark-night medicine of initiation is characterized by a "both/and," not an "either/or" dynamic. The Dark Feminine alchemical cooking process, relatively speaking, is multidimensional. For those who have had despairing death-mother energy activated in their psyche (very judgmental and critical; Lady Macbeth, for example, personifies death-mother energy), they will have to wrestle with the horrific tension of this energy in twilight with the depth of intensity addressed in midnight of dark night. Death-mother energy kills spirit and soul. This is very different from the Dark Feminine that is about death in service to generative life, soul essence. There is a continuous sacrifice and surrender made as a soul works through the enormous defended muscle that each self-part has developed over the years, as well as experiencing varying doses of the black darkness of aridity, a lack of satisfaction in life, and a powerlessness to restore the soul's vitality in any way. The heat of the alchemical cooking process is slowly calling the psyche beyond its defensive protective stance toward a symbolic death that is necessary if there is ever to be a spaciousness for the core essence in the depths of the underground to germinate and to sprout into conscious new life. The organizing principle, with its teleological function, and the life-force energy of Lady Underground is catalyzing the soul toward opening to the deeper more vitalizing nurturance and wisdom in the depths and the psychic fertile soil that contains the seeds of the natural true soul essence in the multidimensional underground.

Again, the reality of sacrifice and surrender and the ongoing, symbolic death experience for the ego is not a one-time event. Twilight of Lady Underground alchemical initiation is deepened and intensified in a more radical purgation in midnight of dark night. Depth work is arduous! In the battleground of darkness and through inner work with split-off self-parts, the soul, through experience, gradually realizes that it is only in being connected to the depths and through the sacrifice and death of archaic ways of being, that a repressed self-part can be freed from inner captivity and integrated into consciousness, and that the soul can be energized toward a more natural essence. As conscious carriers of this liberated, generative, emerging energy, we can all make a more enlivened contribution to humanity. This dynamic is never really overcome sufficiently until the gradual emergence of deeper dimensions of the Dark Feminine energy (virgin and conduit of wisdom) are embodied consciously in and through midnight of dark-night initiation. This is represented in the climax of the Psyche myth by her reunion with Eros.[84]

Hence, John and Mary, as noted earlier, like Meredith, Frank, Psyche, and any one of us, are summoned in darkness of twilight to endure the tension of the opposites, to sacrifice, surrender, and give oneself to night initiation, as each one is seduced toward his or her soul essence by Lady Underground or by some other image of the Dark Feminine. To accept and yield to what is erupting in psyche constitutes the gradual death of structures and patterns of the ego that are no longer appropriate. From the ego's perspective, the process of sacrificing and letting go of familiar restrictive ways of being, such as an attachment, a dependency, vigilant control, naïveté, a charged driver (e.g., *be a dutiful daughter/son, hurry up, be perfect, please others, be strong,* or *be the best,* or *be number one*) is a distressing death. The ego resists and is often unhappy. This reluctance will tend to manifest in some psychological or bodily symptom for each person who experiences twilight. As the well-known Jungian analyst, James Hollis, remarked in a lecture at the Swiss Embassy in Washington, D.C., "The ego prefers certainty over uncertainty, predictability over surprise, clarity over ambiguity, control over anarchy, and decision over ambivalence." Painful though this reality is for John, Mary, Meredith, Frank, or any one of us, the darkness of twilight is designed to bring about alchemical purging for the sake of embodied soul essence.

Furthermore, with regard to the symbolic significance of twilight, the person who embarks on the quest, influenced by the archetypal energy of Lady Underground or some other image of the Dark Feminine, descends into the various shades of the dark-night initiatory experience by a way of "knowing-by-not-knowing." This dark dynamic, which one is drawn into, is the same reality that is reflected in the Norse myth of Odin, hanging upside down on the Yggdrasil or World Tree, seizing the Runes; the Hanged Man of the tarot cards is a similar image. Odin needed to hang upside down and go by a way of "seeing" and "knowing," by "not seeing" and "not knowing" in order to open to a deeper internalized psychic space of embodied wisdom. The Hanged Man seems to "know" that his head will not serve him and that his vision springs from beyond intellect.[85]

Joyce a 56-year-old university professor and trial lawyer noted in a session, "I like reading and talking about the Dark Feminine, but I struggle to tolerate and like whatever is going on for *me*. I don't understand my experience. My whole life has been about knowing and being in control *via* my head. Not knowing what is going on is ungluing me. I've always prided myself on my knowledge, my capacity to articulate clearly, and my appearance of having it together." Also, Hunter, a 70-year-old man in a vowed religious community described himself as trusting his intellect, his ministerial work ethic, his discipline, and his rational, predictable, manageable, ordered life. However, Hunter finds that his sexuality and his heart's desires are like a fire cauldron that's been ignited since he fell in love in his late 60s. He sees himself as if in a dark wood; the terrain and the way are not known. In Hunter's words, "My rational way of being is my familiar and trusted form. I always have prided myself in my discipline, control, and management of life. But now, at this stage in my life, my interiority is turned upside down. My instinctual desires have my thinking function scattered. I feel out of sorts, uncomfortable, skeptical, and embarrassed. I tell myself that the desire that is awakened within me is healthy. I think that the Spirit, St. John of the Cross, Thomas Merton, and Jung would see my desire as a potential for growth. My rational mind concurs with this view; however, I am leery of what seems irrational and intense, whether it is anger or erotic sexual feelings. I feel very conflicted within myself. I don't want to be stupid and blow my long-standing reputation and my legacy. I have a public persona, and I feel a responsibility about protecting it. I can't get my mind wrapped around all my sexual feelings and fantasies. I feel disoriented in a dark wood." Hunter pauses, "I sure wish there was light!" When we are in the dark thicket, don't we all have some magical thinking creep in, some longing for relief by the light? Lady Underground's twilight of dark-night initiation is going by a way of knowing-by-not-knowing.

Thus, each person who is drawn by Lady Underground in the twilight of the night sea journey gradually comes to realize that one does not discover new interior lands without consenting to lose sight of the shore for a very long time. Furthermore, on this arduous journey, what may seem to the rational collective mindset like interruptions and delays in life are in time perceived by the night journeyer as challenges and opportunities that enrich growth in a practical, grounded, sensory manner. Lady Underground's initiation occurs not in a vacuum, but in and through our human psyche, our earthly body, and in the ordinary of everyday life. Metaphorically, Lady Underground's dark-night initiation is the descent into our inner world. Odin, the Hanged Man, Joyce, and Hunter reflect an interior state tending toward an overdeveloped, one-sided attitude. The journey toward healing, reconciling the opposites, and embodying consciousness is only through befriending and integrating the energy that engages any of us in twilight of dark night. The only way out of the original state in which one finds oneself is to accept it and to give oneself to the inner journey of the twilight of dark-night initiation in the night sea journey of individuation. According to Jung's description of this perilous journey, it is only by passing through and assimilating the night experience that one discovers the hidden treasure of new life.

Twilight of Dark Night of Initiation: Psychological Significance

Psychologically, what is occurring within the human personality that is moved by Lady Underground at twilight in the dark night of initiation? At this pivotal time, more of one's soul essence is calling to be heard and integrated into consciousness. In midlife one suffers the strain, tension, and conflict of the growing split between the altered personality, with all its adaptations and drivers (e.g., *be perfect, please others, be strong, hurry up, try hard, be dutifully responsible*), and the authentic personality with more of one's natural, core essence. This split is constellated and charged as a result of having developed an altered personality in reaction to prenatal, infant, and childhood experiences. Continuing to emerge into adolescence and young adulthood with this accommodating, unnatural identity, one subsequently continues to react, make so-called choices, and decisions that further self-estrangement. Or, as Emily Dickinson expressed it, "Ourself, behind ourself concealed, should startle most . . ." Rilke conveys a similar sentiment, "Disguised since childhood, haphazardly assembled from voices and fears and little pleasures, we come of age as masks. Our true face never speaks" (p. 112).[86] Thus, with the onset of twilight, a positive disintegration begins to occur in the psyche as polarities are seeking reconciliation. The dynamics of night bring about the ego becoming decentered, the persona beginning to crack, the shadow erupting, the complexes getting triggered, and the contrasexual side wanting to be heard in the psyche. The organizing principle of the psyche, with its teleological function, and the archetypal energy of Lady Underground are summoning the soul to embody one's essence.

With the intensification of the opposites in the self-regulating system of the psyche, the ego begins to darken, and one tends to question one's identity, meaning, and existence. The ego, having developed during the first half of life, has had a sense of feeling "at home," as the conscious gatekeeper of the personality. One knows oneself to be a certain way; knowing this identity in a relatively consistent way, seemingly provides a more assured grounding. However, at twilight the ego, which functions in a manner that's more estranged from the deeper, vitalizing, and nourishing sources of the psyche, is purged so that more of the Self can be heard and integrated. At twilight of dark-night initiation, the ego feels as if it is losing its secure, "known" grounding. Since the ego tends to cling and rest in its own knowledge and control, it is not aware of the psychic charged forces that can undermine and sabotage its stance. Purgation is experienced by the ego as a darkening phenomenon, as a losing of control and command of one's life. In Rilke's words, "We are not much at home in the world we have created" (no. 1, lines 11-12).[87] Tennessee Williams sharpens our awareness of this poignant truth in his play *Sweet Bird of Youth*, in which we see the purgation reality through the personality of Chance, who manifests characteristics of one who is alienated from his depths and far from his inner home. As the dynamics of positive disintegration and purgation begin to happen in his psyche, Chance realizes that the lovely past, with all its fresh promise, cannot be retrieved.

In like manner, Jack, a 60-year-old professional businessman who has suffered from low self-esteem for most of his life, finds himself lost and not at home in his inner depths. Jack lost his mother in early childhood, and his father was both emotionally unavailable and often physically absent during Jack's developmental years. Jack accommodates and pleases others in an attempt to be accepted and loved. After doing in-depth marriage counseling over the years, including *imago* marriage therapy and still experiencing major marital dissatisfaction, Jack separated from his wife of 30 years. He finds himself plunged into painful dark waters of grief and loneliness. He is dealing with the eruption and demagnetization of his parental complexes and his inner swamplands. Jack is realizing that his longing for warmth, connection, acknowledgment, and to be with a woman has a large layer of projected energy of wanting a woman to be mother for him and for a woman to bear his soul's loneliness and wounds. In becoming aware of his attachment hunger, Jack has begun to withdraw the energy of asking another to carry and to be for him in a way that he psychologically needs to be and do for himself, as he differentiates from his mother complex and grows in his capacity to bear his own distress and loneliness. This is a challenging reality for any one of us. We need to be able to stand alone and know from within what supports us, as well as to grow in our capacity to bear our suffering until we begin to be grounded consciously in our own depths and to discover the meaning and direction of our soul's summons. No person can carry our soul for us, live for us, and/or die for us. No human being or thing can take the place of the mystery/Mystery. No one can be a god or goddess for us. A lesser god/goddess means a more restricted psyche and subsequently a diminished humanity. Withdrawing our clinging attachment and infantile demands and taking responsibility for this energy is necessary if we are to grow in inner freedom, maturity, and capacity for authentic Eros. Jack is just beginning consciously to take responsibility for his own inner happiness and well-being, particularly with respect to his interactions with women. He is starting to be able to tolerate some time alone with his depths without bolting to call another, to text, or to run from himself as he looks on the outside for what can only be found from within. As Jack notes, "Detachment sucks, and I know this is my soul's task right now." In addition, he is attempting to take responsibility for exploring and honoring ways of nurturing (being mother to) his own inner soul. For Jack and for any male, this growth dynamic is an important stage of masculine development, for their own souls's maturity; this integration enables men to relate to women in a healthier, conscious, and more meaningful way. Jack continues to be attentive to his process even as he realizes that he has slid down the slippery slope of reenactment and then consciously chooses anew, as we all do many times. He recently noted, "I am committed to my soul work and my journey. Coming home within is really tough work. The process is like a roller coaster with so many ups and downs."

Psychologically, the sense of being lost and the hard-earned process of coming home interiorly is an arduous task of differentiation. Like Jack, Jennifer also feels lost. Jennifer is a single, environmentally conscious dentist who exasperatingly utters, "I tried so hard to develop a clear, organized, sound foundation in every step of my personal and professional development, and now at 54 years old, I feel bewildered, bored, and no longer at home within myself. How can this be?" Jennifer and Jack are experiencing a time of human development that Paul Tillich described as "existential estrangement." In twilight of dark-night initiation, one feels lost and not at home.

Furthermore, the persona begins to crack. The persona is the mask worn in response to social situations, the demands of tradition, and one's inner needs.[88] [89] A person needs a healthy persona to function in this life. We do not relate to life around us as raw psyches, but rather as learned roles in communicating with the outside world. Nevertheless, in performing necessary functions, there is the danger of getting lost in one's role or of defining oneself by one's role. Just as the ego does not represent the full personality of the individual, neither does the persona. A sense of boredom, feelings of growing stale, or a lack of meaning in one's role can manifest themselves at this pivotal time. Along with the ego's darkening, there is the impression that one's persona is falling apart. The "clothes" that were once appropriate no longer fit. This psychological dynamic is reflected in the dream of Mary Beth, who had been a nun for 20 years and reported this recurring dream: "Even though I attempt with great effort to put the attire on my head, I still am unable to fit into the traditional headdress and veil, and the traditional nun shoes that my order wears as part of the habit." In Mary Beth's words, "I no longer fit into the collective mindset. I no longer can 'cover over' my consciousness and my 'stance' of truth."

An additional sign that this pivotal time is beginning to occur is the eruption of the shadow. The shadow consists of all those psychic qualities within the personal unconscious that are unacceptable or not acknowledged by the conscious personality. The shadow includes all those aspects of ourselves with which we are uncomfortable and would rather forget and/or deny. Furthermore, the shadow is the object of one's fear, judgment, hatred, loathing, and dislike, but it is also the object of one's secret longing and desire. Jung writes, "By shadow I mean the 'negative' side of the personality, the sum of all those unpleasant qualities we like to hide, together with the insufficiently developed functions and the contents of the personal unconscious" (par. 66).[90]

Jung believed that the shadow is 90 percent gold. It is not only the negative aspects and destructive possibilities of one's personality, but also the unlived potential of an individual. This positive dimension of the shadow represents unactualized life that is a rich resource if owned and integrated into the conscious personality. Forfeiting this central part of oneself can lead to isolation, alienation, stagnation, loneliness, and death. In the words of the *Gospel of Thomas*, "If you bring forth what is within you, what you bring forth will save you. If you do not bring forth what is within you, what you do not bring forth will destroy you" (p. 134).[91] [92] Hence, psychologically, Lady Underground in twilight brings to light the shadow, which contains all that is problematic yet vital, such as jealousy, anger, arrogance, narcissism, and power, but also joy, humor, playfulness, lush energies, and untapped creative fires. Psychologically, as we descend, explore, engage, and befriend our inner world of the unconscious, the underground masculine and feminine energies in all of us are being summoned toward a more enlarged conscious differentiation. In doing our shadow work, Lady Underground is calling us to consciously unearth our unconscious matter. This great excavation is the portal to embodied consciousness.

At twilight, another major aspect that manifests from the unconscious is the complex. Jung referred to the complex as the "*via regia* (the royal road) to the unconscious . . .which is the architect of dreams and of symptoms" (par. 210).[93] Out of the wounds of infancy and childhood, the feeling-charged constellation of energy becomes activated; the more intense the initial hurt, abuse, neglect, or trauma, and the longer it was repeated, the more power the complex has in a person's life and, subsequently, the more apt it is to be triggered. Self-limiting beliefs, charged emotions, physical sensations, will-directed decisions, and energy held somewhere in the cellular memory of the body and the energy field are some of the aspects associated with each complex. The complex is not experienced in a vacuum, but in our psyche and body. The issue is not that we have complexes, but that complexes would have us to the point that we unconsciously identify with them: for example, unconscious overidentification with the mother, father, bully, victim, superiority, inferiority, money, sex, and/or power. An overidentification with any complex is a great deal of charged energy running one's life. Thus, armored reactive responses to another are less conscious replies and far more the triggered complex rearing itself and driving us, whether any one of us is conscious of it or not. Hence, at twilight, what gets stirred and is being engineered in the depths of the psyche is a deeper call by the Self and Lady Underground for a recovery of what is undifferentiated, repressed, split off, and projected. If one is to become ensouled in the deeper aspects of the Dark Feminine energy (virgin and wisdom), differentiation of the mother energy in twilight is an aspect of inner soul work that is unavoidable!

In summary, twilight of dark night of initiation in the Dark Feminine ushers in a passage wherein life circumstances are erupting, and subliminal anxiety is cracking through as meaning evaporates from one's life. As a result, suffering is experienced. Anxiety and fear can engulf one when there seems to be no direction, how-to YouTube video, app, and/or a GPS for the uncharted journey. One can feel bewildered, lost, and without a hope for happiness again. There can be a strong tendency toward attempting to grasp and to cling to known familiar ways. Alchemically, the *nigredo* is occurring for the person in twilight. This painful psychic night is felt in the very muscles and structure of the body that houses the psyche. Such hollow meaninglessness, aching loneliness, and heightened anxiety can be profoundly unsettling. There are no "aspirin answers." The intensity of the energy in the unconscious fires this eruption, which causes the settled known conscious life to start positively disintegrating at this pivotal time. Jung views this time as a spiritual crisis, and, according to him, healing is not known until one has regained one's religious outlook.[94] Moreover, Lady Underground's medicine of darkness is designed for the initiate because, in Jung's words, "We cannot live the afternoon of life according to the program of life's morning; for what was great in the morning will be little at evening, and what in the morning was true will at evening have become a lie" (par. 784).[95]

Midnight of Dark Night of Initiation: Symbolic Significance

To release, to metabolize, to embody, and to live the full energies of life in response to the summons of the soul's intentionality and the energy of Lady Underground require a radical process of transformation, often accompanied by a very demanding rite of initiation. Nietzsche realized this reality, which is reflected in his insight that the tree that would grow to heaven must first send its roots to hell. Jung strikingly noted the same wisdom: "No noble well-grown tree ever disowned its dark roots, for it grows not only upward but downward as well" (par. 148).[96] Lady Underground's midnight initiation is the journey into the darkest and coldest dimensions of our interiority. Symbolically, it is the courageous chthonic expedition into the deeper dark caverns of our inner landscapes. Midnight initiation is entering the gate of blacker-than-black terrain for the arduous descent into the earth of our dark roots, a venture of death and rebirth that is forged *via* the experience of darkness, nothingness, and emptiness. While many may experience the psychic dynamics of twilight for a shorter or a longer time, and/or spiral around the twilight stage on and off many times throughout middle and later years of life, not everyone will enter the portal of blackness to make yet a deeper descent at midnight into the dark caverns of their underground-earth.

What explanation is there for this varying pattern of occurrence? Dag Hammarskjold wrote in *Markings*, "The longest journey is the journey inward" (p. 48).[97] How true this reality is for the person in the second half of life who is making a descent, but it is especially true in a deeper, dark, black night of initiation. There are many possibilities for avoiding and not enduring psychic excavations at midnight. Some primary explanations may be: that given the summons, the sacrifice seems too great on many levels; that there is little stamina and patience to reflect symbolically and do the inner work; that soul work of holistic growth and healing is time consuming, as the depths require more than a shallow passing over in the journey toward conscious embodiment; that flight in the face of suffering and death seems easier than maintaining a perduring attentiveness to the process; that primitive and primary defense structures are too strong; that the unconscious, wounded, autonomous, dark, imprisoned parts that drain, seethe, trigger, sabotage, and define our outer life are determined to maintain safety, security, and a *No* stance at all costs; that there is not a strong-enough ego development to hold the tension of the opposites; that a psychic container is not sufficiently developed to be able to hold the tension of the opposites in this blacker terrain of midnight; that the distractions of life are more enticing than the discipline required for inner soul work; that there is a lack of knowledge about the benefits of holistic active-imagination exercises, including body-energy modalities that could assist in the process of enduring, metabolizing, and integrating the dynamics and energy at midnight; that there is a lack of conscious guides who have done enough extensive, dark, entrenched, shadow work to accompany consciously another in doing the black-of-midnight inner work; that the payoff for staying unconscious and living by collective values seems more ego gratifying and rewarding; and that midnight rites of initiation are not everybody's fate.

As in twilight, each person will enter midnight with varying gradations of intensity and duration. Individuals will experience midnight of Lady Underground's initiation medicine in a range of different doses as each unique soul struggles to endure and to persevere in the process. Some may go through midnight for a shorter or a longer time, and/or spiral around midnight on and off many times as they are summoned to a more expansive conscious embodiment of spirit/Spirit in the ordinary of life. The blacker-than-black medicine of midnight is an intense dose of the alchemical medicine of *mortificatio*. Lady Underground's midnight descent is the adult school of human interiority in intense psychospiritual learning in the virgin and wisdom-depth dimensions within the continuum of the Dark Feminine's inexhaustible energy. The call is toward a fuller range, expression, and freedom of our soul's essence and potential within the relational web of life.

Furthermore, as in twilight, the process in midnight is a choice not made once only. As Jung writes, "There is no linear evolution; there is only a circumambulation of the self. . . . [E]verything points toward the center" (pp. 196-197).[98] Regardless of where we are developmentally in the night and for how long, the mystery/Mystery remains the invisible source and engineering power of the journey. The awareness of conflict and struggle is staggering in engaging the tension of the opposites. Sometimes the reality is agonizing, even horrifically, and especially in midnight; yet, one's choice still remains to pursue one's individuation and to honor the intentionality of the soul as one is in service to the mystery/Mystery. How wonderful it would be if growth in midnight were completed by going through only once the experience of the distress of the opposites and by enduring the tension until something new arises from the depths! This psychic alchemical development occurring in and through one's body in the excavation of one's essence is a process of choice made many times in the spiral and meandering journey of metabolizing and befriending the soul's energy. The conscious choice must be revisited daily in one's inner work, especially with one's dreams and the images and symbols that engage one's depths, while always remembering that we meet ourselves in a thousand different disguises on the road of life. Making this conscious choice daily means choosing it, despite fear, lethargy, anxiety, flight, loss, the slippery slope of rational justifications, and often in the most exhausting of times as one struggles to embody consciousness. Equally so is consciously discriminating and selecting what any one of us says *Yes* to in the joy, delight, pleasure, and fun of life. Thus, the process of midnight initiation involves an ever-growing capacity for a conscious, keen sense of discrimination, discernment, choice, and sacrifice.

Most of us are not educated in darkness, suffering, sacrifice, surrender, symbolic death, and/or physical death as essential ingredients in this evolutionary process and journey called *life*. Midnight is the passage in which the heartfelt soul is matured. One does not enroll in the school of Lady Underground's advanced curriculum of midnight initiation. The soul's intentionality activates and beckons one to the deeper journey of human interiority. Dark night of initiation symbolically moves from twilight to midnight to dawn in the progressive, alchemical purification and transformation of the psyche, housed in the earth of one's body, the manifestation of the psyche. For the sojourner called to this deeper dark descent, twilight is a preparation for midnight, which is an intensification of twilight *par excellence*!

Midnight is the darkest time of the night. We reflect on the symbolism of this dimension of night to unearth a deeper understanding, appreciation, and discovery of the value of this intense journey of consciously birthing and embodying our soul essence. The growth toward our true nature, activated in twilight, is expanded in the summons in midnight. This stage is not only a continuous realm of going by a way of knowing-by-not-knowing, but it's also a more intense purging and stripping through darkness and emptiness to the bare bones of nothingness. The *modus operandi* is slow, repetitive, difficult, and intense as one experiences the *nigredo* state of midnight. It exposes human fragility, woundedness, brokenness, neurotic dependence, and what is not our essence. The black alchemy of midnight uncovers our deepest wounds and/or our greatest attachments. The 14th-century Buddhist mystic Lalleswari encourages a soul in this intense interior state of growth, asserting that one must bear the lightning and thunder along the path. The wise one notes that one must endure the difficulties in the dark midnight of *sadhana* by staying calm and not turning back, for it will seem as if one is being crushed like powder between grinding stones. These intended words of support are daunting to digest! The 16th-century Carmelite St. John of the Cross sees this state of enveloping darkness as analogous to being in a sepulcher of dark death and facing the sorrows of hell or in the belly of the whale. Jung thought that the dread and resistance to this state of being was related to the fear of the journey to Hades. Regardless of one's tradition, Lady Underground's midnight initiation in the Dark Feminine is a horrific reality to embrace and metabolize.

Midnight is the black void of utter nothingness. This stage is the descent into hell, into Hades, which, paradoxically, is not an absence but a hidden presence, even an invisible fullness that is only known in retrospect on the other side of midnight. In Hades, there is the feeling "as if" Lady Underground or the mystery/Mystery has abandoned one, for one is stripped and emptied of any sense of her presence or the mystery/Mystery. The experience of sheer dead nothingness is a suffering for the ego, and often the human tendency is to take flight in some way. Also, from the perspective of the ego, it is as if what one was certain of and depended upon as a source of strength, consolation, and reassurance has vanished. Midnight descent is an eclipse of mystery/Mystery. For the ego, Lady Underground is obscured from awareness. In the seeming utter absence and abandonment of her, some other image of the Dark Feminine, or any sense of the mystery/Mystery, there is an existential felt awareness of annihilating aloneness. The soul does not realize in the stark darkness of this alchemical process that midnight of dark-night initiation in the Dark Feminine is less about the cruelty or harshness of the goddess or nature, and more about the anguishing state of the soul. This arduous experience addresses the finite limitations, attachments, constriction, rigidity, neurosis, defense structure, false identity, masks of self-hatred and the idealized self-image, or masks of the collective ideal of good, love, accomplishments, money, power, or a mixture of these. During this time, a dream will sometimes be like a PET scan of the psyche, revealing metaphorically the scope of healing needed in the deeper caverns of the soul. The heat of midnight of dark night brings the soul's extensive driven, compulsive, and painful splitting wounds to consciousness. The *modus operandi* is slow, repetitive, difficult, and severe as one experiences the *nigredo* state of midnight. This intense affliction is the night of utter blacker-than-black, desolate, cold darkness and emptiness. The dose of midnight medicine in this excavated state of being, however short or long the time of the experience, is so dark, deadening, and empty that the thought of physical death is often welcomed, as a soul can't imagine any good or value coming from such a wretched condition. As one person described this reality: "All desire is gone. I feel stripped of all that has mattered to me. There *is* nothing to live for. No one seems to tolerate, let alone be able to hear this blacker-than-black, cold state of being. The space is so dark and just raw emptiness. It is as if I'm dead bones with utter lifeless nothingness. The deadness is stark. I always liked listening to music, and I can't bear it, not even classical music. It is too passionate, and everything is dead. I feel dead." This agonizing experiential state of being reflects the same motif found in the oldest known myth, *The Descent of Inanna.* In this story, Inanna, the Sumerian queen of heaven and earth, descended into the underworld. Through the rites of initiation in entering the Netherworld, Inanna is brought naked and humbled, crouched and stripped bare; her corpse is hung on a peg to rot. This is the symbolic death that the soul traverses through Lady Underground's midnight of dark-night initiation in the Dark Feminine. The soul is undergoing an alchemical cure to regain its healing, balance, wholeness, essence, and psyche's *telos.* Midnight is a major operation of a progressive positive disintegration and symbolic death to open the night sea journeyer to: the goddess/god/mystery; living the symbolic life; the call to transformation, which includes an inner psychological marriage of equals; embodied consciousness; the summons of a more authentic relationship with others, the Other both inner and outer, the earth, and respect for animal life; and to the conscious discovery of the soul's true nature and intentional path. This seemingly annihilating process is death to the ego and fuller life to the Self. The Dark Feminine is death in service to life! The intense alchemical extraction brings forth a more expanded range of conscious embodied essence and authentic aspects of the soul's true nature, meaning, and direction.

This was evident in the life of one married 86-year-old, contemplative, dying man named Rafik. In twilight of dark-night initiation, Rafik knew descent into darkness through loss on many levels. Some of the issues addressed in his descent were loss through the Great Depression, the death of his father and two close siblings, the end of a career of 30 years not by choice, the struggle with cancer, unemployment for nine months, spirituality, and dealing with some hubristic tendencies. Rafik had a remarkable, resilient spirit in the midst of his suffering and metabolizing the energy in twilight. Essentially, his struggle in this stage echoed the struggle of Job. Rafik emerged from this growth stage with an overall humble attitude and a more grounded authentic relationship to himself, others, the universe, and the Mystery.

Now, in midnight of Rafik's journey of dark night, he spiraled into a yet-deeper descent. With one look at Rafik, one could perceive that the skeleton like body of this suffering soul was being devoured by the archetypal energy of Kali, the Dark Feminine Hindu goddess who is perpetually destroying and paradoxically, at the same time, creating. Her energy is death in service to life and life in service to death. She is indifferent to the bargaining or demands of a dying soul. She is nature as process, which includes the harsh human stripping in the darkness and emptiness of metabolizing, accepting, and surrendering to death, however this is experienced for any one of us at any stage of life, including the last and final frontier. For Kali, and for Lady Underground, the nature of life as well as death is all one. In the words of Jim Hollis: "There is no contradiction in nature—nature is merely *naturing*; no contradiction in the gods—the gods *god* [similarly, there is no contradiction in the goddess—the goddesses *goddess*]; but with so much contradiction besetting the ego, we have historically sought to resolve the problem by splitting into opposites rather than by embracing the mystery" (pp. 178-179).[99]

In *Hamlet*, Shakespeare refers to death as "the undiscover'd country." Rafik was entering this bleak, blacker-than-black frontier. He was facing the cliff's edge, anguishing over the stark darkness and emptiness of his state, questioning his very center. Rafik was embarking upon the journey into silence from which no echo returns. As a man who had withered to a mere 110 pounds, Rafik came to know his finite nature on many levels. What was heaviest for him in midnight was questioning the very existence of the mystery/Mystery and an afterlife. This is a real horrific existential struggle for any one of us to face at any time in our life, and all the more so when one is at the doorstep of death and the finality of life as one has known it. For Rafik, the experience of the mystery was the encounter with God. Rafik needed to own and to express what was welling up in his depths. While the nature and the dynamics of his process can be seen and understood through the lens of Kali energy or Lady Underground's dark night of initiation medicine, for Rafik this would not be his language or template to describe his horrific, agonizing experience of life-death. Psychologically, he was enduring the most intense aspect of midnight of the night sea journey. Spiritually, he was experiencing what St. John of the Cross described in his commentaries on adult spirituality in *The Dark Night, Book Two,* found in *The Collected Works of St. John of the Cross* as the passive night of midnight of dark night of the soul.

With a look of annihilating despair, Rafik, who sat with his eyes cast down and his small, frail hands folded on his chest, said with a pressing certitude, "Eileen, I need to talk about something that has been weighing very heavily on me." Pause—a deep silence emerged for almost five minutes as we sat together. Then Rafik began to express very slowly: "The worst is I've come to this point, and it is dark, empty, empty, so empty, and absolutely nothing. And worse yet, it is a dreadful, stark, cold, empty nothingness." The heaviness of Rafik's gripping plight and the felt crushing suffering of his soul were palpable. Again, silence transpired as we were together. Then, Rafik said: "My whole life (pause) I've been a believer because I came to experience God in a real way that made a difference in my life. The Presence was my guiding center (long pause). To come to this point (very long pause), this is all there is?

(pause) Just empty, dark nothingness? I don't know (pause). I don't know (pause). I don't know if there is a God or (pause) if there is anything after this (pause), anything after this life." As Rafik expressed his honesty and his raw vulnerability about his genuine depths, silent tears began to roll down his thin, sunken face. Rafik's agonized suffering was real. Silence . . . silence . . . a depth of silence arose in Rafik and in me as we sat together in the interactive field of his midnight death of dark night, spiritually and psychologically. The annihilating pain of Rafik's suffering soul was undeniable, both his withering, frail body and his utter poverty of spirit. Tears continued to roll down Rafik's face. There were no words, only the tears and silence of such a blacker-than-black midnight for about five minutes. Then, seemingly out of nowhere, what arose in the interactive field was an undeniable felt sense of a benevolent Silent Stilling Presence. The gracious grace of the numinous energy was quieting, utterly stilling, and phenomenally irrefutable. Stillness speaks! After a period of time, Rafik drew his hands together, gazed across at me, and quietly nodded his head, as I also did to him. This was the last time I saw Rafik in my office. He died two weeks later. As Rafik left that day, I gave him a hug. He proceeded toward the door, stopped, turned his head, looked me in the eye, and said, "I'm going home, going with a still, inner peace."

John of the Cross describes in *The Dark Night, Book Two* (Chapter 9 in *The Collected Works of St. John of the Cross),* that the moaning and clamoring in this state of being is such a painful disturbance because the annihilating sorrow of the soul is such a deep suffering. According to John of the Cross, sometimes dissolving in tears is a rare reprieve and release for a soul who is experiencing this indescribable anguish and suffering. In the intensity of symbolic death in midnight of dark-night initiation, all supports are failing, the center is questioned, and nothing seems trustworthy. Rafik owned and experienced consciously this phenomenon.

Metabolizing midnight entails a suffering, and nothing could be more normal in the human condition than a reluctance to suffer. Eckhart Tolle says that if one can let go of the unwillingness to suffer, and focus on owning and allowing the pain to be, or in Rafik's case, permitting himself to fully experience his sense of doubting, questioning, and feelings of being duped and abandoned, then one may notice and discover a subtle inner differentiation and separation from the pain, or a slight space between the sufferer and the pain. With this subtle opening, one may freely and consciously choose to include the reality of acceptance and surrender to it. D.H. Lawrence reflects in his poetry some of the arduous dynamic at this stage of midnight: "Are you willing to be sponged out, erased, cancelled, made nothing? . . .dipped into oblivion? If not, you will never really change" (p. 614).[100] Midnight initiation in the Dark Feminine and the night sea journey involves having a willingness to suffer consciously. This latter-noted reality was reflected by Meredith (see the *twilight* section) as she struggled and endured doses of darkness, emptiness, nothingness, and the tension of the opposites. With a grimacing face and a despairing voice, Meredith declared: "There is nothing, nothing. The darkness and emptiness were horrific this weekend. It was just horrendous, and I finally wrote *Psalm Zero* to express the empty nothingness at my core." Then, Meredith began to read her poem:

> Psalm Zero
> Is the Lord my Shepherd?
>   I am grievously in want.
> He makes me lie down in desert wastes
>   and leads me beside dry streambeds.
> He crushes my soul
>   and goads me along empty pathways for no one's sake.
> As I walk through the valley of the shadow of death
>   I fear much evil.
> You are with me;
>   Your rod and Your staff, they chastise me.
> You strip me naked in the presence of my enemies.
>   You waterboard me with boiling oil,
>   and my cup is crumbling to dust.
> Surely sorrow and wailing shall follow me all the days of my life,
>   and I will dwell in the wilderness forever.

After reading *Psalm Zero*, Meredith paused and then muttered with a disgusting tone, "What the hell kind of God are you!?"

About three months later, Meredith was working with an image from her dream in session. She was doing an active-imagination exercise that involved being aware of an image from her dream that caught her attention. In her process she did deep-belly breaths as she worked with her image in her body. She reported what was arising within her. Meredith said, "What is coming to me is a flash of Rilke's poem, from *Rilke's Book of Hours: Love Poems to God*, where Rilke says to God, press down hard on me, break in that I may know the weight of your hand, and you the fullness of my cry." In Meredith's experience, she said that what had stunned her were the words, "the fullness of my cry." "For me, 'the fullness of my cry' was never heard. My mom could not hear when I was under my mom's hands. How could God? Part of me wants to sob and part of me wants to yell." Meredith's process continued to unfold in session as she expressed sorrow and rage through core energetic body work. What was most shocking to her from her inner work was her awareness about her attitude toward God. "Wow (pause), I just realized I have really put a trip on God (pause). I'm shocked how much I have put on God, and it is not God at all. This is about my imprisonment of my psyche, my constriction, and about my complexes." This was a humbling realization for Meredith and a significant turning point for her. Since then, Meredith has had a steady attentiveness to her inner work of demagnetizing, separating, and continuing to differentiate from her overidentification with Death Mother energy, befriending various psychic parts such as *No No*, and opening to the benevolence, protection, still-silent nurturance, empowerment, and symbolic dialogue with an earthy primitive Dark Feminine Figure that appeared in one of her dreams. For Meredith, who thought she was unlovable, this Dark Feminine Presence has been a very welcomed blessing and a generative mysterious surprise to her. Working with her dreams and images, doing body-energy work, various forms of active-imagination exercises, EMDR, EFT, and especially painting have been the portals through which healing, nurturing, and expanding her journey in conscious ensoulment have emerged.

For any one of us, midnight darkness is hard to bear and to metabolize. Given the brutal dynamics, it is inconceivable for a soul to realize that a process is transpiring in which the Otherness is drawing our depth of authentic soul essence into proper conscious focus and realization. Through varying doses of dark alchemical medicine, a soul gradually becomes differentiated with a more authentic sense of identity, purpose, and realization that nature natures, gods god, and goddesses goddess. Only in retrospect, does a soul begin to perceive that the Dark Feminine's Otherness is a love that darkens to vitally restore soul essence. John of the Cross conveyed a similar tone in his perspective of dark night as a night that guides, an absence that unmasks, and a flame that recreates. Or, as Meredith recently tried to describe the intimations of the energy of the primitive Dark Feminine Figure in a numinous healing active-imagination exercise: "Her energy is like a black that is light, a silence that is stilling, nurturing, and strengthening. I experience being in her presence as black/light, that is a black/light energy that is dark, but not oppressive, rather the dark black is light, expansive, and generative." Paradox is operative in dark-night initiation.

Midnight of dark-night initiation is intense desolation, emptiness, aloneness, confusion, abandonment, and despair. For some people the experience activates frustration, anger, and depression because they are powerless to "call the shots" or control the outcome, or because in Jim Hollis's words, "[E]go consciousness is obliged to face its greatest nightmare, that it is so profoundly limited."[101] Part of the hell of this rite of passage is that one does not know the duration of the process, and it seems unimaginable that anything good could come from this wrenching suffering. Life's limitations are harshly experienced. It is annihilating. In the deepest levels of night, the realities of disbelief, loss, despair, and death are experienced in ways unimaginable. One is stripped naked of all controls and of the support systems that provided meaning, affirmation, and empowerment.

The grip of the Dark Feminine in midnight *nigredo* is one of deconstruction of all that is not of one's soul essence, for example, the deconstruction of one's self-limiting beliefs and emotionally clinging to attachment-hunger feedback. Physically, one feels as if one is "dead bones," for one has no energy. As one person described this stage: "I'm like, I'm dead. There is nothing in me. Usually, a shot of B-12 makes a difference, but even B-12 seems unable to energize me." Midnight initiation is Gethsemane and Calvary. This *nigredo* medicine is about stripping us from all that is not our natural essence.

During this darkest stage of growth, one is blinded in seeing and understanding the hidden presence or what, if anything, the process is leading toward. This reality is part of the anguishing hell. Transformation does not happen at the end of the road; it is in the making *now* while we are *experiencing* the absence, abandonment, darkness, emptiness, loss, surrender, and death. If one essentially knew the underside of this Hades's pivotal stage, one would undoubtedly realize that it is already resurrection. However, the sojourner is veiled from awareness in the descent into hell, as the dark medicine of Lady Underground works its way through the psyche of a person in the "heat of the night."

Midnight of Dark Night of Initiation: Psychological Significance

The psyche is the medium of the bitter struggle of midnight. As in twilight, in midnight, psychologically there is no linear development, only a deeper circumambulation of the Self with the unfolding process pointing toward the center, the *Imago Dei*. Fundamental to the midnight journey into the dense dark caverns of the psyche is excavating, metabolizing, and integrating the deep-rooted dark shadow of the most deprived, repressed, neglected, undeveloped, abandoned, and dissociated aspects of the psyche. We all have a great deal of muscle developed around our dark shadow that keeps it well-hidden, buried in the depths, and often imprisoned. For all of us, we have our trigger-conditioned "go-to" response, whether we are conscious of it or not, which acts as a shield to avoid dealing with what is within our inner swampland of blacker-than-black muck. In midnight a deeper sense of our core essence is attempting to be heard and integrated. Psychologically, what occurred in twilight will greatly intensify in midnight as positive disintegration begins to occur around archaic, armored, primitive defense structures. If we are ever to incarnate the deeper dimensions (virgin and wisdom) of the archetypal Dark Feminine energy of Lady Underground, we will have to metabolize and assimilate her midnight of dark-night initiation. While this is death for the ego, it is life for the Self, as this is the very work that opens us to a greater depth of ensoulment. Again, the dynamics of holding the tension of the opposites, sacrifice (of archaic infantile and protracted adolescent ways), surrender, and death will be operative and deeply felt by the ego. Our entrenched shadow possesses incredible potential for generative good as well as horrific destruction. In midnight, psychologically what we resist and avoid bearing and metabolizing consciously in ourselves, we will spew out on others, the mystery/Mystery, politics, society, and planet Earth. Keeping our psychic antenna up for signals and clues of the many ways our depths have of revealing themselves, including listening to our body, is essential in midnight. As Jung notes, "The substance that harbors the divine secret is everywhere, including in the human body . . .and can be found anywhere, even in the most loathsome filth" (par. 421).[102] Remaining soulfully attentive to what seems like dismal and/or dead like realities and/or self-parts is crucial, if we are ever to know a grounded, more generative expanded interiority.

Often, these rather constricted, deprived, disheveled, and sometimes very infantile and adolescent psychic parts, which perhaps even look as if they've been in a concentration camp, are self-parts that we prefer to repress or wish would leave us. However, it is these very unassimilated self-parts that reveal themselves in one form or another and most often through the inferior function of the psyche. This fourth function tends to be the most undeveloped and normally the least differentiated function. And yet, as Jung points out, "It is precisely the least valued function that enables life" (par. 444).[103] While the inferior function, for the most part, remains in the unconscious, this function is frequently the "back door," our shadow, especially our blacker-than-black shadow that comes through in an attempt to be heard and integrated into consciousness. It needs to be understood and appreciated that our darker shadow aspects or disassociated self-parts that are received, embraced, and attended to consciously and with compassion are a depth dimension of our generative soul. These energies, which are often banished, concealed, traumatized, and/or undeveloped within the deep dark roots of the psyche and soma, are knocking at our door, sometimes banging at our door, in order to be heard and integrated into ego-consciousness in midnight. Considerable libido is needed in order to have an enduring and perduring attentiveness to ever so gradually, respectfully, and with compassion assimilate and befriend these undifferentiated, unconscious, impoverished self-object parts, the skeleton in the cupboard of perfection, and undeveloped psychic energy. Thus, the unconscious content within the inferior function, according to Jung, "...seeks, and itself is, what I have elsewhere called 'the treasure hard to attain'" (par. 205).[104] "Psychologically it means of course that the mystery always begins in our inferior function, that is the place where new life, regeneration, is to be found" (p. 954).[105]

Often, when the darkest aspects of the psyche are manifesting and sometimes erupting, including in the body because the self-parts have been so neglected, the split both within and without often emerges with a tendency to view light energy as good, right, and valuable, and shadow as bad, wrong, and not worthy of our consideration and exploration. Most of us tend to resist our swamplands, and this opposition and flight to avoid or escape the deep, darker, inner shadow work usually rears its face in midnight initiation. Individuals, by and large, struggle and are reluctant to accept and warmly greet dark shadow! Even though we live in a quantum world, there seems to be a lack of understanding of the interdependence of dark and light. This dynamic is core to the Dark Feminine and to the energy of Lady Underground, which allows dark and light, as well as all other opposites to coexist creatively in the psyche. Usually, as the energy is activated in the depths, urging attention for more of the hidden aspects, the ego-consciousness will tend to experience some degree of denial, resistance, lethargy, anxiety, depression, or a bodily restlessness. Furthermore, when dark, repressed shadow is calling to be heard and integrated into ego-consciousness, most of us will be inclined to initially label, judge, criticize, condemn, and deny what is foreign, unknown, unfamiliar, and uncomfortable. Many act destructively toward self-parts of their unconscious that are attempting to emerge, in the same discounting manner that they were treated initially by parental or authority figures.

For example, Jack, a 60-year-old self-employed accountant who had lost his mother at age 7, laughed anxiously and shrugged off wanting to own, deal, or be conscious about his inner child or his wild adolescent self-object shadow parts. He, impulsively and with an infant like neediness, wants to do whatever he wants to do and whenever he wants to do it. His father indulged his *puer* drives and ignored and emotionally abandoned his son. He never, for instance, showed up for even one of his baseball games, something that was a great source of pain for Jack. Jack not only felt abandoned by his mother in death but had always felt embarrassed, hurt, rejected, and abandoned by his father, as well. Jack's pain is real, and it is a tragedy that his mother died young and that his father's behavior was so self-absorbed that he could not be present to Jack physically or emotionally. Jack had no control over his father, and he is unable to change history. However, the greater tragedy is that Jack, who is aware of these self-object parts within, chooses to perpetuate that wounding by continuously rejecting and abandoning himself, acting out that split within himself. Until Jack stops living the victim role, seeking reassurance from others, judging, and abandoning himself, he will continue to experience his charged complex of rejection and abandonment. He takes people's *No*, their lack of interest or withdrawal very personally. For all of us, it is much easier to judge or blame another for what the other lacks or has done to hurt us than to examine our interior and do our own inner work around the dark, slippery, shadow parts that we bring as we constellate the interaction, e.g., an underlying power issue that fuels the need to control in a relationship.

Another example of a lack of receptivity initially toward dark shadow is Meredith, who was very critical, judgmental, and discounting toward *No No*, a part of herself that was revealed in a dream. *No No* personifies Meredith's feeling realm, which was banished to the unconscious in early childhood because of trauma caused by her mother and the family milieu, which did not value feeling. At first, she was terrified, skeptical, controlling, and untrusting of this dark shadow part. Meredith was scared and cautiously ambivalent toward this vulnerable self-part fearing that her scorned, disregarded, imprisoned aspect would manifest in public, a reality that she not only dreaded, but was fiercely defended against. For Meredith and for all of us, to descend into the blacker-than-black world of the inferior function and to face and befriend what is there is a twofold cutting edge: We dread descending into the blacker-than-black of Hades. We fear coming apart at the seams, unable to hold ourselves together, and yet, here in the unimaginable darker-than-dark black hole, of almost seemingly dead unreachable reality, we are humbly summoned in all our utter emptiness and nothingness to hold a perduring patient attentiveness in the black of midnight. It is here, without our knowing, that the gradual releasing of the generative soul within begins to unfold. It is precisely in the descent into the seemingly unimaginable, impossible, blacker-than-black midnight of dark-night initiation that the important impossibilities are significantly possible! Also, Dwight (described in *twilight* section), the CEO, businessman, and golfer who desired to maintain his very guarded and idealized self-image, who needs to be "number one," and who tends toward an overidentification with the good while splitting off his dark side, is very reluctant to consider his shady growing edges. He acknowledged recently that he secretly checked into a prominent golf training program for two days to perfect his game, chuckling, "I have to avoid embarrassment regardless of the price tag." How Dwight is with golf is how he is with life: controlling. He avoids exploring his golf dreams for fear that they may reveal something about his idealized way of being, which he wants to maintain at all costs. For example, Dwight hates the disheveled, poorly dressed, emotionally deprived, little orphan dream figure who continues to manifest in his dreams and who longs to be Dwight's caddy, and who shows up at the country club just before an important golf tournament. Dwight wants this nagging youth expelled from the golf course before he is distracted from his game and embarrassed publicly. Little does Dwight realize that he whom he most despises holds, perhaps, the potential generative energy to loosen and unlock the energy in the tightened muscle of his shoulder, free him from his "iron" mindset and skewed swing, and his unresolved shame and over concern about embarrassment. For most of us, myself included, it is challenging to have a spaciousness within to welcome the dark-shadow "stranger" knocking at our door, barging into our home or office, showing up at a golf tournament uninvited, and emerging upstairs unannounced from the coal room of our cellar. To hear this call with graciousness and receptivity is difficult. Within our personal depths and the collective psyche, we need to have a greater openness and inquiry to understanding the light and shadow of consciousness, not as good/right and bad/wrong in themselves. In an evolutionary quantum world, they are simply different rich dimensions of the visible and invisible mystery/Mystery waiting in midnight initiation to be liberated and realized for the tremendous potential for a more expanded, generative life.

The deeper descent into the dark unconscious, the perilous adventure of the night sea journey at midnight, aims at the restoration of life and the resurrection of life over death. "Death therefore represents the completion of the spirit's descent" (par. 436).[106] During the various doses of midnight medicine, in the heat of this intense alchemical night, psychologically, the tension of the opposites between succumbing to the darkness of total despair and surrendering to the mystery/Mystery in the darkness is at the greatest agonizing stretch within the psyche and felt sense of the body. As we experience this night, the psyche acts "as if" it is questioning and doubting the trustworthiness of the *Imago Dei* at the center.

The power of midnight reveals and uncovers the pathology that is the suffering of our psyche. Pathology in the Jungian sense is that which has become one-sided, exaggerated, overidentified with, or too archetypal. Jung does not see pathology in a negative sense, but as an attempt (even though insufficient) in the psyche to move toward wholeness. For Jung the psyche is a self-regulating system that maintains its equilibrium. Given this reality, every process that goes too far immediately and inevitably calls forth compensations. Without these, there would be neither a normal metabolism nor a normal psyche. Thus, psychologically, midnight is a summons from the psyche to progress toward balancing and embodying more fully the soul's true nature, its essence. Lady Underground's midnight initiation in the Dark Feminine is psyche's call to demagnetize the complexes and befriend the self-object parts that have become split off in order to restore balance, reconciliation, and health to the psyche. Psychologically, the dark medicine of midnight is a remedy for our neuroses, which Jung saw potentially as being positive and as stimulating new values or a more generative attitude toward life. The neurosis is a miscarried effort to incorporate the unrecognized side of the whole personality into conscious life. *The values that we lack are to be found in the neurosis itself.* Therefore, psychologically, midnight initiation is the arduous journey of discovering the jewel in the wound.

With this understanding of midnight, we are unavoidably obliged to deal with the ego and its restrictions. Psychologically, in the sacrificing, holding the tension of the opposites, and surrendering process, all masks and suits of false attire are stripped away, and the inescapable naked truth of our finite humanity becomes visible. At this time, polarization of the opposites is at the greatest tension and is unavoidable. This blacker-than-black darkness reflected in the symbolic Calvary event is the underside of resurrection. Without the ego going through this alchemical dynamic, no rebirth or transformation of consciousness is possible. Old ego structures must die if the energy that is repressed, held, and locked within the muscles of these somatic unconscious psychic aspects are ever to be released, directed toward maturation, and constellated in higher levels of consciousness. Psychologically, death represents the most definitive and unbearable of all sacrifices that must be metabolized, accepted, and processed fully.[107] Death asks us to surrender and to make a leap of faith, the inner act that changes *my* will into *Thy* will be done. With this change in perspective and in locus of control, we are able to move through an impasse that seems hopeless, an impasse where we feel stuck, perhaps even despair, and locked in with no exit. About this reality, Jung writes that those who find themselves on the road to wholeness cannot escape this characteristic suspension, which is the meaning of crucifixion.[108] When the ego has exhausted its own resources, has reached an impasse, and has realized its essential impotence and utter poverty of spirit, the experience of the supportive aspect of the archetypal psyche is most likely to occur.[109] For this reason, the archetypal Self is experienced by the ego as a defeat.[110] Hence, death is in service to the Self for the greater purpose of transformation. Analytically, midnight initiation is a rite of passage, of stripping, dismembering, and symbolic dying, which is central to a kind of sacramental act undertaken for the purpose of birthing our transformation and embodying our soul essence.

Importance of the Body in Lady Underground's Dark-Night Initiation

The experience of the archetypal symbol of Lady Underground (and/or any other image of the Dark Feminine) and of the dynamics of her dark-night initiation do not happen in a vacuum, but in and through our psyche, contained and manifested through the body. Jung emphasized: "[S]ymbols of the self arise in the depths of the body, and they express its materiality every bit as much as the structure of the perceiving consciousness. The symbol is thus a living body, *corpus et anima*" (par. 291).[111]

Early in the day of development, most of us learn that the expression of primitive affect in any form seemingly is unacceptable. It is rare for space to be respectfully held for a child, a young person, or for anyone, to allow one to communicate intense anger or fear as healthy emotions in a constructive way that is not harmful to oneself or anyone else without being wronged, judged, and shamed. For many adults, it is hard to hear any intense feeling in a grounded way. Some can be fearful of intensity or take the strong expression of emotion personally, hear it as an attack on one's identity or authority, and become triggered with emotional upset. An individual's capacity for intensity can be controlled by internalized parental tapes that only allow certain emotions or what is rational to be communicated. The exception to this may be the tolerance of a wider range of emotional expression considered acceptable by the collective at gatherings such as sporting events, political rallies, and conventions. Otherwise, feeling, especially intense emotion, is often banished to the unconscious. Controlling human affect is the mode of operation for many. If we have an internalized intrusive, perfectionist critic or an attacker who is not consciously integrated, we will launch this toxic energy outward toward others and life. For example, Jack (described in the *twilight: psychological significance* section) had no supportive adult figure to help him process his anger and grief about the early death of his mother and his emotionally absent and unavailable father. His intense emotions were exiled most of his life to his stiff, tight neck, sore shoulders, and his abdomen. It was only through the body-energy work in the form of EMDR and EFT that his holding and blocking pattern began to loosen in his muscular structure, and the intense emotions and self-limiting beliefs were able to be released, expressed, and metabolized in a safe analytical framework. Through the process of body-energy work within the frame, Jack's psychic container began to grow. Perhaps Jack's story is not your narrative. However, because there is no such thing as perfect parents, family, neighborhood, school, or religious system, we all to one degree or another have deported unprocessed emotion to the somatic unconscious. Marie-Louise von Franz once reflected that emotion is the carrier of consciousness. If any one of us is to open to the deeper roots of our embodied soul essence, we will need to become sensitized and to learn to attentively listen kinesthetically to our inner sensory receptors to befriend a wider range of our emotions, which are longing to be heard and integrated into consciousness. Body-energy work moves the process from just thinking about a dream image in our safe, controlled mind, to allowing us the discovery of breathing that image into our body and experiencing a fuller range and vitality of the gift of it. Through relaxing and allowing more spaciousness for an image to be explored, we can open to greater awareness of the pulsating, vibrating energy, and meaning of the image; unlocking unprocessed stifled emotion held in the somatic unconscious; and an overall greater unleashed generativity for the life of the soul. Part of the value of an approach that allows for somatic awareness and body-energy modalities to be included in the analytic framework is the possibility for more of the deep roots of the breadth and depth of each soul to be heard and birthed into life. *The body is the sacred vessel of the soul.*

Lady Underground's energy is drawing us to be more consciously embodied. The journey in human interiority of Lady Underground's dark-night initiation is the quest to come home in the body, as the core dwelling of incarnational engagement with the depths in an ongoing transformative process. There is no conscious embodiment of spirit, of the archetypal energy of Lady Underground, without twilight and midnight of *dark-night* initiation. In midnight the grip of the Dark Feminine ultimately is experienced as a psychological death. This death of old internal psychological structures manifests in the physical body and in the auric configuration of people in this stage. Some people become physically ill in the shift, as there is a breakdown (positive disintegration) on every level of our being. The emotions that erupt are experienced in the body. We see this reality in Psyche's felt sense of overwhelming fear and despair with each task she is given by Aphrodite, but especially with the fourth task, to go to the underworld. Also, we notice this intense experience of body sensations in the myth of Inanna, the Sumerian queen of heaven and earth. As noted previously, Inanna is the oldest known myth that describes the descent motif. Like Psyche, we see in Inanna's descent that as she passes through each of seven gates, the intensity increases in the sensory experiences of temperature, sound, and touch. She is progressively emptied and ultimately stripped, bowed low, and hung from a hook on the wall. In midnight, we are psychologically stripped naked and experience ourselves as dead bones in Hades. It is a horrific sense of one's raw vulnerability and utter poverty of spirit. This is a cold, empty feeling, as it was for Inanna, who experienced the passage of each gate with an increase of coldness, loss of feeling, and wailing.

Jung stressed the importance of the body in almost every volume of the *Collected Works*. He held that the body is the visibility of the soul, the psyche, and that the soul is the psychological experience of the body. Spirit and soma cannot be separated. The body is the soul in action. When body and psyche are split, life becomes an intellectual and will-directed phenomenon. Hence, the energy field, of which the body is a manifestation, mirrors a life that is ego or will-directed, and the current of driving energy is power. Jung wrote, "[A]ll will is a demonstration of power over fate" (par. 74).[112] and "[W]here love reigns, there is no will to power; and where the will to power is paramount, love is lacking" (par. 78).[113] The enslavement in will-directed energy and in overidentified, adaptive behavior (compulsive tendencies to *please others, try hard, be strong—don't feel, be perfect, hurry up, and/or be the responsible dutiful daughter or son*) are manifestations of being cut off from the vital energy of the instinctual life. When an infant or toddler is cut off early in development from the natural, grounding, pulsating energy of instinctual life, there is a tendency toward intellectualization. Subsequently, the body's capacity for flexibility, softness, pliability, and flow of the life force becomes crystallized; rigid energy locks in the nadis, trigger points, muscles, and the very cells of the subtle body.

Thus, there is no dialogue with the unconscious without listening to the body. A patriarchal perspective that favors and assigns credibility to reason and mind over instinct and body is no longer tenable. One of the dark, shadow aspects of patriarchy is primitive groundlessness. Nietzsche's paradox is realized only in working through the primitive emotion erupting in the rugged terrain of the body, with a sense of courage, patience, acceptance, compassion, and love. Every step of the process affirms the paradox: The ascension to spirit/Spirit demands the descent into ground.[114] Opening to the depths through body-energy work is soul work. The somatic unconscious communicates and reveals itself with its stiffness, tensions, constrictions, skeletal muscular rigidity, blocks, impasses, and disruptions in the energy flow. Body-energy work can help to loosen energetic aspects of dysfunction. Furthermore, it can be a rich resource in assisting in a more holistic process of unearthing, metabolizing, integrating, and embodying the shadow, especially the charged dark shadow. There are many different forms of body-energy work, as noted at the end of each chapter. These various modalities are portals to objectifying, assimilating, and making our depths conscious in a *grounded way*. This soulful work facilitates opening to our inner sensory receptors, learning to trust the subtle pulsating energy of our instinctual feeling in our bodies, and discovering the possibility of having our hearts stirred and inspired by embodied intuition arising from deep within the inner well, the inner crypt, the depths of our soul.

What is key is finding the access for our soul's way to our inner terrain being attended to and incarnated, while remembering that there is *no one way*. Honoring and respecting this truth allows our soul's path to unfold more naturally as we attempt to perceive and respond to the summons of the mystery/Mystery. As a result, we begin to discover the subtle shift of being more consciously present in one's body, in one's interactions with others, and in one's connections with all of life. The overall, evolving development supports the gradual forming and birthing of a conscious container. As we begin to come home to honoring our body with a respect for our instinctive rhythms, we open to the awareness that this is our most natural and deepest connection to the web of all of life, our home planet, Mother Earth, and the Great Mother of our pulsating universe. Hence, we realize little by little that Lady Underground, as an archetypal image of the Dark Feminine, acts as a connector linking body and psyche in the inner soul work. Active imagination, a vital tool in various forms, including body-energy work, serves as the bridge between psyche and soma in the journey toward embodying consciously our soul essence. Through dark-night initiation into the Dark Feminine, the soul slowly emerges more consciously embodied. Lady Underground's twilight and midnight initiation is an arduous summons in excavating our more natural self from the dark caverns of our depths. This heroic journey of incarnating consciously is a celebration of human embodiment, in which the mystery/Mystery is experienced in the ordinary of our sacred vessel, our *body*. In a quantum creative universe, part of the fabric of our *deep inherited roots* is the potential and capacity for conscious human interiority, ensoulment of our core essence. Opening to conscious human embodiment releases a humble, deep, felt instinctual awareness that we are a part of the cosmic web of life that is fundamentally interconnected and interrelated. Human embodiment furthers consciousness. The very embarking on this psychospiritual quest is the road less traveled, is the journey of unearthing, metabolizing, humanizing, and embodying consciously the archetypal energy of Lady Underground.

Ancient Path Makers Inspiring Today's Soul Seekers

Given the reality and challenge of midnight initiation, the question arises: Are there any pioneers of humanity who have endured twilight and midnight initiation and are attempting, in an ongoing way, to live consciously embodied lives? Today, where do men, women, communities, institutions, societies turn to find their souls stirred and their imaginations inspired by conscious path makers who have dared to make the descent, endure dark-night initiation, and are a conduit of wisdom in empowering others to hear and to respond to the summons of the Dark Feminine? Who are some of the ancient pioneers who dared to make the journey and manifest some of the universal themes, values, and aspects of the quest? Jungian psychology invites us to remember that mythology is a rich resource that offers us psychological insight and truth about human behavior, the journey, and significant rites of passage. Mythology stirs, inspires, empowers, and guides us with lessons for viable psychospiritual growth and development. Because the mystery/Mystery and paradox are part of a quantum evolutionary world, mythic stories about the encounters with the mystery/Mystery, a power greater than ourselves, can offer us a broader and more inclusive perspective than collective religious traditions and the sometimes "pat" answers of science. Often times a mythic tale can be a mirror of our own situation, and the realization that we are not alone is a source of strength and comfort. Outstanding classics, especially literature and sacred texts, as all great art, reflect the wisdom of the human condition. Myths are a particular type of literature. They are not written by one person, but rather emerge gradually from the collective imagination and the experience of an entire era and culture. Even though myths are not of scientific or rational creation, they are nonetheless real. They contain certain motifs that portray a collective image about life that is common to all. Subsequently, because of the manner of its development, a myth carries a powerful collective meaning. Myths are not simply stories of happenings and themes in the remote past but eternal dramas that are living themselves out repeatedly in our personal, societal, and global lives. Examining mythic characters such as Lilith, Inanna, and Psyche, we ascertain some of the energetic qualities that Lady Underground symbolizes as an archetypal image of the Dark Feminine. We begin to get a better feel for the energy of Lady Underground and characteristics embodied by ordinary people in everyday life that reflect Lady Underground's energy. Like Jung, we can discover in these mythic figures an expression of basic psychological patterns that can enrich our perspective and empower us, especially during midnight of dark-night initiation in the Dark Feminine within our individuation journey.

The archetypal pattern of descent/ascent in Lady Underground's midnight of initiation is the same theme manifested in the ancient Sumerian myth of Inanna (as noted previously); also parallel to this process is the Jesus story in the Christian tradition. The descent/ascent myth of the goddess Inanna, sometimes referred to as Ishtar, manifests a symbolic image of the journey toward wholeness. Inanna's descent into the underworld symbolizes the healing and bridging journey of the split between above and below, between the collective ideal and the split-off, banished, dark shadow represented by Ereshkigal, Inanna's sister and goddess of the underworld.[115] Inanna descended to the great below of her own volition. She embodied more of herself after going through Hades, making some choices and sacrifices on her return. Through being stripped of her identity in the underworld, surrendering, dying to herself, and becoming receptive to whatever must take place between above and below, Inanna opens to a life more integrated, generative, and full. In the process, Inanna's dark shadow, Ereshkigal, is also transformed and revalued. Ereshkigal is no longer "kept down," and Inanna is no longer "high and mighty." A gate has been opened between the two realms. With Inanna's courage and prudence, an exchange of energies has taken place. The myth challenges both men and women to ask themselves, "In what way do I act 'high and mighty?'" and, "What aspects of my humanity are being 'kept down?'" When any one of us fails to integrate our darker sides, others suffer for what is our neglected inner work.

Inanna as an ancient path maker reflects one who came through midnight more aware of her generative power and how she wanted to exercise it. She emerges with compassion and with a depth to love that suffering brings. As queen of above, Inanna was the fertility goddess of plants, animals, and humans. After her descent to the underground, she had a greater respect and perspective about the mysteries of death. She was exposed, stripped, flogged, killed, hung on a peg to decay, miraculously revived, and returned to earth transformed.[116] Thus, we see that Inanna, the highly cultivated, civilized one, seeks the initiation of the deep and dark primal chthonic powers that her shadow sister held in the underworld. Here, Inanna endures a divesting of her power, control, death, decay, and resurrection. As goddess in all aspects, she is "Lady of Largest Heart" because of her transformative initiation experience. By going into the great below, into the blacker-than-black darkness, she emerges with an awakened heart of compassion and has a wisdom about death and rebirth, which makes her a source of inspiration for us because she has *been there* and she *knows.*

Another ancient mythic figure who informs us is Lilith, an irresistible, long-haired feminine character who personifies lunar consciousness, dark chaotic creativity, grounded inner authority, and an instinctual, earthy aspect of the Dark Feminine. Lilith represents the body that is lush instinctuality and sexuality. She animates natural, pulsating, primal sexual energy. Lilith is part of the Great Goddess whose origins are shrouded in Sumerian, Assyrian, Babylonian, Canaanite, Persian, Hebrew, Arabic, and Teutonic mythology. She appears in the Sumerian culture, dating back as early as 3000 B.C.E. Talmudic *midrash* reports that the primordial Lilith, who had been the first wife of Adam, was made from the same dust as he (Genesis 1:27) rather than from his rib (Genesis 2: 18-24). Desiring mutuality, equality, and unwilling to be Adam's inferior, Lilith refused to lie beneath him, and consequently, the lady of dynamic, sumptuous sexuality was expelled from the Garden of Eden.

Thus, she is a manifestation of some of the specific qualities of the Dark Feminine that existed prior to this split or banishment from the garden. For Lilith, to be denied the freedom to be her essential nature and to be banished symbolically is to split off dynamic dimensions of the quantum energy-flow of the body that she so represents. This would include a sense of initiative, inner authority, lush sexuality, creative fire, instinctual wisdom, inner marriage of the masculine and feminine as equals; and capacity for mutuality and equality in outer relationship in which neither is sacrificed or subordinated to the other. Imagine our world today: What if more of these aspects of the Lilith energy of the Dark Feminine were embodied consciously in men and women in our society and culture? Lilith refused to sell out, to collude, or enslave herself through constraint and submission to the controlling judgmental patriarchy. It is important to realize that she was not about equality and likeness in the sense of identity or merging. On the contrary, Lilith was for equal freedom and respect to move, change, and be her natural soul essence. Her exile is the rejection of a certain aspect of humanity, and as such, it recedes to the underground of who we are and even becomes demonized in the process. Women suffer from this banishment, as do men, and subsequently society and culture. In Lilith we find some of the energy of Lady Underground (also known as Lady Wisdom, as noted in Chapter One) depicted as both the vitality of sexuality and the richness of natural instinctual wisdom. Because Lilith is often equated with the serpent of the temptation in the garden, she is the goddess of kundalini, the hidden creative fire of sexuality and creativity that lies coiled as a serpent at the base of the spine, waiting to be aroused, awakened, liberated, and expressed in a variety of generative ways.[117] [118] [119] [120] [121] Like Lady Underground, Lilith challenges us to not sell our soul, to make the descent into the dark, which means a shattering upper-world adaptation (the false suit of clothes of compulsive drivers such as *be perfect, please others, try hard, be helpful, hurry up, be strong—don't feel, and/or be the responsible dutiful daughter or son*) in order to reintegrate the Dark Primordial Feminine that has been held below. In fulfilling this task, the symmetry of *as above, so below* is embodied consciously within us.

In further mythological consideration of Psyche, we note that the archetypal descent/ascent dynamics of Lady Underground's midnight initiation call are similar to the energetic patterns that are operative in Psyche's descent into the underworld in the *Eros and Psyche* myth. This myth, recorded for the first time in Apuleius's *The Golden Ass*, was written in the second century C.E. Aphrodite instructs Psyche to make the arduous journey to the underworld to obtain from the hand of Persephone herself, who reigns in the underworld, a little cask of her own beauty ointment and to return it to Aphrodite. Psyche becomes curious about the beauty ointment, opens the cask as she comes to the surface of the earth after having endured all the obstacles, challenges, and trials, and is suddenly overcome with a death like sleep.

There is a multitude of possible interpretations, one of which is realizing that Persephone is the goddess who, like Psyche, entered into the underworld; yet there Persephone became a queen on her own, a knower of the dark side of life. Her attractiveness is enriched by suffering, which is a different beauty than that of the young Psyche. Persephone reflects the beauty of the mature Dark Feminine that is rooted in its depth of knowledge, wisdom, passion, interdependence, and interconnectedness. Psyche's undoing the cask could also be motivated by her vanity; however, this view seems shallow and culturally biased. Perhaps, given the focused attentiveness and the enormous amount of psychic energy required to go through a dark-night rite of initiation, Psyche was exhausted, vulnerable, and more susceptible to the regressive pull of the unconscious. Maybe, like most of us, she thought that the worst was over and that she was basically finished. Imagine any one of us having that thought! For Psyche, to open the cask of beauty ointment is, perhaps more strongly than she had ever known before, to be seduced yet again into circumambulating, incubating in the dark, dying symbolically, waiting for guidance to arise from deep within, owning, claiming, and embodying her "roots" within the ground of her own Dark Feminine soul essence. If so, this is a necessary stance in the process of the restoration of her true nature, an inner beauty that is paradoxically a hidden light (to the ego) that arises in the black emptiness ever so slowly through dark-night initiation in the Dark Feminine. In this sense her falling into a deep sleep was a necessary psychological death in the renewal of the feminine and the transformation from one level of development to another in the journey toward embodied consciousness. Consider also that Psyche may be going through the regressive pull of the unconscious and a slippery slide into the old consciousness that is known, familiar, and seemingly easier. We saw her being subjected to this temptation in previous tasks. In the overall dynamics, is this, then, a necessary further purification, a symbolic psychological death into the dark depths of the unconscious, circumambulating her core once again in the process of restoring the new conscious feminine, who Psyche is in her essence? Whatever is so, Psyche must explore it, experience it, fall into its spell, and metabolize it if she is ever to arise embodying the new differentiated inner feminine consciousness. Sinking into the deep sleep of unconsciousness, passing through yet another dimension and assimilating the experience of the blacker-than-black night, sacrificing and dying symbolically, Psyche revisits her own woundedness and thus becomes one with Persephone, the goddess of suffering.

Paradoxically, this regressive act becomes the source of Psyche's transformation; she circumambulated her "root" issues at a deeper level than she had ever known before, and by so doing, she discovered her true desire, which reflects her natural soul essence and beauty. Furthermore, her desire has matured through her suffering in the underworld. The story of Psyche and Eros describes this integration through various steps, whether it is viewed from a male or female perspective. Thus, for Psyche, the developmental task is to balance her earlier emphasis of suffering and surrender with that of her heroic rise; for Eros, however, it is to encounter suffering, surrender, and compassion as a creative complement to his heroic stance.[122]

To cross over to this myth is to further our understanding of the complexity and the depth of the midnight, pivotal time *via* the door of Lady Underground. Exploration of Psyche's challenge uncovers the fact that there is a crucial experience within the rite of initiation that distinguishes it from other developmental stages; namely, being shaped and formed anew in the heart of the mystery/Mystery, through darkness and emptiness, and a deeper befriending of the roots of our scars and wounds in order to discover the jewel in the wound. Jung once noted that our inner emptiness conceals just as great a fullness if only we would allow it to penetrate us. Mystery is not outside of this process. The intimations of mystery/Mystery are a penetration by a formlessness that is full (although possibly obscured from the ego's comprehension), a darkness that guides and renews, an absence that reveals and liberates, a suffering that opens to potential meaning, wisdom, and compassion, and a love that heals. The invisible mystery/Mystery is at the heart of the whole transformative dynamic. The mystery/Mystery is the source and the engineer of the summons to wholeness. Without this phase of night, the process of gradual emergence and embodiment of natural soul essence is impossible.

Maturing Through Dark-Night Initiation in the Journey of Interiority

Nothing is left out of Lady Underground's dark-night initiation, including desire, which imbues the fabric of the great cosmic web of life. In a quantum world, desire is an essential dimension of all creation. Desire is the powerful dynamism that permeates the cosmic-planetary life, pulses in our yearnings and longings, stirs and moves the human heart, and fires the teleological process. Without desire, we humans would never choose anyone, anything, or make the journey. Desire is a good and because it is god/goddess inspired, it is sacred. The issue for any one of us is not desire in itself, but rather the way in which desire runs us and the degree to which desire engulfs consciousness to the point of obsession, attachment, possessiveness, loss of growth and creative potential. As desire is awakened in the imagination and in the human heart, we are opened to possibility and vulnerability, our depths are stirred, and this enlivening gift precipitates the experience of darkness and limitation in all of our loves. This includes the tapestry of all our significant loves, which weaves the variegated threads and textures of our path: marriage, significant others, vocation, work, vital soulful projects and committed endeavors, solitude, and the journey. The dynamic touches not only individual lives but potentially can also impact a group, organizations, communities, institutions, and nations, although many are bankrupt in their capacity to consciously reflect on their darkness and see it as potential for growth and renewal in the context of a quantum evolutionary world. Lady Underground's rite of initiation is an intense adult seminar on the education of desire. Through twilight and midnight, we are drawn, summoned, or plunged into the extraction process for the revealing of our essence. Part of this vital growth is the education of our desire and of our capacity for a differentiated, conscious, embodied relationship with self, others, the planet, and the whole of the cosmos, including all forms of inhabited life, and the mystery/Mystery. There is no one way for this alchemical operation to occur.

Thus, the innermost sanctuary of one's heart and desires is purged, emptied, and matured through Lady Underground's night initiation, as its negative force deprives consciousness of dependable and comforting notions of consolation and support. *In* the experience of this *dismantling* darkness and emptiness, and *in* this suffering and withdrawal of accustomed pleasure, restoration and transformation transpire. One is stripped, broken and raw, not just for the sake of suffering in itself, but to open to a greater depth and meaning of an embodied, conscious interiority. The alchemical cooking and restoration of the soul occurs not outside what we value and hold dear, rather the night purgative cleanse is precisely *through* all that one cherishes, loves, relishes with meaning, and demonstrates invested energy. One is drawn to abandon certainty and is invited to embrace detachment.[123] Consciously knowing that one must end a relationship that is not life-giving, for instance, and struggling to do so because one realizes that some of the dependable and comforting securities that the relationship has provided will be lost is one example. Lady Underground's *dark night* educates one toward the capacity for conscious, embodied relationship, both in one's interiority and in one's outer relationships, including the cosmic web of all life. If one's intellect, memory, and will (or to put it another way, one's energy grid) have not been touched and altered by the darkness, dryness, nothingness, and emptiness of night initiation in the Dark Feminine, then the rite remains a barren intellectual undertaking that bears no fruit. What one resists will persist. Nothing is left out of the process.

Subsequently, the dark, shadow side of desire is confronted in twilight, but the deeper and more charged embedded roots need to be faced, explored, and dealt with in midnight. For any one of us to carry this vital aspect of our humanity in an embodied, conscious way is dependent on us making the deeper descent to discover, befriend, and integrate the unconscious, charged energies of our nature. Unless we do inner soul work with our dark side of desire, including its blacker-than-black dimensions, such as power issues and masochistic and sadistic tendencies, we will never know a fuller range of transformative, potent, creative, generative dimension. Our gold is in metabolizing and assimilating our darkest, most charged shadow. If we rationalize, deny, or are afraid of the distortions in our desire (we all have some), we limit our capacity for vital and healthy self-expression. By remaining wedded to our idealized self-image and denying that we have dark shadow, we are more apt to act out our charged attitudes and emotions unconsciously as a defense against feeling the hurts and traumas of our wounds of origin. Some examples of distortions are attachments to power, infantile unmet needs, victimization, sadism, masochism, competitiveness, criticalness. The more our charged distortions go unprocessed, especially regarding the destructive impact on others and ourselves, the more we will tend to feel insecure, inadequate, or incompetent, and then usually blame others for our misery and misfortune. Through dark-night initiation, desire is not subverted, suppressed, or destroyed, but gradually purified, metabolized, integrated, transformed, and set on fire. The dark, shadow side of desire is purged of distortions, infantile neediness, demands, and ego-centeredness liberating vital, potential energy for greater generativity as our soul essence is extracted. Desire that is laden with charged, dark, unconscious material is revealed through a person's dreams, fantasies, body, relationships, solitude, life events, art forms, and/or how one relates to the cosmos. As Helen Luke described it, we must be willing to open our eyes and look at ourselves objectively in the mirror, confessing openly to that which we see (as Dante did in the dark wood), accepting the black, the journey into darkness where we shall be ground to pieces.[124] Night medicine breaks the old paradigm; it dissolves whatever we are attached to and rely upon as real, secure, supportive, and dear.

For all of us on the journey of individuation, Lady Underground's rite of initiation is a process of being seduced and drawn into the black void of nothingness and emptiness in order to birth and to embody one's soul essence within the context of the interconnected web of all life. One way or another, we are exposed to the sobering realization of our "dirty laundry," which is the deeper, darker, shadow aspect of the personality. It is only by working with and befriending the images "knocking" and "hammering" at our door in twilight, and most especially in midnight, that we begin the serious excavation of our underground. This incredibly challenging process of befriending is soulful inner work that engages messiness, stench, untidiness, irrationality, imperfection, chaos, tumult, and complexity as part of life dimensions that are inherent in a quantum evolutionary world. There is no psychic room, in the earth of who we are as persons, to house consciously Lady Underground's archetypal energy without serious shadow work being done at this stage. New wine cannot be put into old wineskins. Talk of incarnating Lady Underground's energy is easy; doing the inner work is hell. In the words of Rainer Maria Rilke's poem, *Turning Point*:

> Work of the eyes is done, now go and do heart-work
> on all the images imprisoned within you; for you
> overpowered them: but even now you don't know them.
> (pp. 133-134) [125]

Or, do heart-work on what Emily Dickson refers to as "Ourself, behind ourself concealed, should startle most" (p. 225).[126] It takes courage to enter the dark caverns of archaic energies, to face and to work with our inner terrorist, dictator, narcissist, xenophobist, witch, killer, saboteur, supreme court judge, sadistic attacker, know-it-all critic, stingy one, masochist, planner of hidden agendas, bully, fabricator, abuser, and all the other dark and lurking figures that roam the various regions of our underground, subtly or more obviously. The process requires an immense amount of heat: to melt our defenses, especially the primitive defensive structure; to demagnetize the heart of stone; and to release the blocked heart of shame and grief for the part of us that has been belittled, humiliated, judged, condemned, rejected, abandoned, imprisoned, and dissociated. The shadow redeemed is transformative energy for life, love, and creativity.

Even if we have not yet realized it, the night also afflicts our memory. It is the cavern of our soul that houses the inner video of our journey, including experiences of beauty, love, and knowledge, as well as those of life's crippling hurts and traumas. Treasured memories of persons, events, and successes that once offered exhilarating reassurance, or were catalysts of the revelatory process, are no longer sources of strength and meaning. Our recall still serves us; however, it is devoid of meaning. We feel as if all support systems have lost sustaining power. The purging of this cavern can evoke the eruption of the dark side of the personality. As primitive defenses give way, archaic terror, anxiety, instinctual anger, rage, and automatic default responses of criticism and blame may surface as we struggle with utter vulnerability in facing, remembering, and dealing with whatever arises from our depth. At this deeper level of midnight, subtle forms of self-hatred, buried in the earth of who we are, can manifest as a disguise. Self-alienation that is masked can appear as withdrawal (many expressions, including workaholism), disregard, coldness, rejection, agitation, obsessiveness, lack of feeling, violence, and hatred toward another. If we are unable to metabolize this energy, it can rear itself to confront the body. Depression may emerge and commonly does at this time. In the recurring cycle of life-death-rebirth, decay and death are operative. When everything seems absurd and hopeless, it is difficult to perceive that anything good or valuable could ever emerge from such stark meaninglessness. This hopelessness elicits the painful and yet healthy tension between the haunting temptation to escape through manic flight or despair, and the choice to accept and to give oneself over to experiencing the reality that is arising within oneself in all its dimensions. For all of us, the mystery/Mystery is not outside the excavation of this memory cavern, but rather in the very process for the sake of new life, whether we realize it or are unaware of it. As the Persian poet Rumi reminds us, welcome, treat well, and even be grateful for all (dark feelings and thoughts, violent "storms," shame, joy) that comes to "visit" us in this adventure in being human, for it really is no accident that the "visitor" arrives. Jung reported that he himself knew people who had experienced this phenomenon, "which, as Hildegard [of Bingen] implies, brings into awareness areas of psychic happenings ordinarily covered in darkness. . . .Its effect is astonishing. . .it almost always brings about a solution of psychic complications and frees the inner personality from emotional and intellectual entanglements, thus creating a unity of being which is universally felt as 'liberation.'"[127] This clearing is an aspect of Lady Underground's medicine in unearthing and liberating our soul's unique essence, thus contributing responsibly to furthering the web of planetary consciousness.

Moreover, perhaps the steepest energy gradient of the psyche to purify, in twilight and especially in midnight, is that of the will. The determined drive to create, manipulate, control, and possess what we desire, value, and love is deeply rooted in the personality. Most people do not give up easily what they are wedded to in life. The will to power strives to insure and maintain life's blueprints at the cost of not being authentically human. At the time, we do not realize the subtle narcissistic motives that are embedded in our control and will-to-power tactics and that dominate our way of being and our so-called loving. Also, many function from an underlying belief in an anthropocentric view of life, while others give only lip service to being interconnected and interrelated to the cosmic-planetary life. Only through the gradual disclosure and recognition resulting from inner soul work on the darker aspects of the shadow do we realize the hidden, destructive darkness of the will to power woven throughout the subtle, often-unconscious, variegated levels and patterns of our life, including our attitude toward the Earth, herself. During this growth period of the will being purged, it is difficult to envision a way of being and loving that is more beneficial than the accustomed, adaptive way of being and loving. As all support systems are found wanting, we can feel alone, estranged, and abandoned. This renewal through intense purification provokes a tremendous sense of annihilation and an agonizing cry from the human heart. This is reflected in the last words Jesus utters, "Father, why have you abandoned me?" This psychospiritual state of annihilating, dark emptiness is a stripping that evokes the excruciating tension between the temptation to succumb to the belief that one has been screwed and the courageous choice to experience all that is arising within oneself in the immediacy of feeling and sensing the unfolding occurrence. This is a death to our meddling and a *yes* to a fuller range of being authentic.

To open to deeper depths of our conscious human interiority is to discover the well within.

During the progressive journey in interiority through twilight and midnight, gradually a psychic container is being formed that is strong enough to hold the tension of the opposites and flexible enough to receive the awakening inherent life force of the spirit/Spirit. Throughout this extensive rite, we are faced with our limitations, flaws, growing edges, and need to stay attentive to the process while remaining fluid and flexible in an inner, unknown terrain of uncertainty and absurdity, which is a difficult summons for any one of us, a call that will disrupt and scramble our known, familiar, comfortable order, structure, and ego-directed agendas. Unequivocally, the heat of the night will confront our entrenched hubristic attitudes and behaviors, which will have to be sacrificed if we are ever to open to a humbler stance and wider range of conscious ensoulment. The journey is never one of having arrived; we are always in process, and as such, we need to retain an abiding humility while remembering that the inexhaustible and incomprehensible mystery/Mystery remains the source of the journey, not we, ourselves.

For this reason, Jung warned that most of us can tolerate attending to the least among us, but if God were to knock at our very door, we would not be humble enough to recognize that the least among us resides in our very own self.[128] An alchemical excavation needs to take place in the dark caverns of our human soul if we are ever to open, to house, to release, and to live in the everyday ordinary, the energetic resonance of Lady Underground and consciously embody the inherent spirit/Spirit within us. Her archetypal energy is unearthed, metabolized, personalized, and embodied through doing our soul work on the dirty laundry, foul garbage, and undeveloped energy of our dark deep-rooted shadow. Liberating the generativity and the intrinsic life-force energy is the underside of this befriending process. Humility is needed, not just while the laundry is being done, but rather as *a way of being* throughout the night of initiation. As we shall see in the next chapter, this includes dawn.

To sort through, own, and process our most repulsive dark parts is to accept and to befriend our deepest wounds: life's sorrows and betrayals. From this deep gesture we begin to discover the jewel in our wounds and the meaning in our illnesses. What were once perceived as our greatest stumbling blocks have become our greatest stepping-stones. To paraphrase from Friedreich Nietzsche's *Beyond Good and Evil*, the great epochs of our life are at the points whereat we gain sufficient courage to rebaptize our wounds-complexes-shadow parts as the best in us. The gift of Lady Underground's dark-night initiation, especially midnight, is reflected in the Rumi's poem that begins, "This being human is a guest house." As noted earlier, Rumi empowers us to welcome and embrace all who come to us as unexpected visitors to our "home," even those who arrive intrusively and violently, those who may come and empty us in sorrowful ways unimaginable. Hard as it may be for any one of us to be thrilled about this guidance, Rumi wisely suggests that we receive, accept, and respect each guest, for their task may be to empty us for a greater gift than we can imagine. To what purpose might Rumi offer this wisdom to journeyers of the darker night? The clue is in the last verse of the Sufi mystic's poem:

> Be grateful for whoever comes,
> because each has been sent
> as a guide from beyond. (p. 109) [129]

In the unceasing cycle of destruction and reconstruction of the slow, repetitive *modus operandus* of twilight and midnight, the release of our old, adapted, false self comes at a price: nothing short of facing death. The price is paid in the letting go of all that we hold and believe ourselves to be, a gradual stripping away until only more of our soul essence remains. In entering the gate and traversing the passage of twilight, but more profoundly in midnight, we come to know another eternal reality: the discovery of a hidden secret that was already/always present, that the elements of the unceasing cycle of birth-death-rebirth are not separate; they are one in the quantum context. (As noted in Chapter One, in a quantum-physics perspective, everything we perceive and experience is a great deal more than the initial, external impression we may obtain, that we experience life, not in isolated segments, but in wholes, quanta.) Renewal of life comes by dying. In facing death, we are free to live life unencumbered by the barriers and shackles of the adapted false self. We open to a wider, more enriched, conscious embodiment within the context of the dynamic, interconnected, and interrelated cosmos.

Formed Anew in Solitude of Dark Nothingness: Inexhaustible Wellspring

In midnight it is precisely as dispirited, vulnerable, empty, and powerless that one is opened to the dark mystery of Lady Underground, or some other image of the Dark Feminine, in the solitude of dark nothingness, and yet, paradoxically, fullness. It is only in retrospect that the *dark-night* initiate gradually begins to realize that the dark abyss into which one is drawn is not an empty experience, but rather a pregnant phase of being formed, directed, empowered, and loved anew into one's emerging embodied soul essence and path. Twilight and midnight initiation are a progressive experience of being in the dark unknown while being formed anew through the destructive-reconstructive and recreative energy of the alchemical night. Blind though we are in this solitude of black nothingness, paradoxically, *in* and *through* the darkness, a positive disintegration is occurring, which loosens, dissolves, and opens psychic space for a greater capacity of our human embodiment of the Dark Feminine energy.

The latter insight is reflected in the comments of Marietta (referred to earlier in this chapter) regarding her descent and her experience of Lady of the Valley, an image of the Dark Feminine from the coastal region of Venezuela. Marietta states: "She is with me, yet she is so still, incomprehensible, and hidden. I've had to look at and own what I would rather not see and know is mine. I don't know where this process is taking me. I've been stripped of my 'white-wash wall cover.' I'm in the dark, and the dark is killing me; and yet, in the killing, I'm emerging more myself than I have ever known or imagined myself to be. I feel like I'm but a grain of sand and glad to be so." Marietta made a silent retreat for eight days where she spent a great deal of time outdoors in the country. The archetypal experience with the outer, rich, fertile nature was a portal to her plunge into a deep, dark, intense descent and to the loosening of some of the barriers that had kept her wounded self and instinctual roots imprisoned in a barren interior, wanting to awaken at a deeper, interrelated level. Through her experience of the Dark Feminine in solitude, and in her soulful process that included various forms of inner work (dreamwork, mandalas, journal writing, body-energy work, EMDR, EFT, and deep-belly breath—image work), Marietta, over a very long period of time, is opening not only to all that she has been defended against in her life, such as sexuality, intimacy, abusive power, and other dark, shadow elements, but also to the inexhaustible wellspring of the *invisible* world. In the experience of the dark, silent nothingness of Lady of the Valley, Marietta is being deconstructed, reconstructed, and formed anew. She is finding her voice, truth, and path of contribution. Her process has been a slow, repetitive operation, as she has been attentive to honoring her call toward an embodiment of a conscious interiority.

Furthermore, Marietta is beginning to discover, in her ordinary life and times of solitude, intimations of the reality that there is no separation between the *visible* and the *invisible* worlds. The possible range of self-experience in *dark-night* initiation is awakening to the realization that her journey is not about the discernment and mastery of night initiation, but about letting go, sacrificing, surrendering, receiving, and responding to being grasped by the mystery/Mystery that is present and yet ever distant, known and yet ever unknown. The other side of utter, dark nothingness is an inexhaustible wellspring. Gradually, we discover that the idea of separation, seeking, and striving is an illusion. As June Singer wrote, "The only barriers to breaking through from one stage to the next reside within ourselves" (p. 196).[130] Some initiates who do their dark-night soul work open to the intimations of the eternal *present* and discover the paradox that we are not going anywhere. Midnight initiation in the Dark Feminine is about coming *home* and being educated in the integrative seminar of darkness, with the primary lessons being an emphasis on being *present*, entering into *process*, and allowing *paradox*.

In midnight we gradually open to the inexhaustible mystery of *no experience*; that is to say, hidden, secret, and ineffable, the work of mystery/Mystery in the soul.[131] Where Marietta is or where any of us are going is *here*. Marietta, like Jung, is discovering what Jung said at 81 years old in telling his own story: "The difference between most people and myself is that for me the 'dividing walls' are transparent. That is my peculiarity. Others find these walls so opaque that they see nothing behind them and therefore think nothing is there. To some extent I perceive the processes going on in the background" (p. 355).[132] What Jung is referring to as the "background" is what Pauli and Jung jointly perceived with their quantum imagination as an inexhaustible, creative vibration of energy: particles/waves, that is, a life-force field that is fundamentally one and mysterious. All humans, at the subatomic level, that is, within their energy field or the earth of who they are, have this imprint of the life force in their makeup or "background," whether they are conscious of it or not, whether they accept it or not. This imprint of the life force is a wholeness, which is largely unmanifest and dynamic, and is the wellspring of all possibility. Jung's pioneering, comprehensive psychology provides an informative framework and a language for a contemporary, progressive interpretation of the energetic dynamics that are operative and evolving individually and collectively.

Jung and Pauli invite us to perceive ourselves and our world through our quantum imagination, and Jung, moreover, challenges us to view ourselves and the cosmos through our experience of our embodied conscious depths, which requires a change of focus from the foreground of consciousness to its background. In opening to the solitude of dark nothingness, we grow in our capacity to trust, to treasure, and to be present to the *whole* of the moment, while always remembering that the *whole* is far beyond what we can finitely grasp. This process is a shift from seeing oneself as central in the universe to seeing oneself as a part of the evolving cosmic-planetary interconnected and interrelated web of all life. In other words, to paraphrase the Zen proverb, before midnight illumination, we chop wood, carry water; after midnight illumination, we chop wood, carry water. We may find it helpful to realize that this shift in perspective is a viewpoint within a wider lens of long-held rich traditions that support this stance, especially the esoteric branches of the Judeo-Christian culture, including the contemplative and monastic orders, mysticism in Christianity, Kabbalah in Judaism, and the Sufi tradition in Islam.

In quantum theory, the creative potential emerges (evolves) from *within* the cosmos, both collectively and individually. Marietta is beginning to grasp that she already is and always was a unified whole. She is now ever so gradually becoming conscious of this oneness within as she does her ongoing inner soul work, especially with her blacker-than-black shadow.

Whether we are drawn by the archetypal image of Lady Underground, or some other face of the Dark Feminine, and/or an image that incorporates the Dark Feminine energy, the mystery/Mystery asks that we be willing to open to and trust the spiral of descent/ascent growth. This process of gradually opening to the *invisible* world of seemingly dark nothingness happens progressively as we are able to develop a deeper capacity for solitude, that psychic state wherein we are present existentially to our self-experience in the *visible* world and in the *invisible* world. Both are real and need to be consciously experienced without getting stuck in either, as Edith Wallace, M.D., Ph.D., a Jungian analyst and artist wisely noted at 92 years of age, in her presentation "Contemplation and the Visible and Invisible Worlds," at one of her Six Day Retreats—Opening to the Creative. Moreover, Edith soulfully held that, while we live between two worlds that are really *one*, only in experiencing being *present* to mystery/Mystery in the *invisible* world are we able to be more *present* living in the *visible* world.

The *visible world* is finite and limited. The *invisible world* is infinite, hidden, an incomprehensible and inexhaustible mystery. Most people are aware of both worlds. However, given the pace of our Western technological society, we tend to forget about the existence of the invisible aspects of reality. We have a diminished or distorted perception of the deeper dimensions of human interiority, thinking for example, that the experience of these deeper realms is available to just a few. Individuals suffer from the diminishments and distortions of the eclipse of mystery. The different gradations of intensity range from ordinary experiences of unrealized blessing to ordinary, conscious, numinous experiences to contemplative states. The differentiation is determined by the various degrees of free acceptance of the ever-present source and the ability to reflect on it and to objectify it. Writing in *Apologetics and the Eclipse of Mystery*, James Bacik, Ph.D., a pastoral theologian, noted that some people, such as poets, artists, and mystics, are more in touch with their deepest experience and have a greater ability to verbalize it. Others are in close existential contact with the mystery of life but have very little ability either to reflect on it or verbalize it. Bacik concludes that there are degrees of existential closeness to the mystery and various degrees of both existential and reflected religious experience.[133] June Singer concurs with this sense of the various gradations of self-experience of the invisible world. She suggests that if anyone feels called to begin the perilous path that leads into the unknown reaches of human potential, that person should proceed.

However, Singer also warns us to remember that the more primitive aspects of human development are not very far from us either. Nor is the middle stage, the personal stage in which we identify ourselves as persons who can cope effectively with the intricacies of life.[134] Thus, it is wise for all of us to remember that within *dark-night* initiation, the danger of hubris always remains, regardless of the stage of solitude and gradation of intensity of self-experience that is occurring for any one of us.

Conclusion

In this extensive chapter, we have explored how darkness pervades the "night sea journey" of Lady Underground's dark night of initiation in the Dark Feminine. This archetypal energetic pattern draws and summons us to a depth encounter, to a deeper conscious interiority. This arduous rite of passage is the very process that a soul experiences in consciously unearthing, metabolizing, humanizing, embodying, and relating personally to the archetypal energy of Lady Underground. Whether we clearly know the language, stages, and patterns of initiation is not as important as acknowledging, sacrificing, surrendering, and befriending the inevitable turmoil, struggles, suffering, and challenges of our soul in everyday life. What is important to realize is that *in* the very experience of darkness in twilight and midnight, inner renewal and transformation are taking place. The conscious restoration of the depths of our more natural soul essence does not happen at the end of the journey in interiority and embodied consciousness; it is *in* the alchemical making *now*. If we could see the underside of this intense night of suffering, sacrifice, surrender, and death, we would realize that it is already rebirth and resurrection. However, since we are not educated for dark-night initiation, we tend to view this experience, because of the ambiguous, unfamiliar dynamics, as an indication of failure and defeat. Lady Underground's twilight and midnight of dark-night initiation are instead a manifestation of growth, of the life-death-rebirth cycle, of restoration, and of human development in the summons to incarnate our soul essence.

Whether the image is Lady Underground or another face of the Dark Feminine such as Inanna, Lady of the Valley, Grandmother Earth, Tara, or another image that incorporates the Dark Feminine, the primordial archetypal energy seduces us toward liberating and embodying consciously our soul essence as men and women in the here and now within this evolving Universe Story. This happens only in making a descent into the "crypt" of who we are and having the courage, openness, honesty, humility, and trust to assimilate the night. As a grain of sand causes the illness in the oyster that creates the exquisite pearl, so too Lady Underground's dark-night initiation, activated in a person and metabolized consciously by the individual, births the humanizing dance of *"dawn"* in a soul. One benefit from the inner work of the alchemical night, when it has been effective, is that the unrecognized or neglected aspect of the psyche assumes a conscious embodiment. What was formerly a tendency to favor one side of the personality now opens to receive its opposite in a conscious way. This is true for Marietta in her rite of passage, guided by Lady of the Valley, and it is also true for those who find themselves lured into this night of initiation by Lady Underground. The gift of this night liberates the generative soul within us. The process opens us to more enlarged horizons, including a more embodied interiority, humbler attunement to the intimations of the mystery/Mystery, and greater attentiveness to solitude, the planet, psyche's telos, and the restoration of the soul's essence. *Dark-night initiation* is a coming *home.* In the words of T.S. Elliot:

> [T]he end of all our exploring
> Will be to arrive where we started
> And know the place for the first time. (p. 59) [135]

And moreover, the wise poet reminds us that this journey in conscious ensoulment is:

> A condition of complete simplicity
> (Costing not less than everything). (p. 59) [136]

Following the section on Inner Work, Chapter Four will explore dawn as the ever-emerging, evolving, and unfolding conscious embodiment of Lady Underground's energy. The text will attempt to make her energy and her challenge more visible. Hopefully, we will recognize her when we see her and welcome her among us.

INNER WORK

The beauty of the Way is that there is no "way."
~Loy Ching-Yuen, *The Book of the Heart*

Naturalness is called the Way.
~*The Secret of the Golden Flower—The Classic Chinese Book of Life*

The way is not in the sky. The way in in the heart.
~Gautama Buddha

I give you news of the way of this man, but not of your own way.
My path is not your path…The way is within us,
. . .[Who] should live your own life if not yourself? So live yourselves.
The signposts have fallen, unblazed trails lie before us. Do you not know that you yourselves are the fertile acre which bears everything that avails you?
~C.G. Jung, *The Red Book*

The right way to wholeness is made up of fateful detours and wrong turnings.
It is. . .not straight but snakelike, a path that unites the opposites. . .a path whose labyrinthine twists and turns are not lacking in terrors.
~C.G. Jung, *Psychology and Alchemy*

Don't be satisfied with stories,
how things have gone for others.
Unfold your own myth.
~Rumi

to suffer the healthy and necessary guilt involved in differentiating consciously from parents, siblings, and the collective, and to begin to honor the summons of your soul?

- In twilight and midnight of dark night, the regressive pull toward prolonged and arrested development is manifested by infantile and adolescent self-parts desiring nothing to change, wanting safety, security, and comfort. What areas and issues of life do you refuse to risk and to grow in opting to remain compliant, constricted, and cautiously vigilant in controlled, protected, or dependent states? Where do you need to give yourself permission to override parental and authoritarian introjected voices and rules, and a well-developed defense system for a more expanded consciousness?
- What aspects of your humanity are "kept down" and subsequently cause others to suffer because of your neglected inner work?
- What are the ways you stay busy as a mode of defense to avoid discovering what lies deep within you and learning to listen to psyche's summons?
- How do you attend to the rich hidden treasure within the dark inner crypt of your depths?
- Our culture is absorbed with charged issues concerning power, money, and sex. Consider each of these topics and explore what your shadow issues are in these dimensions of life. What is your growing edge in each of these aspects of life?
- Describe the deeper descent in your soul's journey toward embodied consciousness. What dark shadow issues have you had to grapple with, suffer through, and befriend in discovering a deeper meaning, identity, and purpose?
- What are the facades, roles, strategies, and denial schemes you use in perpetuating your destructive shadow? What is the payoff that you receive for maintaining your falsities and maze of illusions? What aspects of your authentic self, do you sacrifice in upholding the maze?
- What do you perceive are some of the charged polarities that are operative in our politics, institutions, culture, country, and global world? What are ways of demagnetizing the charged polarities you

have noted? In dialoguing with another, what is your capacity to tolerate a point of view very other than your perspective? How do you imagine growing in your ability to dialogue and to respect an opinion of another that is different from yours?

- How have you experienced and discovered your darkest shadow becoming a potential source for creativity and generativity?
- What are the signs and symptoms manifesting in the global community that would indicate that our world is in a dark-night growth period? What do you perceive is needed in the global community if we as a human species are to grow toward a more expansive and humbler human consciousness in this interrelated, interconnected evolving cosmic-planetary life?

~Process Exercises

- After reading Chapter Three, consider the image that captures and engages your awareness. Bring your attention to your breathing and take a few long, deep-belly breaths, allowing the belly muscles to relax. Then, begin to exhale slowly as you allow your body to relax and let go as you open and enter into the silence. Stay with the relaxing deep-belly breaths until you are present to yourself in your body. When you feel attuned to yourself, begin to call to your awareness the image that caught your attention in Chapter Three as you continue to breathe naturally. Take another deep-belly breath and, as you exhale, focus in and notice what is arising within your body as you are present to yourself. Maintain this process of deep-belly breathing, of exhaling slowly, and then focusing in and paying attention to what is manifesting in your body as you are present to yourself. Do this exercise for about 20 minutes. Then, take another deep-belly breath and, as you exhale slowly, focus in and see what you notice as you are present to yourself. When you are ready, begin to open your eyes as you reorient yourself to your outer dwelling. Take some time to recall your experience. You may want to record it as a way to honor and to further objectify your depths. Some possible reflection questions to consider might be:

    - If your image could speak, what would the image express to you?
    - What was it like for you to experience your image?
    - As you focus on your body, listening kinesthetically to your sensory receptors, what are you discovering within your body as you are aware of your image and present to yourself?
    - What is being revealed to you from your somatic unconscious?
    - Has your image changed in any way during the exercise?
    - What is the psyche attempting to engineer as you are attentive to your process?
    - If you were to speak to your image, what would you want to communicate?
    - Finally, as you focus again on your breath, acknowledge yourself and your depths for your inner work as you bring closure to your process.
- What stirs you and engages your attention in Chapter Three? Consider allowing yourself to enter into an active-imagination exercise, with this part of yourself, or with a Chapter Three mythological character *via* the right-hand/left-hand technique. Remember in this exercise, your dominant hand represents your conscious voice and your nondominant hand represents the unconscious aspect of you that is attempting to engage your attention. The purpose of the active-imagination exercise is to dialogue and to relate to a part of yourself that is surfacing from your unconscious. The exercise can assist in giving voice to this part of you. In relating to this part, hopefully, you will gain an expanded awareness and integration of an aspect of yourself that is endeavoring to be heard. Begin your dialogue with your dominant hand and allow to arise what comes forth from within you, as you start to write spontaneously what is emerging within you to the part of you represented by your nondominant hand. Then change hands and hold your pen or pencil in your nondominant hand as you allow to arise what comes forth from within you in response to the communication from your conscious voice. Remember, allow the dialogue to flow and to continue until it naturally feels complete for

you. What have you learned through the active-imagination exercise? What do you sense your psyche is attempting to engineer, or what do you perceive is the summons of your soul? Finally, acknowledge yourself for being attentive to your inner work.

- Reflect on your experience and understanding of dark night in your life. If you were to visit an art museum what painting or sculpture captures for you the energy of your reality? If you were to write about the painting or sculpture, what would you say about the piece that speaks to you about your dark-night experience? What art piece manifests the energy of Lady Underground for you?
- What theater experience have you had that stirs your imagination, moves your heart, engages your spirit, and captures symbolically for you the energy of dark-night initiation? If you were to record in your journal how this theater event spoke to your being, what would you express?
- Allow your imagination to wander and to consider what style and what piece of music captures for you the energy of your dark night? Consider listening to the music and allow to arise whatever emerges within you. You may want to write about the music that reflects meaning to you concerning your dark-night experience and to record any further sensations, emotions, and/or insights that may have been stirred in your listening process.
- Consider taking a walk in nature and let your senses be attentive to the experience as you allow yourself to be engaged in the arena of nature by being present in the here and now. Take some deep-belly breaths and attune your hearing to the more subtle sounds in your nature walk. You might discover that you are becoming more still inside, as your pace of walking begins to slow down. Look with a curiosity and a reverence as you open to the "other" and as you are engaged. What moves your imagination? What speaks to your soul? What does nature teach you about the arduous journey of Lady Underground's dark-night initiation and the call to embody one's authentic being? After you walk, you may want to record your experience in a journal or to write a poem about the dynamic as a

possible further way to objectify, metabolize, integrate, and honor your process.

- What words would describe your dark-night experience. Make a list of these words. Obtain a poster board or something smaller if you prefer, scissors, glue, and several magazines filled with pictures. In a quiet, reflective space, sit with all your materials, recall your dark night, and look over your list of words describing this reality. After your recollection, consider taking some time to be with yourself in solitude. Next, when you are ready, begin to look for pictures that capture your dark night, cut them out, and then glue them on the poster board as you create a collage that expresses your dark-night experience. What was this exercise like for you? What did you discover and learn through the process? You may want to record your thoughts, feelings, and sensations that emerged within you in this exercise as a further way to objectify, to metabolize, and to integrate your experience. Also, when your collage is finished, consider putting it in eye's view of where you are sitting. Allow yourself to take some time reflecting on the whole of the collage. If you like, take some deep-belly breaths and, as you exhale, allow yourself to be with your collage in silence. After your time of stillness, you may want to focus in and be attentive to your body and your process, to see if anything further has emerged in your unique experience. If you like, you may want to record what your collage experience was like for you and what you learned through your experience. Finally, take some time to acknowledge yourself and your depths as you complete your exercise.
- Jung writes in *Psychology and Alchemy (C.W. 12,* par. 439*)* that the dread and resistance that every natural human being experiences when delving too deeply into himself [herself] is, at bottom, the fear of the journey to Hades. The realization of a deeper descent and a further summons of your soul can activate fear and even terror. Your immediate impulse may be to put the brakes on your energetic system. However, the summons to a deeper, dark night of initiation, to face yet another layer of defense and the subtle aspects of our darkest shadow and charged complexes, holds the potential and invitation to a greater expansiveness. Explore your darkest shadow.

What are the subtle, diffuse, and elusive ways you squelch and constrict the flow of your energy in your life? Consider doing an active-imagination exercise by writing a short parable about your dark shadow characters and the subtle, diffuse, and elusive ways you say *No* to incarnating consciously the unique gift of yourself and your soul's path. What would be the title of your parable? Who are the main characters and the underlying theme? What is the paradoxical challenge and lesson in your parable? Are there any surprises or shifts in the parable? As you reflect on your parable, what are your growing edges? As you focus on the present and the ordinary of everyday life, what are you willing to take responsibility for in honoring and envisioning your soul anew?

- Consider having a real dialogue with another who has a polarizing perspective on some issue in life from your view. After the dialogue, reflect on what the experience was like for you. As you focus on your body, what did you notice during the dialogue, and currently, what do realize as you are attentive to yourself? What did you learn from the dialogical encounter?
- What wisdom figure from your life, religious tradition, spirituality, or from a favorite mythological story speaks to you about insights, wisdom, and guidance regarding dark-night growth experiences? Consider doing an active-imagination exercise with this wisdom figure. You may choose to use the right-hand/left-hand modality, a slow meditative walk with the wisdom figure, the empty chair exercise, or some other modality of your choice. What would you want to express to the wisdom figure? What would you want to ask the wisdom figure? What do you imagine the wisdom figure would want to communicate to you? You may want to record in your journal what you experienced and learned from your active-imagination exercise. Remember, as you bring closure to your process, acknowledge yourself and your depths for your inner work.
- Draw or paint a mandala of the image of your dark night experience or the image that engaged your attention in Chapter Three, "Dark Night of Initiation." Or consider what do you most question, wonder about, or struggle with as you reflect on the material in Chapter

Three. If your wonderment, question, or struggle, had a color or an image, what would it be? Allow yourself to express this color or image in the form of a mandala. When you are finished, notice and record the feelings, thoughts, or sensations you experienced while drawing your mandala and after completing it. If your mandala had a title, what would it be? What awareness have you discovered through your mandala exercise? Remember to take some time to acknowledge yourself and your depths for your inner work.

- Lady Underground's midnight of dark-night initiation can seem unending. Given the intense state of annihilating darkness and the sense of being stripped raw, thoughts of death can seem like a welcome relief as one is plagued by the blackness of midnight. In this repugnant state, messengers don't help anymore. In the black darkness of this night, energy is zapped, even for inner work. Silent solitude is a realm of being and a domain of the soul to be honored. Consider taking some time in silent solitude.

~Body-Energy Exercises

- After reading Chapter Three, consider what has captured your attention that currently is challenging you to a deeper interiority and a more expansive self-awareness. With regard to this reality, what, if any, are the discounting beliefs, attitudes, or charged feelings that you have about yourself that are gripping you and driving you in your present life? What aspect of your shadow has been triggered through the reading, reflection, journaling, or exercises? Record your responses to both of the former questions. Consider doing an EMDR exercise with a trained EMDR practitioner as one possible way to demagnetize any shadow material, including discounting attitudes and beliefs, charged emotions, and/or cellular memory surrounding the reality that is challenging you. This process is a creative way to access the active imagination in the experience of differentiation, healing, and integration.
- Reflect on the recorded list from the previous exercise. Consider where you tend to withdraw and say an inner absolute *No* or a strong verbal *No* to issues, to invitations, and to challenges for expansive growth.

What are the ways you squelch life, what are your manipulative behaviors, what are the controlling ways that you attempt to pull the wool over others's eyes under the auspices of appearing and sounding good, and what are the subtle, diffuse, and elusive destructive self-defeating attitudes that prohibit your generative growth? What is the price your body pays for perpetuating your shadow? Given the reading, these reflective questions, and what was activated within you, ask yourself, in this present moment, what captures your attention the most that is longing to be heard, metabolized, and integrated in embodied consciousness? We cannot change everything all at once, so remember, take what captures your attention right now, or what currently has the most energy for you. Consider finding an EFT practitioner and do an EFT sequence. This is one way to do an active-imagination exercise to demagnetize the charged shadow that is gripping and driving you, to honor your depths, to objectify what is attempting to be integrated into consciousness, and to release the energy for creativity. The tapping is a modality of body-energy work that touches into the active-imagination process and potentially offers a more integrative approach in the process of inner soul work. When you are finished with your session, you may want to record what your experience was like for you. Also, note how you experience your body as you are present to yourself right now. What did you learn through the body-energy exercise? Remember, when you feel complete with your exercise, take some time to acknowledge yourself and your depths for your inner work.

- Reflect on what part of you do you attempt to disregard, deny, or disown. Consider doing a body-energy exercise by allowing the part of you that you reject or disown to sit symbolically on an empty chair and allow the whole of you to sit in another chair. Begin the active-imagination session by taking some time to be quiet, and when you are ready, begin to speak to the part of yourself that you disregard and deny. Express what you feel and think about this part of yourself to that part that now is symbolically sitting in the empty chair. Then, realizing that physical movement can change the energy flow and the energy field, let yourself stand up, move, and take the empty chair. Allow to arise what wants to emerge spontaneously and express it to the whole of you that is symbolically sitting in the opposite chair. Continue to allow the active-imagination dialogue to flow back and forth between the whole of you and the self-object part of yourself that you are in dialogue with in this exercise. When the dialogue feels complete to you, bring closure to the experience by taking a few moments to acknowledge yourself for your active-imagination body-energy session. You may want to take some time to record in your journal what you learned in the process.

- Consider finding a quiet and safe setting where you might have space to move and not be interrupted in any way. Reflect on what captured your attention in Chapter Three, or perhaps from one of the discussion questions or exercises. Allow yourself to take a deep breath as you become present to yourself and focus on what image is emerging in you. Where do you sense the energy of this image in your body? In this exercise of soulful, arising movement, your breath, sound, and movement are a direct form of active imagination. The conscious focus is on the imaginal as it expresses itself through the breath, sound, and/or movement. In this process the body is the medium; the breath, sound, and movement are the message. In this particular form of tracking your image within the experience of your body, the active-imagination dialogue is a felt physical and emotional engagement through the medium of the body. Allow yourself freedom in your body movement and when your experience feels complete, take a deep breath as you find your way to bring closure to your process. When you are finished, you might want to record your experience as another way of objectifying and befriending your depths. This body-movement exercise can also be done with two others: One person holds consciously the space for the individual who is the body mover, and the other is the observer. For the exercise you can allow 10 or 15 minutes for the movement component and then time for processing the exercise. Again, if you do this body-movement exercise alone, or if you do it in the presence of two others, remember, before you finish, to take time to acknowledge yourself and your depths for your inner work.

CHAPTER FOUR

BIRTHING AND EMBODYING THE PROGRESSIVE DANCE OF DAWN

Without the soul the body is dead, and without the body the soul is unreal.
~C.G. Jung

No matter what the world thinks about religious experience, the one who has it possess a great treasure, a thing that has become for him [her] a source of life, meaning, and beauty, and that has given a new splendor to the world and to [hu]mankind.
~C. G., *Psychology and Religion*

Pouring out a thousand graces, you passed these groves in haste;
and having looked at them, with your image alone, clothed them in beauty. . .
When you looked at me your eyes imprinted your grace in me. . .
~St. John of the Cross

O leaves of love, O chlorophyll of grace
~Jessica Powers

Only now can we see with clarity that we live not so much in a cosmos as in a cosmogenesis, a cosmogenesis best presented in narrative; scientific in its data, mythic in its form.
~Brian Swimme and Thomas Berry

[E]very one of us, is ready to plead: tell me a story. For the role of stories is to explain life, and the good stories, in their very substance and in the structure of their language, become revelation.
~Andrew M. Greeley

To lose oneself in the unfathomable, to plunge into the inexhaustible,
to find peace in the incorruptible, to be absorbed in the definite immensity,
to offer oneself to the fire. . .and to give one's deepest self to that whose
depth has no end.
~Pierre Teilhard de Chardin

In your light I learn how to love. In your beauty, how to make poems. You dance inside my chest, where no-one sees you, but sometimes I do, and that sight becomes this art.
~Rumi

A condition of complete simplicity
(Costing not less than everything)
~T.S. Eliot

Naturalness is called the Way.
~*The Secret of the Golden Flower*

. . .silent music, sounding solitude, . . .
~St. John of the Cross

So the darkness shall be the light, and the stillness the dancing.
~T.S. Eliot

Dawn

At this historical time, the Eternal Feminine, and specifically the Dark Feminine, the *Unknown She who is,* arises, births, and reveals her face like a vital current in multiple ways within the inner and outer landscapes of the web of all life. She is embedded in the primordial energy and the catalyst for the yearning and unfolding creative process. Recognizing, assimilating, and navigating consciously this resurging archetypal energy during this accelerated shift in evolution ignites the potential for a more passionate and compassionate embodied awareness and presence of ourselves personally and collectively within the dawning of the emerging new Cosmic Story.

Central to this unfolding Universe Story is the flaring forth to imagine, live, and consciously embody an Earth-centered norm of reality and value, versus a human-centered (anthropocentric) stance. Moreover, biblical stories and traditional sacred texts containing creation stories need to be read and understood in light of the scientific nature story of evolution. Realizing and appreciating consciously a more expansive anthropology of who we are, within the full dimension of the Universe Story, stirs our deepest sacred depths, awakens our imaginations, causes us to ponder, and contemplate its mystery dimension, and obliges us to share in the care and responsibility for coauthoring and codirecting the potential emerging process in a sustainable way of life.[137] [138] [139] This includes conscious befriending and living in a mutually enriching relationship with the shared body, the Earth herself, as well as being open and committed to exploring and discovering ways to be human while being in harmony with the Earth community. By our quantum interconnectedness and interrelatedness, the entire universe is bonded in a comprehensive inclusiveness and unity. At our core essence, we are all one.

Approximately 14 billion years ago, the primordial energy containing all the archetypal *unfolding potential* of the ongoing evolving universe flared forth creatively! Spirit is the creative power, the wellspring of all possibility within the primordial flaring forth of our mysterious, dynamic, evolving universe. Core to the primal energy is the ancient ever-new foundational archetypal feminine energy of the Great Mother Goddess, with the masculine principle being the other foundational energy of our evolving cosmos. In the last 60 years, the feminine has returned and has been reclaimed by many, which expanded our horizons. However, the Dark Feminine is a deeper dimension of the gradations of the Great Mother Goddess energy (mother, virgin, conduit of wisdom), which is calling to be heard, metabolized, integrated, and embodied consciously at this historical time, given the intense polarities and the environmental crisis. On the continuum of the archetypal energy of the Great Mother, the Dark Goddess is the deeper, earthy, immensely powerful "Other," more shadowy, and often hidden, unknown, sublime, and mysterious dimension of the Goddess. In general, while the Western world has experienced gradually more of the emergence of the feminine principle in the process of recovering, reclaiming, and befriending this foundational energy, it simply is shallow and insufficient to speak about an overarching global aspect of the Great Goddess's energy that has emerged, more notably in the latter half of the 20th century and in the unfolding 21st century, without recognizing and speaking specifically about the Dark Goddess. Her energy is within the inexhaustible continuum of the Goddess's potential archetypal energy patterns and possibilities for development personally, collectively, and planetarily. Of the Dark Goddess's many faces, Lady Underground is one image of the Unknown She. Her archetypal dark-night initiation is an arduous journey in befriending and embodying consciously the manifestation of her energy in a more awakened-passionate awareness and compassionate presence as we navigate this unparalleled shift within the evolving comprehensive Earth community.

Given the more expansive anthropology that underpins the emerging Universe Story, we recognize that a greater emphasis is placed on the encounter and experience with the mystery/Mystery in the here and now. However, while we realize this value, we also are aware, paradoxically, that within our soul's depths, all our questioning, seeking, knowing, desiring, and loving are sustained and drawn by a source that always remains unknowable and exceeds our finite grasp. Lady Underground's twilight and midnight of dark-night archetypal initiation opens us to the dark nothingness and emptiness of divine energy that is experienced as mystery/Mystery, and as such, always remains hidden and incomprehensible. This inexhaustible, beyond-understanding, and essentially unsolvable mystery/Mystery is the infinite horizon and ground of our being and of the great cosmic web of all life. Religious experience is not an experience of mastering the mystery/Mystery, but rather letting ourselves be grasped by the mystery/Mystery that is present and yet ever distant, known and yet ever unknown.[140]

Dawn is awakening to letting ourselves be touched and grasped by the mystery/Mystery. Dawn is discovering that we co-share in the responsibility of furthering the conscious evolution of the comprehensive Earth community. Dawn is birthing more of the *essence* of who we really are, that is to say, *liberating the generative soul within us.* It is showing up in everyday life with a more awakened-passionate awareness and compassionate presence. Dawn is the progressive journey of coming *home, of conscious embodiment within the evolving Earth community.* We live, grow, and develop consciously in an interconnected and interrelated web of all life. The mystery/Mystery is not outside of this dynamic, rather as Karl Rahner, S.J., one of the most esteemed and finest theologians of the 20th century noted on November 11, 1974, at a private gathering at the Jesuit Residence in Chicago, "The deepest experience of self is the experience of Mystery."[vi]

Gradually in dawn, more of the depth and breadth of our true nature emerges into consciousness as we befriend consciously the "Otherness" that exists hidden in all of us, in the best of us, and in the least of us. Dawn is metaphorically about the ever-widening realization and embodiment of the progressive journey in service to larger life and humble service to the mystery/Mystery. The ongoing call to the emerging and evolving way of dawn, in embodying the fuller potential of our humanity and our soul's path within the Earth community, is reflected in Rilke's *Book of Hours: Love Poems to God* in his imaginative poem of the Mystery's empowering self-communication to a soul that is evolving into life.

[vi]Karl Rahner, S.J., the famous German theologian (1904-1984), was in Chicago, Illinois, in November 1974, for a celebration of St. Thomas Aquinas's anniversary and to lecture on "The Incomprehensibility of God." On the evening of November 11, 1974, my friend Michael Montague, S.J., a theologian, invited Kathleen Russell Navarre and me to a social event at the Jesuit residence. As we entered the large residential community home, I asked if there was a special reason for the occasion. My friend Mike said, "No, just a small gathering of about 25 people." Of the group assembled, Katie and I were the only women.

As I sat down in the circle of guests, I introduced myself to the gentleman sitting next to me, who identified himself as Bernie. I presented my friend Katie to Bernie and discovered in the exchange of dialogue that he was Bernie Lonergan, S.J., a renowned theologian. At this point, a waiter was presenting Katie and me with canned beverages on a tray. We each made a choice, and suddenly we heard a deep, distinguished, strong, emphatic voice say, "Get the ladies a glass; you never serve ladies a canned beverage without a glass!"

I turned to Bernie Lonnergan and said with wonder, "Who is that man?" Bernie responded, "Karl Rahner!" Needless to say, Katie and I received a glass rather quickly; we both nodded to Karl, and he smiled! Then, with a shift in the pitch of Rahner's voice to a softer tone and a more relaxed pace, Karl began to address the group. Sitting in a large leather chair by the blazing, crackling fire burning in the earth-stone hearth, Rahner spoke in conversational language about the topics of love, prayer, life, and death, and what these themes meant to him personally at this stage in his journey. Rahner shared that his mother was dying. He conveyed, with a tender tone of voice, that for him love and prayer were the lived presence of attending with intention to the human experience in the here and now, and for Rahner at that time, it was the ordinary human experience of holding his mother's hand, combing her hair, and washing her face as she was in the process of dying. His closing comment to the group, was: "Remember, in the words of Thomas Aquinas, 'It is all straw,' unless we probe and live fully the depth dimension of human experience in the ordinary of everyday life."

> You, sent out beyond your recall,
> Go to the limits of your longing.
> Embody me. . . .Don't let yourself lose me. . .
> Give me your hand. (p. 104) [141]

We turn now in this chapter to consider "dawn" as the third stage of "night" in Lady Underground's dark night of initiation in the Dark Feminine and to continue to explore what it means to embody her energy at this phase of night and in the 21st century. Through twilight and midnight, we are challenged to embody consciously a more expanded sense of our authentic self, our deepest possibilities. *Death* in midnight opens us to *birth* in dawn. As T.S. Eliot noted well in "Little Gidding," it is "A condition of complete simplicity (Costing not less than everything)" (p. 59)![142] This soul work emerges through the alchemical cooking via the three stages of *nigredo* (black-darkness producing: loosening, suffering, and death of rigid psychic structures), *albedo* (white: emerging new phase of greater consciousness and freedom), and *rubedo* (red: pulsating aliveness of life). This evolving process constitutes the dissolving and death of old dominant principles and archaic structures and patterns of the ego that are not in service to our soul's summons and the gradual birthing of a more expanded sense of our true nature.

As these interactive dynamics of the alchemical operation occur, there is a gradual increase in the light of emerging consciousness (dawn) in the psyche, that at a somatic level is experienced as a gradual opening to a greater spaciousness within our being, along with a greater flow of pulsating energy sensed as warmth, and a more felt aliveness within the soma. With a more expanded sense of self comes a greater capacity for containing our emerging, embodied essence. This growth development has occurred, as one has lived and endured the inner battle of the opposites with enough awareness, with adequate capacity to reflect on one's experience, and with sufficient strength to bear and to hold the still point within until the unity beyond the opposites emerges. (This is a transcendent-function experience.) This process of living, enduring, and suffering through the tension and inner war of holding the opposites with a perduring attentiveness until something new arises from the depths is the life-death-rebirth dynamic that forges and grows soul. This is the energetic underpinning that cultivates and liberates the generative soul within us. Through this progressive alchemical operation, dawn of soul is born.

Furthermore, it is important to realize that this soul reality is true at a personal level, a conscious group level, especially a group organizing as a conduit for change from the ground up, and at a leadership division for an organization, institution, country, and/or a global cause. For example, at a leadership level, as president, because of Abraham Lincoln's humanitarian vision and a depth of indomitable sense of purpose, Lincoln carried and bore the responsibility of the agonizing tension of acutely realizing the potential disintegration of the Union, the terrible human cost of the loss of life in the darkest horrific months of the Civil War, and the reality of slavery that was constitutionally protected already, and yet consciously Lincoln held that it was morally, socially, and politically wrong.[143] Lincoln bore this inner battle of tensions while rallying his disheartened countrymen, soothing the animosity of his generals, mediating the friction and conflicts of his often-contentious administration, attending the daily demands of his office, bearing the excruciating loss of his son Willie, and subsequently, because of his wife's distraught grief, primarily parenting his dear son Tad.[144] Not outside of this chaos and annihilating dark night, both for America and for Lincoln personally, but in the midst of this horrific dark night of our country's history and of Lincoln's personal agonizing dark night of the soul for his family, Abraham Lincoln pondered, held, reflected, endured, and awaited insight and wisdom to arise within himself, and only then, he began passionately and gradually to draft and to edit the Emancipation Proclamation. Lincoln read for the first time to his cabinet the preliminary draft of the proclamation on July 22, 1862, at his cabinet session. As recorded in the diary of Gideon Welles (secretary of the navy who was present for the draft reading), Lincoln saw this declaration of freedom and amendment to the constitution as "absolutely essential for the salvation of the Union, that we must free the slaves or be ourselves subdued" (pp. 463, 459-472).[145] Thus, through Lincoln's embodied inner authority and his constitutionally sanctioned war powers as president, the abolition of slavery by constitutional provision was settled on January 31, 1865, when the House of Representatives passed the Constitutional 13th

Amendment, abolishing slavery.[146] The process of the passage of this historical amendment to the constitution was birthed gradually by a man who had the courage to live, to bear, and to suffer the tensions of a tormenting haunting dark night of the soul personally and professionally as the leader of the United States. A little over 150 years has transpired since Lincoln pondered within his depths his evolving and unfolding perspective, as well as his formulating the lines of the Emancipation Proclamation. As a country we have come a long way. However, the dark, deep-seated seeds of unconscious, destructive, annihilating shadow still toxically contaminate our country's collective soul and the souls of all of us who are enslaved and imprisoned by patriarchal power, greed, injustice, and hatred in any form. This includes violence manifested by anyone, or any group, such as the KKK, white nationalists and supremacists, and neo-Nazis. Only through living and suffering the tension of the opposites, and metabolizing and integrating our darkest shadow, will we know the embodied potential of dawn and the possibility of a new horizon personally, for any one of us, in our soul's journey, and collectively in our organizations, institutions, country, global world, and planetary community.

Thus, through the birth-death-rebirth cycle of dark-night initiation, in dawn a greater expanded felt sense of meaning, purpose, identity, and direction arises from within, and one knows oneself in a more grounded, conscious way. Through this process, often the rigidity of our narrow one-sidedness, manifested in the energy controlled and locked in the restrained tight muscles and neuropaths of the body, is loosened and relaxed in going through the struggle of the opposites, which also develops one's container. Without this essential reality, one cannot hold the higher resonance of incoming energy or be a conduit of the divine/Divine energy in a grounded integrated and humble way. Many have numinous experiences, but because of the inability to endure the tension of the opposites for whatever reason (inner soul work), there is no well-developed conscious container, and thus one is not able to hold the energy in a consistent way as one is about the ordinary living of one's life. The development of one's conscious container is essential, and one way this occurs is through the process of enduring the suffering of the opposites and the overall befriending of the shadow. This inner night war is reflected in the opposing psychological functions that are operative in navigating, befriending, and integrating our psychic energy in the journey toward embodied wholeness (as mentioned in the previous chapter). Jung realized this wisdom, noting that "beneath the neglected functions there lie hidden far higher individual values, which. . .are of greatest value for individual life, and therefore vital values that can endow the life of the individual with an intensity and beauty he [she] will vainly seek in his [her] collective function" (par. 113).[147] Having the courage to go into the inner caverns, metabolize the chaotic war of opposites, and birth values of greater depth not only widens the individual soul with greater possibilities and insightful wisdom, but ultimately, in a quantum evolving universe, it widens and impacts the web of all life. Furthermore, as one navigates and assimilates the tumultuous struggle of the opposites somatically, rigidly held energetic patterns in the neuromuscular system of the body gradually give way, and there is a less constricted and natural flow of energy released in the neuropaths of the body. As this occurs, one can viscerally experience the pulsating energy flow. The body parts that were tight, inflexible, and blocked become more relaxed, agile and supple. Hence, the body becomes more pliable and soft. This relaxing, opening, and yielding of the neuromuscular system creates soul-body space for the birth and embodiment of the progressive *dance of dawn* incarnating in the natural earth of our being. In the gradual emerging to dawn awareness, we become more sensitized and attuned to incarnation as a conscious *celebration* of conscious embodiment and to the expansive interconnection with all creation. Cosmogenesis is furthered through conscious embracing and embodying personal and collective potential. In awakening to dawn, we begin to realize that body is the vital sacred vessel, container, and medium of the psyche through which the invisible mystery/Mystery is revealed. A further realization or deeper perception is that within this quantum evolutionary universe, which pulsates with the originating, creative, generative spirit/Spirit that animates all life, the entire cosmos is mystery's/Mystery's first manifestation of embodiment, along with planet Earth, which is also a body, and every creature and organism within the corporeal earth is endowed with body. Thus, in the words of Diarmuid O'Murchu, the internationally known social psychologist, author, and lecturer, "Our human embodiment is an inheritance of a creative universe, whose existence and flourishing is intimately linked to embodiment. In its fuller meaning, incarnation finds expression in all forms of embodiment" (p. 242, Note 190).[148]

Dawn is the grounding awareness of the continuous journey toward conscious ensoulment, accompanied by an ever-growing realization of a deep solidarity with the cosmos and all its paradox of opposites: light and dark, joy and sorrow, promise and peril, constriction and expansion, chaos and creativity, life and death, and so many more! Thus, in dawn we open to embodied consciousness with an underlying awareness that the inner and outer landscapes of all of life are imbued with relatedness and with generative energy that animates the cosmos. As Hildegard of Bingen observed: "Everything that is in the heavens, on the earth, and under the earth is penetrated with connectedness, penetrated with relatedness" (p. 146).[149] The ever-present nature of all life within the cosmos reflects an abiding reality wherein the invisible plane underlying and supporting the visible one is manifest. The Sufi Master and great Persian poet, Hafiz, conveys this reality, "I hear the voice of every creature and plant, every world and sun and galaxy—singing the Beloved's Name" (p. 16)![150] The poet Jessica Powers, O.C.D., addresses this tenderly, "O leaves of love, O chlorophyll of grace" (p. 83),[151] and John of the Cross notes in *The Spiritual Canticle*, "Pouring out a thousand graces you passed these groves in haste; and having looked at them, with your image alone, clothed them in beauty" (p. 472).[152] Further in the poem John writes, "When you looked at me your eyes imprinted your grace in me" (p. 476).[153] Last, the famous Jesuit poet Gerard Manley Hopkins reflects this dawn of inner and outer awareness of embodiment in his verse: "The world is charged with the grandeur of God" (p. 855).[154]

Thus, we realize the soul's ongoing journey of individuation in dawn involves an ever-progressive process of differentiation, interiorization, unification (deeper communion), and a continuous opening to a greater awareness of a more expansive relational cosmology that is not mechanistic in nature. Rather, at core, the modern, evolving, quantum worldview sees relationality woven within the archetypal patterns of energy in which everything in creation grows and flourishes as our essential humanity emerges from a vast web of relationships. For each of us in dawn, our soul emerges with hopefully a greater embodied humble awareness of the interface of archetypal, cosmic, planetary, cultural, social, and personal influences. For dawn is awakening beyond the narrow boundaries of the ego's frame to a wider, more intricate, colorful woven tapestry of our soul's life and relational narratives that in some small way interconnect with the web of all life in a participatory, evolving, creative universe.

Hence, in dawn we are opening to a deeper dialogue and communion with our center, the *invisible world of the mystery/Mystery*, potentially experienced as what one analysand described as "dark light," John of the Cross contemplated as "silent music," and T.S. Eliot conveyed as "the stillness in the dancing." This conscious experience of dawn ultimately brings us renewal. As professor/coach Morrie Schwartz conveyed to Mitch Albom (America's No. 1 sports columnist for the *Detroit Free Press*) in *Tuesdays With Morrie,* "When you learn how to *die*, you learn how to *live*" (p. 104).[155] In the process of death and dying from the crippling Lou Gehrig's disease, Coach Morrie's final days were a symbolic dance of living because he knew well how to die throughout his life, and through it all, he did one of his favorite joyful realties—dance!

Symbolically, dawn is the manifestation of the spirited dance of the conscious, well-differentiated masculine and feminine energies as one, and yet, distinctly two. The feminine energy incorporates a conscious sense of living and being in the present with a spirit of receptivity and a capacity to surrender, embracing process, and allowing the paradox of the opposites to coexist creatively. The masculine energy encompasses a conscious laser-like focus for discriminating and guiding in life. Again, remember that we are speaking of these energies symbolically and not from a gender-related basis. In the language of spirituality, dawn is the inner mystical marriage. From a Jungian perspective, psychologically, dawn is the inner partnership of the masculine and feminine energies, the *coniunctio*. This conscious embodiment of the masculine and feminine energies is the new conscious partnership that Lady Underground beckons us to incarnate in this 21st century. This new conscious relationship is an emerging, evolving, unfolding dance of an ever-growing embodiment of both a conscious differentiated masculine energy and feminine energy in which the dynamic inner symbolic relationality of these energies is one of mutual equality and respect. Also, neither of the two distinct energies are in any manner being sacrificed or subordinated to the other.

This creative aspect of the progressive, generative dance of dawn is reflected most pointedly in Camille Claudel's most famous work of art, her bronze sculpture piece, *The Waltz,* completed between 1891 and 1893 (to see, Google: the bronze *Waltz* by Camille Claudel). The work was created to be viewed and received from all angles. The phenomenal sensuous, lush, rhythmic, passionate sculpture conveys a flow of movement and a depth of intimate feeling revealed in the contours and attention to elegant detail, illustrated in the alive felt sense of the resonance of energy between the two of them in their waltz, and yet portrayed as one moving exquisitely in their dance. Camille's sculpture of the body in *The Waltz* manifests the interior soul. Reine-Marie Paris wrote about this quality of interiority that's reflected in *The Waltz*, stating that "Her domain is not the sun but the shadows inside a house. Just as there is chamber music, so there is chamber sculpture" (p. 22).[156] [vii] The inspiring, twisting sculpture, made in the image of dance, obliges viewers themselves to move around the piece several times to view, ponder, appreciate, and imaginatively open to its creative effects.

So too, in the progressive *dark-night* journey of initiation, we circumambulate, enduring the holding of the tension of opposites, sacrificing in the cycle of life-death-rebirth, and befriending the ignored or demeaned shadow many times before coming to a more conscious embrace of our shadow, especially our deeper, blacker-than-black aspects of shadow and the inner conscious partnership of the masculine and feminine energy in the earth of our bodies as men and women. Within the experience of these deeper levels of the psyche, we open to the potential of the wellspring of wisdom, compassion, and vision that arise out of the depths of the metabolized energy in dark-night initiation, and thus we open to a wider horizon of consciousness of all life. This enriched expansion into broader channels of awareness summons us back into the human circle enlivened by greater consciousness, responsibility, and humble service. For any of us, only through the progressive embodiment of a conscious, well-differentiated feminine energy and a

[vii] The private owner of *The Waltz* sculpture gave The National Museum of Women in the Arts, in Washington, D.C., permission to reproduce a print at the time of the Camille Claudel Exhibit in 1988.

conscious, well-differentiated masculine energy within the overall process of housing and befriending our questions of our own story, will any one of us know the possibility of a greater inner freedom and capacity to love and relate more authentically to the "other" and to all of life. Again, for all of us, in our soulful inner work, costing not less than everything, it is well to realize and remember that the inner work remains ongoing and evolving, and that the mystery dimension will always continue to surround the journey.

Also, once more, keep in mind that without twilight and midnight, there is no dawn. You may recall in Chapter Three we noted that there were four primary stages to a rite of initiation: separation, ordeal, encounter with the holy, and return. Given the dynamics of the self-regulating system of the psyche, twilight and midnight primarily involve many doses of grappling with the darkness as one navigates through the journey of separation and ordeal stages of dark-night initiation. As noted in the previous chapter, this reality from the view of the ego is an experience of death. Horrific as it is for the ego, the separation and ordeal stages are a necessary prelude to the growing awareness of the Self and the conscious embodiment of the dance of dawn. Jung refers to this experience of symbolic death as "a defeat for the ego"; Edward Edinger describes it as "a crucifixion of the ego"; St. John of the Cross speaks of it as the "dark night of the soul"; Kierkegaard calls it "despair." Psychologically, they are all referring to the state of alienation that often precedes a religious experience.

What is important to remember is that normally growth and expansion are never a clear, cookie-cutter process in the archetypal experience of the four primary stages to a rite of initiation. As the inner cooking and emerging dynamics accelerate, often our ego tries to cling to our old patterns out of fear and self-limiting beliefs that we would be left bereft. From the controlled, limited ego's view, it is easier to maintain the *status quo*, and to cling to what is familiar, known, secure, and safe, even though it is dysfunctional, especially in a career, marriage, relationships, ministry, and/or vocation, than it is to sacrifice the old, let go, and surrender, as we are fearfully traversing the tightrope of life. For anyone of us, going by a way of knowing-by-*not-knowing* initially tends to trigger anxiety! Letting go and surrendering are horrific. Scary is an understatement! When legs feel like Jell-O, with no grounded stance, anxiety and terror plague us! We don't know who we are without our constrictive armor of defense and our sophisticated, compartmentalized, mastermind-numbing, denying control system. For most of us, our go-to defensive response is on automatic pilot. In the grip of the angst of life, thoughts of thinking the unthinkable and bearing the unbearable are often cut off automatically as being completely out of the question of being experienced and endured. Frequently in the struggle of life's realities, we flounder as we attempt to listen to the nudges of our body's inner sensory receptors, to discern clues from our dreams, and to stay attuned to the hint of discarded, pushed-down, and objectified self-parts attempting to rear up from the underground within us. For many, loosening the grip of control beyond the familiar self-experience is a sense of ungluing anxiety, sheer panic, and paralyzing fear. Nonetheless, terrifying as it is, our task is to forge ahead, befriend, and liberate the unassimilated energy represented in psychic parts of ourselves that have been imprisoned underground, sometimes with a sign on the locked cell gate reading, "It is unthinkable and unsafe to allow this unbearable part out." However daunting and seemingly impossible, we need to bite the bullet, to bear the suffering, and to have the courage to proceed as we are engaged by underground self-parts that are longing to be heard, released, and integrated as we endure the dynamics of a particular stage in the initiation process. Trust grows gradually every time we overcome our resistance to accept the inevitable and to endure the resulting pain with fortitude as we let go into the void of surrender, giving up our narrow, strong self-will. Again, keep in mind, it is less important that we recognize the particular stages of initiation by name and far more significant that we consciously metabolize, integrate, and embody the dynamics of the energy that is engaging us in our journey. Given a person's psychospiritual development and the archetypal inner landscape of an individual's soul, there may be shorter or longer periods of separation-and-ordeal dynamics in the initiation process, as well as opening in dawn to varying degrees of realized moments and/or longer periods of the emerging and unfolding stages of the encounter with the mystery/Mystery and the return.

Edward Edinger points to the image of wilderness as a classic symbol for alienation. Throughout this writing, the symbol of *dark-night initiation* conveys the same connotation. In and through the wilderness or the *dark night*, characteristically, some encounter or revelation of the divine/Divine occurs.[157] We see this manifested in the Old Testament in the life of Moses when he encounters the Divine at the burning bush on Mount Horeb. Also, the first 31 stanzas of the "The Spiritual Canticle" of John of the Cross, composed during his oppressive nine months of imprisonment in the Carmelite Monastery in Toledo, Spain (beginning December 2, 1577), reveal his ineffable encounter with the Divine during his horrific confinement. Psychologically, when the ego has exhausted its own resources, aware of its essential powerlessness, and is at an impasse, then the experience of the supportive dimension of the archetypal psyche is most likely to occur.

While the encounter of the self-communicating mystery/Mystery in a rite of initiation may reflect many different dimensions for a soul, the encounter can be one that is potentially healing and strengthening. It is the mystery/Mystery that heals. In dawn the "encounter with the holy" is an experience of an emerging conscious awareness of intimations of the mystery/Mystery that can manifest in a variety of forms in nature, solitude, a dream, a vision, within a relationship (including the analytical relationship), through the creative arts, an illness, deathbed experience, as well as in a community ritual and celebration. This ongoing journey of opening to the inexhaustible continuum of deeper levels of relationship and communion with the invisible mystery/Mystery is the birthing and embodying of the dance of dawn. Lady Underground is the seducer (remember what this means from Chapter Three, being beckoned toward one's soul essence) in twilight and midnight of night initiation in the Dark Feminine within the overall archetypal summons by the organizing principle of the psyche (Self) that is drawing us toward a more enlarged life in our soul's journey in service to the mystery/Mystery within the evolving Universe Story. Lady Underground's empowering self-communication of compassionate love and wisdom is an opening to the gateless gate of inexhaustible mystery/Mystery in the dawn of initiation. Dawn is the experience of being touched and summoned by the mystery/Mystery. As such, because of the overall experience of growth and integration in dark-night initiation, potentially one can tend to become more sensitized and attuned to being attentive to the intimations of mystery/

Mystery, as manifested in the multiple levels of all life. Furthermore, growth over time can strengthen one toward a greater capacity to honor, contain, hold, and endure the suffering of the tension of the opposites with a perduring attentiveness to the depths until something more arises from within to give meaning, purpose, guidance, and direction. This ongoing stage of development can conceivably be less will-directed and ego-driven, and tend more toward being animated by the creative spirit/Spirit source from within that permeates and is reflected in all of us and in the whole of the cosmos. However, all this being noted, dealing with one's ego and shadow, especially one's blacker-than-black shadow is an ongoing reality to be befriended not just once, but even as one advances in age, if one is to assimilate the deeper dimensions of the virgin and the conduit of wisdom energy of the Dark Feminine. The process of incarnating consciously is a lifetime journey. Furthermore, expansion in dawn consciousness is not a state of magical thinking or delusional fantasizing; nor is it outside the mundane reality of everyday living. Rather, the journey remains one of conscious responsibility and humble service, as one continues patiently to listen with an inner-attuned antenna for the intimations and call of the mystery/Mystery in the midst of the ordinary of life with all its *demands, disappointments, betrayals, tragedies, injustices, losses, challenges, as well as its abundant goodness, joy, pleasure, love, and gratitude.*

Encounter With The Holy

From twilight and midnight of *dark-night* initiation—whether in the "crypt" of Lady Underground of Chartres; the "caves" of the Buddhist anchorites; in the "underworld" of Inanna, Psyche, or Persephone; the "deep unknown dark river" of Ancient Woman; in the "cave-tomb" of Jesus; the "hermitage" of Einsiedeln; the Monastery of the Black Madonna at Santa Maria de Montserrat in Spain; or in the Jasna Gora Monastery of the Black Madonna of Czestochowa—comes the means of renewal, rebirth, and resurrection. Whether in the crypt, monastery, hermitage, tomb, caves, river, or underworld, the archetypal process of the life-death-rebirth cycle is the same. Each of us must make the inner descent, which is to enter a symbolic "crypt," if we are to find our identity, meaning, purpose, and direction in life. Without an inner descent, there is no embodied conscious ascent. Jung writes about this in *Symbols of Transformation:* "The treasure which the hero [heroine] fetches from the dark cavern is *life*: it is himself [herself], new-born from the dark maternal cave of the unconscious" (par. 580).[158]

A significant part of a rite of initiation is the "encounter with the holy." Lady Underground's dark night of initiation in the Dark Feminine (or some other image of the Dark Feminine, for example, Grandmother Earth, Lady of the Valley, Lady Guadalupe, Kali, Lilith, the Black Madonna, Sheba, Tara, Kuan Yin, or Sister of the Algonquin Indians, etc.) is a gate to the *invisible world* in the ordinary of everyday life. In the dance of dawn, Lady Underground invites us to enter more deeply into our lives, to allow our stories to unfold, and our souls to be birthed and embodied in our emerging, earthy soul essence. Regardless of how the encounter occurs in the progressive birth of dawn, the intimations of Lady Underground's self-communication with a soul are real.

Jung borrowed the word *numinous* from Rudolph Otto, who coined the term in his 1923 book, *The Idea of the Holy.* Otto held that the essence of holiness, or religious experience, is a specific realm that remains inexpressible and eludes apprehension in terms of concepts. To convey its uniqueness, he used the word *numinous* from the Latin *numen,* meaning a god, cognate with the verb *nuere*, meaning to nod or beckon, indicating divine approval. The numinous announces itself by stirring a strong affective state, which Otto refers to as a feeling of the *mysterium tremendum.*[159] For example, we may sense the numinous by a presence of consolation or be gripped by a holy dread. Physically, the body may experience a wide variety of sensations ranging from a quiet stillness within, a being-held phenomenon, a felt opening in the heart and a sense of enormous warmth and love, a vibrating, a flow of pulsating energy through the subtle body, possibly including an orgasm, a release of kundalini through the entire body, and/or any combination of these awarenesses. For Otto, *Mysterium* means the feeling that one is in contact with something that is *wholly Other.* He describes the encounter with the numinous as a visitation by the Other that may come like a soft tide pervading the individual with a quiet tranquil sense or humble speechlessness in the presence of "whom or what?" One senses "that which is a *mystery* inexpressible and above all creatures" (pp. 12-17, 26).[160]

Rudolph Otto's account of the experience of the *numinosum* was so influential to Jung that "numinous" became a central organizing word for Jung's views on soul and religion and for his psychological formulations. What is the significance of the "numinous" for Jung in the history and development of Analytical Psychology? In an August 20, 1945, letter to a Mr. Martin, Jung wrote, "[T]he main interest of my work is not concerned with the treatment of neurosis but rather with the approach to the numinous. But the fact is that the approach to the numinous is the real therapy and inasmuch as you attain to the numinous experiences you are released from the curse of pathology" (p. 377).[161] Thus, he viewed the presence of the numinous as a dimension of religious experience and a key part of the healing process. For Jung, a numinous experience is synonymous with religious experience.

The *numinosum* became for Jung the foundation on which he constructed the remainder of his psychological theory. The cornerstone of Analytical Psychology is the archetype, the primordial universal patterns of energy inherent to all of humanity. For example, birth, death, father, mother, the hero, and the child are just a few of these common motifs of energy. A particular quality of the experience of an archetype is the feeling of numinosity that accompanies it. Psychologically, the experience of the archetype within the psyche is a numinous encounter and a manifestation of the divine. Often, these experiences move our hearts, compel our attention, and stir our depths. We need to be attentive in a qualitative way to this powerful energy that transcends our ego awareness. This encounter is occurring and influencing our ego consciousness to draw us toward our essence, in other words, to enlarge it and /or to defeat it. The summons is to inner "cooking," metabolizing, assimilating, and embodying this energy. This call to a deeper human interiority is a beckoning to finally grow up, a signaling to stand humbly and to make a contribution responsibly, with awakened awareness and compassionate presence, in this interactive evolving universe, and it's a stepping into the expansive horizon of this adventure of life, our unique journey. We are not the initiators of this inner dynamic. Numinous experiences are not ego crafted. Individuals who have had an encounter in dawn with Lady Underground, or another image of the Dark Feminine, describe this numinous sense. They also report what Jung notes about any archetype: It has a "specific charge" (par. 841);[162] it "either exercises a numinous or a fascinating effect, or impels to action" (par. 109);[163] it often intervenes "in the shaping of conscious contents by regulating, modifying, and motivating them" (par. 404);[164] and/or it has the character of revelation. A numinous experience is felt as a personal revelation; importantly, its significance may be accepted or rejected, as well as metabolized and integrated consciously within a wide range of degrees.

In birthing dawn, the encounter with Lady Underground (or some other image of the Dark Feminine) is an encounter within oneself in relationship to the *wholly Other*. As the numinous manifests in our life, the transcendent Other is experienced in some surprising, subtle way, or perhaps in an incredible, poignant way that transcends our ego's rational understanding. This undeniable experience is a rebirth in the psyche. It is not so much that the Other has "come in"; rather, the Other has already-always been within one's inner unfolding psychospiritual archetypal landscape. Through the numinous encounter with the Other, the soul experiences receiving the transpersonal energy (communication) consciously in one's body and being affected by the self-communication of the Other. It is like something is *happening* to the soul! The creative potential for life, the eternal seed of germination, has been already-always within, but the energy pattern has been unmediated, and thus inactive or undeveloped within a soul. However Lady Underground's *dark night of initiation* is activated in our journey, the evolving process includes rebirth and renewal in dawn.

The incarnational "encounter with the holy/Holy," that is, the archetypal energy that is experienced through the symbol of Lady Underground (also referred to as Lady of Wisdom, or Seat of Wisdom, as noted in Chapter One), is creatively depicted in numerous ways through the arts and the dreams of many. The poets, artists, and mystics give us a lens to view images that evoke the mysterious depths in the inner well of human experience. Each hears the murmur of the mystery's/Mystery's self-communication and responds through their own creative self-expression via the poem, painting, opera, dance, sculpture, theater, writing, and/or solitude. The power of image in the creative arts ignites the imagination, stimulates thought, provides enjoyment and pleasure for the soul, and is a gateway to encountering the mystery/Mystery. One such creative image of the Dark Feminine, which is potentially a door to the archetypal imagination and to a compassionate encounter with her in dawn of dark-night initiation, is the painting by Michael O'Neill McGrath, OSFS, of the Black Madonna called *Mary, Seat of Wisdom* (To see image, Google: www.trinitystores.com). Michael's painting flows from his interiority. His journey has been shaped and influenced ever since his first numinous encounter with the Black Madonna while being on pilgrimage in France and Spain several years ago. He painted the Black Madonna, *Seat of Wisdom,* along with a series of 12 others, after spending six months in solitude at a small monastery of Visitation nuns. While showing me *Seat of Wisdom* during an interview in his *Bee Still Studio* in Washington, D.C., he said, "Mary's blackness suggests a rich, fertile soil; a symbol of depth reflecting new beginnings and growth."

What are these new beginnings to which Michael makes reference? Lady Underground, Black Maria, Lady of Wisdom, is not a woman sitting passively on a throne. She is not an antiquated statue collecting dust in a cold damp crypt of the Chartres Cathedral. She is an alive, dynamic presence within the psyche of Michael, and alive in others, as she allures and inspires them toward their emerging soul essence, through the alchemical separation and extraction process of *dark-night initiation.* As Michael creatively incarnates her energy in his life and in his imaginings of her, he notes that he does so from a space of "not knowing and feeling relatively in the dark, even though I experience painting light out of the dark." Paradox, presence, and process are part of his way as an artist, which is akin to qualities of the energy of the Dark Feminine. There is a oneness between his solitude and his painting as he experiences the felt sense of "spirit/Spirit" take over. The brush, paints, and canvas have a life of their own in the dance of dawn that flows in the pliability of the body figures and the playful dance of vibrant color in his paintings.

Unlike Lady Underground on a throne in the crypt of Chartres, Michael's *Seat of Wisdom* is not on a throne. She is seated on a modern "simple" chair—a rocking chair—which he notes, "is reflective of her down-to-earth simplicity," or she is her essence, *She Who Is*! There is an emphasis on her inexhaustible, illuminating wisdom of heart. Lady Wisdom's self-communicating healing energy is a felt sense of being "held" in her dark, immense nurturing silence of nothingness in solitude. Dark silence of nothingness is not an absence of sound, but rather paradoxically it is a stillness that speaks. Gradually in dawn, in the depth of still dark nothingness, and almost as if nothing seemingly is happening, Lady Underground, who is one image of Seat of Wisdom, conveys a subtle, nurturing, empowering energy that forms us anew and summons us toward our essence. These more sublime interior spaces of darkness reveal a hidden hint of light that forms and strengthens us anew in our more authentic true nature. Rilke validates the value, gift, and wisdom of these interior spaces of darkness in the journey of individuation, in his poem, "You, darkness, of whom I am born" (p. 57).[165] And John of the Cross writes how within these experiences of darkness in dawn, Secret Wisdom awakens, empowers, and summons us to a wider vision of life, "How gently and lovingly you wake in my heart. . ." (p. 53).[166] Through Lady Underground's self-communication in dawn, the generative soul within us is liberated. Dream processing, various imaginal techniques including body-energy work, and other forms of inner soul work continue to be avenues she accesses in our conscious awakening, unfolding, and evolving. Dark Wisdom beckons us toward new vistas. In dawn, very gradually we are potentially drawn into a deeper interiority and a deeper inner communion. This dimension of human interiority is reflected in the theology and spirituality of St. John of the Cross and St. Teresa of Avila. We equally see this depth dimension of formation and this pioneering human potential reflected in the contemplative experience within the Jewish tradition of the Kabbalah, the contemplative black-light experience of the Sufi mystics, the practicing Buddhist experience in the notions of the void—the great silence, the Hindu mystical tradition, and the Chinese Wisdom tradition of Taoism.

Again, remember, the Black Madonna is one image of the presence of the Goddess as Wisdom. Dark-night initiation in the Dark Feminine is the overall process of Lady Underground-Wisdom summoning and forming a soul in one's more expanded embodied essence. To be initiated into her Dark-Feminine way is to experience the harsh reality of crucifixion from the ego's perspective. Psychologically, this crucifixion is the intense pull of the opposites experienced within the psyche. Throughout this time of agonizing suffering, Lady Wisdom functions as incomprehensible, secret, hidden, obscure, and yet loving "Other." The *Unknown She* is forming us anew in a way of knowing-by-not-knowing. The experiential continuing adult-education course of dark initiation is the symbolic womb experience of her black nothingness, which opens one to a horizon in dawn more than one can imagine. *In the still secret dark,* she is slowly awakening and summoning us to more of our true essence, which we consciously come to embody in dawn of night. Rather than oppressive dark, the phenomenon is subtly forming and inspiring us anew in quiet solitude in her generative ways. This insightful formation in wisdom is reflected in Rilke's poem about his value of darkness, which he realizes he was born from in life. In the lyrics, he expresses his love of darkness as more than his love of the flame, which, he considers, limits the world as it illumines only what it surrounds, barring the rest. Moreover, the wise poet observes that the dark accepts and includes all, which is also characteristic of Lady Underground. Rilke writes, "[T]he dark embraces everything; shapes and shadows, creatures and me, people, nations—just as they are." And finally, Rilke proclaims, "I believe in the night" (p. 57).[167]

For most of us, myself included, our genuine capacity and freedom to express that "I believe in the night" arises from a more enlarged vision that we are able to own only in retrospect because our inner soul work allows us to metabolize and integrate the separation and ordeal stages in twilight and midnight. And then, only further in the ongoing circumambulating process within dawn stage, through Lady Underground-Wisdom's (or some other expression of the Dark Feminine) self-communication, dreamwork, imaginal techniques, and inner soulful attending do we gradually begin to consciously understand and embody a wider horizon of the value, gift, and wisdom of night initiation. Blinded and pierced at first, we are undone and stripped naked, and only in hindsight do we discover and realize that *someone—totally Other,* beyond our ego's grasp, has been engineering our recreation. Within the confusion, bewilderment, messiness, and chaos of dark-night initiation, there is an *alive someone—a presence, totally Other,* bidding us toward a more expansive enlivened ensoulment! The *ancient hidden One of luminous black* is an *ever-present powerful One,* beckoning us into conscious incarnation. This *mysterious Other,* who has been a life-force catalyst in the night, is orchestrating a gradual interior makeover that outer, collective-reality-TV-show directors and producers could not even begin to imagine, comprehend, appreciate, or hear! Throughout the global overview of our journey, there has been an invisible presence, the *Unknown She,* who has been a container of all of our story, even parts of our life that seem unthinkable, unspeakable, and/or unacceptable because of unbearable wounding, loss, betrayal, angst, addictions, anger/rage, and/or trauma. Significant to night initiation is the encounter with the holy/Holy. However this occurs, if the healing numinous experience is integrated, one's perspective is broadened and subsequently one is freer to embody consciously a greater inner and outer spaciousness in one's journey with a deeper sense of identity, meaning, purpose, and direction. Lady Underground-Wisdom's summoning gaze is hidden in twilight and mid-night, but her *beholding presence* in dawn reflects a beckoning energy of benevolence, empowerment, and unconditional love. This is keenly reflected in John of the Cross's poetry *The Spiritual Canticle,* "When you looked at me your eyes imprinted your grace in me. . .and left in me grace and beauty. . . " (pp. 47-480),[168] and in *The Living Flame of Love,* "How gently and lovingly you wake in my heart, where in secret you dwell alone; . . .how tenderly you swell my heart with love" (p. 53).[169]

This awareness reflected in the poems of John of the Cross is also creatively portrayed in Michael O'Neill McGrath's, *Mary, Seat of Wisdom. Dark-night initiation* is not primarily *some thing or some event,* an impersonal darkness like an adverse disagreement, tense situation, or an afflicting, distressful condition, but *someone/Someone,* a numinous presence stirring and moving our depths and heart in an undeniable way. This encounter with this numinous *someone/Someone* who is hidden and unknown empowers the soul and, potentially, forever impacts and changes the course of one's life.[170] Within the expansive spectrum of potential human interiority, her extracting ways are through an overall darkness of going by a way of knowing by not knowing in the journey of transformation. Her "seduction" of love calls us to hell and back! There are multiple doses of symbolic death experiences to our shallow, arrogant self-confidence, our sense of ego control and will-direction, our power plays, our sly-fox moves in an attempt to "pull the wool over" another, our hidden agendas, and our attachments. This symbolic black night of death undercuts and demagnetizes our innocence, infantile affective sentimental life, narcissistic grandiosity, slippery rational compartmentalized defensive self-talk, suave manipulative games, wolf-in-sheepskin behavior, arrested development, patriarchal control moves, and wounds of origin. Through this progressive night of initiation and transformation, the conscious relationship with Lady Underground slowly develops by attentive soul work that nurtures the inner dialogue in the budding relationship with Black Maria (or some other image of the Dark Feminine). This conscious relating with Lady Underground is how she, as Lady Wisdom, becomes a *revealing presence* that forms, guides, and empowers our life, and liberates the generative soul within any one of us.

Value of Intentional Solitude

While there are many ways that this conscious relating is nurtured by individuals, *one* vital source is the experience of the practice of intentional solitude that is honored in various ways. Intentional solitude is *one* valid means to cultivate the dialogue of the ego-Self axis, in the language of depth psychology, or in the language of spirituality the soul-Divine communication. Attending this interchange is also a way to further the development of the inner dialogue with the Dark Feminine, which is one aspect of the Great Mother energy, and this archetype is one dimension of the Self. There has been a great deal of conscious expansion, individually and collectively, with the resurgence of the Goddess in the last 60 years. The progressive summons to journey into her "other side" within the deeper interior caverns of the psyche presents a soulful call and opportunity to bring forth a greater depth of her wisdom into the light of consciousness. *One way* this vocational summons to her deeper "other side," known in Jungian psychology as the Dark Feminine, can be nurtured and strengthened is through intentional solitude. Purposeful solitude is an opening to the *invisible world.* In ancient times, having a perduring attentiveness (solitude) to the mystery was both palliative and preventative, as it was used to heal fatigue and to prevent weariness. Solitude was also used as an oracle, as a way of listening to the inner self for instinctual and spiritual guidance, otherwise impossible to detect in the hubbub of daily life.[171] This was significantly brought home to me in a dialogue with Koka, the medicine man in the Bush of the Tongua people in Zimbabwe, noted in Chapter Two. I asked Koka how he maintained a balance in his life and how he knew how to be for people who came to him with various requests for healing. Koka's response was simple: "I go out, away from the village, sit in silence as a regular ritual within a circle that I have drawn on the ground in the center of the cornfield, beg the ancestors for inspiration, and wait in silence." I persisted in asking, "How long do you wait, and what do you eat or drink?" He smiled and said, "I do not drink or eat while in the circle. I'm fed by another means not seen by the physical eye." He points to his third eye. "I wait sometimes eight days and sometimes the ancestors talk to me sooner—like in one day (he laughs!). The guidance comes in an inner voice with a message I have not thought of before (he pauses). And many times, I receive a clue from a dream when I go to sleep in the circle." I was amazed, despite our distinct backgrounds and obvious diversity, at the depth of commonality that Koka and I shared about solitude.

Marietta, who was mentioned in Chapter Three, takes an hour at home in intentional solitude each morning in her created sacred space, which includes her image of the Dark Feminine, Lady of the Valley. She sometimes begins by recording her dreams from the night, and/or sits in silence, focused on an image, a felt feeling, or some unknown reality that is stirring in her body. Then Marietta breathes into her visualized image, her conscious feeling, or the unknown reality within her body, which she barely senses subtly moving but captures her attention. Marietta's process unfolds in silence as she is present to herself and what is arising within her. Eventually, she is simply present to her depths, and her depths to her, in silence. At the end of her hour she often writes in her journal as a way to further objectify her inner soul work. This has been her primary way that her relationship and inner dialogue with the Dark Feminine has unfolded in her inner descent/ascent in the journey of human interiority.

When he entered analysis, Thomas, was a 50-year-old Asian doctoral student in theology. When I think of Thomas, I think of a contemplative man of depth and presence who embodies the value of silence and solitude. He is one of the few people I have met who reflect the words of Lao Tzu (founder of Taoism) on the wisdom of silence: "Those who know, don't talk. Those who talk, don't know" (ch. 56).[172] As a young child of 4, Thomas daily accompanied his father to the family plot of land to attend to the crops. As they walked, his father held his hand and taught him a mindful, contemplative walking exercise. They began their walk when it was still dark and walked their way together into dawn, as it was cooler to be about their work on the land early in the morning. The mantra that they used as they walked one step at a time was, *I love you.* With each step one word was expressed. This contemplative practice became a deep part of Thomas's soulful way of being. Thomas is a man who has endured a depth of blacker-than-black dark night of the soul. He has known the crushing massacre and loss of his family through the horrifying atrocities of a country bombed and torn by war, and the hideous suffering and annihilation of soul, in being a prisoner of war. Thomas tends to his inner soul work. He has a daily practice of taking time in silence. Also, each day and often several times a day, Thomas took the staircase rather than the elevator at his residence on the fourth floor as he practiced his mindful contemplative walking exercise. While Thomas mindfully placed each foot on a step, he said one of the words from his mantra that his father taught him as a child. During his time of studies in the United States, he went through an inner descent and an outer struggle with an authority figure that was most trying. At the height of Thomas's dark night of trial, a significant turning point for him was a profound numinous experience that he had while walking the four flights of stairs to his residence. The following day he came for a session. As Thomas entered the consulting room, I could sense a depth in his quiet disposition. Silently, we nodded to each other in recognition of one another and then sat together in silence for some time. Then Thomas began to speak: "You know all that has been." He paused. Next, he started to tell me that a day earlier he was walking the stairs to his dwelling and doing so mindfully, one step at a time, saying the mantra *I love you*, as he had done so many times in his walking practice. Then Thomas's eyes filled as he struggled to speak and express, "As I took my last two steps and mindfully put my feet on the top floor, I heard within myself the words (Thomas paused, closed his eyes, then opened them, and began to struggle to say what he heard) *I love you, too*."

Words fall short and do not capture the felt depth of soul that Thomas attempted to convey about his numinous experience. Numinous religious experiences are often ineffable, and yet in our humanity it matters sometimes to experience affective soulful silent witnessing to what is essentially inexpressible. *Silence* arose within Thomas and between us in the interactive field. I empathetically, in silence, witnessed what was for Thomas an undeniable, soulful, heartfelt, emotional experience for him. Thomas was never the same. With resilient courage and integrity, he stood his ground and attended continuously to what he needed to deal with in his outer journey. In the ordinary of life, Thomas encountered and experienced the extra-ordinary.[viii]

The value of intentional solitude was also recently conveyed to me by Anne, an analysand who is retired and still very active in life at 80 years old. For Anne, solitude grounds and nurtures her soul. The form of her solitude is to go out into her backyard, sit in silence under the oak tree, and breathe in the fresh air while holding and sipping hot tea. At a certain point, she put her cup down and explained that her eyes close, and her focus on her breath takes her inward for about 45 minutes. "In this temenos," says Anne, "I connect with Sophia, who is dark and yet not oppressive. I'm present to more of my day and life because of this experience of solitude." There is *no one way* in regard to the form of solitude. What seems important is the conscious intentionality and the ongoing, potential impact solitude has for birthing and embodying the Dark Feminine in dawn and the opening to a fuller inexhaustible spectrum of the mystery/Mystery.

[viii] After completing his doctorate, Thomas returned to his country of origin. I wrote to him to ask his permission to share his experience. After five months, I had heard nothing. On the day that I began this section of the writing, I was moved, humbled, and surprised to receive an e-mail from him. He wrote that the grace of that day remains an eternal source of empowerment and gratitude for him, as he is present to and about his day-to-day life. I was very grateful, also, that Thomas gave his permission to write about this part of his process and story.

Ongoing Process In Dawn

Also, for all of us, there is never an arrival or completion in dawn, in intentional solitude, or in exhausting the unconscious! For Jung the individuation journey is a spiral process of an ongoing circumambulating around the center, the Self. Thus, the spiral journey is continuous even in dawn, as we experience greater interior freedom and open to a deeper capacity for awareness, presence, relatedness, and embodiment. Dawn encompasses an ever-emerging gradation of dimensions. In dawn we need to humbly remain open, keeping our soulful antennas up and receptive, inquiring to the underground sources of our distress or whatever is arising within us, which offers us unending opportunities to befriend the depths and grow in ensoulment.

Part of the continuing attentiveness to psyche and one's form of solitude is opening to the further potential of generative untapped energy that is hidden and bound up in the deeper pockets and caverns of the unconscious manifesting in the somatic unconscious through tensions, blocking postures, and interruptions in the flow of energy. Our very joints, muscles, tissue, cell receptors, proprioceptors, and membranes can be impacted by subtle, blocked, hindered, or prohibited energy flow in our bodies. Being attentive to the ongoing, unfolding, evolving journey in dawn is a challenge!

Time and again, we might "think" we are basically integrated, and yet anyone of us can be blind, naïve, inflated, and oblivious to the many signals from a controlling unconscious self-part that attempts to be heard and integrated. It is a loss, and in many cases a tragedy, that a self-part had to go "underground" in infancy, childhood, or adolescence. However, the greater tragedy would be that anyone of us would begin to gain insight into an unconscious, haunting self-part and would continue to perpetuate, over and over, the wounding of this psychic part through further reenactment. We can intellectually hold that we are for change, conversion, and transformation, and yet our underlying attitudes and behaviors reflect a stance of avoidance through the never-ending flight of an orientation toward the future. For all of us, it is easy to slide down the slope of rationalization and excuses in our mental compartmentalization of our behavior, which is supported often by an inner gremlin of lethargy who says, "Oh, wait until tomorrow, or another day!" Subsequently, through our perpetuating our woundedness, we further harm our imprisoned self-part and contaminate others with our shadow. These unconscious, deep-seated energies of an alienated or traumatized self-part will manifest usually in some form of a deeply buried, elusive, imprisoned, or self-defeating belief. This reality creates restriction in the flow of energy in the body and the human energy field, resulting in constricted emotions and adaptive defensive attitudes that further reinforce our misconception. These embedded energies, with which anyone of us can be overidentified, unconsciously define, effect, and limit our true soul essence. The deeply concealed energies impact our vision and experience of life; they haunt, sabotage, and prevent us from experiencing our true nature and our life more fully, as it really is. Our ongoing transformation is not outside of these unconscious, veiled, imprisoned self-parts, but rather this is precisely where some of our finest gold resides in our depths. It is here in the hidden recesses of our unconscious that our most vital and creative resources lie untapped. To compassionately unearth, metabolize, befriend, and consciously embody an autonomous wounded part is to open to a wider and deeper capacity of our soul essence and our ability to be a conduit for compassionate presence in our everyday world. Moreover, it is this exact buried, imprisoned energy that is the source and precise fertile "underground" that Lady Underground-Wisdom accesses in her call to any one of us in her summons to liberate the soul within us in our ongoing transformation in dawn. The conscious, expansive horizon of new psychospiritual dimensions in the journey in individuation emerges from the fertile, subtler grounds within us, including our blacker-than-black energy in the inner caverns of our depths. If we could realize the underside of these alienated, often traumatized, banished, shamed and despairing, split-off, charged self-parts, we would already begin to experience resurrection and the releasing of our generative soul within us!

Thus, being attuned to our sensory antennas and to the many ways our depths attempt to capture our attention in befriending our charged fertile "underground" is an ongoing summons in dawn. Unless we soulfully and compassionately deal with this energy, which is often represented in deeper, split-off self-parts that can manifest in unconscious, subtle, vague patterns of relating, compulsive attitudes and behavior, desires, fantasies, dreams, and/or somaticized symptoms, we will project this alive, unconscious energy, which is longing to be heard and integrated, onto our wives, husbands, partners, friends, analysands, clients, spiritual directees, students, co-workers, neighbors, congregations, and society to whom this energy does not belong at all. For this reason, Jung held that "[W]hen an inner situation is not made conscious, it happens outside, as fate" (par. 126).[173] Our wounds are our responsibility. Individuation does not occur in a vacuum. Jung often noted that individuation is not individualism. We are by our nature relational, and thus we do not individuate alone. "The unrelated human being lacks wholeness. . .and the soul cannot exist without its other side, which is always found in a 'You'" (par. 454).[174] Furthermore, for Jung, "Individuation does not isolate, it connects" (p. 504).[175] For any one of us, we cannot come home to embodying our true and essential nature by being an island. "One cannot individuate without being with other human beings. . . .Individuation is only possible with people, through people" (pp. 102-103).[176] Thus, the very process and experience of individuation opens us to a more expanded involvement and intimacy with others, the world, and the whole of the interactive cosmos.

In reflecting on both Jung's observations as well as listening to our instinctual wisdom, birthed from our inner soul work, we come to realize that others and life can mirror and stir our soul's swamplands. We meet ourselves in a thousand different disguises on the road of life and especially in and through relating with one another and reflecting on our experience. For all of us, as we interact with one another, unconscious self-parts can become constellated in the interactive field. However, it is not another's task to do our soul work or to be burdened by our unconscious, infantile, unmetabolized needs, which we refuse to carry, to bear that cross, and to do the necessary psychological work to integrate the deeper splinter parts. For each of us, the summons of individuation obliges us to endure the unavoidable suffering of the conflict inherent in our core essential nature. The issue is not that we have these splinter self-parts. The concern is that these unconscious autonomous charged parts would own and drive us. These self-parts are not the whole of us. They are a part of us. They had to go underground because the reality of life was such that there was no parental figure who had enough time or attentive emotional awareness and presence, given their own flaws and wounds, family and cultural circumstances, demands of life, and/or crisis, to hear and give us the necessary mirroring or the empathy to be seen, heard, attended to in a felt, caring way, and to help us metabolize what was perhaps wanting, distressing, frustrating, overwhelming, and/or wounding for us. Energy that has not been metabolized and assimilated consciously does not evaporate or cease to exist; it goes unconscious. Any one of us can have a split-off self-part, and/or a traumatized part that is three, six, or nine years old, *et cetera*, as well as a repressed self-part that is still adolescent. Again, it is important for all of us to realize that the issue is not that any one of us has a splinter unconscious part, but that an unconscious part would have us and drive us in our relationship to ourselves, others, Other, work, and life. Also, it is key for all of us to remember that there is no such thing as perfect parents or the perfect family system. The countless variables that impact a marriage, parenting, and family life can be complex. Most parents have done the best they could, given their psyche and their inherited family, historical experiences, and cultural milieu. With this being noted, everyone suffers some degree of psychic scarring, including a mother and/or father wounding. Also, there are unequivocally others who endure various forms of impoverishment and/or abuse due to the lack of healthy, supportive parenting and the complexity of cultural variables and oppressive realities of discrimination and alienation. Subsequently, these individuals will have more activated wounds in their psyches to process, assimilate, and integrate in the journey of healing and becoming whole. This is especially true if more of the death instinct, Thanatos energy as opposed to Eros, the life instinct, was activated in the psyche of an individual in his/her familial, historical, and cultural milieu. If the Death Mother (Medusa Complex—critical, judgmental, devouring mother; some examples are the female president played by Meryl Streep in the movie, *The Giver*, or the mother in the contemporary movie, *Brooklyn*, the mother of Camille in the animated film, *Leap*, or Lady Macbeth in Shakespeare's play), and/or the Death Father complex (Cronus-Saturn Complex-devouring, dominant father; one example is the father in the movie, *Dead Poet's Society*) has been constellated in one's psyche, the depth of inner work that will be required to consciously unearth the horrendous defensive structure, paralysis, fixation, destructive power force, and bondage will be immense. Regardless of our family backgrounds and our historical and culture experiences, all of us are wounded to some degree, as we have grown and developed within an evolutionary quantum world that is flawed and marked by shadow. Nonetheless, we are *more* than our history.

As various cellular repressed memories of shadow energies are befriended, both the ego and one's container become stronger. Subsequently, one is able to do inner soul work with deeper, well-guarded, dissociated, shamed, wounded, and/or traumatized younger and/or adolescent self-parts. These latter self-parts take an incredible amount of psychic energy and perduring attentiveness for the shift and integration in consciousness to occur so that we may incarnate more of the depth and breadth of our true essence.

The value of body-energy work is essential in birthing these deeper caverns of the soul if the treasure of great value is to be unearthed, discovered, and unleashed. Even if one has done major inner psychospiritual soul work with the adolescent or some other self-part in the overall twilight and midnight of Lady Underground's dark-night initiation, one can still find oneself in an ongoing way being summoned to circumambulate in what is yet another unknown, deeper, and subtler inner swampland terrain on the journey of transformation in dawn. The roots of inner wounding stretch deep, and in direct relationship to this depth is the potential rich harvest of befriending and liberating generative dimensions of the diamond of one's soul, for any one of us and for those we are called to serve in the outer world. We never exhaust the unconscious, or any aspect of the depths that the inexhaustible mystery/Mystery can summon us to befriend. Usually, the same issues and complexes are being addressed again that were befriended in earlier growth. However, now there seems to be a deeper psychic dimension being encountered at a level not known before. Time and again, we can regress into a fantasy and can engage in magical thinking that someone else is going to be the spark of life, the fun, the reward, or the answer to our angst, restlessness, loneliness, and sometimes depressed soul. This ungrounded magical thinking, which is rather short-lived, due to the lack of embodied consciousness, is reflected in the contemporary film, *Into The Woods,* in which an unconscious, romantic *puer* prince encounters the unaware, shallow baker's wife and flirtatiously flits around in their exchange. Both are still looking on the outside to find in another that which can only come from within one's depths through one's personal inner soul work. Even in dawn of dark-night initiation, any one of us at times can engage in a hurry-up mentality of magical thinking. There are no real shortcuts for the ego in the life-death-rebirth cycle of inner soul work. Dawn is never a dimension of consciousness having arrived. Coming home is an ongoing journey.

Befriending Deeper Depths In Ongoing Dawn

While the path home is unfolding continually, nevertheless for any one of us, even if we are very accomplished individuals who are chronologically in our forties, fifties, sixties, seventies, or eighties, can even now still look to the outside for what can only come from within. For all of us, we can have an unconscious self-part that is longing, looking, and wanting a particular need to be met from an "other" and/or "others." We fail to realize that, in the process of our desire being projected, we often unconsciously objectify the "other" and/or "others." We all realize that eros is the life force imbuing all of creation. Desire is core to our nature. The erotic arises naturally toward relationality and deepens in the conscious relational domain. Mature relationships can enrich our souls with enjoyable companionship, possible sexual intimacy, enlivening spiritual sharing, stimulating intellectual conversation, and at times encouragement and affirmation. However, for all of us, it is also of value to remember that as we progress in incarnating consciously, through the ongoing life-death-rebirth cycle of the ever-evolving dawn of our life, our relational capacity, and especially our vivifying erotic energy, can have a shadow aspect, just as any other dimension of our life can have a shadow component.

For example, *one* aspect that often can manifest for anyone of us is an *unconscious*, wounded, affective, young, split-off self-part arising within us and experienced as charged eroticized energy because the very human *need* for the young unmet fundamental longing for greater emotional and physical intimacy was deficient due to a lack of parental affective mediating and empathetic mirroring presence. This autonomous, unconscious, splinter self-part tends to have some hidden, conclusive, self-deprecating belief created by us, usually in reaction to early infant/childhood (or even adolescent) pain and the perceived limitation of our parents or significant parental figures. The internalized, unconscious, false or self-limiting belief squelches, restricts, or blocks the energy flow in the electromagnetic field and in the body, resulting in constricted emotions and shielding attitudes that further support our perceiving or misperceiving our surroundings. Consequently, this energy of the split-off self-part tends to be charged. It is like an unconscious attachment hunger within us that longs for connection. This strong autonomous energy reveals itself through the body, through an attachment, an impulse, acting out, and/or in very subtle, vague, diffuse, and sometimes shrewd ways that keep the deep-seated energy locked and concealed in the underground. Even when we become conscious of this self-part, the journey in the battle from an unconscious attitude of a *no* current of energy moving within us to a *yes* current of energy pulsating within us involves a perduring attentiveness to the inner and outer psychic life, requiring a great deal of inner-soul work in befriending this underground, imprisoned self-part.

Sometimes individuals assume and think that all highly charged eroticized energy that stirs within us and is constellated and sensed with another is to be pursued and acted on as a relationship that is magically "meant to be," rather than consciously holding, having an inquiry, unearthing, metabolizing, discerning, and integrating the energy arising within them. For example, consider having an inquiry about the erotic energy that is arising within you in which you probe and reflect on the psychic content activated by the erotic attraction that stirs interest in an actual other. Furthermore, ponder having an inquiry about your sexual fantasy triggered by the erotic attraction in a real other and what your fantasy might reveal psychologically about yourself. What is perhaps the hidden alive psychic material evoked by the erotic attraction that is trying to get your attention and summoning you to more conscious development and embodied maturity? What is the allurement in your erotic attraction? How might you work with this inner psychic material? Who could you be honest with and discuss this psychic material that is arising within you and engaging your fantasy and attention? We meet our depths on the stage of life in a thousand different disguises on the journey, and especially in the other. Just because we experience this arousing libido and constellated "chemistry" with an actual other doesn't mean that the energy is one to be acted on with another.

We can only gradually honor and embody our generative transformed desire and healthy sexuality by first honestly facing and befriending any undifferentiated form that anyone of us may possess. Then, through inner soul work, we can begin to gradually discriminate consciously our natural instinctual pleasure from the painful charged reality activated in infancy, childhood, and/or perhaps adolescence. We do this by circumambulating around the deep inner recesses of the caverns of our soul as we uncover the original infantile, childhood, and/or adolescent pain concealed within the charged erotic energy arising within us, within distorted beliefs about intimacy and sexuality, within our blind, distorted perception of the other as object, within our loveless sexual fantasy, and/or within sexual expressions charged with undercurrents of masochism and/or sadism. We cannot dismiss and sweep under the carpet any shadow aspect around this issue and minimize the essential task of consciously bearing and enduring the psychic inner battle that needs to be faced in the journey toward freedom. Consciously doing the necessary inner soul work makes a meaningful difference for the individual, for the other and/or others with whom one is in relationship, and ultimately for the collective and the planet. When any one of us attends to this deep, obscure, shrouded pain, feels and expresses the energy, releases it from the neuromuscular system and electromagnetic field, and metabolizes consciously the core initial pain that had been covered over and sexualized, then we advance the extrication and differentiation of our imprisoned desire and genuine gift of sexuality, from charged currents of, perhaps, a mother, father, or power complex, and/or of trauma, masochism, or sadism without losing the natural essence of our lush, hot, erotic sexual enjoyment!

Lady Underground-Wisdom is not outside of this process. She is summoning us all the way to recover and to reclaim the whole of who we are, including our conscious, natural, erotic desire and healthy sexuality, and to liberate and embody generatively the ever-widening realization of our creative core essence! Most of us have not been educated about the quest toward our soul's homecoming, including the conscious embodiment of desire and sexuality, especially our erotic desire and healthy sexuality, and yet we do have a conscious responsibility for our energy. For all of us in the journey of individuation, attending to conscious relationship calls us to work on both the outer relationship and the inner psychic content.

In a lecture (at Mount Sinai Medical Center, New York City) titled "*Responding to the Erotic Transference,*" adapted from "*Countertransference and the Erotic,*" Ann Belford Ulanov noted that "[C]onsciousness is our protection against falling into the soup with our patients" (p. 109),[177] also our clients, spiritual directees, parishioners, neighbors, and coworkers. We all as clinicians, spiritual directors, chaplains, those serving in a helping occupation/ministry, leaders in any professional form, and/or adults seeking conscious psychospiritual growth need to be aware of our eros experience. This requires ongoing inner work for any one of us, including me. There are times in our eros experience that we need to remember the wisdom of Jung when he reflects "that the least amongst them all, the poorest of all beggars, the most impudent of all offenders, yea the very fiend himself [herself]—that these are within me and that I myself stand in need of the alms of my own kindness, that I myself am the enemy who must be loved. . .," or otherwise, we are "merely an unconscious fraud" (par. 520-521).[178] There is a wide range in the gradation of our erotic desire from our arousing alive libido to consciously befriending and embodying the flame of love as revealed in John of the Cross's poem, *The Dark Night:*

> One dark night,
> fired with love's urgent longings
> ah, the sheer grace!
> I went out unseen,
> My house being now all stilled (p. 50). [179]

Ulanov further keenly observed that eros is the function of psychic relatedness; however, relatedness, as libido with instinctive backing, is not equivalent and does not mean conscious relationship. The latter requires conscious participation with an evolving growth in soulful feeling toward one another in the interactive communication in an unfolding and developing conscious relationship. The former urges one to connect, reach out, get involved, and invest libido whether this is in others, projects, causes, or pursuits. Regardless of how the energy is constellated for anyone of us, the fire stirrings of psychic relatedness "may initiate erotic embodiment in connection with another person, with one's God, with what conveys to us the loving of life, and the transpersonal source and value of it" (p. 107).[180] Furthermore, the conscious befriending of this energy through soulful inner work opens us to a deeper embodiment and more of the potential and fuller incarnation of our essence, and potentially a compassionate wisdom and soulfully a keener discriminating and discerning capacity in our inner psychic life and our outer human relating, including our service to others.

Again, the issue is not the erotic energy in and of itself or even us having a shadow dimension to our erotic energy. The concern is our shadow having us, driving us, and burdening others with our unconscious aspects that are material for our inner soul work. We live in a quantum evolving universe with all of creation endowed with erotic intentionality. Our pulsating fire of desire can be avenues that Dark Lady Wisdom accesses in our ongoing transformation in shaping and recreating us anew in being grounded in our bodies in the here and now with a greater capacity to be *present* to one's self, others, and all of life. A practical aspect of our intentional solitude in our growth toward grounded consciousness is the summons to being with the question of how to live with this lush, pleasurable, joyful energy and to do so with conscious responsibility and ethical awareness. The seeds of our dark shadow, which are imprisoned in the cellular depths of our being remain unconscious, and take time—a long time in realizing and befriending the energy for a higher good and the enlargement of consciousness. Psyche summons, and through one's form of solitude, dreamwork, and imaginal techniques of inner soul work, one can pay attention to the dimensions of shadow energy that are attempting to be heard and integrated, while realizing that we never exhaust the unconscious. Birthing and embodying insightful wisdom and empathetic presence is generated from the deeper depths of inner soul work. The particulars of this process in being formed in the secret Dark Lady of Wisdom throughout night initiation is unique for each person summoned by this archetypal energy. However, there is, in general, an overall sense of growth in incarnating a fuller spectrum of one's enlivened nature, bodily wisdom, and compassionate presence in the journey of individuation. Thus, dawn of dark night is opening to the enlargement of embodied consciousness within the relational network of universal life in the here and now. This deeper growth in awareness expresses itself in our vivifying way of being, relating to others and all of cosmic life, and our vocational path.

Value of Witnessing Religious Experience

The creative arts portray various aspects of the wisdom of these deeper levels of night, including in dawn, as we have seen in some of the previously noted examples in this chapter. However, oftentimes people are reluctant to speak of their experiences, given the humbling, intimate, and ineffable nature of the numinous visitations. We are not educated for darkness, especially the more sublime dimensions of darkness, as reflected in various gradations of contemplation. Subsequently, because we lack experience, and/or some informative awareness about these deeper psychospiritual levels, we sometimes are deficient in our ability to maintain an attuned presence, respect, and capacity for holding the *temenos* for another's sharing of soulful realities, especially experiences of the "encounter with the holy" in rites of initiation. In the analytical relationship, or in any soulful relationship, "witnessing" another's numinous experience, as well as any aspect of a soul's journey has great psychospiritual value. Inner spaciousness and greater inner freedom can arise within a person when one is heard, understood, and seen in a deeply felt, empathic way. Witnessing is an archetypal experience that assists self-development. Because of this occurrence for a soul, the potential within can arise to open to a deeper capacity for a perduring attentiveness to the mystery/Mystery in the ongoing psychospiritual journey toward individuation.

This was true in the case of Maureen, a 52-year-old, tall, attractive physician, who has known dark-night initiation. Maureen is a gifted woman with a quiet, passionate manner and a generous, compassionate heart; she is widowed and a mother of an only daughter. While Maureen is a musician and an artist, her primary professional training was as a neurosurgeon and transplant physician. Being highly specialized, she had lived her life for several years responding to the calls of a hospital beeper. Twelve years ago, she resigned from her active practice in order to care for her dying husband, who was also a physician. The years that followed were a dark night of initiation in the Dark Feminine for Maureen. A significant turning point came because of a dream she had had of an unknown black woman whom she described as being numinous in character and a modern-day Black Madonna of Wisdom:

> I'm in the center of the floor in a round auditorium. A black woman of great inner strength and benevolence enters the auditorium and stands right in front of me. She begins singing a slow, methodical, and very beautiful love song. She sang the song standing while I was on the floor at her feet. I was deeply moved. The music was so sweet, so very sweet, that I began to cry. She seemed to know me and seemed to know that I liked the song. When she finished, she looked down straight into my face and eyes, smiled, and held me with her gaze.

As Maureen slowly told her dream, we entered a space of silence together for a few minutes. The tears rolled down Maureen's face as she spoke of the deeply felt sweetness of the song, the loving tone of the woman's voice, and the numinous presence. She said that she felt as if a sacred ointment of consolation had touched her depths. What was ineffable for Maureen was any attempt to describe the contemporary Black Madonna of Wisdom's look into Maureen's face and eyes and the effect of the gaze on her being. Maureen recounted the very beautiful love song and how, after the dream, she wrote the musical notes that she had heard within her being. For a long time, she played the love lyrics on her piano as a refrain ritual when she did her inner soul work in her growth process. Maureen's dark night of initiation, guided by her personal experience of this modern-day Black Madonna of Wisdom, was a journey from an overdeveloped one-sidedness of rational thinking to consciously experiencing feeling worthy, receptive, and responsive in her body as an adult woman. She experienced an inner renewal as she opened to the generative love of the Dark Feminine. Maureen's dream awakened her toward developing a conscious relationship with Lady Wisdom. Her attentive contemplative practice, soulful inner work of various imaginal techniques, including painting, and her analysis were avenues in her opening to a generative, more expanded, embodied consciousness. Today, Maureen's journey continues to unfold and evolve. She has discovered that her dark night of initiation in the Dark Feminine gradually opened her to sensing and experiencing a wider dimension of intimations of the invisible mystery/Mystery within her, in her relationships, everyday living, and service in her local community.

In dawn, a soul not only encounters the holy/Holy but is empowered with the fire of Lady Underground's spirit. Potentially, this experience is a dance of expansive awareness and empowerment as we open to a wider resonance of her revealing presence and her self-communicating wisdom. This enlivening energy releases the flow of long-held unconscious energy for living and life. The lens with which we view our inner and outer landscapes is forever changed by the dawn of Black Maria-Wisdom's spirit of immense benevolent love. This dance of liberating the soul within us to a whole new resonance of consciousness with love in dawn is dynamically portrayed in Michael O'Neill McGrath's, OSFS, painting of the Black Madonna, *Our Lady of Light* (To see the image, Google: www.wlp.jspaluch.com/373.htm). The energy is also reflected in John of the Cross's *Living Flame of Love*: "How gently and lovingly you wake in my heart. . .," and further, ". . .how tenderly you swell my heart with love" (p. 53).[181]

We now proceed to consider the last stage, the "return," in Lady Underground's dark-night rite of initiation. This final stage of formative renewal in our being recreated in a more expanded sense of our true soul essence is a significant part of our transformation in being formed in the energy of the Dark Feminine. As we begin to explore this last stage, we recall the wisdom with which we began this chapter; that is, all our questioning, seeking, knowing, desiring, and loving are sustained and drawn by a source that always remains unknowable and exceeds our finite grasp. Living the challenge of the everyday conscious embodiment of the wisdom of the progressive dance of dawn remains very practical and down to earth, as was noted in Chapter Three. For anyone of us, we would do well to remember the wisdom of the Zen Buddhist proverb, in our day of development before Lady Underground's dark night of initiation: "Chop wood, carry water." During twilight and midnight of dark-night initiation, it is "chop wood, carry water." In the progressive challenge of embodying the dance of dawn, we choose to show up in life even with all of life's engaging and varying dimensions, and we attempt to be present consciously in the journey of "chop wood, carry water." There is no retirement from "chop wood, carry water!" What is different through the process of dark-night initiation is the soul's *consciousness* and *meaning* with which we "chop wood, carry water" in the ordinary everydayness of our life. The *consciousness* and *meaning* broadens, empowers, and sustains us toward our soul's destiny. With the experience of Lady Underground's dark night of initiation in the Dark Feminine, we open to living a more expanded, consciously incarnated life, connected and supported by the ongoing ego-Self dialogue, or in the language of spirituality, the soul-Divine dialogue. Even as the deepening in interiority occurs, we still continue the journey of attuned, discerning attentiveness to the intimations of the mystery/Mystery, however this self-communication emerges as we are about living our ordinary, everyday lives, responding to the summons of our vocations.

When more of Lady Underground's energy is metabolized and incarnated, there is a natural effect on all with which we relate. Embodied consciousness impacts the interactive field. This reality is part of the fundamental theory of quantum physics, as noted in Chapter Two. This is the conscious reality that is so needed in our 21st century if our interconnective world is to know a deeper, evolving, interiority and awareness. Chapter Two addressed this call, need, and challenge of the new paradigm to make a deeper descent/ascent in the night sea journey to bring forth a more expanded, incarnated consciousness and an emerging, unfolding, embodied wisdom to our planet. Hence, Lady Underground-Wisdom ushers in a greater emphasis on the importance of presence, process, and allowing the opposites to coexist creatively in the journey of consciously incarnating individuation. Today, given the intense polarization in our country and the global community, more than ever there is a need for the conscious journeyer to seek balance in the psyche by bearing the suffering of the tension of the opposites inherent in one's depths. Honoring and embodying consciously Lady Wisdom's energy offers us a deeper, broader, and more grounded, holistic way of perceiving the night sea journey within the creative complexity of our evolving cosmos.

The Return

The last stage of Lady Underground's dark-night initiation in the Dark Feminine is *the return*. The journey inward is never in and for oneself. Black Maria-Wisdom's dark night of initiation summons us back into the human circle with greater consciousness, responsibility, and humble service. Lady Wisdom's call to conscious living is embodying spirit/Spirit in the ordinary of our daily life within the comprehensive Earth-community.

To offer perspective on this last stage of Lady Underground's dark night of initiation, we turn to Analytical Psychology's rich resource, the world of fairy tales, and specifically to the tale of the *Black Nubian Woman*. Sir Laurens van der Post, a longtime friend of Carl Jung, recorded this tale in one of the volumes of fairy tales that he collected from the Kalahari, (now most commonly called "the San") of South Africa. Sir Laurens had always been fascinated by the aboriginal inhabitants of Southern Africa. In 1957, he led an expedition over the Kalahari Desert in search of the remnants revealing the account of this unique people. *The Lost World of the Kalahari* consists of eight cassettes containing Sir Laurens van der Post's interviews and descriptions of the circumstances, customs, mores, rituals, and fairy tales that chronicle the remarkable survivors of an ancient world. The fairy tale of the *Black Nubian Woman* was told to Sir Laurens van der Post[ix] by a Zulu wise man in Africa. Sir Laurens, in his lectures and conferences, often retold the fairy tale as an offering of gratitude, respect, and honor to the Dark Feminine, as he felt that this world was losing its spiritual identity to modern technology, prejudice, empty values, and a lack of realization of the relational dimension of all life. Old fairy tales often address the subject of making the journey in life, transformation, and of how one finds the courage to make the voyage and

[ix]Sir Laurens van der Post was born in 1906 in the interior of Southern Africa. He lived among the people who created the first blueprint for life on Earth, becoming the main chronicler of the Stone Age Kalahari Bushmen. He was also one of Jung's closest friends for 19 years. Van der Post dedicated his life to teaching the meaning and value of indigenous cultures in the modern world. He was concerned that this world was in danger of losing its spiritual identity to modern technology, prejudice, empty values, and a lack of understanding of the interconnectedness of all life on earth. Sir Laurens was awarded knighthood in 1981. He died after his 90th birthday in December 1996.

prevail against overwhelming odds. Such tales were passed down through the generations by oral tradition, using archetypes as a mirror held to daily life. While no one tale can reflect all of the dimensions of the universal basic patterns that are available for the growth of the self in the human journey, we can gain some insight into some recognizable themes of human life by exploring a tale in which an Ancient Wise One gives some grounded direction about the return phase in dark-night initiation. We turn now to consider the wisdom of the last stage of initiation in the Dark Feminine, from the perspective of an old tale, because we have all set off into unknown woods or into deep, unaccustomed waters at one point or another and have had the need to find our way back to the circle of conscious living. In the words of Lisel Mueller's *Why We Tell Stories*, it's ". . .because we had survived. . . , we discovered bones that rose from the dark earth and sang. . .because the story of our life becomes our life" (pp. 150-151).[182]

The Return: Tale of the Black Nubian Woman

The Black Nubian Woman deals with primordial universal human themes that draw their inspiration and power from the archetypal world that is common to people of all traditions, cultures, and times. The people of South Africa and other parts of the world have many versions of this valuable tale. The images and their meaning in each culture may differ slightly; however, beneath these nuances are the central themes of descent/ascent, initiation, and individuation. In this tale, a beautiful African woman who maintained herself well and who was of generous heart but naive has been duped by a group of jealous women from her village into a well-meant-but-foolish act, as a result of which the heroine finds herself in the chaotic situation of having lost what is most valuable to her, namely, her necklace. In Africa, a necklace is reflective of significant feminine values, and a necklace of a particular woman reveals something of her soul's unique identity and giftedness. The jealous women had banded together in a plot to humiliate and to reject the Nubian Woman. The envious ones perceived the Nubian Woman to be "different" because she valued solitude and took time to be alone, and time to be with others, but mainly because her necklace of exquisite beads seemed to them to be more beautiful than their necklaces.

As the tale unfolds, the jealous ones who are gathered on the river's shore see the Nubian Woman coming and say, "Come on, be like us, and throw your necklace into the river." Desiring acceptance and inclusion in the group, the Nubian woman was tricked by the other women, lured into throwing her special necklace into the river as an offering to the river, which they claimed that they had done with their necklaces. The naïve woman readily does this, and then the group begins to laugh mockingly and maliciously at the deceived woman, as they pull their hidden necklaces out of the sand, and then run off to the village. The sad, distraught, stricken Nubian Woman wanders along the riverbank, alone and in tears, realizing what she had done. In her great loss, she cries out three times to the river, hoping somehow that her necklace would wash ashore. As she searches, a growing sense of weariness and desolation comes over her. Time passes, and there is no necklace and no response to her calling out to the river. Then she hears from within a voice summoning her to plunge into the deep, unknown, dark river. She obeys the voice at once, and without hesitation, she leaps and dives into the river's depths.

The Black Nubian Woman's journey takes her to the bottom of the riverbed. There, she encounters an unknown Ancient Woman with repulsive, open sores, and through her experience with the Old One, the Nubian Woman discovers her inner, grounded, unique, feminine core, her essence, beauty, and empowerment for her unique path. This Old One is another image of the Dark Goddess. The Ancient, Ever-Present Woman summons the Black Nubian Woman: "Come and lick my sores." Unlike her earlier response to the directives of the outer collective by relinquishing, foolishly, what was most valuable to her, now the Black Nubian Woman hears the call of the inner voice and responds soulfully with a heart that is open, receptive, and responsive. This woman of generous, compassionate heart is so moved by the horrific plight of the Old One that she lets go of her agenda and obeys the request of the Old One. This touches the Old Lady and leads her to bestow upon the Nubian Woman her original necklace, now adorned with additional, even more phenomenal, exquisite beads and gems that makes the necklace more valuable than the original one given by her family. Moreover, the Ancient One anoints the Nubian Woman's forehead with the finest hippopotamus fats, strips her of her old garb, and clothes the woman anew in beautiful attire. And, from then on, the Old One promises to protect the younger woman, especially from the devouring monster at the bottom of the river.

After that, the Eternal Wise One instructs the woman regarding her return journey and the direction for her soul's way of being in life. The Old One looks into the eyes of the Woman, saying to her, "After you ascend from the depths to the riverbank, regardless of whatever occurs, do not look back, but fetch a round stone in the path a short distance from the river and pick it up. Then, after taking some time to pause, which is essential, and remembering not to look back, heave the round stone over your left shoulder and into the river so that it will return to me. Next, begin walking slowly and steadily until you meet someone who will give you water to drink. When you drink the water, drink deeply, then you will be more able to live your everyday life with greater clarity. Finally, my dear friend, continue on your path home and resume your ordinary life in your village." Then the Wise Old Woman from the bottom of the deep, dark river gives the Nubian Woman a final blessing; she says to her, "Go slowly."

Upon her return to the village, the Nubian Woman meets the jealous ones, who immediately inquire about her magnificent necklace. The Woman tells them, but before she could warn them about the devouring monster at the bottom of the river, they run off in haste, eager for a valuable, magnificent necklace from the Old One, too. But when the Old Lady asks them to lick her sores, they refuse her, disgusted. They laugh at the Old Woman, demanding to be given necklaces at once. Then, unseen in the midst of all this, comes the monster, which devours them all.

The directives for the return in the last part of this tale are now our focus as we reflect on the final stage of initiation in the Dark Feminine. The time came for the Nubian woman, as for all who make a descent into the depths, to ascend and to return to the circle of life and to be about her daily, ordinary tasks, relationships, and vocational destiny within the interactive web of the evolving universe. Whatever the path may be for the woman of the tale and for all who embody the Dark Feminine, the summons and responsibility to listen to the intimations of the mystery/Mystery and to guidance from within, to take time in solitude to do one's soul work, to reflect on one's experience, and to discriminate and discern what is essential, to have the courage to be one's unique self, and to be about humble service through one's vocation is a daily challenge. We become responsible to show up and to be present to, in an ensouled way, what we have become aware of through our inner journey.

Encountering the Dark Feminine—the Old One and the Black Nubian Woman

After the depth experience with the Ancient Woman, the Black Nubian Woman could never think of herself in the same way. Because of the healing, heartfelt, transformative encounter between the Ancient Wise Woman and the generous, compassionate Nubian Woman, the heroine emerges from the descent into the dark depths with a deeper, embodied interiority. The Black Nubian Woman is now a changed woman. In recalling the initial details and dynamics of the tale, we realize that to bravely attend to the wounds and scars of the Ancient Woman is to give birth to the mending and healing process of what is ancient in her and in all of us. For we realize that the Old One with the repulsive open sores is an image with a twofold dimension: She represents the contempt for, and the inadequate acknowledgement of, the evolved spectrum of the energy of the feminine principle in our many cultures and civilizations; she also signifies, at the personal level, our most despised, rejected, shamed, traumatized, and dissociated parts of our psyche. Hatred and repression of the feminine impacts and wounds *all* women, men, children, and the Earth herself. This horrific wound and its shadow symptoms are manifest in all institutions of societies, cultures, and the global planet. When the Nubian Woman, or anyone of us, addresses this issue and works on these personal and ancient, deep wounds to the soul, we each effect, in a very small, minute way, the larger, interconnected, creative design of cosmic life pulsating within each of us and the whole of the interactive field in the evolving, global world.

So we see that through progressive, inner soul work, the protagonist's growth process, at the personal level, proceeds from a distorted self-perception, impacted by naïvete, emotional depravation, and outer adaptation to collective values and expectations to an emerging, embodied consciousness with a more expanded awareness of her true soul essence and of her summons to be about her vocation in her everyday life. Perhaps our heroine's initial way of being resulted from inadequate empathic parental mirroring, socio-economic historical factors, and/or cultural injustices and oppression. The courageous Woman's commitment to the inner soul work, which involved processing, metabolizing, and integrating deep, dark-seated shadow work with the Old One, was significant to the Woman's emerging soul essence. Exhausting as the soul work is because of the energy it takes to deal with our split-off pain, the only way out of the black nothingness and emptiness of the swamplands of the soul is through bearing and befriending the dreaded, charged, unbearable wounds and "sores." There are no shortcuts! Furthermore, in the return, there is no retiring, having arrived, and/or sitting on one's laurels! The inner work is ongoing throughout life. The Black Nubian Woman's psychospiritual identity was expanded because she consciously suffered and befriended the process of her dualities. The Nubian Woman arises from the depths with a self-esteem and an inner identity that's grounded in her instinctual wisdom, her soul having been nurtured, anointed, guided, protected, and empowered by the loving spirit of the Ancient One. Because of her transformative inner work in her relationship with the Old One, the Nubian Woman ascends with greater inner freedom and attunement to the murmur of the mystery/Mystery from both within and without.

As we center our attention more deeply on the return, we have to wonder about what exactly transpired in the encounter between the two that augmented such a shift in consciousness in the Black Nubian Woman who was thereafter forever changed. Prior to her descent, the Nubian Woman experienced the chaos of loss, grief, and despair. What once had seemed to have energy for her no longer holds true. Raw reality quickens consciousness. The Nubian Woman is emptied of her attachments to shallow, insubstantial realities and deceptive relationships that were devoid of depth and meaning. Her false suit of clothes and armor of defense are positively disintegrating. She is at an impasse in the dark night of her psychospiritual journey. It is precisely in this interior dark-night space of blacker-than-black nothingness and emptiness that the Old One summons the suffering Black Nubian Woman to attend to and deal consciously with the repulsive "sores." She does not deny, avoid, or take flight from the Ancient One, but rather is receptive, surrenders, and gives herself to the call. James Hollis, an internationally known Jungian analyst, describes well this challenge: "It is in the swamplands where soul is fashioned and forged, where we encounter not only the *gravitas* of life, but its purpose, its dignity and its deepest meaning" (p. 9).[183]

Healing Path To Wholeness: Opening to the Inner Wellspring

From a Jungian perspective, the Nubian Woman's suffering is due to her neurosis, her suffering soul, which had not yet realized its meaning. The Woman's neurosis is her one-sidedness and defense against the pain of the "sores," wounds of life, traumas, and meaninglessness. Her conscious facing, sensing, and feeling into the pain, metabolizing, and dealing with her authentic suffering is her portal to an epiphany, a rebirth, and a discovery of meaning.

The encounter of the Old Lady and the Nubian Woman in the interactive relationship occurs in the dark depths of the river. We are told in the tale so little about the initial meeting. As we engage the tale and allow the tale to speak symbolically to our depths, we can only imagine what transpired between them, given the depth of generativeness of the Old Lady's outpouring gestures to the Woman. Because of the Old One's response to the Woman, we realize that the Nubian Woman had to have experienced some form of healing and an opening to the inexhaustible inner wellspring within her soul. Presence of the Ancient One, who is *totally Other* and hidden in absence that seems like nothingness and emptiness, now reveals herself in abundance and fullness. Mystery is experienced. Presence manifested in a depth of caring empathy, kindness, mercy, and compassion is encountered in processing the emotionally charged swampland of "sores," including that which seemingly is unthinkable and unspeakable. In the depth encounter, the experience of mercy is often part of the unfolding potential in the recovery and rebirth of soul essence. Mercy *is* a powerful, incredibly bonding love, felt deeply in one's whole being. Mercy is the invisible mystery/Mystery as weaver, binding and mending all the fragmented threads of the Nubian Woman's life, and for anyone of us the threads of our life, together in a developing, splendid, colorful tapestry of a soul.

Furthermore, we need to realize that mercy is *not* to be mistaken for some sentimental, pious, routine ritual devoid of meaning, but rather, a deeply conscious encounter of a generative unconditional love. The Old One's self-communication *is* mercy. In enduring the suffering of the tension of the opposites, sacrificing, letting go, and surrendering, one is *embraced* by the Ancient One, who is mercy. Wording is difficult for what is in reality rather ineffable. What unfolds is healing and liberating. Mercy is the outpouring self-communication of unbreakable love of the invisible mystery/Mystery, graciously and freely given to the Black Nubian Woman, which cuts through everything, touches deeply, and heals. Loving, nonjudgmental empathy, kindness, mercy, and compassion transform. Mercy renders one to utter silence as one experiences forgiveness as unconditional love. The process with the Old One opens one to experiencing mercy and being forgiven. We clearly know it when it occurs! And with this experience, often there is a greater conscious awareness and psychospiritual spaciousness within, which allows one the inner freedom, possibly, to forgive oneself. This is key if one is to open evermore to the potential inexhaustible wellspring within one's depths.

Inevitably, as mercy is experienced, we will be summoned unavoidably to befriend the more pitch-black aspect of our shadow's core reality and to surrender our control, the patriarchal power stance in whatever form it manifests for anyone of us, in the journey to forgive another, or others, as we have known mercy. For some, this is an incredibly intense inner war of opposites as one sacrifices and relinquishes whatever blocks one's process toward reconciliation and wholeness. The sacrifice will vary from one person to another. Some realities that individuals may have to forgo in order to forgive include superiority, one's "knowing," hate, prejudice, being right, self-righteousness, judgment, feeling that "it" is not fair, pride, and omnipotence. An exception to this reality is a person who has been traumatized. Because the "scar" may be deeper, the grounded attentiveness to "licking" the "scar" in the process of recovery will take time and will require the unfolding, developing readiness and grace of mercy. Internationally known Jungian analyst Ann Ulanov reflects on this very sensitive issue, indicating that to reach an inner union (*coniunctio*) ". . .in terms of the weight of hate and forgiveness is not to forget or condone injury; it is to become immune to trauma's power to obliterate and then deny such obliteration happened" (pp. 209-210).[184] It is only with time, when a person is more grounded, safe, and secure within his or her interior, that the capacity to forgive may occur in the process of untying a "knotted" wound. Regarding the dynamics of this experience, the emerging process with the Old Lady at the bottom of the river will be unique for each as his/her soul essence is recovered. Also, it is important to remember that if we continue to avoid (or take flight) embodying the capacity to extend mercy, we run the potential risk of not dealing with transforming the potential monstrous power/energy within us and between us, and thus we become capable of being like the tale's devouring monster, however overt or covert, verbal or nonverbal, and sadistically or masochistically this energy may be expressed. In receiving and in extending mercy, there is a loosening in one's psychic structure as a greater, relaxed spaciousness opens within, and a softening occurs in one's overall manner of being in life.

To experience the life-giving encounter of mercy and to extend it to others is to know a new dance in the dawn of a bright sunshiny day! Nelson Mandela demonstrated this in his life, in his acts of forgiveness, which showed South Africa a path away from apartheid. Mandela spent 27 years in prison for attempting to end violent white-minority rule. He became a conduit of peace by reconciling with the individuals who had been the instruments of oppression during his captivity. He forgave, for example, Paul Gregory, his prison warder and on becoming president of South Africa in 1994, he invited Gregory to the inauguration ceremony.

Referring back to the tale, any of the previously noted potential various graced developments of the Nubian Woman could be understood as a manifestation and an expression of the humanized and embodied archetypal energy of the Ancient One, who is *totally Other.* Again, in the words of Ann Belford Ulanov, Jungian analyst, author, and professor of psychiatry and religion at Union Theological Seminary in New York City: "We know something powerful transcends our knowledge and has met us, conjoined with us, linked to our life in the here and now. To move from a religious experience to sustained religious life is to remember this binding and seek its unfolding, to name who has addressed us and practice relationship with this Other" (p. 210).[185]

Through the relationship with the Old One, in recovering and nurturing self-parts, including traumatized parts, navigating and metabolizing the tension of the opposites, enduring the suffering, opening to reconciliation, and continuing to attend to the process toward wholeness, the Woman experiences an epiphany of depth, meaning, and vision. In all the experiences of weaving together the various threads of the tapestry of the soul, the unfolding, emerging, and evolving alchemical conjunction, *coniunctio,* is occurring for a person as [s]he circumambulates many times toward the center. Psychologically, the union of the opposites and the birth of new generative life are taking place. Sometimes, a symbol can emerge in a dream that reflects this reality. While images of the inner sacred marriage or *coniunctio* may manifest for a soul and serve as a symbolic guidepost in the process, we need to remember, still, that the symbol does not arise as an indicator of our having arrived, of having it all together, and/or of achievement of the goal, which in reality is never attainable. The symbol of the *conjunctio* points to a deeper communion and union in the ongoing, ever-expansive journey in human development in the individuation process. T.S. Eliot expresses it well:

> We must be still and still moving
> Into another intensity
> For a further union, a deeper communion. . . (p. 32) [186]

We can only imagine that in circling to the center, the Nubian Woman opens to depth, an inner wellspring. Here, mystery/Mystery in stillness speaks, and silence shapes and forms her anew in the healing encounter with the Ancient One. In the hidden dark stillness of silence, a state of conscious awareness beyond thought and concept, the Woman is bejeweled, and gradually her inner soul essence begins to emerge. More of our heroine's essential nature is born, meaning is discovered, and vocation is realized in the unfolding encounter. To open to the inner wellspring of stillness is to encounter a depth of transforming love in the silence. In conscious, embodied interiority: creativity, imagination, and vision arise, all of which is potential, valuable energy for the return journey in service to the outer circle of life.

We realize from the tale that the Woman does not perpetuate her neurosis and further the wounding of the Dark Feminine by having a seemingly infantile temper tantrum, as the envious women seem to demonstrate through their disgusted, greedy, and entitled response to the Old One. Like the Nubian Woman, we can be receptive to the experience, giving ourselves over to the inner alchemical cooking process of transformation (transforming something from an unconscious raw state to a conscious digestible one), or we can avoid, take flight, or offer excuses if we are about living an unenriched, constrained life with a bankruptcy of meaning. At various times, for any one of us, we may oscillate about choices many times, including being jealous, envious, greedy, acting narcissistically entitled, embodying a controlling power stance, and/or having an infantile temper tantrum as we struggle to endeavor and to honor our journey in individuation. When we act out our shadow, we need to remember that it is a part of us and not the whole of us. However, we need to address this self-part and work with it; otherwise it will be driving us, and our toxic energy will impact others in a destructive, dominating, "monstrous" way. Because of the Woman's generous reply to her soul's summons, she comes into a new and expanded, embodied awareness and meaning. So, too, the tale calls all of us, men and women, to befriend the "sores" of the neglected, repressed feminine energy, both personally and collectively, throughout the planet and over millennia. Like the Nubian Woman, hopefully we, too, will open to the inner wellspring, to a more enriched, embodied consciousness, and to the discovery of meaning, for as Jung noted, "The least of things with a meaning is worth more in life than the greatest of things without it" (p. 67).[187]

Love Experienced As Ancient Recognition—Already/Always Present

The Ancient One addresses the brave Woman of compassionate and generous heart as "My dear friend." The personal, intimate greeting, being addressed with loving recognition, breaks through and melts the iron archaic defense structures, opening the door of being seen and known in a profound, unconditional way, as if you had always been known. This is true even though you may have thought you were your shame or were somehow deficient, a failure, nothing, unworthy, bad, not good enough, damaged goods, unwanted, not safe in this world, inadequate, insecure, unlovable, incompetent, unintelligent, and any other self-limiting belief due to life's traumas, wounds, and/or a lack of empathetic parental mirroring. The reception of the Nubian Woman by the Ancient One is such that the Nubian Woman realizes that she already/always has been loved by the Old One, even when she was not conscious of it. The welcoming greeting is about the Old One's recognizing the Black Nubian Woman's soul essence. The Woman is seen for her true nature, which is deeper than name and form. The salutation is about being known, loved, acknowledged, empowered, and summoned in *coming home:* the journey toward wholeness that is individuation. The Nubian Woman experiences herself as an alive presence. As an ensouled someone, she is inhabiting her body consciously, having developed and grown through an empowering relationship with the Ancient One, rather than colluding, being a codependent object of other people's trickster aspects, both conscious and unconscious. The experience between the Old One and the Woman is something like the enlarging experience of conversation between Jesus of Nazareth and the woman of Samaria. If one perceives the greeting simply as a welcoming (literal thinking), one has approached the inner world from an egocentric view and missed the deeper, soulful potential of the encounter with mystery/Mystery. An indescribable depth of soulful intimacy seems to have been experienced and appears to be core to the relationship between the Ancient One and the Nubian Woman. While dark-night initiation in the Dark Feminine liberates the soul within us, what could be emphasized far more is the unequivocal, immense outpouring of self-communication of the mystery/Mystery. The Ancient Lady, who is so touched, lavishes the Woman with a more magnificent necklace, anoints her, clothes her anew, gives directives of wisdom, and empowers her with a blessing message. The Wise One's gestures indicate an expression of profound, gracious, generous, and generative love. Someone *totally Other* and beyond the Black Nubian Woman's ego grasp has been orchestrating her recreation.

Dream time and fairy-tale time are symbolic (not literal) earth time. We need to realize that licking the "sores" by the Nubian woman is not a singular, one-time event! The process for the Woman, as it is for any one of us, is sometimes incredibly slow, and at other times amazingly swift. There are surges of growth and expansion in awareness, then temporary contraction, and sometimes regression to a state of fusion and impasse. Having patience and compassion for ourselves and a perduring attentiveness to our process is important as we attempt to remain consciously present and to await our unfolding and emerging soul. We cannot push the river. We need to allow the river to flow and to remember that in all things, the mystery/Mystery is the mover. For the Nubian Woman and for most of us, our psychospiritual development tends to proceed in a spiral manner, as we circumambulate our issues many times, each time hopefully, at a deeper dimension, as we have the courage to face and metabolize the more pitch-black aspect of our core reality. Here, for the Woman and for all of us, in this seemingly despicable, unbearable psychic swampland of "sores," are buried the *unknown* and often the most despised, dissociated self-parts, which hold the potential energy for the greatest growth and for the depth and expansion of soul. The underside of the nub of our dark, destructive shadow is our capable inner gold awaiting liberation for creativity and contribution in humble service through our vocational summons in life. In this most desolate, dismal swamp of psychic space is the jewel of potential energy for releasing the soul within the Black Nubian Woman and within each of us.

Vast Potential—Birthing New Frontiers in Human Consciousness

In the unfolding, soulful relating and attending to wounds both ancient and of a lifetime, something profound has transpired between the Old Lady and the Black Nubian Woman that is ineffable. As reported earlier in some of the clinical examples, attending the depths through soulful inner work can liberate pulsating energy and bring one to an abiding contemplative silence that is most loving and profoundly healing. In the words of Karl Rahner, S.J., expressed earlier in this chapter, "[T]he deepest encounter of the self is the encounter with the Divine." The experience of the gracious mystery/Gracious Mystery occurs in a thousand different disguises on the road of life. There is *no one image or way that the mystery/Mystery draws, touches, loves, and heals.* The Ancient One hidden in the luminous black depths of the river is an ever-present powerful One. Given the heartfelt anointing, some type of empowering affirmation and blessing of grace is given to the Woman. There is, in essence, an overall experience of a loving inflow communicated to the Black Nubian Woman. St. John of the Cross speaks of contemplation as the loving inflow of the Divine. Symbolically, this encounter between the Old Lady and the Black Nubian Woman manifests something of the vast potential of contemplative depth experiences that are possible in the human journey of transformative embodied consciousness. Through the positive disintegration of the Nubian Woman's way of presenting herself in outer life, the sacrifice of letting go of her "shoreline" shallow state of constricted ego awareness, and the surrendering and receptivity to the summons of the Old One, even in the blacker-than-black soul work, the Nubian Woman opens to more depth and intimacy than she ever imagined possible. A jewel is discovered in the journey of dark-night initiation in the Dark Feminine.

Thus, in the return or ascent from the depths, the Black Nubian Woman who emerged was very different from who she had been prior to her experience of descent. Now her inner beauty is carried from within, and she is about her path in a more humble, embodied, conscious way. She possesses a more expanded, grounded, psychospiritual interiority. Through the soulful, tender, heartfelt exchange between the two in the still pitch-black nothingness of the rock-bottom depths of the river, the Black Nubian Woman's unique and true essential nature begins to emerge in a body-felt way. This inner soul work is the portal for the Nubian Woman's transformation. The heart and soulful depth of this woman has been touched by the mystery/Mystery, causing an inner renewal and transformation. The ungrounded, insecure Woman, who once was lured and influenced by superficial, jealous, envious, and manipulative others and who had to face these dynamics in herself, now returns more consciously embodied to be about her ordinary life in her unique way. Having been called to face, examine, metabolize, assimilate, and transform these possibly charged, shadowy qualities in herself, other "sores" of origin, and unknown and undeveloped gifts that have been dormant in her unconscious, she now emerges with a more humble, balanced, and authentic sense of her true nature. She knows her felt values and can live and speak her truth. When you have experienced integral healing through the mystery's/Mystery's self-communication, however this transpires, you then see with a clearer, differentiated perception, the heart opens to a more expanded, awakened-passionate awareness, embodied consciousness, and your way of being in service becomes more humble. For the Black Nubian Woman, as well as for all of us, we become responsible to show up and be present in an incarnated, conscious way, to what we have been given through the inner journey. Jung put it this way: "Anyone with a vocation hears the inner voice. . .the voice of a fuller life, of a wider, more comprehensive consciousness" (pars. 300, 318).[188]

The Woman of the story, and all women and men who know interiorly their grounded self-worth from their interactive relationship with the Old Woman in the river (or some other image of the Dark Feminine) and their differentiation from this relationship, are not driven compulsively by the collective norm to achieve, continuously to accomplish, or to live one's vocation seeking approval and validation from the outside for what can be found only within. The journey toward consciousness is about the process of differentiating, about the gradual detection and discernment of the summons of the soul, and about having the courage and the strength to honor what one feels obligated to obey in service to the mystery/Mystery. There is but one true jewel that remains forever ongoing and living: the inexhaustible life of the soul in relationship to the mystery/Mystery. The progressive journey for the Black Nubian Woman in her return, as for any person, is to have a perduring attentiveness to the intimations of the mystery/Mystery. We are in service to the mystery/Mystery. People and groups will always have their opinions and judgments about who any one of us is and what any one of us should be about: Discerning and honoring humbly the soul's summons is the key obligation in our service to mystery/Mystery. Furthermore, the return requires remembering to be mindful of the continuous process of the life-death-rebirth cycle, of demagnetizing the wounds, "licking" the sores (the shadow in all forms, including the old dominant parental complex, and complexes of the wounds of origin, both individually and collectively). The Old Woman's call to "lick my sores" is an invitation that remains part of our lifelong journey in "the return" to living in an evolving, flawed world as we interact and relate to all dimensions of life. Consequently, it is important to remain grounded and connected to our soul's center in mining our leaden darkness and metabolizing and containing the potential "devouring monster" of power, greed, and aggression in any one of us and in any form that may threaten us, whether from within our psyche or in the outer collective. This is especially true in a polarized society and a world driven by power, greed, and aggression in many forms. If we have not dealt with the subtle and the blacker-than-black shadow of our own overt and covert patriarchal power issues, greed, anger, rage, shame, hatred, jealousy, envy, narcissistic tendencies, addiction, and the racist, terrorist, xenophobist, and misogynist within us, we will add to the horrific, destructive swampland in life. Others and the Earth herself do not deserve this reality.

Thus, we realize that the mystery of the Dark Feminine principle heals and that this is a progressive process. The Dark Feminine is a fundamental human pattern of energy that is available for the growth of the self. This energy is "a connector" in the quantum context (as noted in Chapter Two), as it embraces the vitality of the opposites, supported by a potential for wholeness within the psyche that is already/always present whether we are conscious of this reality or not. Furthermore, when we are engaged consciously in this Dark Feminine energy, as manifested in Lady Underground, psychospiritually we are "in proper relationship to the Dark Feminine," and as such, the opposites are allowed to coexist creatively within the fuller potential of the flow of life in all its dimensions.

Renewal of life that makes a difference at our roots cannot be by way of any kind of technical, intellectual, spiritually mass-produced, prescribed remedy or by rational talk that patronizes the Dark Feminine with "lip service" only. The tale reveals that only through "licking the sores," which involves one's saliva, will healing occur for any one of us and/or collectively. What does this mean? Saliva, which is primarily water, is a healing symbol of curative liquid that represents the energy flow being mediated between healer

(Old Lady) and client (Black Nubian Woman) in the interactive field of the transformative relationship. Sucking and licking is a natural human behavior for a baby, and for an animal it is the instinctual way of cleaning and healing wounds. Jesus restored sight to the blind man with his own saliva.[189] Shamans often will use saliva in a healing ritual. I personally witnessed this reality with Brant Secunda, a shaman of the Huichol people, in November of 1991, when I participated in a 12-day retreat in the rites of passage with the Huichol Indians, who are a small tribe living in central western Mexico near Ixtlan in the Sierra Madre Mountains. Human saliva is 99.5 percent water; the other 0.5 percent consists of electrolytes, mucus, glycoproteins, enzymes, and antibacterial compounds. Waters are symbolic of the Great Mother and associated with birth and the feminine principle. Water as a liquid can be symbolically reflective of dissolving, purifying, washing away, and regenerating new life; it is associated with abundance of possibilities and spiritual refreshment or the primal origin of all being, the *prima materia*. Thus, wet saliva may be seen as a liquid bodily secretion possessing a spiritual power and effecting purification, bringing together, connecting, soothing, healing, and rebirthing new life.[190] All people have this substance. Hence, the Nubian Woman is called to bring forth from within her, her own unique feminine moist essence in the process of attending the "sores," not by pontificating cerebral words out of her mouth, but by the healing, life-giving, symbolic saliva from her mouth. What is being brought together, metabolized, healed, called forth, birthed, embodied, and renewed is the lost Dark Feminine energy that has been repressed personally and collectively. The return is about living more fully this conscious embodied Dark Feminine essence. For all who are intent on the path of individuation, the return is made with a more grounded, realistic consciousness of entering and living with a more expanded self-understanding, which includes a well-differentiated feminine energy and masculine energy. This awareness will continue to grow out of repeated spiral descents into the fertile dark of the imagination, where the opposites are allowed to dance in a creative tension. This creative imaginal *temenos* is the arena where ongoing connecting and healing arise, and every archetype is capable of endless development and differentiation. It is the place where prophetic vision is birthed for the path and for new frontiers of human consciousness in our interconnected, evolving cosmos.

Specific Directives from the Dark Feminine in the Return

In the latter part of the fairy tale, the Old Woman gives some particular instructions to the Nubian Woman on her return to everyday life. She is told that she is to find a round stone on the shore, pick it up, throw it back into the river to the Old One without looking back, and then go on, taking up her ordinary life in her village. What is the meaning of the round stone and the significance of picking it up and throwing it into the river to the Ancient One? For many cultures, stone is symbolic of divine power because of its strength, durability, and permanence. Helen Luke considers the stone in all cultures as the symbol of the immortal Self.[191] Marie-Louise von Franz notes the same reality and further states, "They [stones] represent the secret of eternity and uniqueness, and the secret of the essence of the life of the human being" (p. 150).[192] Stone generally has not been perceived as something rigid and dead but rather as something life-giving. Perhaps the roundness of the stone is symbolic of the innate wholeness of the Self and that to which we are all called in the journey of individuation, the journey of coming home, which is a symbolic directive given by the Wise One to the Nubian Woman: "Continue on your path back home." Thus, it is the round stone that is the appropriate offering to the Dark Feminine, not one's necklace, as the Nubian Woman had been led to believe by the jealous trickster women of the village.

We realize from the tale that in the return the Woman has a more internalized sense of self-worth (the necklace) and is less at the mercy of the cause and effect of others. A closer look at the symbolic meaning of the necklace can offer insight into the nature of the incarnated energy in the return. Moreover, I believe that there is a relationship between the "embodied necklace" and the interiorized possession of the Woman's grounded inner authority, voice, and capacity to access her creative power. This would also be true for any one of us.

As noted before, in Africa a necklace is a highly prized symbol of enduring feminine values, soul identity, giftedness, and worth. Importantly,

"The symbolism of the necklace also includes that of chains of office and the collars of civil and military orders of chivalry, as well as the collars put round the necks of prisoners, slaves, and domestic animals. In general terms, the necklace or collar symbolizes a bond between the wearer and whomever has given it to him or her" (p. 697).[193]

Another fairy tale in which a woman receives a necklace in her individuation process is *Maid Maleen.* She receives a precious chain necklace around her neck when she is married. Being bestowed with this treasured jewelry piece is a symbol of unity and matrimony. Furthermore, it represents "unity with diversity," as individual parts are united to make a whole.[194] In this tale, the gift of the chain necklace suggests psychic bonding and integration. It is the symbol of a newly acknowledged identity.

As we continue the discussion of the meaning of this necklace and its relationship to having our inner authority, voice, and capacity for creativity in the return, we have to consider what caused the Black Nubian Woman to experience her journey of *dark-night* initiation into the Dark Feminine. The Nubian Woman has easily fallen into the trap of the jealous women and, as directed by them, has thrown her necklace into the river as an offering to the river. Considering the general meaning of the necklace as a collar that symbolizes a bond between the wearer and the giver (which in this case was her family), we have to wonder: What did the woman really throw away symbolically? Was it a necklace that was too binding to her neck because of rules, regulations, oppression, suffocation, and expectations, or a collar that was holding her back and "chaining" her, denying her a deeper, more fulfilling and life-giving way of being? Does the necklace, which the generous-hearted female so quickly threw away, suggest that she was a pleaser and in need of external group acceptance, validation, and affirmation and so was influenced by the group norm and collective behavior? Does this mean that she interiorly lacked a relationship to her unconscious or to herself in any real grounded way? When any one of us, male or female, lacks self-identity and self-worth, it is easy to be seduced by directives, slogans, videos, social media, philosophy, political leader or group, or YouTube descriptions of some collective group purpose, cause, or crusade, fine in itself, perhaps, and sponsored by people we aspire to please for acceptance, validation, and love. I recently saw this reflected in the play *The Book of Mormon* in which two "Elders," who are young, male missionaries, and who lack both grounded, inner self-worth and identity, initially obey the rules (e.g., they want to go out at night for a social event but discover that missionaries are not allowed to be out after 9:00 P.M.); as dutiful sons and missionaries, they comply in order to gain acceptance, approval, and validation from the Mormon President. Lack of grounded self-worth, naivety, and passive, unquestioning compliance blind us and keep us unconscious and enslaved as dutiful sons and daughters in what we agree to so readily. We are called not to collude with patriarchal authority, but to differentiate consciously and incarnate our soul's summons.

Also, we see this reality, or stories of it, manifested in covert, manipulative, masterful ways almost daily on certain television networks, social media, and internet sites. Advertising, gangs, terrorist groups, drug and sex trafficking solicitors, and various fundamentalist organizations's recruitment tactics reveal similar dynamics. If our identity is not grounded from within, we can rather quickly part with our capacity to reflect, to discriminate, and to choose decisively, and in this manner we forfeit, sell out, and discard our potential, unique voice of truth and identity. Nevertheless, while the Nubian Woman's ungrounded self-identity may have rendered her more susceptible to participating in what appeared to be an innocent event, this duped naïve choice was a pivotal experience, activating an alarming "wake-up call" that augmented a necessary, positive disintegration and dark-night initiation in the Dark Feminine. The woman's naive innocence and, perhaps, sentimentality needed to be shattered if she, or any one of us, is ever to become detached from collective group norms, opinions, and judgments and begin to mature in opening and discovering our grounded inner authority, voice, and capacity to access our creative power. In the journey of individuation, conscious differentiation from our family of origin and the collective is vital if we are to unleash and awaken to meaning, identity, and purpose as individuals on a much deeper soulful level and spirit/Spirit-directed way of being in life.

Healthy inner authority and the capacity to access creative power for a higher good in life is grounded in a realistic sense of self-worth. This wholesome self-esteem emerges from a proper relationship to the instinctual life and spirit, and a proper relationship to the Old Woman who *empowers within us our authentic spirit of beauty, love, power, and wisdom.* The return is made with much more grounded interiorized identity and personal authority. The need and call, noted in the opening paragraph of Chapter Two, for a more embodied personalization of the archetypal Dark Feminine energy is consciously embraced through the *dark night of initiation in the Dark Feminine.* This potential for growth and conscious ensoulment of the Dark Feminine is only birthed by making the descent, be it into the dark woods or to the bottom of a riverbed, crypt, hermitage, or cave. The descent/ascent in dark-night initiation in the Dark Feminine is the process of humanizing this archetypal energy.

The Old Woman further instructed that once the stone had been thrown into the river, the Nubian Woman was to continue on without looking back and to resume her ordinary village life. What does it mean to resume one's life "without looking back"? What is involved in taking up our ordinary life in our local community, city, village, town, or country? Symbolically, to not look back is to avoid the potential sad entrapment of being pulled into the net of sentimentality and what we have been wedded to or in service to unconsciously in the past. To not look back is, paradoxically, a call and a warning to be aware and to remain grounded as we courageously take responsibility to go forth and to live consciously in the *present* in the return. Psychologically, the message is an alert about the real power of the psyche's regressive pull, especially as we move toward a greater differentiation from various psychic parts in the unconscious. This can manifest in fantasy and in the longing for our attachment and ego desire to abide in the known, safe, secure, familiar, and comfortable. To be aware and to remain grounded is to consciously remember the easy susceptibility to becoming inflated, which is common to most of us. The summons to descend, the mission to ascend, and the inspiring, obliging stirrings to honor humbly the soul's call in the return are intimations of the thin gold thread of self-communication and the movement of the gracious mystery/Mystery in the lives of any one of us.

Symbolically, to take up our ordinary life in our outer world is to take responsibility, to go forth courageously, and to live our new self-identity and awareness. It is to "chop wood, carry water" consciously! The very reality of "the return" to everyday life requires each of us to live consciously the gift of the light and wisdom of the Dark Primordial Feminine. Part of the responsibility of the return is to bring the treasure from the underworld. Jung considered it a moral responsibility to share that of which we have become conscious in the night sea journey. Furthermore, psychologically, to take up our outer-world daily life is to live consciously what Jung considered one of the hardest tasks: *to be our simple self,* which in actual life requires the greatest art.[195]

In the return from night initiation in the Primordial Dark Feminine, we hope, in our ordinary lives, to be aware and present with a heart that is more flexible, passionate, and compassionate toward ourselves, others, Other, and the Earth herself within the context of the great evolving Cosmic Story. The softening and relaxing of dogmatic, rigid, and oppressive controlling qualities give way to a wiser consciously incarnated presence that is neither self-absorbed nor fearful. To be ourselves in our ordinary lives is to embrace the healthy, creative tension of the opposites and the authentic suffering that may arise from holding and containing the energy in all aspects of life. To be ourselves in our ordinary lives is to know that we are more than our history, and thus to give ourselves permission to dissolve self-limiting, gripping, insistent beliefs, labels, and the adaptive drivers (e.g., *please others, try hard, be the dutiful responsible son/daughter, be perfect, be strong, be the good helper*) that tend to fuel and keep us small, entrapped, imprisoned, emotionally infantile, and that sabotage dimensions of our lives. No one, and certainly not the mystery/Mystery, is ever served by repressing who we really are and remaining psychologically and spiritually small. To be ourselves in our ordinary lives is to have a healthy acceptance and greater respect for diversity in all forms and expressions of life in this interconnected universe. To be ourselves in our ordinary lives is to be in relationship. In living practical everyday life and honoring the teleology of the soul, we are obliged to incorporate our new, expanded consciousness into our manner of being, including advocating for justice, peace, and care of the Earth. To be ourselves in our ordinary lives is to have the courage and humility to embody consciously our soul's summons in life through living our unique vocation. To be ourselves in life is to be in service to the mystery/Mystery. To be ourselves in life is to know that the seasons of life will continue to unfold in our evolving, quantum universe, and that the life-death-rebirth cycle of growth will reveal itself in development in all dimensions of life. We have but one life, and in the return, we can choose consciously how we show up in living our ordinary lives. Can you tolerate being embodied and open enough to live in the *present* and to discover and to delight with gratitude about the marvelous in the mundane, the tedious, the dull, and the painful, as well as the beautiful, the joyous, the playful, and the "ooh-la-la" of life? For George Bernard Shaw, the Irish critic, playwright, and social reformer who won and refused the Nobel Prize for Literature in 1925, living his life fully meant making his splendid torch burn as brightly as possible and holding it before handing it on to future generations and desiring to be thoroughly used up when he died. For the Nubian Woman and for all of us, the final curtain call will come, and each of us is the only one who is accountable in the final act of our life's living play: *Coming Home*. What it is to be for the Nubian Woman and what it is to be for each of us remains to be answered as we continue to make the journey Home. Jung reminds us of an important insight in *The Red Book:* "My path is not your path. . . .The way is within us. . . .So live yourselves. The signposts have fallen, unblazed trails lie before us. . . .May each one seek out his own way" (p. 231).[196]

How are you tending your way in the emerging story of your life? What is your way of showing up consciously in everyday living and making your journey in individuation? We realize, ever more, that life is a challenge and a summons to live as courageously and as fully as possible the symbolic life in the *present* time, which will never occur again. The refreshing contemporary poet Mark Nepo, after being informed that he was dying of cancer (which ultimately did not occur), composed the poem "For That," which captures amazingly the call to live fully our unique lives in the *Now*. He challenges us to discover this wisdom. "My purpose, at last, to hold nothing back. My goal: to live a thousand years, not in succession, but in every breath" (p. 51).[197] Gerard Manley Hopkins, the gifted Jesuit poet, also empowers us, through his inspiring lyrics, to live fully our soul's call in the ordinary of life:

> Each mortal thing does one thing and the same: . . .
> Selves—goes its self; myself it speaks and spells,
> Crying *What I do is me: for that I came.* (p. 67) [198]

Hopkins further reflects an appeal to us to live justly in our everyday life:

> Acts in God's eye what in God's eye he is –
> Christ—for Christ plays in ten thousand places. . . (p. 67) [199]

The Black Nubian Woman's developing and emerging, embodied consciousness arises from her process of befriending her own depths of darkness and suffering, and thus she remains "virginal" (meaning "one in herself," an inner attitude of the soul. The virgin energy is an aspect of the feminine principle rooted in the instincts, in a woman or man, who has the courage to be her-/himself with an ongoing flexibility to evolve in her/his true nature.) In the psychological sense of being one-in-herself, she is living more of her essence in the ordinary of her life in the return. The Nubian Woman, the heroine of this tale, is virginal, since her grounded self-identity is truly and uniquely individual and not acquired through approval by the collective, or the *status quo*, and/or through identification with another male or female. She has become an initiated virgin and is not to be confused with the adolescent maiden, for as an initiated virgin, she has grown through her metabolized and assimilated experience of developing more of her differentiated, conscious, masculine and feminine energy. From her underground process she has emerged more attuned to her own inner rhythms, depth of feeling, and wisdom within her body, and thus she is able to be herself, speak her voice and her truth from her authentic center. Also, she possesses an awareness of feeling present and recognizing that it is she, herself, who is present. For a male or female, an initiated virgin is born by making our matter conscious. (The Latin word *esse* in the word "essence" means "to be.") Being virginal is attempting to be nothing more or less than who one is in one's natural embodied conscious *essence*. For a woman or a man to be virginal is to be one-in-oneself, or to paraphrase Gerard Manley Hopkins's lyrics, "*s/he is who s/he is and does what s/he does.*" Mary Esther Harding offers further clarification on this term. One who is virginal does what one does, "not because of any desire to please, not to be liked, or to be approved, . . .not because of any desire to gain power over another, to catch his interest or love, but because what she does is true" (pp. 125-126).[200]

Harding continues: The virgin's "actions may, indeed, be unconventional. . .as she is not influenced by the considerations that make the nonvirgin. . .trim her sails and adapt herself to expediency. . . . She is what she is because that is what she is" (pp. 125-126).[201]

Thus, a virgin is a person who fundamentally has a well-differentiated, conscious feminine and masculine energy, is grounded in inner authority, and has the capacity to speak and to live her/his values and truths. The male or female who has come to incarnate the initiated-virgin energy is one who has discovered an inner freedom to be true to his or her essence and to know that intrusive, self-defeating thoughts or plagues of shame do not define one's core. This symbolic image of virgin reflects the conscious, mature, feminine energy for a woman or a man, which is born from the inner soul work and transformational process of separating and differentiating from the maternal unconscious. The initiated virgin is a person who has done significant inner soul work in the ongoing differentiating process from ego-centeredness and the dominant unconscious parental complexes, especially the basic instinct for merging and union with the mother energy (which is often both projected out and acted on with others) into an embodied, conscious spirit/Spirit-directed life that is attuned to one's depths of being in service to the mystery/Mystery and the summons of the soul. Some variations of this archetypal experience, noted by Francis Parks, are exemplified in diverse images such as "solitary Artemis":

> [I]t is Persephone hidden away in the underworld; it is Demeter wandering alone, searching in grief for her lost daughter; it is Joseph waiting in prison in Egypt; it is Mary waiting with her cousin Elizabeth and again, waiting at the foot of the cross; it is Mary Magdalene who provides us with a beautiful example of individuation out of love. It is the Buddha beneath the Bo tree. (p. 12)[202]

Perhaps you have other examples of individuals whose lives reflect various gradations of the manifestation of this archetypal energy. Who symbolically inspires your life toward a more expanded sense of being your natural virginal self? Whether that may be Mohandas Gandhi, Hildegard of Bingen, Abraham Lincoln, Dorothy Day, Joseph the Nazarene Carpenter, Nelson Mandela, Sonia Sotomayor, John McCain III, Maya Angelo, Elijah Cummings, and/or someone else, the choice and responsibility to do the necessary inner soul work still remains ours and ours alone. No one can live or die for any one of us! The Black Nubian Woman challenges us, both men and women, in the return to show up in the present and be about living more consciously our embodied essence in the ordinary of everyday life.

Directive: Call to Nurture Soul-Divine Relationship and Embody Wisdom

Finally, the Ancient One imparts an explicit directive that reflects a depth of wisdom to empower the Nubian Woman, or any one of us, in the return and the journey home. The Old One instructs the Woman that once she has ascended to the shore, "after taking some *time to pause*, which is essential. . .; begin *walking slowly and steadily*. . . ; when you drink the water, do so by *drinking deeply*." The blessing message is "*Go slowly*." Taken as a whole, the words of wisdom seem to communicate one primary directive that is spoken in four different expressions. This seems to symbolize the Old Lady's way of emphasizing to the Nubian Woman the importance and value of taking time to nurture and to have a conscious, perduring attentiveness to the soul-divine/Divine dialogue (in classical analytical language it is the ego-Self dialogue; and in the language of spirituality it is the soul-Mystery or the soul-Divine relationship and communication) in the lifelong daily journey of individuation, which is also called *coming home*. I sense the Ancient One is reminding the Woman, and all of us, that the path to wholeness and living humbly one's vocation is being present in the here and now, attending consciously to ongoing inner soul work, especially intentional solitude sourced from the deep inner well, if we are to incarnate and live a balanced, conscious spirit/Spirit-directed life within the Earth-centered comprehensive Earth community.

Today there is much offered in continued-education training for those in the helping professions supporting the practice of mindfulness and compassionate presence, and there is specific value for the physician, therapist, clinician, educator, spiritual director, pastoral minister, chaplain, patient, client, and/or student. This practice in its many forms is another way to cultivate living the symbolic, conscious, embodied life. "Time to pause" accesses the focusing sensate and feeling function, while becoming aware is cultivated by paying attention. "Walking slowly and steadily" engages the conscious, grounding, sensate function while being awake and aware in the now. "Drink deeply" summons the soul to a perduring attentiveness to the depths—the mystery/Mystery. "Go slowly," the blessing message, is a communication of affirmation, guidance, and empowerment. It is a directive to be compassionately aware and present consciously in the here and now and to have the courage, as one goes forth in the return, to live one's vocation in the ordinary of life as one continues the journey *home*. The Old One's directives are symbolic expressions of practical, grounding, conscious wisdom that support the dynamic process of embodying wisdom in the interconnective and interdependent web of all life in the *now*. These directives are some of the reflective underpinnings of the various breathing and walking-meditation exercises in mindful Buddhist practice, or the Sufi mantra, breathing, and/or walking meditations of the contemplative dimension of Islam, and/or what is known in Christian traditions as prayer of centering, a form of practice focusing one's awareness on a sacred word, a phrase, or one's breath as the portal to opening to interiority. These practices are more in the nature of what is known in the Christian tradition as "active intentional solitude," "contemplation" being a passive receptivity of the loving inflow of the Divine's self-communication. While the former may open one to a greater spaciousness and inner receptivity for the Divine inflow, the latter is sheer gift—grace. Remember, there is no one way. The Ancient One is *not* articulating the *how*, only affirming and summoning the Nubian Woman, and all of us, to the importance and value of accessing a rich source within us, namely the inner wellspring of the mystery/Mystery, which can strengthen and empower us in living the journey in everyday life.

In the opening of the tale, we discover that one of the reasons the envious others consider the Nubian Woman "different" was due to her taking time alone in solitude. It seems that this "difference," which was a source of criticism, judgment, and envy, was the very reality that the Ancient One affirmed, encouraged, empowered, and to which the Nubian Woman was summoned in her return. Psychologically and spiritually, there is a wide gradation in the potential for psychological depth and religious experience, and what this may mean for one person, is very different from what it may mean for another. Sometimes, what is unknown and unfamiliar is a threat to some people's known reality, and subsequently what seems "different" to them becomes a target for their judgments, criticism, envy, and verbal attacks. Manic talk, gossip, and toxic "noise" can often dominate the collective experience, and many can't imagine the value of taking time in silence, symbolic reflection, and/or contemplative solitude. For some, time alone in intentional solitude is foreign. For other souls, the symbolic directives "take time to pause," "walk slowly and steadily," "go slowly," and "drink deeply" are part of, and perhaps core to, their summons in life, a dimension of their vocation. The Old Lady seems to guide, affirm, and empower the Nubian Woman in this directive and her call. Jung himself valued this reality and was also criticized for it by the collective. In a letter to Gustav Schmaltz on May 30, 1957, Jung wrote, "Solitude is for me a fount of healing which makes my life worth living. . . .I need many days of silence" (p. 363).[203] Jung "drank deeply."

What does this actually mean, to "drink deeply?" Realizing that the language of the psyche is symbolic, we understand that the Wise One clearly is not telling the Nubian Woman to receive the drink of water from the other just for the sake of staying hydrated! Metaphor communicates profound and often hidden insight and wisdom, and Jung understood that water, the most common symbol for expressing the unknown of our psyche, indicates the unconscious. Water speaks to the hidden depths, which contain a great deal of our life. Also, in biblical symbolism, water is reflective of the gift of wisdom ("She will give him [her] the bread of understanding to eat and the water of wisdom to drink"[204]). In the New Testament, the water that Jesus offers to the Samaritan Woman is a living water from an inexhaustible source that will become a spring welling up inside of one (John: 4:14). Within our psyches we are able to experience a reality that is analogous to the spring of water of which Jesus spoke. As John Sanford, the late internationally known Jungian analyst,

Episcopal priest, and pastor wrote: "Something wells up from within the human soul. . .which pours forth life and wisdom. This is symbolized by [the] water. . .[of] which Jesus speaks in his image of 'living water.'. . .It is this source of life within us."[205]

"Drinking deeply" is about the summons to the generative, inexhaustible relationship with the source/Source of life—the inner well within us. Psychologically speaking, we are wired potentially for "drinking deeply" from the inner wellspring in the quest to live life fully and meaningfully. The wellspring is a rich inner resource for living life. "Drinking deeply" is opening to the inner communion with the mystery/Mystery in one's depth within the context of the interconnected web of life. "Drinking deeply" is receiving the healing water that arises from within us to strengthen and heal the weary ego, empower the psyche for the journey, call for sacrifice and surrender, confront crooked ways and distorted lenses, embrace suffering and the life-death-rebirth cycle, reveal the truth and aspects of soul essence, refresh the soul, enliven the spirit, soften and enkindle the heart, offer mercy, call for forgiveness and make amends, revitalize the soul with joy, summon the soul to service, inspire kindness and justice, silently speak in stillness, and so much more in the journey home in meaningfully living the symbolic life, and for some, a contemplative life. "Drinking deeply" is the lifelong endeavor of incarnating consciously, growing from egocentricity to spirit/Spirit-directedness while being about compassionate presence and humble service in the *now*. In the words of William Blake,

> And we are put on earth a little space,
> That we might learn to bear the beams of love. (p. 10) [206]

Lady Underground's dark night of initiation in the Dark Feminine ushers in a summons and an obligation toward a deeper, conscious, embodied interiority (something noted in Chapter Two as essential for today's sojourner). "Drinking deeply" is part of the entire process in the ongoing conscious participative experience in honoring the summons. The Ancient One gives this directive of "drinking deeply" in the context of empowering the Woman so that by "drinking deeply," she will be more able to live her everyday life with greater clarity, as she continues on her path back *home.* Thus, the water is being offered as a source of strength, empowerment, and wisdom to enliven and illuminate one's journey in daily life, while being a presence and in service within this participatory and interconnective universe.

Personal Reflections—"Drinking Deeply"

Of the noted directives of wisdom that the Ancient One imparted to the Black Nubian Woman, the summons to "drinking deeply" stirs my depths and speaks most profoundly to me personally and professionally as an analyst, spiritual director, and educator. There is something about this phrase that opens and moves my heart and entire being, even as I write. In some profound way, these two simple words remind me of who I am and beckon me in my ongoing journey *home.*

"Drinking deeply" has been part of my emerging, unfolding, and evolving interiority throughout my life. The cultivation of soul has been woven by colorful threads of experience that have shaped and formed me in my mythic journey in being attentive to the murmur of the mystery/Mystery. Some of the following brief anecdotes reflect a few of the various colored threads of experience that weave through my soul's tapestry and hint at some of the background and foreground in my soul's felt summons to be attentive to the intimations of the mystery/Mystery.

Like all of us, I grew up having parents and in a family that were not perfect. I have "sores" of origin, complexes. "Drinking deeply" has included the joy, fun, laughter, dance, music, love, and celebrative passion of life, while also facing the difficult, the suffering, and the dark dimensions, including the blacker-than-black aspects of shadow, while somehow instinctively knowing that the only way "out" is "through" whatever may be the reality. When the gas is turned up on all four burners of the stove and the soup is boiling in the pot, I tend to remain in the inner kitchen, attentive to what is "cooking." The mystery/Mystery is not outside of engaging and being engaged by the issue, the "sore," the depth of life; in my experience, the encounter with mystery/Mystery is in and through experiencing and befriending consciously the "sore," the depth of life.

Where did I learn this? One of my teachers was my father; he taught not by speaking, but in his way of being, attitude, and choices in life, especially his capacity to trust the Mystery and choose life in the midst of loss, suffering, and darkness. It is one of the two significant values that I acknowledged and thanked my dad for embodying for me throughout his life before he died 43 years ago. The other value that he taught was about leisure and the ability to play well; to work hard—yes, and to have the intuition to know when to stop, walk away, and play while trusting the process that in letting go and playing, one's imagination opens and creativity arises, which often allows one to return to the work and do it in less time and far more creatively. My dad was a leader and a family man who had a quick wit, warm interactive communication skills, and a spiritual depth. My mother was very much a family-centered person who was also my teacher, especially in her later years. As she grew in her essence, she was attuned to nature in a grounded, simple way. She was a compassionate listener who honored confidentiality and reflected a succinct, insightful, practical wisdom, and she was witty at times in expressing it. In her senior years, I was moved by her contemplative presence and her attentive sense to the intimations of the Mystery. Both parents influenced me in their unique styles, given their wounds of origin, their strengths, and their growing edges.

Life has offered me many growing and learning opportunities, especially meaningful, intimate relationships; but the underlying, developing, dynamic configuration within my psyche, which has been the archetypal pattern of meaning and energy movements, is the formative experience and relationship with Lady Underground. My Jungian training and my life since that training, including the process of writing this book, have been a journey in what St. John of the Cross described as the "dark night of the soul" and, more specifically, Lady Underground's dark night of initiation in the Dark Feminine. *No* leaf is left unturned in her dark-night treatment! Energy that is imprisoned in the underground, at an impasse, irrelevant, unimportant, sentimental, and/or infantile sooner or later gets unearthed, metabolized, processed, and assimilated in the dynamic of transforming growth from undifferentiated energy to conscious differentiated energy, from ego-centered to more spirit/Spirit- and wisdom-directed energy through her doses of dark-night medicine. Initiation in the Dark Feminine has not allowed me to be one-sided within the ultraviolet spectrum of the archetypal energy. As noted in the beginning of Chapter Three, the tree that would grow to heaven must send its roots to hell. Dark-night initiation in the Dark Feminine is about "drinking deeply." The initiation has opened me into a more expansive, psychospiritual, embodied consciousness. In simple language, the universal energy pattern for development and growth has been a summons toward living more of my true nature and path in life. Lady Underground's beckoning has been the portal to opening to a broader awareness of the intimations of the mystery/Mystery and the inexhaustible potential for depth, meaning, purpose, and humble service within this evolving universe. The ongoing endeavor to unearth, discover, metabolize, and to embody my roots consciously has arisen from my lifelong desire and commitment to unmask my defended false self by befriending my core complexes in a multi-dimensional way throughout my psychospiritual process of individuation. My quest continues, as it does for all of us. To paraphrase from Friedrich Nietzsche's *Beyond Good and Evil,* the great epochs of our life occur at the points at which we gain the courage to rebaptize our wounds, our "sores," complexes, dark shadow, for these parts afford us the opportunity to birth, potentially, the best in us, to liberate the soul within us so that we might be more free to live in service to that to which our life's path summons us.

Although I have a wonderful sister who is 13 years younger than I, I primarily grew up being the middle child among five brothers, which had its strengths and, at times, its growing edges. At age 3, for instance, my issues regarding patriarchal power and my voice not counting were constellated in my depths while playing with my three older brothers (The Simon Boys' Club). One time, my feeling-toned concerns were charged further by my mother, who reprimanded and shamed me for my angry behavior with one of my brothers who would not allow me to be the teacher while we all played school. These early "sores" were rubbed in deeper by a rigid, controlling, "letter of the law," first-grade teacher, and by a dominating and bullying, second-grade teacher, especially in an interaction in front of the whole class when this teacher said to me, "You don't know anything and you never will know anything." Befriending these issues, namely powerlessness, my voicelessness, and doubting my way of knowing would be complexes I would address many times in my ongoing, multidimensional process of "drinking deeply."

My maternal grandparents lived on a large farm about 40 miles south of Toledo, Ohio, where I grew up. Visiting the farm as a child and into my adult years was a nurturing experience of many fond memories. I was fascinated by the outdoor and the kitchen-sink water pumps where we had to pump the handle a few times before drinking water began to flow from the well. When we were outside, running and playing in the heat of the summer, it was revitalizing to pump the handle and have cold water flow as we put our mouths near the spout to catch a refreshing drink. Seeking water from the well for all life's necessities at the farm was so very different from life in the city. "Drinking deeply" from the well stirred my imagination and quenched my thirst as a child, and today my soul draws on the inner wellspring, to replenish itself with nurturance and meaning, living the ordinary of life in its many unfolding dimensions.

Once, when I was 6 years old, visiting my grandparents's farm, I stood before my grandmother as she knelt in the dining room altering a beautiful yellow dress that she was making for me. She asked, "Eileen, when you get big, what would you like to be?" "I would like to be myself!" I said. I don't know what that meant to me at 6, but I have always remembered that my grandma warmly smiled and winked at me with delight and said, "How wonderful Eileen, that is terrific!" All these years later, that affirming experience in the early hours of the morning smelling of fresh-harvested wheat, seeing the sunlight streaming in through the dining-room windows, and hearing the pressure cooker whistling in the kitchen as lunch simmered, remains for me a heart-warming, sensory, felt memory of love. Subsequently, I have always lived with a felt sense that to go through life without having been oneself, living one's vocation, and embodying what has been entrusted to us would somehow be a great loss.

When I was 8 years old, I made my First Communion. I have two distinct memories of that day. First, I was excited about the party that was going to take place at my family home in the afternoon! Second, when I returned to my pew after receiving communion and knelt on the kneeler, I became aware, for a brief time, of an undeniable, felt, experience of awe, hearing distinct words within me that I have never forgotten. This happening, with all my sensibilities heightened, has remained over the years in my memory like an indelible mark. Once, I was asked by a Jungian analyst, "When was your first religious experience?" I responded without hesitation, "When I made my First Communion. The only difference between then and now is my having opened to a more expansive circle of perduring attentiveness to the intimations of the mystery/Mystery in the journey of life."

Throughout my childhood and adolescent years, I went with my family to a cottage on Sand Lake in the Irish Hills of Michigan. Fishing from a pontoon boat with my father and five brothers was a real avenue of opportunity during which I developed the capacity to sit still, to be attentive to all that was arising within me and around me, to be patient, and to wait, often in silence, as we fished in a lake that we believed had no fish! We would go out on the spacious pontoon, on water that was 40-50 feet deep, and after baiting the hook, dropping the line, and waiting until it hit the bottom, we reeled in the line by about seven inches, which seemed to be the main activity in the experience of fishing! There was no Garmin fish-finder instrument on the pontoon to help us locate the fish underwater by detecting reflected pulses of sound energy, as in sonar! We would fish for hours and have no bites! Sometimes we would tell jokes, moan, and nag my dad to move to another place, and then maybe *something* would happen!

The wisdom of the psychospiritual journey of individuation, in all its dimensions, and the experience of fishing have a common factor: The ego can't push the river or control the process in any manner. Early on in life, fishing taught me something of being patient, waiting in silence, and being attentive to the murmur of the mystery/Mystery. I have been privileged and humbled to witness the depths of people who "drink deeply." Some of them I have cited earlier in various aspects of their journey in the dark night of initiation in the Dark Feminine. To be of service and to be a witness to people's quests in this manner has been one of the most humbling and deepest blessings of being a Jungian analyst. As any one of us circles to the center and opens to the inexhaustible wellspring of the mystery/Mystery within; words fail to capture and convey the vast potential of drinking from the inner well of our universal heritage, a precious, spiritual, treasure chest within.

In grade school and college, I studied art at the Toledo Museum of Art in Toledo, Ohio. This experience sensitized and nurtured my awareness and appreciation for symbols. In art class, one was instructed to go upstairs in the museum and to be open to what stirred one's being and what captured one's imagination. Often, I found myself in the Egyptian exhibit and would draw the large pottery vessels with their decorative symbols. The primary place I visited was Gallery 14, the Cloister, a reconstructed medieval French courtyard that would have existed at the center of a medieval monastery in southern France around 1150 and 1400. It includes acquired sections of medieval arches and columns with a well at the center. Here, I would often sit and sketch the well with the arches in the background. Also, I tended to visit the courtyard outside of class time, as I felt quietly drawn to the well that was at the center. Today, a framed picture of the French Cloister with the well hangs in the sunroom of my home, and my analytical consulting office is located directly off of an inner courtyard with a well in the center at the Franciscan Monastery of the Holy Land in Washington, D.C.

In my last year of college, I chose to reflect on my life by living at a hermitage for three days. On the third day, I spent seven hours in intentional solitude, sitting under a tree that faced many acres of golden wheat blowing in the breeze. During the last hour, I was moved by an expansive sense of oneness with nature and with all of life, and by a grounding, undeniable, inner peace. I wrote a poem to express the experience as the sun set over the field. Upon my return home, I spent further time in the art studio creating a symbolic design, carving the design into a linoleum block, and making ink prints from that carved-design linoleum block, which helped to further objectify symbolically what was an ineffable soulful reality.

"Drinking deeply," symbolically speaking, has been part of my inner stirring, desire, and core throughout my psychospiritual journey. I associated this dynamic, along with being raised in a family that was conscious about reaching out generously to others, with being a nun. There were also other unconscious dynamics that impacted my choice, as there are for any one of us. My awareness of "drinking deeply" was cultivated in my life choice, in relationships, an attentiveness to shadow, especially the blacker-than-black swamplands, solitude, and in the dark nights of soul, including Lady Underground's dark night of initiatory process into a more expanded, embodied consciousness. Once each year for 40 years I have gone to a hermitage by the ocean to foster listening and being attuned to my depths in the process of doing my inner soul work. Also, one part of my soul's summons has been to research and write a proposal for hermitages to be built for anyone who wants to take some days from the rush and demands of life to "drink deeply." Two hermitages are complete, and for five years they have been available to many of diverse backgrounds to find renewal for their soul before returning to the marketplace to be about their lives. The hermitages are nestled within the natural beauty and quiet of the woods and the oases of gardens on the 42 acres of the Franciscan Monastery of Washington, D.C.

In a dialogue with my father 43 years ago, just two weeks before he died, he expressed to me that he loved me, was proud of me, and realized that I could be myself *and* be a nun. My dad was happy for me in my happiness. After expressing his depth, he also communicated a soulful message to me: "Eileen, continue in life to remember to be yourself. If there is ever a day, no matter what the reason, if you ever decide that you need or want to leave the convent, don't let what anyone says or thinks stand in your way. Your vocation is, first and foremost, to be yourself." My father gave me a phenomenal gift, which still influences my life. After 30 years of being a nun, I consciously chose to leave, as I honored a felt summons from my soul. I recalled my dad's wisdom, which was alive within me and attuned to my spontaneous felt desire to "be myself" and which I had expressed to my grandmother as a 6-year-old child. I have attempted to genuinely continue my journey of embodying my vocation consciously. The verses from Robert Frost's "The Road Not Taken" have had soulful meaning for me, as I chose the road less traveled, and unequivocally, "that has made all the difference."

Also, relationships and intimacy are part of the deep wellsprings of my life. One of the greatest treasures is to have the blessing of cherished relationships, both men and women who live or have lived their lives "drinking deeply" in his or her unique way. We do not come to healing and wholeness in a vacuum. It is in and through the blessing and messiness of interpersonal relationships, including going through the dark night of soul in a relationship, that we become more aware of our shadow and grow potentially in bringing forth and embodying consciously more of our essence, more of our wholeness. Within the relational matrix, one of the best things that we can do for all our relationships is to take responsibility for our own psychic debris, hard and painful as this may be for any one of us. Projections have to be processed; illusions need to be confronted; distortions of reality must be faced; wounded *eros* addressed; and energy integrated and embodied consciously. I have been moved by and have a deep respect for persons who have the courage to do their gripping shadow work. Life is not forever. What we resist, even with a clever masquerading persona, will persist. "Drinking deeply" is about beginning today to befriend our shadow, which is knocking at our door and attempting right now to get our attention, before the final curtain call. Sometimes the reality is missed, and taking flight, rationalizing, justifying, anesthetizing through some self-soothing means, and avoiding dealing with shadow is the chosen route. It is so easy for any one of us to go down this path. Not to do our shadow work, especially the blacker-than-black dimensions, is to alienate oneself further from one's depths, one's significant relationships, and the relational matrix of all life. In essence, it is to refuse to "drink deeply" and to choose in the unfolding now *not to live where one lives.*

Inner soul work is a way to further the empowering directive of "drink deeply." Inner soul work can offer potentially an opening to: a greater spaciousness within; a deeper interiority; a humbler stance in life; a discovery of hidden sources of new life; an expanded capacity for authentic conscious relationships; a fuller realization and appreciation of relationality permeating all dimensions of creation; a greater freedom to be in service; an awakening to contemplative solitude; experiencing a deeper communion with the divine/Divine; and a more discerning heart to the various dimensions in the everyday ordinary revelation and surprise of the murmur of mystery/Mystery. Ongoing inner soul work has expanded my soul more than I could have ever imagined in my life. I am grateful to the mystery/Mystery and to those who generously have assisted me in my inner work, including "teachers" whom I would not have chosen and yet were mirrors for me, affording me many opportunities to grow! For me, to be inattentive to the murmur of the mystery/Mystery in the ordinary of life and my soul's summons would be not to live where I live.

The journey of "drinking deeply" has many twists and turns, and we do not know what will be asked of us, nor the sacrifices required to be true to one's soul in a deep-feeling way to be in service to the mystery/Mystery. All is part of "drinking deeply." Somewhere in the dark unknown, when all support systems seemingly are gone, all the goddesses and gods seem to be silent, and no one else can give us the direction or answer, we have to proceed out into the abyss of the chaotic unknown to really discover and to realize consciously that something more supports us and grounds us from within, something more than we could have ever imagined. When this occurs for anyone of us, we do not forget the grace. In this depth of conscious interiority, we open to an *inner felt* psychospiritual freedom, a profound *felt sensing* of a spaciousness and peace within one's entire body, and an *expansive sense* of soul. We experience in the *now* a felt awareness of inhabiting our bodies in a grounded conscious way with all our sensibilities more awakened. We open to a more extended horizon of being within the web of all life. We discover an eternal ineffable silence/Silence that is the ground of our being. This stillness speaks. This silent inner grounding is a felt sense in the body of a nurturing, empowering, strengthening, "still-energetic," ineffable experience. It is as if one is being held symbolically on the limitless spacious lap of Lady Underground, who in a depth of silence is paradoxically breathing a "still-fire" of love into you. You know *She is*, you are, and the still oneness is real. One is brought to silence. One is moved to profound gratitude. One discovers that one is profoundly supported and loved. There is an awakening to a depth of realization that one is not alone and never has been, even when one might have felt and thought that one was alone. A grounding reservoir of energy springs from deep within as one discovers the courage and the integrity to embody consciously who one is as an incarnated soul and to be about humbly what one is summoned to in life. There is an awareness of essential presence within the experience of one's body that can be described as a greater sense of integration, wholeness, and lightness. Imagination, creativity, and instinctive practical wisdom are generatively liberated in the unfolding enlargement of soul. This progressive differentiation in one's depths is within the interactive universe, where integral to the process of expanded consciousness is the soulful heartfelt realization of hints of the mystery/Mystery as one beholds nature in all her revelations. Ignatius of Loyola refers to this as an experience of the consolation of God; or one might say through a contemplative gaze, the arena of nature is being encountered in its natural essence. (Jung was impressed with Ignatius's Spiritual Exercises and lectured 20 times on the Ignatian Exercises from June 16, 1939, to March 8, 1940.)

In opening consciously to deeper dimensions of soul, including contemplative depths, one experiences a more expansive appreciation and oneness with all of nature. There is an innate archetypal energy within us that is summoning us, shaping us, and so needed by us at this time in history, if a further expansion of the complexification of consciousness is to occur on all levels of life. This deeper element of the archetypal energy of the Dark Feminine, personified in images such as Lady Underground, Ancient Old Woman, Earth Mother, Sister, Lilith, Tara, Kuan Yin, Sheba, Kali, Guadalupe, and Grandmother Earth generate insights and awareness arising from the inner well within that deepen our appreciation of Wisdom, a deeper "Other" dimension in the vast continuum of the archetypal energy. For some scholars, the Wisdom tradition is a basis for eco-theology, the interface between religious wisdom and the pressing ecological and environmental issues of today. Wisdom is not basically a personification in human characterization. She embraces the whole creation, wherein she is its lush, bountiful source and its enduring spirit.[207]

This process of embodying deeper dimensions of soul in the continuum of the Dark Feminine energy is a progressive humbling experience for anyone of us in our unique small way to open to some of the possible human potential for growth and wisdom that lies dormant, in many cases, within the depths of the caverns of the unconscious. "Drinking deeply" involves befriending this potential generative energy. This energy is groping to be heard, unearthed, birthed, and incarnated consciously, so further expansive horizons and dimensions of the universal patterns of energy can be unleashed in the furthering of consciousness for humanity and the web of all life. For example, the Dark Feminine allows differences and opposites to coexist creatively in the interactive and interdependent dynamic of all of life. If we can't accept and respect variances and befriend the opposites within, the likelihood of our capacity to accept, respect, honor, and relate to this energy, manifested outwardly in life, will be low. The challenge for any one of us in our small unique way is to open to the ongoing process of being responsible for befriending and releasing this creative energy for a fuller embodied consciousness. The reality is about showing up and *being present and engaging in life* consciously in the ordinary of life in the here and now, rather than just existing and going through the motions of life in a meaningless and superficial way. The journey continues in the everyday of life with all of its responsibility as any one of us attempts to consciously chop wood, carry water. In the wisdom of the Taoist, "Naturalness is called the Way" (p. 1).[208]

Out of "drinking deeply" from the inner well, the journey in the unknown, with all its perils and promises, continues as reflected in the insightful words of T.S. Eliot: "[B]e still and still moving into another intensity for a further union, a deeper communion" (pp. 189-190).[209] This resourceful energy from the inexhaustible reservoir of the inner well within all of us is the life-giving, creative energy needed to raise awareness and enlarge horizons in the interconnective universe we inhabit, especially in the practical and ordinary of everyday life and the global challenges that face humanity. Questions of depth and practicality arise in life. Some issues need to be addressed with our grounded common sense and instinctual wisdom. Sometimes with the complexity of some realities of life, there are no clear-cut answers and directions. The deeper potential for humanity that Lady Underground and T.S. Eliot beckon us to consider is being attentive to birthing a wider range of the life force that is within and behind the dynamic and resilient web of all life. "Drinking deeply" is awakening individually and collectively to the interconnectedness of all of life and the summons to share in the responsibility "for a further union, a deeper communion." Marianne Williamson speaks to this need in our world today when she emphasizes the need to slow down and learn how to go deep. She says, "The world we want for ourselves and our children will not emerge from electronic speed, but rather from a spiritual stillness that takes root in our souls." Then, and only then, will we create a world that reflects the heart instead of shattering it.[210] "Drinking deeply" will occur to the degree that each of us has the courage to do so in our life through our unique way and path. For me personally, "drinking deeply" has been core to my vocation and my contemplative path in life. And of course, it seems helpful for all of us, myself included, to remember that whatever the twists and turns in the process, remaining humble, honest, and grounded is key.

Dawn: Living the Extraordinary in the Ordinary

Karl Rahner, S.J., the influential 20th-century theologian (referenced at the beginning of this chapter), once noted that the world today needs ordinary mystics who embody contemplative vision; that is, people who live life from a symbolic, contemplative stance in a very ordinary way. We are talking about the potential for embodied conscious *presence*, and as such, one is like a barometer in being that impacts the interactive field in this quantum evolving world just in being one's simple authentic self. This was brought home to me in May of 1988, when I was journeying for a month in Spain, touring some art museums and the historical places related to John of the Cross, Teresa of Avila, and Ignatius of Loyola. I had just completed my doctorate and a dissertation on the similarities, differences, and creative complementarity of the Analytical Psychology of Carl Gustav Jung and the classical spirituality of St. John of the Cross, who were both attentive to human interiority and healing. I wanted to visit the places where John had done his writings, as well as Teresa, another significant Carmelite, and Ignatius, who had influenced my life through making the Ignatian Thirty Day Exercises twice in my life. The latter was a summons I felt moved to honor in my soul's journey, once as an Ursuline nun, and again during my training as a Jungian analyst. For one week, I spent time in solitude during my travels in Spain. I chose to stay at the Montserrat Benedictine Monastery in the mountains of Catalonia, Spain, which is 38 kilometers outside of Barcelona.

Leaving my hotel at dawn, I was at the platform of the train station in Barcelona at 6:00 a.m. with my ticket in hand for Montserrat. I recall seeing only a very old man who was seated on a bench waiting for the train and who appeared to me to be about 88-90 years old, along with two women who seemed to be saying goodbye to him. As the train arrived, the man stood and began to approach the train very slowly. I walked past them, boarded the next train car, which was virtually empty, and took a window seat. Who comes and sits directly across from me, but this elderly man! He made eye contact with me, nodded his head, and smiled warmly three different times. I acknowledged him and then decided to show him a letter from the monastery that was written in Catalan, a language I did not know. I had someone write on a paper in Catalan, *—please, I need cab transportation from the train station in Montserrat to the Benedictine Monastery in the mountains of Catalonia, Spain.* From my pointing to the map, and the bell on the train, the dear man understood that I was asking him to show me where to get off the train for my stop. He communicated a reassuring smile and sense not to worry.

We arrived at a small, one-room train station at the base of the mountains, and the elderly man motioned for me to follow him. We went into the station, and he talked to the man at the ticket booth, who immediately called for a cab. The short, hunched-over, aged gentleman (with many wrinkles revealing his depth of character) gazed at me with laser-light-filled eyes and a warm, kind smile. He extended his hand to shake mine and gave me a nod with a wink. The ticket man, to my surprise, spoke some broken English and I said, "Please ask the man if I can pay for a cab to take him wherever he is going." The ticket man then communicated to me that the older man was saying, "No thank you, I'm going to walk home." Then the service person conveyed to me that the kind man was telling him to inform me that the aged man only has six weeks to live and everyday he asks the Divine to let him do at least one act of kindness a day that would make a difference for someone. The ticket man looked graciously at me, paused, and then continued to express the older man's message: "I knew you were the one who was to receive the kindness today." A tear ran down my face. I was touched deeply and have never forgotten this man and our encounter—his laser eyes communicated a depth of benevolent presence. I felt within my body an alive presence, like a flow of pulsating energy experienced simultaneously with the recognition of the consciousness of this nonverbal experience between us. We walked outside the station, stood and gazed at one another briefly, embraced, and then he stepped back, nodded his head and smiled, turned around, and then began walking down the road. I watched him until he went around the corner. An ordinary elderly man who was dying, being his simple authentic self, living fully in the moment, and extending a simple act of kindness was for me the manifestation of the extraordinary in the ordinary. He was a conduit of the mystery/Mystery.

Charles Williams, the English poet and novelist, once said that the art of living is the capacity to live the ordinary in an extraordinary way and to live the extraordinary in an ordinary way. This simple wisdom of depth for living one's ordinary life is illuminated in the fairy tale of the Black Nubian Woman. The Old Woman communicated this truth by empowering the Nubian woman to be and live her true nature, and to all who would make the return, she offered her guiding directives for initiation, formation, and transformation in the Primordial Dark Feminine in the progressive journey of individuation.

As previously stated, the journey inward is never in and for ourselves alone; it is always to go back out into the circle of life with greater consciousness, responsibility, and humble service in an ordinary way. Each person has a unique gift and capacity for which only each of us can incarnate. What we do to embody and live that gift and path consciously and creatively is our tiny spark of contribution in furthering this quantum cosmogenesis.

Helen Luke, a Jungian therapist and author, believed that whether our talent and capacity is small or great in the world's perspective does not matter at all. What is important is to find and to give our gift—our unique creation. Our bringing forth our ensouled "essence" is within the relational matrix of this amazing interdependent and interconnected universe. In the words of Thomas Berry, cultural historian and theologian: "[O]ur creations are echoes of the creativity present in the entire universe" (p. 254).[211] In birthing and sharing our unique soul essence, we participate in the reciprocal relationship of responsibility for directing and energizing the ongoing evolutionary process and for cocreating the emerging Universe Story. Our "drinking deeply," showing up responsibly in the natural world, and giving generously of our unique essence, opens us to a more felt sensory experience of knowing, appreciating, and respecting the natural design of the archetypal patterns of opposites within all the various depth dimensions of life. In the mystery of the process, as with the Black Nubian Woman, we continue the journey in the ongoing opening to deeper possibilities of the creative dance of dawn, while furthering the unfolding consciousness of the universe. In Jung's words:

> In the last analysis every life is the realization of a whole, that is, of a self for which reason this realization can also be called "individuation." All life is bound to individual carriers who realize it, and it is simply inconceivable without them. But every carrier is charged with an individual destiny and destination, and the realization of these alone makes sense of life. (par. 330) [212]

Conclusion

We began Chapter Four recognizing that the progressive dance of dawn in Lady Underground's dark-night initiation, in assimilating and embodying consciously aspects of the Dark Feminine, is done within an Earth-centered norm of reality and value and the evolving 14 billion-year-old history of the universe. The Great Mother endures as one of the primary goddess images in human interiority. There are light and dark dimensions of the ancient, ever-new foundational archetypal feminine energy of the Mother Goddess. Our exploration has been with the Dark Feminine and specifically with Lady Underground, who is one image of the Dark Feminine. The Dark Goddess is the deeper, earthy, immensely powerful "Other," shadowy, hidden, unknown, mysterious, sublime energy of the Great Mother Goddess. Some core aspects of the goddess energy include mother, virgin, and conduit of wisdom.

In this chapter, our study of Lady Underground's dawn in dark-night initiation in the Dark Feminine has been in the context of the last two stages in a rite of initiation: the encounter with the holy and the return. Befriending consciously these potential patterns of meaning releases an instinctual, creative, and unifying wisdom and more of our virginal essence as we live our ordinary life. Within the continuum of the archetypal Great Mother Goddess energy, there is an inexhaustible potential energy for development in the range of human possibilities of embodied conscious growth from mother to virgin to conduit of wisdom. If our relationships are to be conscious, our planet is to survive, and the well-being of the universe is to further evolve, deeper gradations of the more expanded, hidden, mysterious, sublime depths of the Dark Feminine need to be incarnated consciously in everyday life. Lady

Underground's rite of initiation in the Dark Feminine is an arduous journey of renewal. The dark-night rite of formation calls us to birth and embody consciously a more passionate awareness, compassionate presence, and creativeness of being as we share responsibility in navigating this accelerated shift in the evolving, comprehensive Earth community. At our core, we are all one, which includes being one with the body of Earth herself! Given the intense polarities on every level of life and the climate crisis in our Earth community, Lady Underground beckons us to wake up, "drink deeply," and liberate the inner wellspring of visionary possibilities of who we are and what we can become together as we coparticipate in advancing consciously the unfolding dance of this evolving Universe Story.

We now turn to the final chapter to consider what some of the implications and challenges are for Analytical Psychology, spirituality, and culture.

INNER WORK

The beauty of the Way Is that there is no "way."
~Loy Ching-Yuen

Naturnalness is called the Way.
~*The Secret of the Golden Flower*

The way is not in the sky. The way is in the heart.
~Gautama Buddha

I give you news of the way of this man, but not of your own way. My path is not your path. . . .The way is within us, . . .[W]ho should live your own life if not yourself? So live yourselves. The signposts have fallen, unblazed trails lie before us. Do you not know that you yourselves are the fertile acre which hears everything that avails you?
~C.G. Jung, *The Red Book*

The right way to wholeness is made up of fateful detours and wrong turnings. It is. . .not straight but snakelike, a path that unites the opposites. . .a path whose labyrinthine twists and turns are not lacking in terrors.
~C.G. Jung, *Psychology and Alchemy*

Don't be satisfied with stories,
how things have gone for others.
Unfold your own myth.
~Rumi

~Reflection, Discussion, and Journaling Questions

- In the last 60 years, how do you perceive the feminine principle has returned, been reclaimed, and assimilated in life?

- The Dark Feminine is the "other side" of the Great Goddess within the continuum of the archetypal energy (Mother, Virgin, Conduit of Wisdom). How is the light or dark side of her energy developed within you?
- What image of the Dark Feminine has had meaning for you in your journey?
- There is a continuum in the archetypal formative patterns of energy of the Great Mother Goddess for potential growth and development. These unfolding contents of primal forms need to be humanized, assimilated, and embodied consciously within the context of a unique, particular culture, and a distinct dreamer. What is your experience of the various dimensions of this archetypal energy?
- What do you understand is the relationship between the Dark Feminine and our historical time given the intense polarities, the divisiveness in the nation, and the climate crisis in our Earth community?
- What does the Dark Feminine have to do with the new unfolding Cosmos Story?
- How have you experienced unearthing, birthing, assimilating, and embodying consciously a more passionate awareness and compassionate presence within the evolving comprehensive Earth community?
- It has been said that through a change in human consciousness, the world will be transformed with the realization that the personal and the planetary are interconnected. In your quest in assimilating new dimensions of growth in consciousness, how do you perceive you are making a contribution to the development of the comprehensive Earth community?
- Describe your desire to experience and to know the mystery/Mystery?
- What have been your significant experiences of the "defeat for the ego" that have been a prelude to a more expanded consciousness?

- When you do not listen to the intimations of your dreams or the images of life that are engaging you, how does the unmetabolized energy manifest in your body?
- How does Lady Underground's archetypal energy stir your depths and challenge your consciousness?
- Describe your encounter with the holy/Holy that has expanded your soul?
- In the dawn of your journey, how have you experienced your sensibilities awakened?
- How has the reality of accepting, holding, and befriending the tension of the opposites until something new emerges opened you to consciousness and more enlarged vision?
- Embracing the value of conscious suffering opens us to fuller dimensions of soul. What aspects of soul have you discovered through your experience? Where do you perceive this dynamic as operative in the global world?
- Character and virtue are being formed and etched in the heart and soul of who we are through Lady Underground's dark night of initiation. How would you describe your growth in character and virtue? Where do you perceive signs of growth in character and virtue in our country, in our global community?
- The teleology of the soul in dawn obliges us to incorporate our new expanded consciousness into the conduct of daily life, including care for the body of Earth herself and the evolving planet. How have you been able to navigate, metabolize, and embody the energy of this experience in a way that furthered the consciousness of your humanity and the awakening of our collective potential?
- Who are some of your heroes/heroines who embody for you a sense of dawn? What is it about their lives and journeys that speaks to you of the conscious embodiment of dawn energy?
- Who are historical figures who inspire you to a wider horizon of living a more conscious embodied life? How does this historical individual or persons engage you in living a more awakened embodied consciousness? If they were to pay you a visit, what do you

imagine they would affirm about you, and how do you imagine they would challenge you in your journey of individuation?

- What is the underside of the nub of your dark destructive shadow that is your gold awaiting to be unleashed for generative creativity?
- What blocks you from embodying consciously your creative soul's summons?
- Describe how you have experienced your destructive, blacker-than-black shadow become metabolized, assimilated, transformed, and a source for generative energy channeled in service in the outer world?
- How has befriending your blacker-than-black shadow been a portal for you showing up in the outer world as a humbler, more powerful conduit in service to the mystery/Mystery?
- Jung reflected that our task is "to light a candle in the darkness of mere being." How do you contribute to furthering consciousness and our collective potential in the interconnected web of all life?
- What is your soul's summons at this time in life and our planet's history?
- How do you honor and live your "ordinary life" within the circle of your family, friends, workplace, civic community, and/or country?
- How have you experienced the "extraordinary" in the "ordinary" of your life?
- Where do you notice the regressive pull of the psyche in your life? What is your way of working with this energy as you are about your path in your ordinary everyday life?
- How do you tend your soul's way both in your emerging story and the unfolding Universal Story?
- What are the remaining echoes of a psyche-soma split that are calling for your attention and inner soul work?
- What is your way of intentional solitude, and how do you experience it nurturing your soul and path in life?
- In your meaningful relationships, what are you projecting and asking of the other that you need to befriend and carry consciously yourself?
- How does the fairy tale of the Black Nubian Woman speak to your soul and vocation?

- Describe your experience of mercy. Whom do you need to extend mercy to in your life?
- How have you experienced the "return" of descent/ascent experience in Lady Underground's dark-night initiation in the Primordial Dark Feminine?
- What is it for you to "drink deeply," and how do you experience this in your life?
- How does the Ancient One's directives for the "return" from initiation that were given to the Black Nubian Woman speak to your life? How do you live the directive/s that capture your attention?

~Process Exercises

- After reading Chapter Four, reflect on what image captures and engages your focus. There may be more than one image, and if so, ask yourself which image stirs your wonderment or captivates your attention the most and go with that image. As you proceed to work with your image, find a comfortable posture that enables you to enter an interior space of silence. Close your eyes. Bring your attention to your abdomen, take a deep-belly breath, and while exhaling at your own natural rhythm, you might begin to consider allowing yourself permission to relax. Take another deep-belly breath, and as you release it, you might do so in a way that is comfortable for you. Again, take an expansive belly breath, and while exhaling at your own rhythm, you may be discovering already that you have begun to relax while letting go even more as you enter your own inner depths. Slowing down, relaxing into your inner dwelling, and opening to silence can be a wonderful opportunity to be with and to explore the image that has moved you and caught your attention in Chapter Four. Take another deep breath, and as you do so, you might scan your entire body and notice what is arising within you. If there is a great deal of "noise" or chatter going on in your mind, simply notice this reality, allow it to be without judgment, and simply come back to your breath. Stay with the relaxing breaths until you are present to yourself in your body. When you feel attuned to yourself, begin to call to your

the dreamer's associations with this particular image? Reflect on the other images in the dream and notice the personal associations with these images. Are there any archetypal themes or characters in the dream? Discern whether the dream images are objective or subjective representations. This will impact how one interprets a dream. A subjective representation entails a symbolic "picture" of the intrapsychic reality. If a character in the dream is unknown or triggers an emotional charge, consider first a subjective interpretation. The objective interpretation refers to external reality. For example, persons, places, and material things in the dreamer's life that appear in the dream with accuracy as they actually are in life would indicate considering an objective interpretation. A rule of thumb is if a family member, significant other, or close friend appears in a dream with photographic accuracy, then consider first an objective interpretation. It may also be that dream images can have both subjective and objective meanings. When this occurs, attempt to reflect on the meaning of the dream with a consideration and perspective of what may be the key issue at hand in the dreamer's life. Also, explore the dream and ask what current attitudes, behaviors, or life situation could this dream be compensating? What could the psyche be attempting to say to the dreamer through the dream? What is a surprise, affirmation, new or unexpected message being given by the dream? Last, be open to the possibility that a dream may have another purpose or message. Some possibilities might be:

a) A prospective dream reflects a future development that may be positive or negative and attempts to capture the dreamer's attention in eliciting a corrective response.
b) A prophetic dream is a precognition experience of detail and events that are of significance.
c) A telepathic dream taps into the psyche of another person conceivably to learn or become aware of a reality or an event that could not otherwise be known, such as a truth about a friend or something like the reality of death of another.

- Consider the Ancient One's symbolic directives to the Black Nubian Woman in "the return" and the "journey home": time to pause, walking slowly and steadily, drinking deeply, and go slowly. Which of these directives inspires, intrigues, concerns, and/or troubles you? Consider entering into an active-imagination exercise with whichever directive captures your focus. Allow the directive to be personified and to enter into dialogue with the personified directive. There are many ways of doing active imagination in soul work. One way is doing a right-hand/left-hand active imagination. Remember, your dominant hand represents your conscious voice, and your nondominant hand in this exercise represents the directive that inspires, intrigues, concerns, and/or troubles you. If you do not want to dialogue with a personified directive, you may want to dialogue with the Ancient One. What would She communicate to you if you gave Her some time within your interior? What would you want to express to Her? What would She have to say to you about the planet, the Universe Story? What would emerge in the soulful experience and dialogue with the Ancient One and yourself? In this active-imagination experience, your dominant hand represents your conscious voice, and your nondominant hand in this process represents the voice of the Ancient One. What may emerge is silence. Can you allow yourself to go with this experience? It is important to have an attitude of openness and flexibility when doing active-imagination inner soul work. There is no one way. Remember, the mystery/Mystery is the mover in the journey. Also, you need a pen or pencil and paper to do this exercise. Take some quiet time to become present to yourself before doing the active-imagination exercise. Then, begin with your dominant hand while allowing whatever comes forth from within you to surface, as you start to write what is arising within you to the part represented by your nondominant hand. Then change hands and hold your pen or pencil in your nondominant hand as you allow expression to what comes forth from within you in response to the communication from your conscious voice. Allow the inner dialogue to flow and unfold naturally and to continue until it feels complete for you. What have you become conscious of through your active-imagination experience? How might you assimilate and honor what you have become aware of in your process? Again, remember to take time to acknowledge yourself for being attentive to your inner soul work.

- Reflect on your experience of birthing and embodying the progressive dance of dawn. If you were to visit an art museum, what painting or sculpture stirs your imagination and captures for you the energy of this psychospiritual dynamic? Consider writing about this in your journal as a further way to objectify and to befriend the energy within you that is attempting to be heard and integrated into consciousness.
- There are many different styles of music. Allow your imagination to wonder and to ponder what type and what piece symbolically expresses for you the energy of dawn in Lady Underground's dark night of initiation in the Dark Feminine?
- Perhaps you have had the opportunity to attend a theater and to experience a creation by masterful choreographers, performed by talented dancers. Is there a performance that stirs your imagination, moves your heart, and captures for you symbolically the energy of dawn embodied consciously?
- Another active-imagination, meditative exercise is the loving-kindness exercise. It is an ancient 2,500-year-old practice within the Buddhist tradition and is also kindred to many other traditions. After recollecting yourself interiorly, start the meditation by first imaging sending the energy to yourself, then to significant others, then to identified others of need and challenge, and finally to the universe. When you begin with yourself, there may be a self-part that you have been working with in your inner work, so you can imagine this part and then send the loving kindness to this self-part. Otherwise, express the loving-kindness to the whole of you. Also, the phrases of the loving-kindness are basic; however, you might experience another phrase flowing in your meditation that arises within you. Trust yourself and go with your way of practice. There is no one way. As you reflect on your experience, you may realize a shift in you, as well

as things shifting with others, and life in the interactive field. Consider journaling about this awareness as a further way to objectify and to honor your experience.

May I be filled with loving kindness.
May I be well.
May I be peaceful and at ease.
May I be happy. (Remember, adapt this to express your sentiment)
May you (name the significant other, person in need, or one who challenges you) be filled with loving kindness.
May you be well.
May you be peaceful and at ease.
May you be happy. (Revise accordingly)
May all beings be filled with loving kindness.
May all beings be well.
May all beings be peaceful and at ease.
May all beings be happy. (Modify suitably)

~Body-Energy Work

- After reading Chapter Four, what reality in your depths is stirred that is challenging you to a more expanded self-awareness? What, if any, are the remaining echoes of discounting beliefs that you have about yourself, others, life, money, sex, power, intimacy, addiction, and/or the planet? Are there any old wounds of origin, "sores," or complexes that are the underpinning of any one of these realities? Note any remaining echoes of your self-limiting beliefs, old wounds of origin, "sores," or complexes and consider doing an EMDR exercise with a trained EMDR practitioner as one possible way to demagnetize the possible charge, feeling-toned response, and cellular memory surrounding the reality that is challenging and/or triggering you. This process is a creative way to access the active imagination in the experience of healing and integration while demagnetizing and releasing the trigger and charge of a complex. This is one resourceful and innovative way to befriend what is arising within us and summoning us toward embodied consciousness. The process is a form of body-energy work that can release the generative soul within us.

- Meridian tapping, of which Emotional Freedom Technique is the simplest and most common form, is an effective tool that can assist in the process of demagnetizing self-limiting beliefs, painfully charged shadow material, complexes, loss, grief, trauma, and/or the struggle with the tension of opposites. The 11th annual Tapping World Summit 2019 was just completed, and this body-energy-work modality is being taught worldwide with remarkable results. The Tapping Solution Foundation is committed to Create Global Healing. Since 2010, the foundation has sponsored a group of trained professionals in trauma relief and resiliency services to go to Rwanda to work with the orphaned genocide survivors, as well as to work with the Newtown, Connecticut, community at all levels with a model of sustainable long-term, community-based humanitarian support, based on Tapping. This is *one* form of body-energy work that you can access and do yourself once you learn some of the basics. You can work with this technique in relationship to a dream and some charged reality in the dream, as well as tapping to open to your creative active imagination as you process and open to a deeper wisdom of your dream. Make a list of the remaining realities in life that are a challenge, have echoes of charged energy, or are a trigger for you. Reflect on the recorded list. Given your list plus your reading of Chapter Four and what was activated within you, ask yourself in this present moment what captures your attention and imagination the most that is longing to be heard, metabolized, and assimilated in embodied consciousness? Find an EFT practitioner and do an EFT sequence as a way to work with your depths, befriend the energy, and objectify what is attempting to be integrated into consciousness. The tapping is a modality of body-energy work that touches into the active-imagination process and potentially offers a more integrative approach in the process of inner soul work.

  After your EFT session, consider recording your experience in a journal as a further way to objectify, integrate, and honor your inner soul work. Some reflective questions that may assist you include:
  - What did you learn about yourself through your EFT body-energy experience?

  - How was your active imagination opened in this session?
  - As you focus now on your interiority, what is arising within you as you are present to yourself?
  - In reflecting on your inner work and your present outlook, what do you perceive the psyche is attempting to engineer?
  - What is the summons of your soul at this time in your life?
  - How are you willing to honor your soul's summons in your everyday life?
  - Take some time to acknowledge yourself for your inner work.
- Reflect on the material from Chapter Four and note what image at the present time captures your attention. As you bring your awareness to your breath and scan your body, where do you sense the energy of this image within your body? Find a quiet and safe setting where you might have space to move and not be interrupted in any way. Allow yourself to take a deep breath and align your attention to being present to yourself and your image. As you proceed, let arise within you whatever is manifesting as you focus your awareness on the image and where you sense the energy of this image in your body. In this exercise of soulful, arising movement, your breath, sound, and movement are a direct form of active imagination. The conscious focus is on the imaginal as it expresses itself through the breath, sound, and/or movement. In this the body is the medium; the breath, sound, and movement are the message. In this particular form of tracking your image within the experience of your body, the active-imagination dialogue is a felt physical and emotional engagement through the medium of the body. Allow yourself to move freely in your body movement and when your experience feels complete, take a deep breath as you find your way to bring closure to your process. When you are finished you might want to write about your movement as another way to objectify and befriend your depths. This soulful, arising, body-movement exercise may also be done with two others. One person holds consciously the space for the individual who is the body mover, and the other is the observer. The exercise may be for 10 or 15 minutes for the movement component and then time for processing the exercise. Again, if you do this body-movement exercise alone, or if you do it in the presence of two others,

remember, before you finish your experience, take some time to acknowledge yourself for your inner work.

- A body-awareness exercise that is helpful to develop and to practice at any time, including doing it before any of the other noted process exercises, body-energy work, or prior to intentional solitude is the body-focus-awareness exercise. Find a comfortable position and take three deep-belly breaths as you focus in on your right foot and bring your awareness to your right large toe. You continue to keep your awareness here until you sense the movement of energy in this toe and then move to the next toe doing the same until you have been present to each toe of your right foot. Then be aware of the whole of your right foot and continue to be present to your right foot until you begin to feel the subtle movement of energy in your foot. Once you feel the energy in a particular area of your body that you are present to, then proceed to move to the next area doing the same reality. So, following your right foot you then would move to your right ankle, calf, thigh, hip, shoulder, forearm, wrist, large thumb, each finger, and your whole right hand.

  Next, you would bring your awareness to your left large toe and continue now to follow the same procedure on the left side of the body that you did on the right side of your body. If you notice that you are not feeling anything in a particular area, simply note this reality, and then after some time, move to the next area of your body and bring your awareness to this area. The more you do the body-awareness exercise, the more you will come to feel the energy pulsating in a particular area and throughout your body.

  Also, if you realize that you are trying hard, once you are aware of this reality take some deep-belly breaths and relax. The exercise is one way of being present to yourself and opening to your depths in your body.

CHAPTER FIVE
JOURNEYING WITH AWAKENED-PASSIONATE HEART AND COMPASSIONATE PRESENCE

And we are put on earth a little space, that we may learn to bear the beams of love.
~William Blake

Don't be satisfied with stories, how things have gone for others.
Unfold your own myth.
~Rumi

Our role is no longer to merely ease suffering, bind up wounds, and feed the hungry,
but through every form of effort to raise the powers of love
upward to the next stage of consciousness.
~Pierre Teilhard de Chardin

In relation to the earth, we have been autistic for centuries. Only now have
we begun to listen with some attention and with a willingness to respond
to the earth's demands that we cease our industrial assault, that we renew
our human participation in the grand liturgy of the universe.
~Thomas Berry, *The Dream of the Earth*

It is not sufficient any longer to listen at the end of a wire to the rustlings of galaxies;
it is not enough even to examine the great coil of DNA. . .These are our extended
perceptions. But beyond lies the great darkness of the ultimate Dreamer,
who dreamed the light and the galaxies. Before act was, or substance existed,
imagination grew in the dark.
~Loren Eiseley

The struggle of today is not altogether for today—it is for a vast future also.
~Abraham Lincoln

The way is not in the sky. The way is in the heart.
~Gautama Buddha

The best and most beautiful things in the world cannot be seen or even touched—they must be felt with the heart.
~Helen Keller

There is a Light that shines beyond all things on earth, beyond us all, beyond the heavens, beyond the highest, the very highest heavens. This is the Light that shines in our heart.
~Chandogya Upanishad

There is a vitality, a life force, an energy, a quickening, that is translated through you into action, and because there is only one of you in all time, this expression is unique. And if you block it, it will never exist through any other medium and will be lost.
~Martha Graham

Our true home is in the present moment. The miracle is not to walk on water. The miracle is to walk on the green earth in the present moment.
~Thich Nhat Hanh

Everything now depends on [humanity]; immense power of destruction is given into [our] hand, and the question is whether [we] can resist the will to use it, and can temper [our] will with the spirit of love and wisdom.
~Carl Jung, *Answer to Job*

The Universe contains the All. We are the context for possibility, made open through grace and surrender.
~George Burr Leonard

Please remember, it is what you are that heals, not what you know.
~Carl Jung

When reverence becomes central to the human experience, the exploitation of all forms of Life by *the human species, including the exploitation of humans by humans, will cease.*

~Gary Zukov

Laws and institutions must go hand in hand with the progress of the human mind. As that becomes more developed, more enlightened, as new discoveries are made, new truths disclosed, and manners and opinions change with the change of circumstances, institutions must advance also, and keep pace with the times.

~Thomas Jefferson

Our human compassion binds us, the one to the other—not in pity or patronizingly, but as human beings who have learned how to turn our common suffering into hope for the future.

~Nelson Mandela

Aware of it or not, each of us is involved in the grand enterprise of evolution. The new information being generated in each of our lives contributes inevitably to the ever-complexity and richness of the universe. Our key choice is whether to become aware of and take responsibility for the power of our intentionality.

~George Burr Leonard

Love and compassion are necessities, not luxuries.
Without them, humanity can not survive.

~His Holiness, the 14th Dalai Lama

You must not lose faith in humanity. Humanity is an ocean; if a few drops of the ocean are dirty, the ocean does not become dirty.

~Mahatma Gandhi

There is no difference between healing your body and healing the Earth or helping another to heal. It is all the same Body. Begin. . .include one small part at a time. You will be healing the Whole.

~Alla Renee Bozarth

God picks up the reed-flute world and blows.
Each note is a need coming through one of us,
a passion, a longing-pain. Remember the lips
where the wind-breath originated, and let your note be clear.
Don't try to end it. Be Your Note. . .
~Rumi

Implications for Analytical Psychology

Having examined Lady Underground's twilight and midnight of dark-night initiation in the Dark Feminine in Chapter Three and dawn of night in Chapter Four, we now turn our attention in this final chapter to explore and to consider what some of the implications are for Analytical Psychology, spirituality, and culture and the world soul. Moreover, at this historical time in the evolution of Analytical Psychology, our focus is to continue to contemplate in what way the symbol of Lady Underground calls and challenges us in our being and doing as Jungians. We now direct our reflection to *how* the archetypal image summons us in analytical theory and practice. In addition, we will consider how this image of the primordial Dark Goddess obliges us to be open to new frontiers in the progressive development of Analytical Psychology.

Theory

Pluralism and diversity among Jungians are a rich and enlivening reality in the field of Analytical Psychology. The unfolding and evolving history of the profession has developed from Jung and the first generation of Jungians to the present with some emerging theoretical differences over the years that include a broad spectrum of views and practical approaches. Regardless of whether our theoretical orientation is some variation or combination of the theoretical viewpoints within the continuum of the classical, the developmental, and/or the archetypal perspective, the Dark Feminine energy, for example, as imaged by Lady Underground, challenges us in this evolving interconnected and interdependent era to befriend the deeper unconscious pockets of our primal energy and to have an awakened felt sensory awareness, compassionate presence, appreciation, and lived reality of a more enlivened, embodied essence.

Analysis is more than an intellectual process. Historically in our patriarchal Western mindset there has been a greater emphasis, value, and respect given verbally and nonverbally to spirit and sound rational thinking *over* the body and grounded, connected, and sensed feeling. The importance of the body can no longer be ignored or neglected in our practice within our consulting rooms and in our conversations about the psyche in depth psychology. We need to listen with our attuned sensibilities to the body for the sake of our soul essence. To have an attentive somatic awareness and to access various effective forms of body-energy work within the analytical process serve as a portal to unearthing kinesthetically stored affect-laden cellular memories, stemming from conception and birth throughout emerging stages of growth. The development of our psyche-soma structure (including our primitive defensive system) and subsequent cellular memory begins to unfold *in utero* and in the awakening encounters with parental figures in infancy.

The energy flow in the body that has been disrupted and blocked due to many possibilities, some being unmetabolized infant anxiety and frustration, emotional and/or physical abandonment, shame, trauma, and the lack of attuned empathic parental mirroring does not disappear or evaporate into thin air. The body carries all memory, including preverbal. The body does not lie. It is the manifestation of the soul. Attention to the somatic unconscious can't be overlooked or left out of the analytical framework. To have an attentiveness to the somatic unconscious within the analytical process is to be alert to manifesting signals revealed by the body, including sounds such as a sigh or a gasp, and holding patterns in the breath and musculature of the body. Primal caverns of the soul hold dormant, vital energy that can be a rich source for more expanded and integrated passionate-felt awareness and compassionate presence in everyday life, analytical practice, interpersonal relationships, and interactive communities. The potential generative seeds of embodied instinctual wisdom, compassionate presence, and empathic respect for differences, which are so needed in our contemporary world, are hidden in the dormant energies lodged and imprisoned in the underground musculature chambers of the somatic unconscious. The process of befriending new frontiers in the caverns of depth within our interiority and the untapped dimensions of the Earth herself is a soulful reality requiring ongoing inner depth work. This soulful endeavor embraces the cellular blacker-than-black aspects of the soul in all its complexity, chaos, anxiety, fiery anger, and messiness, as dimensions inherent to birthing new life, as Analytical Psychology continues to evolve in its development and influence, as we Jungians grow in a felt sensory embodied consciousness, as well.

Hence, the archetypal energy of Lady Underground challenges the ongoing emerging field of Analytical Psychology and us, as Jungians, to move beyond scholarly talk of the psyche and soma. Moreover, the Dark Feminine, as imaged in Lady Underground, is beckoning us to befriend our shadow at deeper levels. What is this reality? One aspect of our shadow is the underside of the long-standing emphasis and value given verbally and nonverbally to spirit and sound, rational thinking, namely, the body and grounded, connected, sensed feeling. The process of individuation is not "one" or the "other." The journey is toward wholeness, which includes a "both-and" perspective. Thus, Lady Underground is inviting us to open to these deeper, more sublime psychospiritual resonances of energy in birthing and integrating a wider horizon of embodied consciousness in the field of Analytical Psychology, in the ordinary of our life, and in our soul's vocation.

While our historical roots in Analytical Psychology reveal that Jung emphasized the body, as he discussed it in almost every volume of the *Collected Works*, a contemporary challenge involves the actual openness to, attention to, and tracking of the body's manifest signals in the interactive field of the analytical relationship. Lady Underground calls us to explore and consider the individuation journey in new and extended ways of perception through particular focus on the quality of energetic resonance of the body, the visibility of the soul. Furthermore, the importance of focusing on and tracking the body's subtle intimations and obvious manifestations during dark-night initiation can assist the analysand or the sojourner in experiencing a more holistic process in the analytical relationship, as the analysand progresses in unearthing, metabolizing, and embodying in an integrative way the energy patterns and movements of the Dark Primordial Feminine.

The body's cues that are both verbal and nonverbal (e.g., facial expressions, eye contact, posture, gestures, sounds, breath rhythm, finger and foot movement, musculature armor, as well as tone, speed, and pitch of voice) are the gate to deeper and more primitive subtle archaic psychic energies in the somatic unconscious. These pockets of unmetabolized energy are potential for development and life. Thus, the significance of tracking the subtle signs of the body is essential in the progressive spiral rite of initiation, if we are to become more conscious of our matter. Otherwise, the process remains more an intellectual, rational analysis rather than a felt resonance of an embodied consciousness of a deeper realm of our cellular depths. The energies that are rigidly trapped in the primitive defensive structure of the neuropathways remain blocked, frozen, imprisoned, and unanalyzed. Given that the psyche is a self-regulating energetic system, the call and gift of the soul being revealed through the language, map, and symptoms of the body go unheard and unmetabolized.

The body has a language of its own. For example, a person who may be struggling with a mother, father, or power complex during an analytical session may tend to have increased movement in the auric field and often energetic movement in the solar plexus (third chakra) area. The degree of intensity will vary, depending on how charged the feeling tone of the complex is for the individual. If the energy field can be seen, the condition and functioning of the solar plexus is more obvious to the analyst. While, undeniably, perceiving the energy field is not a necessary component to being an analyst, the awareness of the auric field does provide another template for understanding and confirming what may be occurring in the interactive field. The body's information can be ascertained kinesthetically, auditorily, visually, through a dream, artwork, written material, authentic movement, various forms of body-energy work, and/or some other symbolic material. However the soul reveals itself, the fact remains that having a keen awareness of the body's self-communicative language can assist an analyst in hearing the murmur of the soul that is attempting to emerge into consciousness. Such awareness of these realities will also help the analyst to ask the analysand appropriate explorative questions. This can lead to an arising, felt, alive sense of presence and connectedness within one's body, to deeper conscious realizations and to raise the awareness of the analyst when the analytical space needs to be held for the greater good and further psychic development of the analysand.

Practice: Somatic Awareness and Body-Energy Techniques

Theoretically and practically, analysts, Jungian-oriented therapists, spiritual directors, and educators might find it helpful, effective, and enrichening for themselves and those they serve to be open to a more expanded process that includes introducing somatic awareness and body-energy techniques that can help to facilitate a fuller sense of a felt, sensory, embodied consciousness. Having a conscious awareness of experiencing our inner pulsating energy within our bodies can lead to opening to a greater felt spaciousness within and intimations of the mystery/Mystery. This process of psychospiritual maturing consciously within the body is a progressive maturation of an interior felt knowing that can lead to a stillness that nourishes and speaks, and a reservoir of wisdom for life and service within this continuous unfolding universe. Whether we are conscious and agree with it or not, each of us is an integral interconnected and interdependent living soul within the emerging web of a larger living body of the Earth, herself. The development of this awareness, does not occur through sound rational thinking or doing, but by virtue of a quantum wholeness that we allow to break through within us in a felt, experiential, grounded way. It is more about a felt, sensory, knowing resonance than rational thinking. Within the analytic frame, body-energy soul work is a portal to a more grounded inner freedom, spaciousness, and a larger at-homeness both within and without.

For all of us involved in inner soul work, it is essential to remember that there is *no one way,* especially with regard to body-energy methods and the interplay with the process of active imagination. Having a sensitivity and a respect for a person's unique way of accessing and processing active-imagination experiences is important. Sometimes, different modalities and techniques are needed, or perhaps, more helpful at various stages of a person's growth. Also, the form will differ depending on the strength and development of the ego and the psychic container of the person, as well as the trust level in the analytical relationship and process. Moreover, it is the mystery/Mystery that is moving and engineering the process. I'm often moved and humbled to silence by the inexhaustible, creative, unique manifestation of the intimations of the mystery/Mystery for each person. Remaining open, with a perduring attentiveness to where or how the soul is emerging, is essential. Sometimes what can help in this reality is to hold the space for a person to have an inquiry. This holding of space includes being curious (what do you notice? what is arising within you right now?); staying with the process (what happens next?); describing the phenomenological experience with as much precision as you can sense and detect; remaining open and flexible in attitude (check assumptions and clarify meanings); embodying attuned empathic listening; showing genuine interest, kindness, and compassion; being nonjudgmental; and staying in the present moment.

Some other simple and nonthreatening modalities that can be weaved into the interactive communication within the analytic frame might be the technique of Mindfulness (defined previously) or what some call Focusing as one processes a dream or attends to what is being presented by the analysand, client, or spiritual directee. For example, after a person shares a dream, one could say to the dreamer, "I'm wondering, as you are present to yourself, what captures your attention the most about this dream as you bring the dream into our interactive space." Let the analysand know you have heard what he or she has shared by empathically reflecting it back to the person. Allow the exploration to unfold naturally as you interact with one another and empathically mirror what the person is communicating. Then, the analyst can say something like, "As you're talking about this image, where do you sense the energy of this image in your body," or "As you're attentive to your image, what are you noticing is arising within your body as you speak about your dream image?" Next, one would focus on this as the process unfolds in the interactive communication. Think of the dream as an alive and embodied energy that has emerged from the depths, which includes the somatic unconscious. The analyst needs to maintain a presence of respect toward the analysand while he/she focuses on the felt experience of the image and the body interacting along with the unfolding imaginal process. Focusing or what is known as Mindfulness is a way to be empathically present to the person, while assisting him/her to let go of the controlling mind and its effort to manipulate everything. Having a sense of wonderment and/or a playful curiosity is helpful to the individual in intentionally attending to what is surfacing in the exploration. In this same regard, another effective way to get out of the head is to be very descriptive of the felt sense that is arising in the body in the emerging and unfolding imaginal dynamic. In this way, the soul explorer learns to allow his/her own unique life's meaning, direction, and instinctual wisdom to arise from the well within one's depths. Thus, soulful and conscious embodiment emerges gradually over time from an attuned process felt directly within the body. Also, accessing this technique does not negate weaving it into the process of a classical Jungian approach to a dream, of being attentive to the exposition, development, crisis or impasse, and the lysis or outcome.

Furthermore, if we intentionally and respectfully are attuned to the body, it will communicate to us whether the revelation is cold, hard, armored, dead, blocked, or warm, soft, receptive, aliveness, and/or pulsating. If someone in the process expresses that nothing is happening, nothing is something. Or, someone who is very much in the head may note, "I can't get a felt sense of anything." The analyst needs to be attuned consciously to the person and the interactive field to know whether to ask, "What is it like for you to experience nothing?" or "How do you feel about not being able to have any awareness of a felt sense?" or simply to make an empathic response and be soulfully present. Sometimes, as the former question is tracked, Focusing may assist in unlocking charged feelings and realization, and at other times, one can be at a psychic impasse, and this needs to be accepted and respected with compassion. Soul work belongs to the individual. It will be unique for each person. It is not appropriate to push the river or *try* to do anything in any manner. For all of us in the healing journey, sometime or other, we may know an image or issue in the mind but do not have a felt sense of it in the body. Having a respectful space held for us, a patience, a nonjudgmental attitude, and compassion for this psychic impasse, unresolved issue, or self-part is key. In time, and sometimes a very long time depending on psyche's reality, and in each person's own unique manner, somatic awareness can occur in a body-felt way that opens one to a greater freedom, spaciousness within one's interior, and creativity. It is a moving experience to finally have a felt, body sense when one's affective dimension has had to go underground in childhood or adolescence due to family illnesses, trauma, circumstances, dynamics, and demands, or if it was not safe to experience and express emotions in one's family, social, or cultural milieu, and/or because of a lack of parental mirroring and empathic mediating. For example, in an analytical session, Saoirse, a perceptive, bright, gifted woman who is attuned to her psychospiritual journey, had a felt, body awareness in session that had a depth of meaning for her. While processing her dream, she engaged in Focusing as she explored her image of a child being released from an underground cave. Saoirse sensed where she felt the energy of the image in her body and was attentive to all that began to arise within her as she breathed into the image and tracked it in session. What was a felt, sensory experience through Focusing opened to a moving awareness of healing for Saoirse and initiating the birth of her unique creativity as an author of children's books.

Another form of body-energy soul work is authentic movement or what I call "soulful, arising movement." This form of body-energy work assists in unearthing charged, unmetabolized, feeling-toned self-parts that perhaps became constellated *in utero* and during early infancy and continue to impact consciousness. Strongly heightened, emotionally charged, preverbal and presymbolic material that has been constellated in early development is less reachable by verbal aspects of analysis. This "underground" energy, trapped in caverns of our inner landscapes, holds potential for regenerativity and creativity. Thus, this movement is a nonverbal modality that accesses the breath and active imagination in the process. One enters this experience nonjudgmentally, accepting and being with what is present. One begins by centering oneself, then bringing one's awareness to the breath while taking a deep-belly breath, and exhaling at one's own rhythm. Next, when one is ready, one gradually begins to move to one's own rhythms, as one allows to arise in the body whatever spontaneously is surfacing as one freely moves. The mover is present to the symbolic depths and whatever is emerging in the moment. As one is present consciously to oneself in this creative contemplative way, the soul mover trusts and learns to allow one's own unique rhythm and process to unfold, to develop, and to be expressed naturally. A soul with a perduring attentiveness that is attuned to one's genuine felt sensed rhythms can open to a resonance in the body, especially in the heart, almost as if the body is being played as a musical string instrument like a violin, a cello, or a classical guitar. One can experience in an alive way the felt subtle-body resonance of the energy. Soulful arising movement is symbolic and can be a profound contemplative experience. Sometimes, what evolves for the experienced contemplative soul mover is the discovery of one's emerging life-meaning and instinctual body wisdom as it arises from the well within one's depths.

While soulful arising movement may be helpful and appropriate for some at one stage, at another point, a whole different way of doing soul work may be necessary. There is no *one* way. What remains essential is the natural way for any one particular soul, whatever that may be for a person. Another modality of choice is a process of holding in awareness a selected valued image from a dream while simultaneously doing deep-belly breathing and allowing to emerge whatever may arise as a portal of entering an active-imagination process. This form can be a deep, felt, sensory way to release pockets of repressed energy and unconscious cellular memory that present themselves in a dream image, and when worked with at a body-energy level, can unleash vital energy and meaning. Again, what is important is there is no *one* way, and moreover, for all of us, what is vital is finding and paying attention to our unique soul's way.

For those of us who are privileged to accompany others in their inner soul work, we need to find the courage in an ethical and professional way (including the necessary continuing education) to hold the space for those who are seeking a more holistic and integrative way that includes somatic awareness and body-energy techniques. As noted in Chapter Two, "New Paradigm," Lady Underground summons us to be voyagers of the night sea journey with particular attention on and keen perception of the importance of the body as we plumb our depths, to find and to embody a deeper human interiority. In the words of John O'Donohue, "New frontiers. . .will emerge as you begin to approach them, calling forth from you the full force and depth of your undiscovered gifts" (p. 20).[213]

Furthering Jung's Insight on the Interconnectedness of the Psyche and Soma

If you haven't realized already, this book has been gradually revealing that the archetypal energy of Lady Underground becomes humanized and embodied consciously through *experiencing dark-night initiation* in the Dark Feminine. It is true that there is no one way for dark night to be experienced, metabolized, and integrated in the journey of individuation. Each person's path in the process is one of a kind—distinctive for each soul. However, the rich tools of Analytical Psychology, both in theory and especially in practice, can offer the sojourner in dark-night initiation guidance in discovering insightful perceptions and instinctual wisdom in the process of *experiencing*, and discerning various gradations of reality, in the alchemical process of transformation. Thus, the Dark Feminine stretches us to consider Jung's body emphasis throughout his writings and to bring the wisdom of his message to a more expanded level of embodied consciousness in our era of Analytical Psychology.

Part of the jewel of the Dark Feminine energy is that in her, the healthy tension of the opposites can coexist: chaos and creativity, dark and light, death and rebirth, descent and ascent, psyche and soma, and peril and promise. The dark-night initiation guides us toward leaving behind the narrow confines of conventionality and of duality. Leaving duality means living life in paradox. Allowing paradox to coexist creatively is a core dimension of the wisdom of the Dark Feminine. The qualities of paradox, presence, process, sacrifice, surrender, and receptivity are key aspects of the energy pattern of the Dark Goddess, who renews everything while she herself perdures. The more we befriend her energy patterns, the more we are opened to the challenge of holding and enduring the suffering in the experience of the tension of the opposites. This process transforms us as something new emerges within us, especially the transformation of our hearts, which are formed anew in her resonance.

Jung, whose thought was ahead of his time, realized the significance of the dynamic interplay between the psyche and the body, something that still seems intellectualized, overlooked, forgotten, and/or unrealized by many, especially in the Western world. As Jung reminds us, "[A] factor exists which mediates between the apparent incommensurability of body and psyche, giving matter a kind of 'psychic' faculty and the psyche a kind of 'materiality,' by means of which the one can work on the other" (par. 780).[214] What keen insight and awareness Jung possessed about the powerful interconnection between psyche and soma. Anita U. Greene, Ph.D., a Jungian analyst in private practice in Amherst, Massachusetts, who incorporates bodywork in the analytical frame insightfully observed that to consider the body as "only flesh, bone, sinew—*materia*—is still to be caught in the old idea of the body/mind antithesis. To introduce somatic awareness and body techniques into the analytic framework is *not* to introduce a suspect or alien element. Rather, it is to heal a split that has haunted the analytic process for generations" (p. 203).[215] In Jung's words, "[I]f we can reconcile ourselves with the mysterious truth that spirit is the living body seen from within, and the body the outer manifestation of the living spirit—the two being really one—then we can understand why. . .the present level of consciousness must give its due to the body" (pp. 219-220).[216]

Thus, in this interconnected and interdependent evolving quantum universe, the Dark Feminine challenges us to hold a "both-and" perspective, rather than an "either-or" view with the psyche and soma. Since Jungian psychology is in "process" in this post-Jungian period, Lady Underground challenges us to move beyond any old resonance of body-mind antithesis or any fixed mentality of one school versus another. She calls us to be open to the creative complementarity of what the diverse perspectives together hold in enrichening our view on any particular case at various stages of a soul's process, especially in dark-night initiation in the Dark Feminine. Again, in the words of T.S. Eliot,

> We must be still and still moving
> Into another intensity
> For a further union, a deeper communion. (p. 32) [217]

Exploring Psyche-Soma In the Analytical Relationship

The school of psychology known as Object Relations can provide us with a more extensive view of the importance, depth, and scope of psyche-soma and early infant development. Object Relations perspective grew from the realization that key to our development are primal objects, namely, mother and father, or whoever the parental figure in our early formation. Object Relations has influenced Jungian psychology, as well as other psychologies and spiritual developmental growth programs, such as the Diamond Heart approach. Also, Object Relations can offer us a deeper insight to understanding better, from another viewpoint, what Lady Underground is summoning us to embody.

For this reason, we will consider how Object Relations and early infant observation further enrich Jung's emphasis on the psyche-soma and complement what the incoming Dark Feminine is stressing, to advance consciousness, individually and collectively. This exploration will be in the context of the analytical relationship. In general, Object Relations and infant-observation theories hold that development takes place in a relationship and that the infant is relationship seeking. The seeds of awakening intimacy, sexuality, and the spiritual/aesthetical dimension of an infant first occur in the early *coniunctio* of feeding and holding in the mother-infant experience. The degree of affective presence surrounding the mother-infant dyad in this initial felt sensory skin experience will impact our psyche-soma cellular memory and our future capacity and style of relatedness. Further developments of activating warmth and desire in intimacy, sexuality, and the spiritual/aesthetical aspect of the newborn are found in an infant's experience of all the senses: touch, taste, smell, vision, and hearing in the close encounter of mother-infant. The development of our psyche-soma structure (including our primitive defensive system) and subsequent cellular memory begins to unfold *in utero* and in the awakening encounters with mother in infancy.

All analysands will have sensory experiences at some point. Realizing that our earliest formative experiences can reveal themselves through the body, it is key to be attentive to the self-communication of the body in an analytical hour. People naturally move in and out of different types of images (visual or auditory), body movements, and proprioceptive responses (feelings in the body). Analysands give them manifestation in their language, gestures, facial and vocal expression. Tracking the revealing language and map of the body can potentially offer a significant opening to the interior psyche. Working with this dynamic, within the repertoire of the session, holds the possibility for a deeper and more integrative or holistic approach. It is *one way* of honoring and "holding the space" of the incoming Dark Feminine energy as we sustain an intentional value for the body and its revelation of the soul in session.

In Object Relations and infant-observation theories, the personality develops through the analyst-analysand relationship as it reflects the mother-infant dyad and works through the transference of primitive unresolved unconscious affect, for example, anxiety, frustration, and aggression, and needs, such as intimacy, sexuality, and/or spirituality in the early *coniunctio*. With these theories, the analyst uses countertransference and projective identification to conceptualize the recreation of the internal object relationships in the transference. As infants and in early childhood, we all need a good-enough, felt experience of being related to with a sensory contact of warmth, holding, gazing, listening, softer voice, touching, responsiveness, and soothing by the parental figures in our environment. In initial development, our natural soul essence is affected, mediated, arrested, and sometimes impacted so that one emerges as a person of necessary adaptations, diminishment, and gradual selling out of soul. Since there are no perfect parents and no perfect family system, everyone has sold out, in some way becoming what they were not, and in so doing split from their natural soul essence, which then goes "underground." As individuals take on a false identity, they turn away from their true nature, by necessity, to cope, survive, and/or for the sake of safety in making so-called choices in conforming to what parental or authority figures expect, demand, or what one senses is needed, skewed though that may be, in the environment, given the family situation. For example, Jack felt he could not express his needs as a child because the wants of his dying mother seemed more important, and Joyce thought that she had to deny her needs to avoid being a burden to her mother, who always appeared tired and overextended because of her full-time care of Joyce's younger sister with special needs. Since we are all dependent on our caregivers in infancy and childhood, we adapt in some way, and in so doing, we disconnect from our natural soul essence to fit into the façade of a false suit of clothes (*be perfect, try hard, please others, be strong—don't show emotions, be dutifully responsible, and hurry up*) of what is referred to as "normal."

The early experience of attachment styles (mother-infant), on the vast continuum from smothering to abandoning, activates a recurring internalized message about relationship and possible issues of self-limiting beliefs about intimacy, sexuality, and/or spirituality in the early *coniunctio*. This is important for we can't have a conscious, meaningful relationship with another/Other when we have pockets of unconscious, unresolved energies and arrested development held in the cellular memory and musculature of our bodies that "drive our car" in our outer life. As one insightful, very honest 25-year-old woman said to me recently, "I'm seeking my value and needs in the mirror of the other that I'm attracted to, as I did with my mother and father. I realize I'm trying to get my narcissistic supply! I'm so embarrassed about this reality, but I have to be honest if I'm ever going to work through my insecurities and my pit of emptiness." And a male analysand discloses, "I go to great lengths and try so very hard to please my significant other and I still get no response from her. I feel like her intent is to withhold from me and to punish me. I really like women and so, besides my significant other, I enjoy other women for their company." Another woman working intensely on her issues reveals, "I had to be vigilant at not being a bother, being perfect, and being strong at not showing any emotion, especially anger, as I knew for a fact that I would be sent to a relative. My whole life has been about not feeling. What mattered in my family home was intellect." For many of us, we do not realize that in living out the charged driver of try hard, please others, be perfect, be strong, hurry up, be dutifully responsible, be good, and don't be a burden are manifestations of a false identity that we took on in becoming an individual of necessary adaptations to cope and to make it in our family, neighborhood, school, and religious systems. Our adapted behavior is an attempt to deal with anxiety, being overwhelmed, neglected, and/or violated and what seems too unbearable to us. We all do the best we can in our unfolding process. Often, what is most precious and some of what is core to our essence is what goes *underground,* is disowned, abandoned, split off, and hidden from ourselves. This is true even in the best of families. For some, what is most precious, one's true nature remains hidden in the depths, forgotten altogether. Subsequently, we seek and long to merge and to "connect" with another/Other for nurturance and security in an attempt to meet unconscious and unresolved infant and young attachment needs and hungers. The task to meet these deeper caverns of unbefriended and unmetabolized energy is an immense challenge. Given this reality, the analytical relationship holds the potential to be an essential container in a person's addressing and processing unresolved laden affect and issues that arise and are experienced in and through our psyche-soma, especially in Lady Underground's alchemical dark-night initiation rite.

Jung's original theory does not give adequate expression to some of the previously mentioned primitive affect and issues, especially sexuality and the issue of the spiritual/aesthetical dimension of the early *coniunctio*. Brian Feldman, informed by his infant-observation studies and following on the work of Virginia Woolf, refers to these experiences as "moments of being."[218] The seeds of the awakening, gazing, delighting, pleasuring, celebrating, and balancing of sexuality and spirituality are rooted in our first mother-infant intimate holding and feeding experiences. These encounters are the origins of incarnating the playful, delightful, and pleasurable Lilith energy. These mother-infant, intimate, human experiences are also the first germination of Lady Underground's lush, human-divine, intimate, rhythmic erotic energy. Brian Feldman considers the baby sucking at the breast to be the first experience of being penetrated, the early *coniunctio*. He contends that the baby and the mother have a capacity for reverie and believes the infant's reverie can be seen as the infant plays with the nipple and breast—the first play object.

Thus, Feldman hypothesizes that during these states of reverie the infant's capacity for introjection develops, and gradually the breast/nipple is introjected and forms the basis of a primal good internal object. In the mother-infant encounter, their "connection" and "relatedness" create the infant's capacity for symbolization, which evolves from birth onward. Feldman perceives the skin as the first experience of container. Through the felt sensory experience of the skin, the infant develops a concept of inside and outside spaces, with a boundary that separates the two distinct areas. When a breakdown occurs, there emerges what Feldman calls "second-skin development." Body components are used in this process. For example, in the early mother-infant dyad, when a baby is consistently pushed away from the pleasure of skin-to-skin sensation and the satisfaction of nursing at the breast, or when the infant is abruptly cut off from physical to mechanical feeding, these changes tend to hasten intellectual development, rather than create a sense of being more grounded in the sensory body domain of matter. Consequently, when the "primary skin" of our normal "connectedness" and "relatedness" to our body does not occur in infancy, it will manifest itself in the analysand's "secondary skin" body language, in the analytical relationship, and/or in the analytical frame. Being attentive to the symbolic manifestations revealed in the body and in the interactions within the analytical frame will reveal what Feldman refers to as "secondary-skin function," where body components are used by the individual in an attempt to contain unbearable primitive anxiety and aggression.[219]

A practical example of the infant-mother bonding impact on adult development and the capacity for relationship is an interaction with an analysand named Susan, who was emotionally abandoned by her depressed, alcoholic mother at birth. One of Susan's early memories of her father was of him snapping his finger at her to come when he wanted her, which was the same gesture he made when seeking the dog. After six months of our work together, Susan arrived 10 minutes before her usual time and went down the hall to the restroom, which she typically did every week. When she passed the consulting room, she noticed a man looking at a painting on the wall of the room and immediately assumed that I had forgotten her, as her mother had, and that her session was being given to the man who was standing in the consulting room. I was in my private office getting a text for that man, who was a student of mine at Washington Theological Union, where I taught. He had arranged to pick up the book 10 minutes before the hour. As I walked out of my office to go to the consulting room to hand the book to the student, I passed Susan and said, "Hello," thinking she was going to the restroom as she usually does before her session. She also smiled and said, "Hello." But

Susan passed the restroom and exited the building down the back staircase without ever saying anything else. When I realized she had left, I called her. Her distant, cold, angry tone erupted toward me. Susan's infant-mother dynamic and her "second-skin" defense were clearly evident from the tone of her voice and her choice of words as she verbally "chewed me out" and then "cut me off" by abruptly ending the phone conversation. The "second-skin function" was more apparent in the following session, during which I noticed a stiffening of her spine, shoulders, and bodily structure as she expressed her anger toward me for what she assumed I had done to her. Furthermore, she informed me that she was not going to be a caretaker to me, as she had had to be for her mother. In hearing her cold, icy verbal attack, I felt as if I had been kicked in my stomach, as well as the cold, annihilating sense of being cut off. I experienced something of what I imagined Susan felt as a child in encountering her Death-Mother energy. This gave me a real felt empathic awareness of what I had surmised already about her experience of the infant-mother relationship. My imaginings were that Susan was often abruptly cut off and harshly pushed away, responses that set up "second-skin development" and can hasten intellectual development. In Verena Kast's comments about the relational aspect of the complex, "Susan had been triggered in her Death Mother complex, unconsciously identified with the cold, distant, judgmental Death Mother energy, and projected unconsciously the abandoned little girl on me."[220] Susan experienced herself as her skin and structural body, which was rough, cold, stiff, and distant. Often, I felt as if Susan wore an imaginary sign that said in bold lettering, "Don't touch." Her fairy tale of choice is "*The Rough-Face Girl*," an Algonquin Indian Cinderella tale. Over time, through arduous, inner soul work, which has included body-energy work, especially on her Death Mother complex and many self-object parts, Susan has softened, relaxed, and warmed up slowly to her own soul's inner rhythm, as she has grown in trust both with me and with the Dark Goddess, to whom she refers as Sister, an image of the Dark Feminine. Sister is represented as the Ancient Wise One in the North American tale of the Algonquin Indian tribe located by the shores of Lake Ontario. Susan experiences Sister as her soul's guide in her ongoing dark-night rite of initiation in the Dark Feminine.

Realizing some of the rich offerings of post-Jungian developments, such as Object Relations and infant observations, and reviewing some of their impact on and value to the theory and practice of Analytical Psychology, we also need to remember, in this discussion, that consideration needs to be given to Jung's early years and their influence on the development of his views. In this regard, most of what has been examined is the archetypal approach, which tends to avoid a personal exploration of his early life. Had Jung's infancy and painful childhood been dealt with from a developmental view, these experiences might have informed his theory. He delved within himself to find healing and left a rich legacy.

In conclusion, we need to realize that Jung could not have developed a coherent theory of child development because of his own childhood wounds and due to his not having had a contained analysis in which to work through his infantile issues and traumas by today's analytical norms. During the first half of the 20th century, the acceptance of sexuality and the rediscovery of religious, transpersonal dimensions were significant in the steps toward individuation and provided adequate answers in regard to healing. In our time, from the perspective of this incoming Dark Feminine energy, a new psychological need has arisen: the need for the unearthing, metabolizing, personalizing, integrating, and conscious embodying of primitive affect and infantile neediness (stored within the cellular memory of the somatic unconscious) for personal validation within the healing relationship. These needs are reflections of the archetypal Dark Feminine, which values subjective experience, affect, sensations, and feeling. The Dark Feminine prizes all self-parts, especially those most scorned, neglected, split-off, and demonized. She embraces our "underground" self-parts that are often judged and disregarded as shameful. For her, the gold is in these primitive energies locked in the caverns of our interiority, and if befriended, they release more of our essence. Lady Underground is for our true nature, that is to say, our unfabricated self, the real you! She is about empowering us to birth the natural true essence within each of us—that is, the deeper dimensions of the Dark Feminine, the virgin and conduit of wisdom energy. The gift of her dark-night initiation in the Dark Feminine is the journey of liberating the soul within us. Our one-of-a-kind natural essence becomes consciously ensouled amid life's travails and triumphs as we navigate in these extreme, polarized times. The sense of a conscious, felt, experiential, embodied, interconnected and interdependent "relatedness," both within and without, is part of the incoming Dark Goddess's energy. This is also a fundamental principle of quantum physics (which was addressed in Chapter Two) in considering the new paradigm for this 21st century and the new emerging Universe Story. The creative complementarity of the wisdom of Lady Underground's energy, as seen and understood through the lens of contemporary Analytical Psychology, neuroscience, the wisdom of quantum physics, the evolution of energy medicine, supportive contemporary body-energy techniques, and contemplative practices offers a combined, more integrative, and holistic perspective of the night sea journey and, especially, if one is drawn into Lady Underground's dark-night initiation in the Dark Feminine. Thus, the challenge for contemporary Analytical Psychology is to be open to the possibility and the consideration of utilizing the insights, benefits, and wisdom of Object Relations and infant observation, along with other mentioned complementary modalities within the healing power of relationship, for holistic, clinical, and ethical practice in these challenging, evolving, polarized times.

Furthermore, it is important to remember that no one discipline, and especially the discipline of contemporary Analytical Psychology or quantum physics, has a monopoly on the truth of ongoing transformation and the implications of such an adventure in human interiority. A creative complementarity is born in considering the distinct but mutually enriching wisdom of both disciplines, as well as the insights of anthropology, neuroscience, theology, spirituality, energy medicine, body-energy techniques, and contemplative practices. This combined pluralistic view is *one* attempt to envision human development in the process of individuation, while remembering that the experience is greater than any particular attempt to represent it. In the words of Jung, "Sooner or later, nuclear physics and the psychology of the unconscious will draw closer together, as both of them independently of one another and from opposite directions, push forward into transcendental territory" (pp. vii-xlvii).[221]

Implications for Spirituality

What does Lady Underground have to offer to contemporary spirituality in our modern time? Spirituality is a broad concept that includes both existential, lived experience and the academic discipline of spirituality. We are oriented toward mystery/Mystery. Hence, the search for meaning arises from deep within ourselves and within creation itself, and as such, spirituality is personal, planetary, and cosmic. In our consideration and exploration of what are the implications for spirituality, we realize that the lens of depth psychology is a rich resource for opening one to both the creative life and the sacred inner well within, for all those who are interested in experiencing and embodying consciously their spirituality. Jungian method and practice are a vital means for deepening and understanding our personal psychospiritual stories, as well as the collective patterns within culture. Spirituality is an innate quality of our essence. It is a portal in nurturing the dialogue and communion with the transcendent manifest in the already/always present Other, both within and without. Jung considered spirituality key to the human journey. He once noted that life was a luminous pause between two great mysteries, which themselves are one. Having a perduring attentiveness to being *present consciously* to experiencing our experience opens us potentially to "drinking deeply" from the inner well while birthing our identity, meaning, purpose, and direction in the mysterious journey of life that is but a luminous pause. This is to live the symbolic life and to be a coparticipator in the divine/Divine drama in the evolving Universe Story.

The paradigm shift referred to in Chapter Two calls us to a new spiritual sensibility of a conscious interiority. The shift summons us to "drinking deeply." This requires new wine and new wine skins. The Jungian psychological approach can be most helpful in this journey toward embodying one's more natural, authentic, soul essence and broadening the horizon of one's lived spirituality in the ordinary of life. Also, for those who are involved in a traditional religious practice, Analytical Psychology can deepen and enrich one's relationship to the tradition of choice and enlarge one's understanding, appreciation, and meaning of its archetypal significance and symbol system. It is within this noted context that we now consider and explore more specifically what Lady Underground, who is both ancient and contemporary, has to offer to spirituality, in our modern time, within the web of all life. There are many aspects that one could address, but the following points seem to be some important ones to consider in our reflection on this question. You may have some other insights and perspectives as you contemplate this reality and as we circumambulate and explore this engaging question.

First, Lady Underground summons us to an ongoing openness and receptivity to envisioning spirituality within a context of a new emerging mythology. This mythology needs to be grounded in an adequate anthropology that sees humanity as a unified whole and as part of the common Universe Story of an evolving 14 billion-year-old history, shared by all humanity; modern, cutting-edge science, including quantum physics; and a dynamic cosmology. Fundamental to this contemporary mythology is having a well-differentiated conscious feminine energy and a well-differentiated conscious masculine energy. The Dark Feminine's gift and call for conscious spiritual sojourners is to balance and honor both masculine and feminine energies. The creative dynamism of this archetypal energy is an integrative "both/and," rather than a dualistic "either/or" vision. This progressive, dynamic interaction, symbolized in the image of a dance of the two energies, can potentially manifest as an inner marriage of respect, mutuality, and equals in which neither is subordinated nor sacrificed to the other. The inner dance of our feminine and masculine energies is a mirror of our outer relational style and capacity. Lady Underground summons us to *conscious relationship* in the transformative journey of coming home, both within and without, on all levels of the web of life. William Blake states it well, "[A]nd we are put on earth a little space, that we may learn to bear the beams of love" (p. 10).[222] And Jung reminds us, "[W]here love reigns, there is no will to power; and where the will to power is paramount, love is lacking. The one is but the shadow of the other" (par. 78).[223] "An unconscious Eros always expresses itself as will to power" (par. 167).[224] Lady Underground's dark night of initiation in the Dark Feminine is a medicine of death in service to generative life and conscious relationship! She challenges spirituality to empower individuals to move beyond an infantile codependent spirituality that avoids being uninitiated, naive, and engages in neurotic suffering versus authentic suffering that purifies illusions and delusions.

Realizing that we live in an interconnected and interdependent evolving world, she challenges us to live an integrative spirituality that also views and lives life from an Earth-centered norm of reality and value, rather than from an anthropocentric stance. To objectify ourselves—our bodies, others, animals, marine species, plant life, bodies of water, forests, and the body of the Earth, herself, is to perpetuate living from the unconscious swamplands of our souls, a way of living that further alienates us from our essence and the evolving well-being of the Earth community. Lady Underground is beckoning us in the interconnected, embodied web of intricate relationships to see the Earth as being here to be communed with, to be related to respectfully and with balance, and to be attuned to the voice of the Earth in an intimate way. When we relate to the natural world from an anthropocentric view, we objectify the Earth by entering into a destructive relationship that is often based on a patriarchal, inflated attitude of power, domination, and greed. The Earth is not ours to do with as we wish; rather, in the spirit of the archetypal energy, we are called to be conscious stewards, cultivators, and responsible cocreators of creation, befriending Earth in her growth and development in a just and sustainable way. All life matters in this unfolding universe: all human life, ethnic groups, nationalities, religious beliefs, including atheism; rainforests, forests, animal life, plant life, marine life, nature in all aspects, and natural resources; and all cosmic-planetary life. Lady Underground is for the evolving growth of the body of life in all levels of creation. Her energy patterns are a catalyst toward holistic growth into higher, more complex levels of conscious interacting with the Earth herself and our unfolding universe. An integrated and meaningful spiritual life is inconceivable without a meaningful and informed planetary-cosmic embodied awareness and way of life. If anyone of us is to live a conscious psychospiritual embodied path, it needs to include a cosharing responsibly and respectfully in the very care of furthering the evolving divine/Divine grandeur in the Cosmic-Planetary Story.

Part of realizing the psychospiritual interconnected and interdependent dimension of humanity, and Earth herself, is being informed consciously of the plight of our common home and awakening responsibly to assisting in the cocreation of the future. We need to reflect and consider whether we are hearing and honoring in a practical way the potential for growth and development of the archetypal energy of Lady Underground, when we engage, contribute, and perpetuate polluting the Earth with our trash and toxic waste; denying the scientific reality of climate change; refusing to understand and to see our part in climate change; being insensitive, judgmental, and uncaring of the plight of the most vulnerable; rallying support for the use of greenhouse gas emissions and fossil fuels; anesthetizing our psyches, bodies, and relationships through our compulsive consumerism or other numbing choices; accepting and tolerating vegetables, fruits, meats, poultry, fish, and grains being chemicalized and genetically modified, which is fueled by greed and profits of individuals and the food industry; and leveling rainforests and burning forests for development while ignoring the destruction of significant ecosystems. What impact does all this have on our bodies, on animal, plant, and marine life, and on the Earth, herself? An embodied conscious spirituality needs to take these realities into account and to find a responsible way to dialogue and deal with these issues. This will be unique for each conscious traveler in the psychospiritual quest. In the journey of unearthing, metabolizing, personalizing, and embodying the archetypal energy of Lady Underground, we share in the cocreating of furthering the common unfolding Universe Story by accepting responsibility, in our unique way, to honor, care, save, and protect creation. Lady Underground invites everyone who is serious about the spiritual path to be true to who we are as creative, imaginative coparticipants in the new unfolding myth. In this interconnected web of life, Lady Underground summons those on the spiritual quest to embody consciously the potential of the archetypal energy, as we all share in the evolving creation of the universe and in the balance needed for the well-being of the entire cosmos.

Second, she challenges those on the spiritual quest and the discipline of spirituality to embrace a realization that the creative life force of the spirit/Spirit is pulsating throughout the universe even in all its unfolding stages of evolution. Lady Underground, who is ancient and ever new, reminds us that the primordial sacredness of the Earth community is because of its inherent spirit/Spirit. The spirit/Spirit imbues and enlivens everything in creation. Spirit is the rich wellspring of all possibility. It manifests in the stirring of desire and the flow of love in the human heart; the arising inspiration of imagination, creativity, and wisdom in the depth of silence; the erupting restless and often chaotic shifts in every stage of evolution in creation; and in the ongoing innate cyclical pattern of birth-death-rebirth that weaves throughout the web of all dimensions of life. Amid life's travails and triumphs, Lady Underground nourishes, protects, guides, and empowers each of us in our unique, one-of-a-kind manner to be attuned to the murmur of the pulsating life force within, to bring forth creatively what is within, and to do so true to both our inner rhythm and the mystery's/Mystery's call.

Third, some features of the Dark Feminine are being present in the here and now, engaging in process that respects dynamic movement, change, messiness, and complexity as the nature of life; allowing paradox to coexist creatively; and enduring the suffering of the tension of the opposites with the capacity to sacrifice, surrender, and be receptive to the divine/Divine inflow. The energy of Lady Underground beckons any authentic contemporary spirituality to embrace these key dimensions, if one's spirituality is to be a conscious, grounded one. Dualistic divisions and the splitting of reality, which can result in one dimension of energy being demonized and the other held as a "good," are the underpinnings of a dangerous and problematic spirituality. We do not live in a truly dualistic world. When we do not allow paradox to coexist creatively, we easily can slip into becoming too one-sided and thus perpetuate a neurotic way of being while thinking that our narrow spiritual path is integrated. For example, light and darkness tend to be split, and often the former is valued over the latter. Many perceive light as good and split off or demonize darkness as bad, thus attempting to eliminate the darkness that actually charges and triggers energy with more intensity. To deny or evade darkness is to live superficially, cut off and dissociated from one's ground, one's instincts, and one's depth. Jung often warned that the shadow we do not befriend will become fate in our outer life. Much of the aggression and violence erupting in our outer world stems psychologically from this dualistic dividing and splitting of reality, then projecting it and spewing it outward in life, and sometimes enacting the energy that we are overidentified with unconsciously. When we metabolize and befriend the darkness and integrate both light and darkness, we grow and embody consciously more of our soul essence, we release a greater potential for respect, tolerance, forgiveness and compassionate presence, as well as furthering the growth energetically of our Earth community. Thus, Lady Underground challenges each of us on the spiritual path and the discipline of spirituality to accept and recognize her face in the here and now by allowing paradox to coexist creatively (above and below, promise and peril, birth and death, creativity and chaos, triumphs and travails, extinction and transformation) in the unfolding process of life, without idealizing one dimension of reality while splitting-off and demonizing the other.

Fourth, Lady Underground calls all of us to be serious about our psycho-spiritual journey and leaders in the field of spirituality, to move beyond rational talk of an integrative spirituality and toward fostering a progressive journey of an embodied, conscious spirituality. Historically, the Western world and major religions have tended, at one time or another, to give greater value to spirit/Spirit and rational thinking than to body and connected feeling, or to emphasize soul over the body. Jung expressed that without the soul, the body is dead, and without the body, the soul is unreal. The tendency toward splitting is another echo of a dualistic mindset. Within the unfolding Universe Story and the new emerging mythos, body is perceived as an alive unified process reality tending toward fuller consciousness within the larger embodied sphere of the Earth herself. The evolving Cosmic Story is an interconnected and interdependent web of all life, as unified subjects teleologically awakening to fuller ensouled consciousness and collective potential. Humans and the Earth herself are not objects! Lady Underground obliges us to embrace and befriend the body, as it is the manifestation of the soul. She challenges spirituality to find ways to foster holistic growth for voyagers of the deeper, dark night-sea journey of the soul to befriend the underground of who we are, including our lower chakras versus constant "flight" upward, and in doing so to open to a greater freedom and spaciousness within the conscious soul-body of who we are in the present. The mystery/Mystery is not outside of this process, but in and through the whole experience. Her progressive dark night of initiation in the Dark Feminine through twilight, midnight, and dawn is an ongoing process toward a fuller birthing of our natural, authentic, soul essence, and as such, is of enormous importance for a meaningful and vital contemporary spirituality.

A one-sided, dualistic spirituality does not serve us in how to live and navigate in these present extreme polarized times. We need a conscious grounded spirituality that is attuned to the whole body-soul of who we are within the context of the unfolding Earth Body herself, and that is inspired and guided by a generative source that arises and flows from "drinking deeply" at the inner well within us.

The journey toward unearthing, metabolizing, humanizing, and embodying the archetypal energy of Lady Underground helps us to understand and appreciate the depth and meaning she can offer the sojourner making the spiritual quest. Again, we are reminded of the wisdom of Nietzsche, that the tree that would grow to heaven must first send its roots to hell. For example, at 65 years old, Meredith, who grew up in an authoritarian, rational, thinking family milieu where she felt her reality of life didn't matter, had to gradually awaken, befriend, and trust her "underground" instincts and feelings in her arduous psychospiritual quest toward conscious embodiment. Also, at 65, Jacob, who has a long-standing history of being a "dutiful son," discovered that for the health of his body, he has had to say *No* sometimes to his wife and to others whom he has tried very hard to please, to be the good, responsible one. Growing up, Jacob thought he didn't have a right to own his needs or to express them without feeling guilty about being a burden to his parents, both of whom worked to support the family. As Jacob became attuned to his body and befriended the self-part of himself that was the dutiful little boy, he was able to gradually open to a greater spaciousness within and to have the freedom to own his needs and to say *No* when it was appropriate for him to do so, without feeling guilty about it. Marietta, who had been attentive to her soul work for a long time, realized to her surprise that she is summoned at a deeper level to befriend her blacker-than-black, sadistic, killing, nonverbal and verbal attacker energy toward those who have wronged her, cut her off in traffic, and hold other than her social, moral, and political views. As she faced the destructive Death Mother energy and the role of power, criticism, and judgment in her shadow, she began to express her creative power in her emerging compassionate presence to the dying in her hospice work.

The universe is in need of men and women who embody consciously the wisdom, contemplative vision, passionate awareness, and compassionate presence that a well-grounded spirituality can offer to humanity at this time in the unfolding Universe Story. In this arduous progressive journey, *symbolically* speaking, the whole of one's soul-body essence becomes the lap that holds the *other* through good-enough, empathic, attuned mirroring and by mediating the new soul life being born. Being a heart-awakened, compassionate presence and holding the space for another in the journey of befriending the various dimensions of soul, including the blacker-than-black shadow, is a profound gift, as the other experiences being seen, heard, accepted, and loved. This symbolic and empathic held-on-the-lap process is healing. This conscious, soulful attunement liberates the generative soul within any one of us. This is the unfolding foundational energy of Lady Underground being birthed in new frontiers. Just as we realize symbolically that Isis holds the infant Horus on her lap and Lady Underground holds the Divine Child on her lap, so too, we awaken to the awareness that in our ordinary way we possess the capacity energetically to hold the space for others, and to be instruments of embodied-passionate awareness and compassionate presence.

The gift of the Primordial Dark Feminine of Lady Underground is both an ancient and an ever-new, unfolding and evolving energy, which is a rich resource for holistic psychospiritual growth and development for today's sojourner. In an era of unprecedented, evolutionary development in the cosmos, Lady Underground calls us to move beyond a selective "split-parts" spirituality to adventuring forth in the ordinary of our life to embodying consciously a holistic, generative, interconnected, and interdependent spirituality within the web of the *whole* of life. Spiritual directors, educators, religious leaders, and those facilitating retreat days, seminars, and workshops can benefit those they serve and accompany by continuing to do their inner soul work of integrating the Dark Feminine energy in their personal lives, and by understanding, appreciating, and fostering in an empowering way the dynamics and underpinnings of this archetypal energy that is manifesting in our time.

Fifth, the feminine principle is one of the two great archetypal foundations of our evolving cosmos, with the other being the masculine principle. Throughout history, there are several feminine archetypal images that have emerged as goddess figures that symbolize various aspects of cosmic nature. The Great Mother endures as one of the primary goddess images in human interiority. Her archetypal energy has various gradations within the continuum of potential energy that is available for growth and development. As noted before, some core aspects of the goddess energy include mother, virgin, and conduit of wisdom. Lady Underground as a primordial image of the Dark Feminine is a deeper, earthy, immensely powerful Other, more shadowy, hidden unknown, sublime, mysterious dimension of the Mother Goddess. It is *insufficient and unacceptable* to speak only about recovering, reclaiming, and befriending the overarching global aspect of the Great Goddess's energy. If humanity is to grow individually and collectively in a greater complexity of consciousness, the depth and expansion of the continuum of the archetypal energy of the feminine needs to be embraced and embodied more fully at this time in our unfolding Cosmos Story. The mystery's/Mystery's summons is to psychospiritual wholeness whether we speak psychologically or spiritually.

Thus, we are beckoned to befriend the Dark Feminine, who is a manifestation of the psychospiritual wholeness to which we are called in an era that has long overvalued the rational. A key sign of her resurgence is chaos, turbulence, disorientation, ambiguity, and messiness, felt personally, socially, spiritually, economically, politically, and within the collective of cultures. In an era of the reappearance of the Dark Feminine, liminality marks the present, unprecedented, evolutionary development. With this noted reality in our awareness, we need to realize that Lady Underground challenges anyone of us who is serious about contemporary spirituality and who is a voyager of the darker night-sea depths to embrace and embody consciously the various aspects of potential energy for development in the continuum of her universal patterns, which arise from the collective unconscious (mother, virgin, and conduit of wisdom). This is true for men as well as for women. We all possess the universal imprints of the archetypal energy within our inner pantheon. Furthermore, we understand that the real meaning of motherhood is not limited to women who have given birth; it is a pattern of energy inherent in both men and women.

Often for an individual and for many cultures, the mother energy (either the Good-Enough Mother or her negative counterpart, the Terrible Mother, of which the Death Mother is the most severe form or manifestation) is lived out undifferentiated at personal and collective levels. Time and again, all of us project the Mother Goddess energy (as well as the Father God energy) outward unconsciously on spirituality (as noted in Chapter Two), a person, a Church, a political system, theory, and/or a campaign, an official leader such a president, a social system, an organization, an institution, and/or our body. Moreover, individuals and the collective in cultures frequently have become attached or fixated unconsciously at this mother dimension of the goddess energy, either at the nurturing end of the spectrum of the archetypal energy or the negative counterpart of the continuum. Either way, development will be protracted for a person. When this energy is constellated unconsciously, the projection of the mother energy can be triggered outwardly (positively or negatively), stirring longing and attachment hunger, and/or as a charged force of the Terrible Mother energy, with the worst possibility on the continuum of energy being the Death Mother energy. Lady Underground beckons us psychologically and spiritually to grow up and differentiate consciously from the Mother energy. A professional man in his mid-50s had tried so very hard, continually for 10 years to please his female significant other, but no matter what he did, it was criticized and never good enough. This is a man who is still unconsciously mother bound. And a 57-year-old female anesthesiologist described how, for her entire life, she had felt constricted and less than who she is as a woman because her mother had always had to be, narcissistically, "number one." This is a woman with an unresolved mother complex.

Some of the characteristics of the Good-Enough-Mother energy are attuned, adequate, empathic, mirroring, nurturing, protecting, providing emotional and physical security with a sufficient sense of the felt presence of warmth and love. Terrible-Mother energy tends to emanate from power; it is critical, judgmental, and perfectionistic, which kills the feminine energy in any one of us, men and women. However, Terrible-Mother and Death-Mother energy are not to be confused with any image of the Dark Feminine, such as the Black Madonna known as Lady Underground. The former diminishes one's core essence, kills spirit, murders soul, cuts off the feminine instincts in both men and women, is without love, and comes from a space of power and judgment. The Dark Feminine is about liberating our true nature and the generative soul within us. Even in her doses of medicine of dark night of initiation, her hidden, unknown, genuine spirit is one of death in service to life. The Dark Feminine is about loving us into our embodied soul essence. The way is through the death-rebirth cycle that is a necessary, innate, universal, transformative dynamic that permeates life at every level in the evolving Universe Story. It is important to note and to remember that the dimension of the mother energy of this Dark Feminine, reflected in the Black Madonna (and other images of the Dark Feminine), consists also of the body and the Earth body herself, all the charged human experiences that can plague our emotional field, the diminishment of our physical being, disease, and all "faces" of the death-rebirth cycle throughout the stages of life, including our final personal death as a transformative union with the inexhaustible mystery/Mystery and the cosmic web of all life.

For all of us, we need to be clear that Lady Underground shatters sentimentality and ushers in a summons to move beyond superficiality by doing our inner soul work. She is *not* the Lady of Perpetual Light who endorses continuous warm, feel-good spirituality of the "light!" The challenge for anyone of us in our spirituality is growth in differentiating consciously from the mother energy in our psychospiritual journey of individuation. Furthermore, the summons of Lady Underground is to progress in embodying consciously the fuller, more expansive dimensions of the potential archetypal energy for growth in human and evolutionary development (virgin and conduit of wisdom). The good-enough-mother dimension of the continuum of the archetypal energy is very much needed to be adequately mediated and mirrored for our children, families, communities, societies, cultures, and all of nature. It is also equally important, especially in these extreme, polarized times and with the Dark Night that looms over the Earth community in so many ways, that the deeper energy of the Dark Feminine on the continuum (virgin and conduit of wisdom) be embodied consciously, if we are to survive and thrive, and if the unfolding Universe Story is to evolve to greater levels of consciousness. In these charged times, the world is in need of the Dark Goddess's deeper "other" gifts of energy and virtue from the inner well within all of us. She challenges us to exploring, experiencing, and embodying consciously our darker depths, including our blacker-than-black shadow and in doing so, to open to an inner spaciousness and a vast inclusiveness. The psychospiritual process is a journey toward reconciliation —an expansive growth in unity with diversity, both inwardly and outwardly. To open to the still point of unknowing, where all is known, draws us in the path of enlarged horizons. In the journey of embodying the fuller range of her potential universal patterns, we become more passionately aware and compassionately present to others, the earth we inhabit, the energetic and resilient web of life, sustaining and transforming us through each summons, including the course of death itself.

For any one of us, men and women, we need a well-differentiated, conscious feminine and masculine energy; otherwise, we will have a truncated spirituality. Lady Underground is calling for the deeper, more shadowy, sublime, potential aspects of her archetypal energy to be befriended consciously. The issue for spirituality and for any one of us who is serious about living a healthy conscious psychospiritual journey is not an attachment or a fixation on one dimension of the archetypal energy to the exclusion of the other valuable elements that hold potential for growth and development for us individually and collectively. The call at this historic time is toward a greater capacity for conscious ensoulment of the various resonances of the Dark Feminine energy: mother, virgin, and conduit of wisdom. If we are to address and resolve consciously the societal and cultural erupting chaotic issues, the intense charged paradoxes of our time, and the challenges of today's unprecedented evolutionary acceleration, we need a grounded, holistic spirituality that supports us toward the conscious embodiment of the virgin and conduit-of-wisdom dimensions of the Dark Feminine archetypal energy. The virgin dimension of the Dark Feminine is the grounded rootedness of the wisdom energy. The virgin energy is the progressive opening to the inner freedom to be who one is naturally. The resonance of wisdom embraces more universal values and the embodied conscious feeling function that is so needed in our Western culture and world-soul community, if we are to open to a greater heartfelt and inspired, compassionate consciousness within the unfolding 14 billion-year-old Universe Story. These deeper expansions of the continuum ultimately open us and empower us toward greater interior levels of differentiating consciously from the Great Mother and the Great Father archetypal energies, as we open to the depths and the ongoing teleological summons of the mystery/Mystery. The progressive, evolving journey home remains one of being in service to the mystery/Mystery, not any substitute—that is *nada, nada.*

Given this fifth point, the differentiation from the mother energy and the movement toward the embodiment of a fuller range of the Dark Feminine, the question remains still: How do we raise awareness in integrating this energy in a practical, everyday way? How do we foster and facilitate youths and adults in becoming aware of the ways of the Dark Feminine? While many ancient traditions, contemporary science, and history stress the enormity of this unprecedented evolutionary era, they also raise our awareness, as did Jung, of the enduring truth: It is our conscious choices that influence and form our growth, development, and future, personally and collectively. How might the discipline of spirituality stir our imaginations anew and empower us to recover, to reinterpret, and to embody consciously the emerging Dark Goddess energy, which permeates and reveals itself on all levels of life? While there is no one answer, no one way, and you may have many ideas on this topic, here is one perspective that I offer. I also invite you to explore and to imagine what may be some other possible creative courses of action.

One promising option for spirituality is to revision generative, interdisciplinary programs, workshops, rituals, community services, retreats, meditative reflections and exercises, psychospiritual direction, and educational seminars in the arts (portal to the imagination) that would foster growth and empowerment in the deeper dimensions of the archetypal energy of the Dark Feminine within the context of the unfolding Universe Story. For example, the cosmology of the Judeo-Christian traditional religious stories no longer speak to informed, educated, conscious individuals who are about a holistic individuation journey. If contemporary holistic spirituality is to influence our psychospiritual homecoming, it needs to be grounded in the context of an interdisciplinary approach that considers and includes modern science, a holistic anthropology and cosmology with an Earth-centered norm of reality and value, contemporary-scripture and sacred-text scholarship, technology, and the arts within the new, emerging Cosmos Story. What this might look like is informative and liberating opportunities that also would emphasize and include a Jungian understanding of the Great Mother energy and the "other side" of the Goddess, namely the Dark Feminine. Other interdisciplinary program opportunities might include teaching practical modalities to open to the possible experience of the "inner well," such as meditation and/or mindfulness; engaging in different resonances of music, various imaginal techniques, mandalas, dreamwork, left-hand/right-hand exercise, journaling, soulful inner rhythmic dance, qigong, tai chi, painting, and various forms of intentional solitude; the value and healthy attitude of the body as the portal of incarnational engagement; the importance of befriending consciously the feminine and masculine energies in the process of embodying the inner marriage of equals in which neither the masculine nor the feminine energies are subordinated and/or sacrificed for the other; the inner relational constellation (or the lack of it) of the masculine and feminine energies as a mirror to our outer relational capacity; the vital need to withdraw and integrate projected parental *imago* energies, as well as shadow material, including the blacker-than-black shadow in the summons to a deeper grounded interiority as we differentiate consciously from the mother energy (as well as the father energy) in opening to the deeper experience of the virgin and conduit-of-wisdom energies in the journey of individuation; a quantum world relationality as core and thus, essential, interconnected, and interdependent networking; and the vital need of being open to exploring, discovering, and experiencing various creative potential portals to the infinite mystery/Mystery in the soul's journey while remembering that there is no one way and our service is to the mystery/Mystery, not a modality. This latter takes courage! Often, many of us have been raised to be skeptical and/or to demonize any modality that is other than what we have been taught or what we've known as cradle believers in certain religious traditions and/or certain beliefs or "truths" taught within our family, ethnic, and/or cultural settings. For example, within the Roman Catholic tradition, reiki, energy medicine, and therapeutic-touch energy work are forbidden by the bishops in Catholic hospitals and health facilities. How pathetically sad!

Ancient modalities of energy work can be a phenomenal avenue for opening to the infinite field of the mystery/Mystery. One of my dear friends, Carole Fisher, a Quaker who died in 2013, at age 90, had volunteered for 10 years at Johns Hopkins University Hospital doing energy work for those in palliative care, bringing them compassionate presence and assistance in their dying process. She was the first person ever who did formal energy work on me and taught me a great deal in her contemplative, compassionate presence. What a profound experience in the journey of opening to more expansive depths in my psychospiritual journey.

The encounter with the mystery/Mystery can be through others, dreams, body, nature, solitude, sacred rituals and places, and modalities of creative imagination that we've not yet explored or considered. There is no one way! Lady Underground invites us and challenges the discipline of spirituality into the unimaginable that is significantly possible. She summons us to bring forth what is within us into the light of consciousness in our unique way, and in doing so responsibly, to make our humble contribution in advancing the unfolding Universe Story.

Like Jung, who at age 12 had a three-day interior struggle, wondering what was God's will for him regarding thinking a particular unthinkable thought, so too for us, we are being invited, challenged, and stretched to imagine the unimaginable individually and collectively. After finally enduring his intense inner battle, Jung gave himself permission to experience thinking an unimaginable thought about the destruction of the Basel Cathedral as he walked past the cathedral in the square near his home. Because Jung allowed himself to experience his reality fully, he opened to an amazing interior expansion, to his great surprise. He felt an enormous, indescribable relief and what he described as a grace of unutterable bliss that he never forgot.

Where is Lady Underground summoning you to expand beyond what is known, secure, and rational, to experience what is unthinkable or unimaginable that you might embody consciously a more expanded and holistic spirituality? How might the discipline of spirituality lead, in an interdisciplinary way, to stir and activate creatively the potential resource within us all, that humanity might expand consciously with a spirit of inclusivity, diversity, and respect for all?

Remember, the gift of the Dark Feminine (Kali, the Black Madonna, Lilith, Sheba, Tara, Pele, Sister, Grandmother Earth, Earth Mother, Lady Guadalupe, and Lady of the Valley, etc.,) does not necessarily reveal itself in the tidy, neat, rational, organized structures of life. She is not a cheerleader for the "perfect" who attempt to look and sound as if they "have it all together," the ideal, or "scoring a 10" in body appearance! Because her energy has been despised, denied, banished, scorned, and repressed, she is not reflected necessarily in the box-office number-one grossing film of the weekend, top "A" list of religious dogmas of various religious traditions, political principles, psychological and other scientific theories, philosophical perspectives, and traditional societal views. If we are to open to deeper depths of the mystery/Mystery, we need to move beyond our limits and give ourselves permission, individually and collectively, to open to new creative interdisciplinary ways of exploring, wondering, and experiencing the unthinkable and unimaginable as we network for the holistic psychospiritual health of one another, our families, our communities, our cultures, and the evolving planet.

Imagine what it would be like for young people if we taught as part of the curriculum in our elementary, secondary, and higher educational systems: conflict resolution; proficiency in heart-attuned empathic mirroring, mediating, and active-listening skills; various contemporary modalities of mindfulness and meditation; respect and care for the body; nurturing embodied self-esteem; befriending growing edges; guidance in reflecting on the symbolic life; opportunities to journal in objectifying experience; exploration in ways to access imagination; embracing diversity and inclusivity; training in modalities like EFT tapping as a way to demagnetize charged, feeling-toned issues; and learning the potential value of drawing a mandala? Might some youths, adolescents, and emerging young adults experience a connection to their depths—a healing, empowering encounter with the mystery/Mystery, as Jung did in being attentive to his experience at age 12?

One place where I have witnessed this reality for youths, adolescents, and young adults was in my travels to Israel on two occasions while visiting the Magnificat Institute School of Music, located just outside Old Jerusalem. It was started in 1995 by the Franciscan Custos of the Holy Land, Fr. Armando

Pierucci, O.F.M. In an area of the world with a prevailing climate of tension, fighting, and killing, this is one creative, generative place, committed through the medium of music (the choirs and the orchestra—over 200 students) to being a gathering place where Christians, Jews, and Muslims come together in peaceful cooperation and mutual respect from diverse ethnic, economic, and religious traditions to learn the art of music together. Students are accepted as early as ages 3 and 4. The mission of the school is to provide music training for all children, regardless of their background. It not only serves as a school of excellence in music, but as a safe haven where peaceful friendships are formed and where healing is known through music. Hearing the choir and the orchestra is nurturing to the psyche. It exists also as a witness to how music is a creative, inspiring portal for opening to healing, and peaceful bonding within a group, in this case, youths of diverse backgrounds. The harmonious melodies and the resonance of the voices (a manifestation of the inner birthing of the feminine and masculine) were soulfully moving to my heart. Important impossibilities are significantly possible!

Some people and organizations lure and recruit the young of our country and the world for terrorism, destruction, and death. What if we had centers for the arts in our major inner cities, like the Magnificat Institute, which fostered and engaged the depths, imaginations, and creative generativity of youths and young adults? For example, ballroom dance instructor Pierre Dulaine volunteered to teach some troubled students ballroom dancing from one school on the West Side of Manhattan to 509 schools in 24 cities around the world. Three-hundred thousand students have completed the dancing program since its inception, which has assisted students in gaining confidence, poise, grace, respect, and other life skills such as learning teamwork. If more individuals, including young adults, discovered and chose consciously various inspiring modalities to "drink deeply" from the inner well, we might arise to creating resilience in a time of extremes through service in our everyday ordinary way, with an awakened-passionate heart and compassionate presence.

Sixth, Lady Underground embraces, accepts, and respects the whole of who we are, including the unbefriended "underground" of our person. Often, what is concealed in our psyche is intolerable, judged, criticized, condemned, disassociated, and constellated in our outer life directly or indirectly: as within, so without. Thus, in these extreme, polarized times, Lady Underground obliges contemporary spirituality to have a bold stance as a trailblazer in raising passionate awareness, in embracing diversity, inclusivity, equality, and respect for all. In an era when news, social media, political rhetoric, and life in our neighborhoods, cities, and nations, can be plagued by such destructive Death Mother energy and the *thanatos* principle, which manifests in a lack of integrity, justice, respect, and tolerance for diversity, inclusivity, and economic inequality, spirituality as a discipline and significant spiritual leaders can be a powerful voice in summoning humanity to their better, true, core essence.

Finally, Lady Underground challenges the discipline of spirituality to be a rich resource in encouraging and empowering men and women who are earnest in living a holistic psychospiritual life in the 21st century to relax, to lighten up, to celebrate, to dance, to have fun, to be here now, and be so joyfully and blissfully in the good, pleasurable, and enjoyable times of life. Again, she is not one-sided in embracing only turbulence, pain, tragedy, illness, decay, death, and loss. She also beckons us to live the fullness of life, which includes joy and sorrow. Lady Underground's dark night of initiation in the Dark Feminine liberates the generative soul within us, including our joyful, lighthearted, blissful, and fun self, as well as our sensual hot oo-la-la self! Joy is not something you crank up; rather, joy emanates and flows from deep within who you are consciously. One dimension of embodying more of our essence is a lighter sense of being in showing up consciously present in the outer world in the here and now. As the outer world is plagued by pollution, so too, our inner world can be weighed down with charged, feeling-toned complexes and constellated dramas of competitiveness, jealousy, envy, anger, hatred, and rage that are draining. The more any one of us unearths, metabolizes, integrates, and embodies consciously the ongoing humanization process of the archetypal energy of Lady Underground, the greater we open to discovering and experiencing the fuller spectrum of the range of her energy, including the joy of embodiment and the celebration of life in all its many pleasures and delights.

While writing this section, I was invited to participate in a three-day qigong workshop in Annapolis, Maryland, given by Dr. Wanping Cheng, a seasoned elderly visiting qigong master from China. Because of the enduring value experienced in participating in a previous qigong workshop some 20 years ago, I decided to attend. The first day was six hours of qigong meditation, the second was four, and the third was three. While being in meditation within the group, Dr. Cheng went around attuning the energy fields of the participants, and after doing eight hours of standing meditations, he did an attunement alone on each participant. One aspect that was obvious was the lighthearted joy that emerged by the third day individually and collectively in the group. The workshop was like a veil being pulled back to reveal an illuminating awareness of certain realities, including that, at the core of us all, is an utter *simplicity*—no drama! It is a gift to discover in a deep-felt way the sheer simplicity within each of us in our core essence. Soul reality at heart is so simple. The realization puts life in perspective. The qigong experience was like opening to intimations of stillness/Stillness—mystery/Mystery in the unfolding now. It was "drinking deeply" from the inner well. It was seeing at yet another level of soul resonance. In stillness, wisdom/Wisdom reveals itself. Like the gift of an unexpected guest's visit, love arose in my heart. When I left the historic grounds of Linthicum Walks in Crofton, Maryland, I felt grounded, my heart open, and filled with a deep gratitude and a quiet inner joy welling up from within my being. While walking toward my car, parked on the grounds, I beheld the beauty of the arena of nature surrounding me, I passed a very old tree of such splendor and stopped to put my hand on it, thanking it for its way of being in this evolving magnificent universe. I drove home from Annapolis in an enduring silence. As I type this even now, I feel the deep resonance of energy within my heart. The more any one of us demagnetizes our drama of complexes in an ongoing way, we open to more depth and the inner well within us wherein stillness/Stillness speaks and reveals itself.

While this interior space of illuminating awareness is possible in the journey in human interiority for any one of us, subsequently this soulful psychospiritual space also stands to activate and to loosen in the unconscious yet even more unknown deeper cells of the muscle of our darkness, as the light brings our infirmities to consciousness. The process of transformation is ongoing. And so, the ongoing life-death-rebirth cycle continues in the journey of birthing and embodying a deeper sense of ensouled aliveness in the emerging present. In this way, the ancient primordial archetypal energy of Lady Underground is born anew in the evolving now. This is something for which we all have the capacity, and it is such a rich resource for life. There are many ways; and for sure, there is no *one* way. Little did I know that in going to a qigong standing-meditation workshop, it would be an avenue opening to depth, to experiencing a hint of mystery/Mystery, and to releasing a greater generativity within, including a quiet, lighthearted joy and a deep inner peace.

Without question, we can draw on rich religious traditions grounded in soulful rituals, inspired by sacred texts, and anchored in spiritual and contemplative practices of a wide range, including opening to potential frontiers of growth in human interiority as viable ways to nurture our psychospiritual journey. However, Lady Underground's deeper resonances of energy challenges us to remain *open* to ways we don't know and perhaps are out of our set, known parameters and comfort zones, including ancient traditions, to discover where the mystery/Mystery may be summoning us in new ways in giving birth to imagination, vision, creativity, virtue, and healing solutions to issues that face our times. Also, whatever the path and modalities we may choose in embodying consciously our spirituality, we all need to remember that the way for us does not have to be a certain religious tradition versus a nontraditional way. For some, it may be within a particular religious tradition, and for others it may be differentiating and leaving a formal tradition. However, in this era of in-between times, it can, and may be for some voyagers of the darker night-sea depths of the soul, a both/and, for the expansive gradation in the ongoing path in human interiority is inexhaustible.

Regardless of whatever the way may be for any one of us in the spiritual journey, what seems key for seekers on all paths is living the wisdom reflected in the story, *Becoming Human*, told by Hafiz, one of Islam's greatest poets and mystical spiritual teachers. The wisdom of this story is the wisdom of Lady Underground as well as the wisdom of any other image of the Dark Feminine. For it is in essence a universal contemplative truth: "drinking deeply" from the inner well has an inherent empowering dimension about returning to the outer circle of life with greater consciousness, responsibility, and humble service. This is the wisdom in *Becoming Human* as any one of us is about living a generative, *ordinary, embodied, conscious* life. The story goes that there once was a man who sought after Hafiz to express to him the profound visions of God that he had been experiencing in order to discern their authentic validity. Hafiz engaged the man in a dialogue inquiring how many goats, siblings, wives, rose bushes, and children he had, whether his parents were living, and did he feed the birds in wintry weather? The man seemed surprised and flabbergasted that Hafiz was asking about goats and feeding the birds when the man was talking of sublime visions. Hafiz replied wisely to the man's wonderment if his visions were genuine.

> I would say that they were if they make you become
> more human,
> more kind to every creature and plant
> that you know. (p. 225) [225]

Implications for Culture and World Soul

Mahatma Gandhi once noted that a nation's culture resides in the hearts and in the souls of its people. While teaching at Washington Theological Union for 20 years, designing and coleading psychospiritual body-energy workshops and reiki workshops for 12 years, and being in private practice for 31 years in Washington, D.C., I have had the privilege of accompanying and witnessing people from various traditions and cultures do their inner soul work. Some of the many cultures have included various regions of India, Africa, China, Japan, Philippines, Caribbean and Fiji Islands, Middle East, Central America, South America, North America, Europe, Australia, Cambodia, and Vietnam. As noted earlier in this chapter, in the evolving 14 billion-year-old Universe Story, many goddess images and archetypal figures of the feminine, from various traditions and cultures, have evolved and emerged over time, reflecting facets of human nature and inner, psychic, universal patterns for potential growth and conscious development. However, within the sacred pantheon of goddesses, a consistent representation of the feminine principle that often surfaces and continues to be enduring in the hearts and souls of many worldwide is the Great Mother. Her energy is foundational in life, with the masculine principle being the other primary, archetypal, foundational energy. In all civilizations, the mystery of the Great Goddess finds expression in the dreams, myths, fairy tales, expressive arts, sacred places, social and cultural customs, mores, traditions, and the everyday pulse of life of the respective cultures. She both gives and nurtures life, and she devours and destroys life in death. For the Great Mother, death is not a curse or a dreaded reality in life. Death and dying are an integral part of the eternal cycle of becoming and decaying in holistic growth and conscious development in an unfolding, evolving cosmos.

Historically, in the last 65 years, abroad and here at home, we have lived through a wide range of interactions on all levels of life of hierarchical structures and patriarchal rigidities being challenged, defied, denounced, and toppled, and of the feminine principle being increasingly unearthed, recovered, welcomed, and embraced. With all major shifts of change, there can be phases of backlash and regressive pull manifested in attitudes, behavior, and sometimes selective, fixed mindsets that blatantly block and exclude all ways other than the "one way," which suggests a very inflexible ego structure and a closed authoritarian system. It also can reflect a fear of change and the new incoming energy, and/or a default response of denial and resistance. We all can recall experiences in times of transition when we have opposed change, and/or have witnessed it in others. Often, a determined, linear, rational outlook or a self-preserving, irrational view can emerge to seek control and security in old certainties and in known and familiar ways of functioning. While denial is human and normal, the price for not changing and growing can be costly on all levels of life. In an in-between phase of development and transformation, awakening, acceptance, and conscious growth take considerable time and patience. A society and culture that thrives on instant gratification, immediate access and transmission of knowledge, and swift communication in social media tends to want efficiency and to demand quick solutions. Embracing and integrating the more expansive and deeper range of the Great Mother's foundational energy does not happen overnight!

Rational thinking, talking, and writing about it is very different from the experience of unearthing, digesting, and integrating a dose of her dark-night-of-initiation medicine. Holistic, inner, soul work is essential if deeper dimensions of the Great Mother's energy are to be embodied consciously. As with any transition, real suffering is involved in unearthing and metabolizing, dying to a static, archaic, rigid energy and way of being, and opening to a new threshold such as recovering and manifesting the more expansive dimensions of the feminine principle.

As a Western culture in the last 65 years, we have participated in and witnessed the ongoing, evolving shift that has initiated progress for women, men, and the planet. When enough carriers of a culture embody this consciousness in their hearts and souls, the generative foundational principle of life is not only experienced personally in a more expanded way but also the very values, attitudes, and ethical guiding principles that affect our institutions and structures of society and culture begin, ever so slowly, to experience a paradigm shift. We have seen the shift occurring *outwardly* in far-reaching ways as women's career opportunities have expanded. Engineers Christine Darden and Mary Jackson, as well as mathematician Katherine Johnson and computer programmer Dorothy Vaughan, have broken through the racial and gender discrimination of an all-male flight research team at NASA to make brilliant contributions to the space program. Recently, they were awarded Congressional Gold Medals, the highest civilian award in the United States. Also, the first female nominee of a major political party has run for the office of president of the United States and won the popular vote, although not the presidency, after 43 men have held that position. While career and ministerial prospects for women have increased in the last four decades of the 20th century and in the emerging years of the 21st century, equal pay for equal work for women is still a reality being sought. Also, as men have befriended more of their inner feminine principle, there is progress in men being mentors, facilitators, Big Brothers, and leaders of male youth gatherings and men's support groups to empower them as they attempt to grow holistically. For example, President Obama launched on February 27, 2014, the My Brother's Keeper initiative to address persistent opportunity gaps faced by boys and young men of color and to help ensure that all young people reach their full potential. Also, the Elijah Cummings Youth Program in Israel is a two-year leadership fellowship for Baltimore teens designed to build leadership skills and international relationships. When any one of us, male or female, succeeds in embodying more of his or her full potential or essence, we all succeed and expand more fully as a culture. In addition, slowly and despite the resistance of many, there has been an effort to raise awareness and address ecological issues for saving the planet, especially climate change—locally, at some state levels, and with the international community.

In general, while the Western world has experienced gradually more of the emergence of the feminine principle in the process of recovering, reclaiming, and befriending this foundational energy, it simply is shallow and insufficient to speak about an overarching global aspect of the Great Goddess's energy, which has emerged more notably in the latter half of the 20th century and in the unfolding 21st century, without recognizing and speaking specifically about the Dark Goddess. She has a profound *interior* gift of depth, which she offers us personally, collectively as a society and culture, and globally: namely, liberating the soul within us as we cocreate and coparticipate responsibly in this evolving universe. As noted previously, on the continuum of the archetypal energy of the Great Mother, the Dark Feminine is the "other side," of the Great Goddess. Just as Lady Underground, an image of the Dark Goddess summons us individually through the dark night of initiation to embody consciously more of our soul essence, so too, as a face of the "Other," deep-rooted aspect of the feminine principle, she challenges the "underground shadow" of our identity as a collective culture, as well as the world, within the context of the whole living cosmos. America is a part of the whole. However, we as a nation are not the center. She beckons us toward unearthing, metabolizing, and integrating more of the soul essence of our American identity within the interconnected global community as a whole.

With this background, we want to consider what has been increasingly prevalent for the Western world in the last quarter of the 20th century and the ongoing present era, namely the Dark Goddess. While her presence is ancient, she is ever new. Intimations of the archetypal undercurrents of the Dark Feminine energy is sensed in: the dreams of modern men and women; various art forms; poetry; theater; film; contemporary dance; song lyrics;

musical compositions; religious experiences; the body, diverse practices of solitude; demonstrations; #MeToo Movement; "March for Our Lives"; expressive outcries for justice, equality, freedom, inclusivity, tolerance, and respect for all, especially for the disenfranchised, marginalized, and the most vulnerable in society; the life-death-rebirth cycle reflected in nature and all dimensions of life; as well as in the shifts in the Earth herself.

These are times of undeniable and unavoidable polarization. As noted in Chapter Two, New Paradigm, there is a tremendous need for the emergence of the feminine principle, and in particular the Dark Feminine in our culture. The old paradigm and the protracted era of patriarchal dominance and control continue to be confronted and to crumble. However, the ongoing difficulty and daunting task, as we attempt to move forward the challenge, are the awareness that doing so calls for an embodied conscious personalization of the feminine archetypal energy (both dark and light aspects) based on the language of Analytical Psychology and a well-grounded interiorized religious development based on the language of contemporary spirituality. Today, many people who lack a well-differentiated conscious feminine and masculine energy, a personal experience of the mystery/Mystery, and a depth connection to their center are lured into, fascinated by, and attached to others rather easily and indiscriminately; they project the mother and/or father archetypal energy "out there" onto other people, "carriers" such as, politicians, celebrities, athletes, spiritual traditions and rituals, religious leaders, groups, gangs, gurus, organizations, and institutions in our culture and world. Often in spirituality, especially within traditional religions, the archetypal energy of the god or goddess is projected "out there" or "up there" onto a God the Father or Mother so that there is little or no interiorized relationship with the mystery/Mystery. People suffer an eclipse of mystery/Mystery. Perhaps some individuals would rather stay "out there" because they fear going within, taking responsibility for their lives, and growing up psychospiritually. Various others, in their illusionary control, will compartmentalize their lives and remain in a protracted psychospiritual impasse. Some will say that it is easier to stay unconscious than to become conscious. Others may give blindly and loyally their power, financial resources, and energy with rock-star like enthusiasm, to such outer carriers, whom they deem powerful and important, in an effort to profit financially, to maintain the status quo, to gain a perceived prestigious position, or to be relieved from misery and angst. A few, because of such emptiness, disconnect, and insatiable attachment-hunger needs, tend to be overidentified with the archetypal energy while arrogantly obsessed with controlling and manipulating others to be their outer carrier via the use of popular prejudices, false claims, and promises, and all for power, greed, and grandiose recognition.

Appropriate outer carriers are understandably needed when people experience utter devastation, anguish, and hopelessness, especially in times of unjust tragedies, colossal weather disasters (such as wildfires, mudslides, earthquakes, tornadoes, and hurricanes), deplorable unnecessary health conditions such as contaminated water, catastrophic illnesses, or no work. These realities are horrific for individuals and their families, and it impacts their stability, self-esteem, health, and well-being. Looking outward for another, for religious congregational leaders, community organizers, various civic organizations, city and state officials, or the federal government to be conduits of human, compassionate assistance in devastating times is needed, essential, and core to who we are for one another as Americans. This latter is different from looking for another or others to be the carrier of one's soul in life. Each one of us needs to ponder, *Am I asking of another to be and do for me in some way what I need to be and do for myself?* Do you have a greater investment in someone else being the carrier of your soul and living vicariously for you the hero/heroine archetypal journey, than in pursuing and embodying consciously the inner night voyage yourself? In addition, we need to remember that there are people in society who, for various reasons (explored in Chapter Three), do not have the capacity to reflect symbolically or to do inner soul work.

For those who are able to reflect symbolically and do the necessary inner soul work in their unique way, there are some key factors that will assist in furthering consciousness in our society. First, a vital step in the evolution of our consciousness as a culture involves naming, owning, and dialoguing openly about our dark, flawed side, withdrawing our projections from outer carriers, and finding ways to network and collaborate for the good of all. Second, at all levels of society, we need to work together through respectful dialogue and acceptance of diversity and inclusivity in all dimensions of being human, if we are to know a more expansive, grounded interiority of our identity as Americans within the relational web of all life. Discerning the universal underpinnings of the face of the Unknown Dark She can give some perspective to these charged unprecedented times. Moreover, it can inspire and encourage us as we navigate attempting to acknowledge and withdraw responsibly our projections on outer carriers and to deal with some of our dark shadow within ourselves, the country, and the global community. Third, this means authentic leadership on all levels of our nation, most especially at the grass roots, having the courage to organize, to stand up, and to be a voice for upholding our core values in a steady, grounded way as we traverse these challenging times. Finally, for us as citizens and coparticipants in this developing country, we need personally and collectively in our communities to accept responsibility to metabolize, bear, endure, and contain the intensity of the opposites within us consciously as we give birth to a new paradigm shift during this era of polarization, accelerated change, and transition both at home and globally. The challenge going forward is one of collaborating, networking, and establishing good, working, honorable coalitions that serve the highest good of all through a dialogical interactive process in which all creation flourishes in our local communities, states, country, globally, and the whole of the cosmos. Nurturing a respectful dialogue with others who differ in our view within a healthy pluralism is key, especially if we as citizens are not to fall into the swampland of a destructive polarization and impasse that "stifles dialogue, demonizes opponents, and makes an idol out of partial truth."[226] This is very important if our identity as an American society and culture is to develop and expand here at home and if we are to differentiate and evolve in our identity internationally as one among others who favor and share values in the coresponsibility and cocreation of the unfolding Universe Story.

Reflecting further, today in the United States, it is the 18th anniversary of September 11, 2001, the day of the deadliest terrorist act in our country's history. This dark night of annihilating horror and so many more heinous, cowardly terrorist attacks have plagued and impacted our country, allies, and the world. The United States has known many abundant blessings, opportunities, freedoms, enormous challenges, and dark shadow, including blacker-than-black aspects of shadow, in its history. The latter autonomous darker splinter self-parts have spewed out from us and manifested in our political, economic, social, educational, environmental, religious, and relational web of all life. As indicated before, Jung notes that what is denied inwardly comes to us as outer fate. What is unconscious is projected outward. The darkness within that we do not address and befriend will unfortunately and sadly end up being discharged on others who do not deserve it. The shadow we fail to metabolize and integrate consciously will be spewed out on loved ones, students, neighbors, friends, employees, parishioners, citizens, local communities, others who look or seem different in some way from us, society, the world at large, and the Earth herself. Our energy field is not isolated. We live and move in an interconnected and interdependent quantum field of energy, and thus our society and culture are affected by the inner swampland of unconscious, dark material that we resist dealing with in our personal and collective lives.

In the last part of the 20th century and the years of the 21st century, especially since 9/11, there have been many charged issues and a very dark erupting shadow that has arisen in America. *Some* realities include wars; enormous sacrifices, losses, and suffering of our military and their families; the financial crisis of 2008, the deepest since the Great Depression; the fraud and corruption of Wall Street without being held accountable for its crimes; the collapse of the housing market; the growing erosion of the middle class; the inadequate minimum wage; the unresolved health insurance crisis and prescription drug costs; the problems of wage inequality, including women not receiving equal pay for equal work, and for women of color the wage gap is even larger; the fading industrial centers in the North and Midwest; the loss of well-paying manufacturing jobs to increased automation and to outsourcing jobs overseas; a decline in moral and ethical values; the Roman Catholic priest sexual abuse scandal; sexual harassment; obstruction and gridlock politics in Washington, D.C.; an authoritarian, patriarchal style of leadership; cultural and historical trauma; opioid epidemic; the plight of the most vulnerable and powerless; unresolved immigration reform; religious discrimination; ethnic stereotypes; racism; sexism; xenophobia, misogyny;

LGBT human rights intolerance; tensions between law enforcement and predominantly communities of color, with tendencies toward racial profiling, excessive deadly force, and discriminatory practice in the criminal justice system; increased gun violence and domestic violence; the rise in homelessness and human trafficking; climate change and challenges with the ecological crisis; terrorism; gangs; cyberattacks; bullying; various hate groups; the threat of nuclear warfare; and the greatest wealth and income inequality than at any time since the 1920s. Many people have experienced varying degrees of anxiety, fear, anger, disgust, confusion, and unrest welling up within them, especially in the 2016 election cycle, the postelection atmosphere, and the present political time. While the country, at different levels of the collective, strives to address the complexity of these issues (some more than others), it does so with limitations in solving them, for no political or economic system is perfect in an evolving universe that will always be fundamentally flawed and ambiguous. However, given this reality, still we as a nation can't use the latter as an excuse for complacency, cynicism, and inaction. Furthermore, we need to realize that these real issues and enormous shadow realms are symptomatic of a much deeper reality in the unconscious psyche of our American culture. An inherent, undeveloped, hidden pattern of energy of multidimensions of meaningful potential is endeavoring to emerge from the depths. Something more is attempting to arise, to be heard, and to be integrated within the conscious, soulful nature of our American identity. Currently, our polarized society is marked by chaos, turbulence, divisiveness, cruelty, hatred, and uncertainty. Old containers, especially the two primary political containers, are struggling to deal with the new incoming energy. The establishment in either party is a microcosm of the macrocosm of the old closed system that has become too one-sided within the structures of our society that are struggling with the same reality. Hierarchical patriarchy is being challenged. For some time, there has been a deeper "other" unknown energy that has been stirring to be heard, befriended, and integrated in augmenting a greater interior balance and consciousness in the hearts and souls of our culture and in the global world soul.

What is this deeper reality and potential energy that is rousing at this extremely polarized, unprecedented evolutionary time? What is the invisible energy and guiding wisdom weaving through our inner foundational landscapes and through history within the unfolding cosmos that is attempting to be heard? What is the expanded consciousness that we lack in our American identity and yet are being summoned to embody especially with the divisive, dark, chaotic 2016 election period, the unfolding turbulent postelection, and the present dangerous political drama? Who is the "Other" that allows the opposites to coexist creatively, nurtures, empowers, and celebrates unity with diversity, and a respect for all, regardless of where one comes from, one's color, race, ethnicity, religious belief or not, gender, and sexual orientation? It is *She Who Is*! It is the eternal *Dark Feminine,* the *Unknown Dark She, Lady Underground*! The Unknown Dark She, the Ancient One, is eternally now. She reemerges as a wake-up call to us as Americans and for the global community. She beckons us to a living, conscious relationship through befriending the archetypal, feminine energy within ourselves and our culture, while intentionally and responsibly nurturing the web of all life.

While the energy of the Dark Goddess has been manifesting, many do not recognize her potential pattern for meaning and growth. Intimations of her energy reemerge and come to us at this time as a reminder and call to embody a greater depth of our soul essence of who we are in our identity as Americans and our place in the larger international community within the cosmos. She appears anew at this time, summoning us to be inclusive and to embrace all people, as we are summoned to by *The Declaration of Independence,* which states that "[A]ll men [women] are created equal, that they are endowed by their Creator with certain unalienable Rights, that among these are Life, Liberty, and the pursuit of Happiness."[227] She returns for the sake of liberating the generative soul within us personally, collectively within our society and culture, and globally. She comes anew to stimulate the imagination with germinating seeds for spiritual and creative renewal, for society and culture, and for the world soul within the context of the dynamic unfolding Universe Story. She summons us to new frontiers of embodying a deeper conscious identity of who we are as Americans at home and abroad through favoring relational webs of coparticipating and cocreating responsibly within the global community as *one body* at the table of "drinking deeply" from the inner well, with equality, justice, tolerance, respect, and inclusivity for all. For in a quantum interconnected and interdependent universe, what happens to one, including the body of the Earth herself, happens and affects all of us.

The Dark Feminine's universal pattern of energy provides meaning and guidance for *potential* growth and development. As an archetype, it gives emphasis to *presence* in the now, to *process* and the allowing of all life forms to develop according to their natural dynamism, and to *paradox* in letting the opposites coexist creatively (life and death, promise and peril, joy and sorrow, light and dark, death and rebirth, order and disorder, etc.). For example, psychologically, through Lady Underground's dark night of initiation in the Dark Feminine, one can grow in the capacity to hold and endure the tension of the opposites, to sacrifice a rigid and outmoded way of being in surrendering to a new, emerging, unknown, expansive way, and thus experience the possible reality that out of chaos and destruction comes new life and recreation. In the crises and seeming madness of chaos is the potential germinating seeds of creativity and transformation. For the Dark Feminine, it is not chaos or creativity, rather it is both/and in a developing, ambiguous process that allows chaos and creativity to coexist naturally in the relational web of an evolutionary universe. The intimations of the Dark Goddess can be noticed in the gradual movement from a more one-sided, either/or, dualistic model of being and working to an emerging, more holistic, both/and model. Chaos is part of the inherent dynamic of living in a complex, quantum universe. When there is little or no consciousness, the tension is not held, and the opposites become too far apart, then the real danger arises for neurotic overidentification, domination, and demonization, as well as perilous acting out. This was reflected in the 2016 election cycle by a presidential candidate in the verbal bullying and insulting spewing on other presidential candidates of both political parties, Mexicans, Muslims, women, a former POW war veteran, a judge, an American Gold Star family, the news media, and the disabled. When anyone of us colludes through tolerating, condoning, and/or offering excuses for shadow being spewed disrespectfully and destructively on others, we contribute to its normalizing and becoming immune to the collective shadow and the gradual interior downfall of the country and the principles of *The Declaration of Independence.* The chaotic dark side, including the blacker-than-black shadow—owned, metabolized, and integrated—allows individuals and the collective of our society to grow creatively in a more expanded, generative dimension of our humanity.

Part of the value of Lady Underground's dark night of initiation, for us personally and collectively, is that it releases the light of consciousness that graces us through drinking deeply from the inner well and potentially empowers us to imagine a more aligned, just society, culture, and global world in a flourishing creation. There is an expansiveness of vision born of the experience of the deeper, more hidden dimensions of the virgin and wisdom energy. As Barbara Fiand notes: "True vision always is a gift. When it graces us, therefore, we do not experience 'sight' as much as the experience of 'being sighted,' being drawn, being enticed into depth. Our answers then will emerge out of that depth" (p. 217).[228] Drinking deeply fosters joy, hope, strength, imagination, and courage for the journey in networking and collaborating to celebrate what is valuable, beautiful, enjoyable, and excellent in our culture, while also empowering the confrontation of systemic injustices of patriarchal power, racism, sexism, xenophobia, inequality, and misogyny in our local organizations, communities, institutions, states, country, and global world. The American culture and the worldwide community very much need the gift of the primordial Dark Feminine energy of Lady Underground in these accelerated, tumultuous times. Within the vast scope of the continuum of her potential energy for growth and human development is the other, more unknown, hidden, and sublime generative energy.

Some of this resourceful, creative energy was conveyed in a letter to me from the late Edith Wallace, M.D., Ph.D., my Jewish contemplative friend and Jungian analyst, when she was 90 years old. She noted that when silence enters, the whole universe changes, and one enters another world characterized by illumination born out of darkness. This experience is mystery to be honored and embraced in light or dark. Edith stated further that this silence was not oblivion or empty, but rather a silence of life, visions, and "such rest comes for all." Evelyn Underhill, in her book *Mysticism,* refers to people opening to drinking deeply from the inner well of these more sublime depths as pioneers and forerunners of humanity. They are beacons of light of what is significantly possible in the journey of human interiority. Hans Urs von Balthasar refers to contemplatives in this range of interiority as like underground rivers and compares the resonance of their energy to an inimitable melody like a great work of music by Mozart or Bach. This contemplative energy impacts our quantum, interconnected relational web of all creation! And yet, what does this look like in real life? It is being here *now* consciously in the unfolding *present.* It is allowing *paradox,* the opposites, to coexist creatively in all forms of life in the unfolding natural *process* of the flourishing cosmos. It is showing up, living, and embodying responsibly who you are in everyday life with a more awakened-passionate heart and compassionate presence in the small, mundane matters as you make your contribution responsibly in your unique way. It is joining with one another, networking and collaborating together, where and how we can, for the higher good of all life in the cosmos. The United States and the international community could benefit from some high doses of this medicine arising from the deeper depths, embodied by soulful conscious citizens and leaders!

Furthermore, it is learning anew to relate in a more holistic and interconnected way that is informed by an attuned, practical, body wisdom that Lady Underground ushers in by her very nature. When we progressively befriend the underground matter of our person, we open to the alive, somatic, wisdom dimensions of the Great Mother archetypal energy, and furthermore, we become potentially more sensitized and attuned to the intimations of the inexhaustible mystery/Mystery. Moreover, for all of us, as we become more ensouled, we realize when we are using our sword and when we are accessing our inner lamplight. Our entire society could benefit from practicing greater respectful listening, mindfulness, and presence, and less reacting. Individually and collectively, we need to metabolize and transform our competitive will-to-power attitude. Also, if we as a society are to befriend more of the Dark Feminine's energy, it is essential to abandon models of being and working that are motivated by dominance, power, and a conquer-and-control attitude, and move toward a more holistic, respectful way of engaging one another. This includes learning afresh how to live in a mutually enriching relationship with the Earth herself through a caring and sustainable means of living. The abundance of the Earth and the wealth of the Western world need to be shared in our networking collaboratively in the global community. Minimizing rigid dualistic divisions at all levels of life and moving toward greater cooperation and partnership within our culture and the world community is essential. Honoring these changes seems crucial for our planetary harmony, development, and consciousness. Lady Underground's energy challenges us to live in a climate and ethos of balanced relatedness in the here and now within the web of all life. Reclaiming the central importance of such relationality is vital in the process-oriented journey of individuation in authentic human and global interrelatedness.

Thus, we realize that the Dark Goddess's energy is foundational, and it is through her that new life comes! However, the irony for our culture and the global world is that we tend to prefer that new life comes through quick fixes and we are reluctant to be patient, to endure dark-night initiation and the night sea journey. For so long, the Dark Feminine's energy has been so scorned, denied, condemned, repressed, and dissociated that today she emerges not in necessarily recognizable ways that we as a society and culture have traditionally prized and valued. Chaos, turbulence, divisiveness, and disorder mark this present historical time, especially in the presidential 2016 preelection, postelection, and current political period. In many cases, the old is dying, and yet simultaneously, the archaic patriarchy is arising in other forms and pushing back with a dictatorial will-to-power attitude, laced with pontificating, dominating, toxic language, which reflects tones, attitudes, beliefs, and vision that reveal a lack of the integration of shadow material. Irrational attitudes and authoritarian, destructive, suffocating, belief systems discharged on others, society, and the global world can be devastating and profoundly dangerous. A psychospiritual dark-night storm of *positive* disintegration is upon us for our country and the unfolding Universe Story. This is a hallmark sign of a "weather forecast" of intimations of the Dark Goddess, and more specifically symptomatic of Lady Underground's twilight of dark-night initiation for our culture. It is *nigredo* time, in alchemical language. Psychologically, a liminal time is upon our nation. The energy field within the collective can be and is in many cases quite tumultuous. The psychospiritual storm that is occurring can usher in a felt sense of upheaval. Often, there is a change and/or a loss of life as we have known it. Eruption within parts of the collective can occur, manifesting through groups arising, organizing, voicing values, and frequently denouncing old, archaic, patriarchal energy. An example of this surge of reproving energy in America manifested in the massive numbers of women and men who joined the Women's March in Washington, D.C., on January 21, 2017, with 600 sister marches in every state of the Union, in several countries and continents of the world, and with record numbers in Paris, London, and Australia. Further manifestations of this emerging momentum include the 2018 Women's March held on January 20, #MeToo Movement, and Power to the Polls. Whatever the issue may be, it is only through individuals connecting consciously with their depths and having the courage to dialogue, organize, work together, and to speak out for significant values and against outmoded hierarchical patriarchy in all forms of life that impact both men and women, that individuals and the collective cultural energy can coagulate in a higher level of integration and consciousness.

So the question arises, will this *nigredo* time be metabolized by our country, and subsequently will America experience a shift toward greater integration and consciousness? It is too early to sense what will occur, as we are in an unfolding, critical, chaotic, growth period in the evolution of our country's identity. The resonance of energy can be extremely charged, polarized, and politicized which undermines democracy. Some leaders seem to play it safe and remain silent even on many immoral matters, societal cruelty, and barbaric behavior like the death of *Washington Post* journalist Jamal Khashoggi. Certain leaders's camouflaged insecurities drive them to manipulate and to attempt to control news media, fueled by a constant need for adulation. While the political tone is turbulent, other realities persist, such as climate change and extreme shifts in weather, which have caused in some cases the loss of life and the devastation of people's homes and communities in many parts of the country and the world. Outcries and protests about police brutality, misconduct, and shootings continue to erupt. Terrorist threats and cyberattacks, including the Russian involvement in the 2016 elections, are real and persist here in our nation and in the world. Devastation, deprivation, betrayal, horror, terror, and death are a daily reality in many areas of our interconnected and interdependent world: Syria; Iraq; South Sudan, Africa; eastern Ukraine; parts of Central America; and Venezuela.

Hence, we live in a time when the signs of the death aspect of the life-death-rebirth cycle of the Dark Feminine are upon us. Essentially, the nation is experiencing a psychospiritual identity crisis of limits. Self-perpetuating, hierarchical, and patriarchal individuals, groups, organizations, leaders, and institutional systems of our society that are primarily concerned with self-preservation are finding their underground shadow is erupting and spewing outward. We see this with the two main political parties, within a bank like Wells Fargo and the massive fraudulent-accounts scandal, with the violence of the armed white supremacists, neo-Nazis, and KKK members organized for an alt-right rally march in Charlottesville, Virginia, with the bureaucracy of various departments in government, and with various religions. This reality is frightening and anxiety-producing for many, and understandably so.

While this unsettling stage of twilight of dark night is vital if we are to grow as a country in a deeper interiority and in our identity, we don't yet know what will unfold for our future as we strive to address our complexity of issues with our finite capacity to resolve them. This is part of the agony of enduring and bearing the suffering, especially for those in various leadership positions, in all walks of life, as they attempt in these turbulent times to be true to our country's foundational values and to hold the tensions in our society in a steady conscious manner as we find our way together in our unfolding ambiguous reality. This phase of change and transition is affecting the social, political, economic, spiritual, ecological, and cultural dimensions of our country's life. The interplay between extinction and transformation (including the regressive pull of the mother complex, the death-mother energy, and the self-preserving, dominant, controlling father complex) of our nation is operative in the unfolding dynamics that we all face and share as citizens. People are worried and afraid, given the charged issues and aggressive political rhetoric, and justifiably so. We are in a huge in-between time of transition.

Chaos, ambiguity, and turbulence will mark this era of history for some time. When we are in proper relationship to the Dark Feminine energy (giving the Dark Goddess her equal due), as manifested in Lady Underground, we are in relationship from a quantum context in the unfolding process of the here and now, and the opposites are allowed to coexist within the flow of life. Lady Underground's energy is an invitation for any one of us, and the collective, to move from our narrow, limited, dualistic worldview toward an ever-emerging, new paradigm shift marked by coresponsibility, coparticipation, and cocreation. Lady Underground's heart of relatedness and practical wisdom, with the underpinnings of oneness and of the dance of opposites, calls us to probe below the surface (the underground) and to discover that within our culture's messy swampland and charged blacker-than-black shadow lie the germinating seeds of new life, vision, and creativity. Within our pitch-black darkness are the light and the gold of the unfolding way forward.

Moreover, at this evolving time, we need to realize that we, as an American society and culture, have not lived through enough bearing, enduring, metabolizing, and befriending these charged issues, and more deeply, the erupting affect from the underbelly of our blacker-than-black shadow to know fully who we are at this stage of our developing history. Like most people in the Western world, we are not raised, educated, and enlightened to access, befriend, and utilize chaos, turbulence, and darkness creatively. The tendency of our shadow's nature to control and manipulate often short-circuits our perceptions; subsequently, any one of us can tend to be biased, critical, narrow, judgmental in our views, and suppress those who disagree with us. Lady Underground's incoming energy is potentially a call to us in our ongoing everyday lives, as we "chop wood, carry water," to stretch beyond our known limits, dualism, polarization, and patriarchal tunnel vision. She summons us to embody consciously a well-differentiated feminine energy and a well-differentiated masculine energy with an inner marriage of equals in which neither the feminine nor the masculine is subordinated to the other. Consequently, this journey of growth in a deeper interiority for us as a country will not happen overnight but will take time, just as our historical "day-of-development" identity emerged over an era of 240 years. We are in process as the tensions mount around the interplay, on all levels of our society, between the various gradations of extinction and transformation. The outcome of our nation's history is unknown. We have not yet lived into our new, unfolding, and emerging identity. The activation of the Dark Feminine archetype releases patterning dynamics that can influence and restructure the constellation and manifestation of energy both in the psyche and in the outer cosmos. The antiquated, closed hierarchical and patriarchal system will break down as a growing number of people are disillusioned with the old mechanistic world vision and with the denial of the creative foundational principle. It is just a matter of time in a quantum unfolding universe. Whatever the new is to be is in a primitive stage as the collective, by and large, struggles to emerge from an embedded codependency on outer carriers and the dark womb of unconsciousness. More individuals within our collective society will have to grow in their interiority and to take responsibility in cocreating and birthing the conscious shift, if a greater complexity of consciousness is to emerge in the relational web. It is important for all of us to realize that this interior growth development for our country may go on for some time. All forms of outer structural and infrastructural cosmetic changes can occur along with flaunting, pontificating statements, and still the charged wounds that divide us will continue to deepen, surge, and become more polarizing. Jung stated it clearly: that until you make the unconscious conscious, it will direct your life. The shadow of our country, not addressed, will manifest as fate.

Thus, change is upon us whether we like it or not. We are in Lady Underground's twilight of dark-night initiation in the Dark Feminine. In alchemical language, we as a country are in the *nigredo.* This turbulent, divisive time contains erupting manifestations of peril and kernels of promise. If we could understand the universal unfolding pattern of the broader scope and the deeper depth dimension that we as a country are being called to embrace, we might realize that the underside, however long it takes to befriend, holds already the signs of awakening, a potential unexpected renaissance, and generative seeds of resurrection for the web of all creation. Resistance assemblies and grassroots organizing groups, on a variety of issues, including women's rights, health care, and climate warming, are indications that some of the collective are no longer passively colluding in embedded codependency. For many others, our country's emerging reality is scary because of the divisiveness, hatred, bigotry, fascist attitudes, deception, and seemingly anything that is out of "order," such as a group attempting to stand up for certain values or an alternative view. As I listen to the news, one can sense the unsettling tone as journalists, and both local and world leaders speak about their grave concerns, especially after America's leader gave no commitment to Article 5 of the NATO Charter at the NATO Summit (the principle that an attack on one member of the military alliance is viewed as an attack on all and requires a collective defensive response; Article 5 has been invoked only once in NATO's history, after 9/11), or to the Paris Agreement at the G7 Summit, or the recent decision to withdraw American troops from northern Syria. The old establishment no longer speaks for many. A leader who slowly erodes democratic norms, praises leaders who are dictators, encourages violence against reporters, and pontificates an explanation for the Paris program exit that is based on dubious facts and spurious claims doesn't seem to offer any credible, coherent vision of conscious depth, integrity, and intelligence. And yet, what is the replacement?

The shift for our country, the Western world as a whole, and the planet is already unfolding and occurring. Within this cultural milieu, we see the face and universal patterns of the Dark Goddess of Lady Underground's archetypal energy stirring the sediment at the depths of our evolving nation's soul and global world soul. The wrath of Kali (an image of the Dark Feminine that personifies death—death in service to life) is upon us; darkness is erupting from the repressed, underground, shadowy flaws of who we are as a country, as we have become too one-sided, psychologically speaking. For example, segments of the nation unconsciously are overidentified with and driven by power, greed, bigotry, xenophobia, and misogyny. Kali's ferocity activates a felt vicious, dark storm for the sake of more expansive growth and new life. She is destruction and death in service to new life—generative soul. Kali and Lady Underground, as images of the Dark Feminine, allow the opposites (e.g., dark and light) to coexist creatively. When our country's darkness is denied and our horrific, destructive, blacker-than-black swampland is "whitewashed," it nevertheless still persists, and sooner or later, it will come back to haunt us and chaotically disturb us, despite our claims to perfectionism (everything is great and amazing) and order in the outer sphere. Hence, the country's underground repressed dark shadow erupting at this time is symptomatic and part of the intricate, archetypal, evolutionary, dynamic pattern that is unfolding. The energy of Lady Underground and Kali now manifesting is death in service to life. The Dark Feminine aspect of the foundational energy of life is moving us toward greater complexification of consciousness in America's developmental growth. Thus, twilight *nigredo* of Lady Underground's dark-night initiation in the Dark Feminine is reflected in the surging chaos and disorder in our society at this time and especially in the charged 2016 presidential race, the postelection, and the current political time. All that is escalating in the culture is not simply a sign that something has gone amiss, rather moreover, it is an indication and symptomatic of a deeper reality of an unconscious energy wanting to make its way known and of a necessary positive disintegration within the larger view of the cycle of growth. Without the conscious containment, metabolization, and integration of the twilight *nigredo* energy for our nation, the country's identity will remain in a protracted developmental stage, and perhaps even regress, because individually as citizens and collectively as a nation, we fail to do our shadow work, and because of a lack of grounded, intelligent, informed, conscious leadership. As Americans, can we sustain weathering, going through, and assimilating the chaotic, dark-night storm of initiation in the Dark Feminine in twilight and in midnight to open to a more expanded, informed awareness in dawn in our nation's evolutionary identity within the Earth community? What will the unfolding path for our country be: transformation or extinction? Abraham Lincoln reminds us that "America will never be destroyed from the outside. If we falter and lose our freedoms, it will be because we destroyed ourselves." What will be our choice—our path?

Furthermore, we need to remember and to keep an overview perspective of the psychospiritual stages of dark-night initiation, which are *day-of-development, twilight, midnight*, and *dawn*. We can't skip *twilight* and *midnight* and expect to experience a renaissance of renewal and a resonance of a more evolved complexity of consciousness for our culture. Our country's emerging essence of identity seems to be in an early twilight manifestation in our journey toward greater conscious interiority. Our trust and hope are in enough good people choosing responsibly from the grounded consciousness of who each is and who we are together as an evolving people hearing the summons to coparticipate and cocollaborate consciously in the direction of enlarged horizons for our nation and the global world within a flourishing creation. This is evidenced by the women and men participating in the worldwide protest of the Women's March on January 21, 2017, the leadership of Greg Boyle, S.J., in the gang intervention program and Homeboy Industries in California, Leonardo Di Caprio's interviewing role in *National Geographic*'s stunning climate-change awareness documentary, *Before The Flood*, the environmental activist Greta Thunber's message to world leaders, and Pope Francis's challenge to Congress, the United Nations, and the new American administration to address climate change. There are some conscious parts of the collective of our country and the global community that are becoming more informed and cognizant of the universe we inhabit and the relational web sustaining and transforming our every choice and venture. This is evidenced in the momentous historical international consensus signing of the Paris Climate Agreement on November 4, 2016. The document is a testament by many international governments for robust global cooperation, grounded in national action, in meeting climate challenge. As of today, 174 countries and the European Union have joined the Agreement. This exceeds the 55 percent threshold for emissions originally set. This is a concrete manifestation of the Goddess—Earth Mother's energy being metabolized and actualized in a more conscious, flourishing manner. However, June 2, 2017, America's administration decided to pull the nation out of the global climate pact. Grave reaction from around the world and in this country has occurred to the president's backward policy choice based on erroneous, so-called "facts" and unbalanced claims that even the consensus of scientists worldwide, including many Nobel-Prize-winning scientists, disagree with this colossal mistake to withdraw from the Paris program. The high to this low is the galvanizing action that has emerged, committed to honoring the agreement, including some states, cities, governors, mayors, large corporations, big and small businesses, several presidents of universities, and significant oil companies.

Moreover, the good news is the realization that the Goddess is the matrix of creation and her universal generative wisdom is available for us in drinking deeply from the inner well within each of us and together collectively. The Dark Goddess is a generative one to accompany, empower, and guide us at this challenging stage. This unfolding accompaniment is not just at the end of the tunnel, but throughout the entire journey of the day-of-development, twilight, midnight, and dawn, and the ongoing cycle of growth in interiority as we open consciously and humbly to potential encounters of intimations of the multiple dimensions of the mystery/Mystery and Wisdom energy. In the words of Helen Luke, "[I]f civilized humankind is to survive the dangers of this century of transition, when all the familiar landmarks are disappearing and the collective structures that used to protect us are crumbling, we must turn to the *goddess*, to the long-despised values of the feminine, to the feeling heart, and the contemplative mind [center]. Perhaps then our culture may see the rising of a new day" (p. 112).[229]

In this accelerated era, my perspective in this exploration is *one* view and in no way *the* viewpoint about the emerging Dark Feminine archetypal energy and the possible cultural and world-soul implications. There is no one discipline, theory, and/or opinion that has the corner on the truth. Momentous changes in our country, world, and planet, given our present plight, demand an ongoing openness in dialogue and collaborative efforts on behalf of all people regarding the complex realities that face us in the United States and in the global community. Genuine dialogue and mutual respect are essential in examining and being open to a *plurality* of perspectives, as we circumambulate the questions that concern our country, world, and the planet, and the potential impact that the Dark Feminine's universal patterns of energy have for our Western region, the international community, and the Earth herself. Hopefully through psychospiritual development, this growth cycle will emerge as a period when the chaotic darkness of the death experience precedes the light of resurrection. The visionary Roman Catholic priest and social psychologist Diarmuid O'Murchu states it well. He believes that a primary issue is our attitude of denial toward chaos because we fear its impact, which arises from an old-paradigm value system that considers chaos to be dangerous, disruptive, and evil, for it threatens the patriarchal, hierarchical orderly system of the status quo. This is a closed system that allows no divergence, variation, or disagreement. Shadow has to go underground! For O'Murchu, denial is the main dynamic for undermining the potential creativity of chaos. We live by the magical thought that we may return to "the good old days" (i.e., make America great again), where things will be "normal" again and an outer carrier will make everything wonderful once more! No, a shift is happening as the old, closed, patriarchal world system crumbles, a new paradigm is emerging, and chaos is symptomatic of a different era attempting to emerge in this accelerated time of evolution. Thus, chaos will be with us for some time as we approach a new, unfolding evolutionary threshold. O'Murchu insightfully notes that chaos is as vital to order as conflict is to harmony and darkness is to light. For any one of us, learning to befriend chaos, recognizing its personal and cultural influence, and attempting to metabolize and integrate its effect, personally and collectively, is a major task of this era. What is really concerning to O'Murchu is the resistance and denial game-playing by our major institutions of church and state, and their subsequent inability to lead, assist, guide, or empower us in this necessary learning of our time. This reality is evidenced daily in the news. "Only when the changing consciousness reaches a more critical mass can we hope to (co)create institutions that will enhance rather than inhibit our evolutionary development. . . .Once more, we encounter the inescapable paradox: in destruction life is redesigned; in chaos life is reformed; in death life flourishes anew" (pp.138-139)![230]

Difficult as it maybe for any one of us, we begin to grasp that extinction and transformation are central aspects in an evolving cosmic and planetary quantum universe. They are as vital to our reflection and dialogue in our holistic conscious growth at this historical period, as we deal with our country's identity crisis. O'Murchu states that extinction and transformation are the evolutionary and psychic equivalents of death and resurrection or Calvary and resurrection. Resorting to denial of our crisis in these divisive and tumultuous times is a human tendency for individuals and the collective. However, denial exacts a terrible price, as reflected in the reality of climate change.[231] The paradigm shift of consciousness to a deeper interiority, unity, and generative identity will need to reach a greater dimension of the American collective, before more of our nation's cultural essence will reside in the hearts and in the soul of its people. Gandhi, in his perspective of culture, offers our nation and the world community a challenge in our psychospiritual interior growth, as we will not come home in the heart and in the soul of who we are without going through the dark night of soul in the journey of transformation. Thomas Berry, cultural historian, warns that this shift in consciousness will not occur until we end the patriarchal pattern of humans' ambition to disrupt the entire functioning of the globe, and Marion Woodman, Jungian analyst, tells us that "we will only stop plundering our bodies and the Earth's body when we connect to our feminine roots and recognize the sacredness in all matter" (p. 273).[232]

Hence, only through working together to unearth, metabolize, and integrate consciously our nation's messy, dark shadow will we open to: the mystery/Mystery that heals; the experience of liberating more of our soul essence; sighted vision that empowers; respectful dialogue that builds bridges; creation of a better, sustainable future for humanity and Earth; and enlightened, intelligible awareness and compassionate presence that births us anew as one within the interdependent, cooperative networking circle of the global and Earth community in the evolving 14 billion-year-old Universe Story. These potential, deeper, human dimensions, born of Lady Underground's dark-night initiation in the Dark Feminine, are valuable qualities needed in any attempt to address and facilitate healing the enormous divisions and lack of respect for equality and inclusivity for all in our society, world, and Earth community. Part of our realization in the individuation journey, individually and collectively, is that we are participatory creatures in a participatory universe. Let us hope that, in befriending the enormous darkness that faces our country, we consciously choose collaboratively to work together in a spirit of Lincoln's wisdom of accessing the better angels of our nature and leaving nothing for tomorrow that can be done today to further, the continuous unfolding Earth community. Through this awareness, we may discover how our ancient future becomes the eternal now for our Western world and global community.

In the words of T.S. Eliot,
We must be still and still moving
Into another intensity
For a further union, a deeper communion. (p. 32) [233]

Conclusion

Transformative images that stir our imaginations and engage our depths are inviting us to awaken to our natural, embodied soul essence and to the instinctual and illuminative wisdom as we traverse the healing path, both inner and outer, in this unparalleled shift in the evolution of the Earth herself and of humanity within the unfolding 14 billion-year-old Universe Story. One such transformative image summoning humankind is Lady Underground, who is *one* image of the Dark Feminine, the other side of the Great Mother Goddess. It is insufficient and unsatisfactory to speak about an overarching global aspect of the Great Goddess's energy that has emerged more notably in the latter half of the 20th century and in the unfolding 21st century without specifically recognizing, and befriending, the Dark Feminine. On the continuum of the archetypal energy of the Great Mother, the Dark Goddess is the deeper, earthy, immensely powerful "Other," more shadowy, hidden, unknown, sublime, and mysterious dimension of the Goddess. Mother, virgin, and conduit of wisdom are aspects of her potential universal patterns of energy for development. This is as true for men as for women. We all possess the universal patterns of archetypal energy within our inner pantheon; the archetypal structuring is woven in the interactive field of the relational web of all life.

At this historical time, having a living, proper relationship to the eternal, primordial Goddess, and more specifically to the Dark Goddess, is key in enlivening and furthering individual, world, global, and planetary consciousness. Awareness of this reemerging vital and foundational energy within a broader evolutionary frame is important, if we are to coparticipate responsibly in furthering the birth of the dawn of new horizons and frontiers in humanity's journey toward greater complexification of consciousness. In this era of a paradigm shift, it is an essential part of the evolution of our consciousness as men and women to plumb our depths, to find, and to embody consciously a deeper human interiority. The dislocations that exist in the outer arena with the horrific threats and the blacker-than-black dark night that looms over our country, world, and Earth community are making it imperative for us to turn inward with courage to locate ourselves in a more grounded awareness. Given the current American culture and global community, it seems essential to hearken to the call of the Dark Feminine, to recognize the symptoms of chaos and sharp polarization as a sign of the imbalance in the inner and outer spheres, especially of the feminine and masculine energies, and to honor the need to integrate the lost Dark Feminine. She enriches our personal and collective lives in our path to enlightened ensoulment.

When Lady Underground's energy breaks through to consciousness, she modifies our awareness. The makeup of our psyche and our self-limiting belief system, held previously as truth from the ego's narrow lens, is being altered and formed anew, not by will-directedness, but by the emerging wellspring of possibility within our psyche stirring, inspiring, and coursing us individually and collectively forward toward wholeness and a greater complexity of consciousness. Her dark night of initiation activates the alchemical cooking process, not outside the context of our body, or just from our neck up, but her initiation is in and through the whole of who we are: psyche and soma. Furthermore, her energy ushers in a grounded awareness of an interconnectedness and relatedness with our inner cosmos and the earth of our body, along with our outer body, the Earth herself. As we unearth buried, hidden, and sometimes imprisoned energies of our dark swamp of shadow, we begin to discover the wisdom of the body, the felt sense of being authentically in our skin, and the inner passion, love, and generativity of being ensouled consciously. Soulful body awareness anchors us in the present moment, is the portal toward a healthier expansive consciousness; it strengthens the immune system, releases endorphins, and energizes the body's ability to naturally heal itself. Any form of natural unfolding embodiment mirrors the primordial energy of the Dark Feminine. Analytical psychology offers fundamental tools and a language to help disclose and guide the venture in befriending this innate energy deep within our lives and within the cosmos, which holds promise for our renewal. As such, Jungian psychology is a rich resource and a portal through which an informed conscious perspective is offered to our Western world and global community.

The ancient, ever-new, Dark Feminine, whom people have been contemplating for centuries is: a foundational principle that generates and births new life; a nature that courses naturally in all her dimensions in the vast universe; a primordial energy that entices essence; a night that darkens and empties; an underground lamp light that reveals psychic swamp; a death in service to life; a mercy that forgives and heals; an absence that reveals; a love that touches and awakens; a hidden darkness that enlightens; a stillness that speaks; a presence that "sights," guides, and empowers; an ointment that consoles; a joy and laughter that lightens and refreshes; a passionate love rhythming within an embodied sense-felt awareness; and a compassion that liberates the soul within us. Her face has manifested as Isis, Lilith, Inanna, Psyche, Persephone, Kali, Tara, Pele, Yemana, Sheba, Old Woman at the bottom of the riverbed, Lady of Montserrat, Lady of Guadalupe, Earth Mother, Sister, Lady of the Valley, Grandmother Earth, Mary Magdalene, Lady of Czestochowska, Black Madonna of Einsiedeln, Lady Underground, and many others. Her name is secondary to the power of her energy and the fidelity of her love. The reality that her inherent emerging patterns and stages in initiation, and/or her potential inherent gift may be so obscured in the noise of our everyday life, politics, culture, and world scene as to be unrecognized by our clouded perception does not negate her energy or the surging power of her influence, individually and collectively. Hopefully, we now more readily recognize her, welcome her among us, and are even more open to befriending and embodying consciously her essential energy. And yet, even while we are more aware of her significant value and innate patterns of universal energy, we also realize paradoxically that within our soul's depths, all our questioning, seeking, knowing, desiring, and loving are sustained and drawn by a source that remains unknowable and exceeds our finite grasp. For all of us, in our soulful inner work, costing not less than everything, it is well to realize and remember humbly that the inner work remains ongoing and evolving and that the mystery/Mystery dimension will always continue to surround the journey. Thus, the unfolding way arises through our perduring attentiveness to the intimations of the mystery/Mystery whose depth has no end.

In due course, through the Dark Goddess's dark night of initiation and our differentiation process, we open potentially to sensing more expansive, multilevel dimensions of inexhaustible depth and to the murmur of the mystery/Mystery revealed in nature, simplicity, silent music, sounding solitude, benevolent kindness, the darkness that is light, and the stillness that is the dancing. Within this assimilation of enlarging experience, we discover that the way of the Dark Feminine is an ancient path for today's psycho-spiritual journeyer of depth. Lady Underground opens us to the *invisible world.* We realize within our expanded, consciously-embodied, human interiority the inner wisdom of the ancient Gnostics who wrote, "Know then, before the curtain of night obscures knowledge, that the truth is to be sought in *this world* and also in *that world,* for the two worlds in truth are one; it is only the rational mind that thinks otherwise" (p. 216).[234]

INNER WORK

The beauty of the Way is that there is no "way."
~Loy Ching-Yuen

Naturnalness is called the Way.
~*The Secret of the Golden Flower*

The way is not in the sky. The way is in the heart.
~Gautama Buddha

I give you news of the way of this man, but not of your own way.
My path is not your path. . . .The way is within us,
. . .[W]ho should live your own life if not yourself? So live yourselves.
The signposts have fallen, unblazed trails lie before us. Do you not know that you yourselves are the fertile acre which bears everything that avails you?
C.G. Jung, *The Red Book*

The right way to wholeness is made up of fateful detours and wrong turnings.
It is. . .not straight but snakelike, a path that unites the opposites, . . .a path whose labyrinthine twists and turns are not lacking in terrors.
~C.G. Jung, *Psychology and Alchemy*

Don't be satisfied with stories,
how things have gone with others.
Unfold your own myth.
~Rumi

~Reflection, Discussion, and Journaling Questions

- How do you experience your body attempting to engage your attention in a more enlightened somatic awareness?
- How do you as an analyst, therapist, spiritual director, psychospiritual facilitator, and/or educator, and/or anyone of us become attuned to your bodily experience? What has been influential in your growth in heartfelt awareness, embodied presence, and empathy? How has working with psyche and soma attentively made a difference for you, and how has it impacted your presence to others and/or your companioning clients in their healing process?
- As one who accompanies others in their soul journey, how do you personally unearth the buried energies in the caverns of your depths in working with your psyche and soma? What are the imaginal modalities or techniques that have assisted you in self-discovery?
- Connecting with "underground" energies in the caverns of the soul opens one to "drinking deeply" and to discovering germinating seeds of our regenerative and creative nature. What are the "underground" energies you have unearthed that have been a source of generativity for you personally and professionally?
- Describe your way of working with dream images. How do you attend to the reality of the somatic unconscious in your work with dreams?
- What part of your "essence" went "underground" in adapting to cope and to make it in your family, neighborhood, school, work, and/or religious tradition?
- Explain how the distinct but mutually enriching wisdom of Analytical Psychology, quantum physics, contemporary neuroscience, theology, spirituality, energy medicine, body-energy techniques, and/or contemplative practices have influenced your journey of individuation.
- How do you view Lady Underground's archetypal, foundational energy challenging spirituality?
- Where is Lady Underground summoning you to expand beyond what is known, secure, and rational to experience what is unthinkable or unimaginable that you might embody consciously a more expanded and holistic spirituality?

- What has it been like for you to differentiate from the Mother energy in your psychospiritual journey of individuation?
- Where do you perceive the dynamics of Death Mother or Death Father energy operative in our culture? What are examples of the manifestations of these energies in the 2016 election cycle and in the current political time? How do you imagine yourself participating responsibly in the paradigm shift so that a different, more conscious resonance of energy can manifest in the unfolding now?
- The paradigm shift calls us to a new spiritual sensibility of a conscious interiority. The shift summons us to "drinking deeply" and making a responsible conscious contribution in our own unique way within the web of life. The Jungian psychological approach can be most helpful in this journey toward embodying one's more natural authentic "essence" and broadening the horizon of one's lived spirituality in the ordinary of life. Describe your experience in the journey toward a deeper conscious interiority. How has the Jungian perspective assisted your psychospiritual, holistic growth?
- Who in the culture do you admire as an individual who seems to embody consciously more of the virgin and conduit of wisdom energy? Explain what it is about this person that inspires you? Who, for you, are some historical figures that reflect the deeper "other" dimension of the continuum of the Great Mother foundational energy (virgin and conduit of wisdom)? How have these historical figures inspired your life? If you could dialogue with one of them, what would you want to communicate to the person and what would you like to ask the individual? What do you imagine this person might like to communicate to you in the dialogue experience?
- How would you describe American culture today?
- At this historical time, what do you perceive are the issues that our country needs to deal with if we are to grow in a deeper, grounded, interiorized identity?
- Identify where you perceive the old-paradigm, dualistic, patriarchal system operative in our American society?

- What benefits do you receive from remaining unconscious and refusing to take responsibility for your adult life?
- How do you imagine yourself living a fuller conscious life as an American citizen and making a generative contribution to the expansive growth of our culture?
- Where do you tend to give your energy and power to "outer carriers" and how might you begin to take your power back, grow in detachment, and take responsibility for your path in life and for growth in your soul's "essence"?
- What are America's blacker-than-black shadow aspects that are divisive and destructive to the country? Explain your perspective and what you believe would be helpful in the healing and transforming process for us as a nation?
- What are the symptomatic indicators manifesting in America, the Western world as a whole, the global community, and the Earth herself that suggest that a deeper dimension is attempting to be realized in life and in the evolving cosmos?
- What is the relationship between the Dark Goddess of Lady Underground and the ecological movement in the 21st century? What is the urgency for the comprehensive Earth community being informed and united in its commitment about the threat of climate change and the plight of the planet?
- Describe your understanding of the current ecological crisis? What is your way of sharing in the coresponsibility of saving the planet and living in a more ecologically sustainable manner?
- What are practical choices you can make today to hasten the implementation of renewable and clean-energy technologies across the planet?
- What are actions that we, as individuals and as an American society, can take to prevent catastrophic disruption of life on our planet?
- How do you experience "drinking deeply" from the inner well in your life? How does this reality impact your being a responsible, conscious, American citizen in our contemporary society?

- What is your vision for America that stirs your depths and excites you to contribute your energy to ushering your dream into reality as you share in the cocreation of the unfolding comprehensive Earth community?
- How do you imagine major and small business companies being involved in raising awareness and educating the public about climate change and the ecological crisis?
- What are three hopes you have for America in your lifetime?
- What are you willing to do responsibly to spearhead and to honor your hopes?
- What do you imagine and hope for in your lifetime for the comprehensive Earth community?
- For what actions, as an individual, are you willing to take responsibility in order to prevent catastrophic disruption of life on this planet? What bold action might society take now to address the defining crisis of our time: climate change?

~Process Exercises

- A valuable active-imagination meditative exercise is labyrinth walking, a symbolic walking meditation that quiets the mind, opens the heart, grounds the body, and illuminates the spirit. This is one form of intentional solitude in "drinking deeply." The labyrinth has one winding path that leads from the outer edge in a circuitous way to the center. It is an archetypal symbol whose earliest origins are over 3,000 years old and are found throughout history in various cultures around the world. The labyrinth, inlaid in the paving of the Chartres Cathedral nave in Chartres, Frances, around 1202, is the largest and best preserved from medieval France.

  There are many reproductions of the Chartres labyrinth throughout the United States and world. Consider researching on the internet the places nearest to you where you might go to experience this exercise. Here in the D.C., Maryland, and Virginia areas, there are eight labyrinths at different churches and a retreat center that offer this opportunity to the public. There is no right or wrong way to walk the labyrinth. Have a perduring attentiveness within yourself while trusting your inner rhythms and sense of body wisdom and intuition. Maintain silence throughout your walk and move at your own pace until you reach the center, where you can remain as long as you like while being aware of whatever arises naturally within your interior, as you focus in and are present to yourself during your experience. When you are ready, you can begin to walk out of the labyrinth at your own rate. After you have finished your labyrinth walk, consider finding a space where you can be quiet, relax, and recall your experience. You may want to record it as a way to honor and to objectify further your depths. Some possible inquiry questions for exploration and reflection might be:

- What was it like for you to experience the labyrinth walk?
- How do you feel about the meditative walk?
- What did you become aware of during your experience at the center?
- What image captures the felt sense of your overall meditative walk?
- What do you imagine your soul is calling you to at this time in your life?
- As you reflect on the whole reality, what have you learned from this exercise?
- How might you continue to honor, integrate, and live in your everyday life what you have become aware of through your labyrinth walk?

Finally, take some time to acknowledge yourself and your depths for your inner work as you bring closure to your process.

- Draw a mandala that expresses and captures for you in some way the felt meaning of your labyrinth experience. This is another way to have an attentiveness to your interior and objectify what is attempting to be heard and assimilated by your soul as you allow to arise what is arising from your depths. When you are finished, notice and record on the back of your mandala the feelings, thoughts, images, insights, and/or sensations you experienced while drawing your mandala.

What have you discovered through this experience? Consider taking some time to acknowledge yourself and your depths for your inner work as you conclude your inner soul work.

- One possible way to nurture intentional solitude and to open to "drinking deeply" within, as well as sending healing vibrations to another, is to do the attuned-heart exercise. The simple method can be practiced when doing inner soul work, choosing alignment with one's heart and depths in solitude, and/or when feeling overwhelmed by the busyness and demands of life. Triggered emotions can be draining to our energy field and soma. We can discriminate and choose consciously to demagnetize and shift the energy. The attuned-heart exercise can aid in this process toward utilizing our life force in a more generative manner. In the shift, one can open potentially to an inner felt harmony and an awareness within one's body. The attuned-heart exercise is simple. First, bring your attention to your pulsating heart. While breathing in and out at your normal heart rate, gradually slow your breath down while maintaining your focus on your heart rhythm and do so as if your breath emanates from the heart. In essence, you are sending a message to your neuro-pathways that you are safe, and you can relax, let go, and trust turning your attention inward. Second, choose consciously to call to awareness a felt feeling like love, gratitude, compassion, or care for someone, something, or Earth herself. What is key is first to sense and experience the feeling, and then emit the feeling in your natural imaginary way toward your brain, whole of your body, and depths. Sustaining the feeling resonance assists the state of simply being and allowing to arise whatever emerges between your heart and your depths. From this attuned-heart space of interiority, one can experience a restorative sense of being and choose to send healing vibrations to another at a distance. In short, the steps to an attuned-heart exercise are: focus, feel, and breathe. When you have completed the exercise, consider taking some time to acknowledge your soul for your inner work.

- Watch the DVD *Before the Flood*, developed by the Academy-Award-winning actor, environmental activist, and United Nations Messenger of Peace Leonardo DiCaprio and the award-winning filmmaker Fisher Stevens. This features and chronicles DiCaprio's campaign to raise global awareness about the dangers of climate change in his role as a United Nations Ambassador of Peace. The DVD presents an informative, riveting account of the clear, dramatic changes occurring around the world due to climate change; it also offers actions that we as individuals and as a society, can take to prevent unnecessary catastrophic disruption of life on our planet.
- After watching the DVD, reflect on what gripped your attention. Contemplate writing down some of your feelings and thoughts as a further way to objectify your awareness. Consider hosting and facilitating a small-group neighborhood, faith community, or an educational sponsored gathering in the local Jungian or civic community to watch, discuss, and plan a course of actions that you can take in sharing responsibly in the prevention of catastrophic disruption of life on our planet.
- Jung once noted that a walk in nature could bring balance to the psyche. Consider taking a walk in nature. Focus on your breath and ever so gradually imagine that you are walking and breathing at your own inner rhythm from your heart. As you become attuned to your breathing from your heart, allow yourself to open to the arena of nature that surrounds you. See and take in the grass, a tree, a flower, plant, a bush, a pond, a lake, or wherever you are focused on in the arena of nature. Allow yourself to be with a tree, plant, or whatever captures your attention, and as you do so, let your awareness be with the tree (or whatever is the object of your focus) as you contemplate it in stillness. In the silence, in the silence, let go and be with the tree (or whatever you are contemplating in nature) as you allow to arise whatever is emerging in your experience in nature. Remember, there is no right or wrong way of doing this process exercise.

~Body-Energy Work

- There is no one particular "cookie-cutter" recipe for every individual or form of body-energy work that is appropriate for one's psycho-spiritual inner work. Some of the noted material in the Body-Energy Work sections in previous chapters may be options for you in your holistic process of befriending and honoring your depths and your soul's summons. Some examples of other modalities of body-energy work that may be forms that can assist in the holistic journey toward healing and wholeness might include: shiatsu, acupressure, acupuncture, tai chi, qigong, yoga, reiki, therapeutic touch, rolfing, bio-energy, sound therapy, and/or Bowen Technique. There may be many other forms that you have discovered that are rich resources for your holistic healing journey. Remember, there is no one way. These various forms of body-energy work can be avenues for opening, nurturing, and promoting the dialogue and communion with the ever-present, inexhaustible mystery/Mystery in the journey of life.

Notes

[1] Baring & Cashford, 1991.

[2] Gustafson, 1990.

[3] Miller, 1997.

[4] Charpentier, 1975.

[5] Matthews, 1992.

[6] Matthews, 2001.

[7] Elder, 1996.

[8] Adams, 1986.

[9] Elder, 1996.

[10] Begg, 1985.

[11] Baring & Cashford, 1991.

[12] Von Franz, 1980a.

[13] Calabria, 1989.

[14] Von Franz, 1980b.

[15] Matthews, 1992.

[16] Harvey & Baring, 1996.

[17] Harvey & Baring, 1996.

[18] Matthews, 2001.

[19] Galland, 1990.

[20] Apuleius, 1960.

[21] Apuleius, 1960.

[22] Pagels, 1979.

[23] Getty, 1990.

[24] Gadon, 1989.

[25] Woodman & Dickson, 1996.

[26] Woodman & Dickson, 1996.

[27] Woodman & Dickson, 1996.

[28] Jung, 1963.

[29] Oman, 1997.

[30] Getty, 1990.

[31] Getty, 1990.

[32] Tarnas, 1991.

[33] Harvey, 2001.

[34] Woodman & Dickson, 1996).

[35] Jung, 1968.

[36] Jung, 1966.

[37] Jung, 1971.

[38] Jung, 1953b.

[39] John of the Cross, 1991.

[40] Teresa of Avila, 1980.

[41] Teresa of Avila, 1976.

[42] Fox, 2000.

[43] Jung, 1971.

[44] Hollis, 1995.

[45] Otto, 1923.

[46] Hollis, 1995.

[47] Welch, 1990.

[48] Hollis, 1995.

[49] Hollis, 1995.

[50] Jung, 1953b.

[51] Meier, 2001.

[52] Meier, 2001.

[53] O'Murchu, 1997.

[54] O'Murchu, 2000.

[55] O'Murchu, 1997.

[56] Grof, 1992.

[57] Grof, 1985.

[58] O'Murchu, 1997.

[59] O'Murchu, 1997.

[60] Luke 17:20-21 (New Jerusalem Bible).

[61] Bacik, 1989.

[62] Eliot, 1963.

[63] Jung, 1953b.

[64] Jung, 1968.

[65] Tillich, 1948.

[66] Eliade, 1958.

[67] Eliade, 1958.

[68] Jacobi, 1967.

[69] Jung, 1953b.

[70] Jung, 1966.

[71] Jung, 1971.

[72] Neumann, 1970.

[73] Samuels, Shorter, & Plaut, 1986.

[74] Jacoby, 1999.

[75] Von Franz & Hillman, 1971.

[76] Underhill, 1961.

[77] Marlan, 1997.

[78] Jung, 1969a.

[79] Bly & Woodman, 1998.

[80] Jung, 1963b.

[81] Jung, C.G., 1963b.

[82] Jung, C.G., 1963b.

[83] Jung, 1968.

[84] Ulanov, 1971.

[85] Gad, 1994.

[86] Rilke, 1996.

[87] Rilke, 1967.

[88] Jung, 1971.

[89] Jung, 1966.

[90] Jung, 1966.

[91] Robinson, 1988.

[92] Meyer, 1992.

[93] Jung, 1953b.

[94] Jung, 1969.

[95] Jung, 1953b.

[96] Jung, 1968.

[97] Hammarskjold, 1964.

[98] Jung, 1963a.

[99] Hollis, 2007.

[100] Lawrence, 1973.

[101] Hollis, 2015.

[102] Jung, 1968.

[103] Jung, 1971.

[104] Jung, 1968.

[105] Jung, 1988.

[106] Jung, 1968.

[107] Gad, 1994.

[108] Jung, 1954a.

[109] Edinger, 1972.

[110] Jung, 1963b.

[111] Jung, 1969b.

[112] Jung, 1966.

[113] Jung, 1966.

[114] Harris, 2001.

[115] Perera, 1981.

[116] Meador, 2000.

[117] Hurwitz, 1992.

[118] Matthews, 2001.

[119] Leonard, 1993.

[120] Kamerling, 2003.

[121] Koltuv, 1986.

[122] Labouvie-Vief, 1994.

[123] FitzGerald, 1986.

[124] Luke, 1993.

[125] Rilke, 1982.

[126] Dickinson, 2003.

[127] Jung, 1967a.

[128] Jung, 1969a.

[129] Barks, 2004.

[130] Singer, 1998.

[131] Turner, 1995.

[132] Jung, 1963a.

[133] Bacik, 1976.

[134] Singer, 1990.

[135] Elliot, 1943.

[136] Elliot, 1943.

[137] Berry, 1998a.

[138] Berry, 1998b.

[139] Berry, 2015.

[140] Rahner, 1973.

[141] Rilke, 1996.

[142] Eliot, 1943.

[143] Goodwin, 2012.

[144] Goodwin, 2012.

[145] Goodwin, 2012.

[146] Goodwin, 2012.

[147] Jung, 1971.

[148] O'Murchu, 2008.

[149] Clendenen, 2009.

[150] Hafiz, 1999.

[151] Powers, 1989.

[152] John of the Cross, 1991.

[153] John of the Cross, 1991.

[154] Hopkins, 1983.

[155] Albom, 1997.

[156] Paris, 1988.

[157] Edinger, 1972.

[158] Jung, 1967b.

[159] Corbett, 1996.

[160] Otto, 1923.

[161] Jung, 1973.

[162] Jung, 1953b.

[163] Jung, 1966.

[164] Jung, 1953b.

[165] Rilke, 1996.

[166] John of the Cross, 1991.

[167] Rilke, 1996.

[168] John of the Cross,1991.

[169] John of the Cross, 1991.

[170] FitzGerald, 2000.

[171] Estes, 1992.

[172] Lao Tzu, 2007.

[173] Jung, 1959a.

[174] Jung, 1954b.

[175] Jung, 1973.

[176] Jung, 1988.
[177] Ulanov, 2014.
[178] Jung, 1969a.
[179] John of the Cross, 1991.
[180] Ulanov, 2014.
[181] John of the Cross, 1991.
[182] Mueller, 1996.
[183] Hollis, 1996.
[184] Ulanov, 2014.
[185] Ulanov, 2014.
[186] Eliot, 1943.
[187] Jung, 1933.
[188] Jung, 1954c.
[189] John 9:6.
[190] Chevalier & Gheerbrant, 1966.
[191] Luke, 1995.
[192] Von Franz, 1972.
[193] Chevalier and Gheerbrant, 1966.
[194] Cooper, 1978.
[195] Jung, 1969a.
[196] Jung, 2009.
[197] Nepo, 1994.
[198] Pick, 1953.
[199] Pick, 1953.
[200] Harding, 1990.
[201] Harding, 1990.
[202] Parks, 2013.
[203] Jung, 1953a.
[204] Ecclesiasticus 15:3 (New Jerusalem Bible).
[205] Sanford, 1999.
[206] Blake, 1992.
[207] O'Murchu, 2012.
[208] Cleary, 1991.
[209] Eliot, 1943.
[210] Williamson, 2004.
[211] Ryley, 1998.
[212] Jung, 1968.

[213] O'Donohue, 2008.

[214] Jung, 1959b.

[215] Greene, 2005.

[216] Jung, 1933.

[217] Eliot, 1943.

[218] Feldman, 2002a.

[219] Feldman, 2002b).

[220] Kast, V., supervision session, 2002.

[221] Meier, 2001.

[222] Blake, 1992.

[223] Jung, 1966.

[224] Jung, 1969b.

[225] Hafiz, 1999.

[226] Bacik, James, "Sunday Meditations," *Seventh Sunday in Ordinary Time, A Cycle*, February 19, 2017.

[227] U.S. Declaration of Independence, Paragraph 2 (1776).

[228] O'Murchu, 2016.

[229] Taylor, 1998.

[230] O'Murchu, 2004.

[231] O'Murchu, 2004.

[232] Ryley, 1998.

[233] Eliot, 1943.

[234] Singer, 1999.

References

Adams, H. (1986). *Mont Saint Michel and Chartres.* New York: New York Books.

Albom, M. (1997). *Tuesdays with Morrie: An old man, a young man, and life's greatest lesson.* New York: Doubleday Publishing Group, Inc. and Company.

Artress, L. (1995). *Walking a sacred path.* New York: Riverhead Books.

Bacik, J. (1976). *Apologetics and the eclipse of mystery: Mystagogy according to Rahner.* Notre Dame, IN: Notre Dame Press.

Bacik, J. (1989). *Contemporary theologians.* New York: Triumph Books.

Baring, A., & Cashford, J. (1991). *The myth of the goddess: Evolution of an image.* London: Penguin Books.

Barker, C. (2001). *World weary woman: Her wound and transformation.* Toronto: Inner City Books.

Barks, C. (Trans.). (2004). *The essential Rumi: New expanded edition.* New York: Harper San Francisco.

Becker, K. (2001). *Unlikely companions: C.G. Jung on the Spiritual Exercises of Ignatius of Loyola–An exposition and critique based on Jung's lectures and writings.* Cornwall, UK. MPG Books, Ltd.

Begg, E. (1985). *The cult of the black virgin.* London: Arkana, Routledge & Kegan Paul.

Berry, P. (1982). *Echo's subtle body.* Dallas, TX: Spring Publications, Inc.

Berry, T. (1998a). The sacred universe. In Ryley, N. (Ed.), *The forsaken garden: Four conversations on the deep meaning of environmental illness* (pp. 237-250). Wheaton, IL: Quest Books.

Berry, T. (1998b). The soul in nature. In Ryley, N. (Ed.), *The forsaken garden: Four conversations on the deep meaning of environmental illness* (pp. 223-236). Wheaton, IL: Quest Books.

Berry, T. (2015, June). Developing a cosmological spirituality. Lecture presented at the Franciscan Center, Sylvania, OH.

Blake, William. (1992). The little black boy. In S. Appelbaum, & P. Smith (Eds.). *Songs of innocence and songs of experience* (p. 10). Mineola, NY: Dover Publications.

Bly, R., & Woodman, M. (1998). *The maiden king: The reunion of masculine and feminine* (New York: Henry Holt and Company.

Boe, J. (1992). Messiness is next to goddessness. *Psychological Perspectives, 27,* 104-109.

Bolen, M. D., & Shinoda, J. (1984). *Goddesses in every woman: A new psychology of women.* New York: Harper and Row.

Bolen, M. D., & Shinoda, J. (2001). *Goddesses in older women: Archetypes in women over fifty.* New York: Harper Collins Publishers.

Braden, G. (2015). *Resilience from the heart: The power to thrive in life's extremes.* New York: Hay House, Inc.

Buckley, M. (1979). Atheism and contemplation. *Theological Studies, 40,* 680-699.

Calabria, M. (1989, November). The goddess re-awakening: Isis. Paper presented at the New York Theosophical Society Lecture, New York.

Cameron, R., ed. (1993). *Non-canonical gospel texts: The other gospels.* Philadelphia: The Westminster Press.

Campbell, J. (1968). *The mystic vision: Papers from the Eranos yearbooks.* New York: Princeton University Press.

Campbell, P., & McMahon, E. (1985). *Bio-spirituality: Focusing as a way to grow.* Chicago: Loyola University Press.

Charpentier, L. (1975). *The mysteries of Chartres cathedral.* New York: Avon Books.

Cheavalier, J., & Gheerbrant, A. (1996). *The Penguin dictionary of symbols* (J. Buchanan-Brown, Trans.). London: Penguin Books.

Claremont de Castillejo, I. (1973). *Knowing woman: A feminine psychology.* New York: Harper Colophon Books.

Cleary, T. (Trans.). (1991). *The secret of the golden flower: The classic Chinese book of life.* New York: Harper Collins Publishers.

Clendenen, A. (2009). *Experiencing Hildegard: Jungian perspectives.* Wilmette, IL: Chiron Publications.

Clow, B. H. (2011). *Awakening the planetary mind: Beyond the trauma of the past to a new era of creativity.* Rochester, VT: Bear & Company.

Cooper, D. A. (1998). *God is a verb: Kabbalah and the practice of mystical Judaism.* New York: Riverhead Books.

Cooper, J. C. (1978). *An illustrated encyclopedia of traditional symbols.* London: Thames and Hudson.

Corbett, L. (1996). *The religious function of the Psyche.* New York: Routledge.

Corbett, N. Q. (1988). *The sacred prostitute: Eternal aspect of the feminine.* Toronto: Inner City Books.

Corbett, N. Q. (2002). *Awakening woman: Dreams and individuation.* Toronto: Inner City Books.

Cousineau, P. (1998). *The art of pilgrimage: The seeker's guide to making travel sacred.* Berkeley, CA: Conari Press.

Cowen, P. (1979). *Rose windows.* San Francisco: Chronicle Books.

Culligan, K, & Jordan, R. (Eds.). (2000). *Carmel and contemplation transforming human consciousness.* Washington, DC: ICS Publications.

Culligan, K. (1997). *Experience of God in chaos* (Video). Lecture presented at the eleventh seminar on Carmelite spirituality, Notre Dame, IN.

Culligan, K. (1998). *Love and kenosis as prayer: A teaching of St. John of the Cross* (Audio Cassette). Washington, DC: ICS Publications.

Dison, P. (1999). *Nietzsche and Jung: Sailing a deeper night.* New York: Peter Lang.

Dorgan, M. (1991). *The mystery of my being* (Audio Cassette). Canfield, OH, Alba House Communications.

Downing, C. (1990). *The Goddess: Mythological images of the feminine.* New York: Crossroad.

Edinger, E. (1972). *Ego and archetype.* New York: Penguin Books.

Edinger, E. (1985). *Anatomy of the Psyche: Alchemical symbolism in psychotherapy.* La Salle, IL: Open Court.

Edinger, E. (1996). *The new god-image: A study of Jung's key letters concerning the evolution of the western god-image.* Wilmette, IL: Chiron.

Egan, K. (1987). *Teresa and John: Search for justice and peace* (Audio Cassettes). Canfield, OH: Alba House Communications.

Egan, K. (1991). *Prayer as love: John of the Cross–The experience of darkness* (Audio Cassettes). Canfield, OH: Alba House Communications.

Eliade, M. (1958). *Rites and symbols of initiation: The mysteries of birth and rebirth.* Woodstock, CT: Spring Publications.

Elder, G. (1996). *The Body: An encyclopedia of archetypal symbolism.* Boston: Shambhala Publications, Inc.

Eliot, T. S. (1943). *Four quartets.* New York: Harcourt Brace Jovanovich, Publishers.

Eliot, T. S. (1963). Four quartets: East Corker. *Collected Poems, 1909-1962* (pp. 189-190). New York: Harcourt, Brace, & World, Inc.

Elizondo, V. (1999). *Guadalupe: Mother of the new creation.* Maryknoll, NY: Orbis Books.

Engelsman, J. C. (1994). *The feminine dimension of the divine: A study of sophia and feminine images in religion.* Wilmette, IL: Chiron Publications.

Estes, C. P. (1992). *Women who run with the wolves: Myths and stories of the wild woman archetype.* New York: Ballantine Books.

Favier, J. (1988). *The world of Chartres.* New York: Harry N. Abrams, Inc.

Feldman, B. (2000). Dissolving and creating: On the development of internal space and the capacity for symbolization. *Journal of Jungian Theory and Practice, 2.* 43-53.

Feldman, B. (2002a, October). *Post-Jungian analysis in childhood: A developmental approach.* Paper presented at the inter-regional Jung Institute training, Playa del Carmen, MX.

Feldman, B. (2002b, October). *The lost steps of infancy: Symbolization, analytic process, and the growth of the self.* Paper presented at the inter-regional Jung Institute training, Playa del Carmen, MX.

FitzGerald, C. (1986). Impasse and dark night. In J. Wolski Conn (Ed.), *Women's spirituality: Resources for Christian development* (pp. 410-435). Mahweh, NJ: Paulist Press.

FitzGerald, C. (2000). Transformation in wisdom. In K. Culligan, & R. Jordan (Eds.), *Carmelite studies 8: Carmel and contemplation, transforming human consciousness* (pp. 303-325). Washington, DC: Institute of Carmelite Studies Publications.

Fox, M. (2000). *One river, many wells: Wisdom springing from global faiths.* New York: Penguin Putnam, Inc.

Gad, I. (1994). *Tarot and individuation: Correspondences with Cabala and alchemy.* York Beach, ME: Nicolas-Hays, Inc.

Gadon, E. W. (1989). *The once and future goddess.* New York: Harper and Row, Publishers.

Galland, C. (1990). *Longing for darkness: Tara and the black Madonna.* New York: New York, Penguin Books.

Getty, A. (1990). *Goddess: Mother of living nature.* London: Thames and Hudson.

Godwin, G. (2001). *Heart.* New York: Harper Collins Publishers, Inc.

Goodwin, D. K. (2012). *The team of rivals: The political genius of Lincoln.* New York: Simon and Schuster Paperbacks.

Greene, A. U. (2005). Listening to the body for the sake of the soul. *Spring Journal, 72*, 189-204.

Grof, S. (1992). *The holotropic mind: The three levels of human consciousness and how they shape our lives.* San Francisco: Harper.

Grof, S. (1985). *Beyond the brain: Birth, death, and transcendence in psychotherapy.* Albany: State University of New York.

Gustafson, F. (1990). *The black Madonna.* Boston: Sigo Press.

Hafiz. (1999). *The gift: Poems by Hafiz, the great Sufi master* (D. Ladinsky, Trans.). New York: Penguin Compass.

Hammarskjold, D. (1964). *Markings.* New York: Ballantine Books.

Harding, E. (1993). *Kali: The black goddess of Dakshineswar.* York Beach, ME: Nicolas-Hays, Inc.

Harding, E. M. (1963). *Psychic energy: Its source and its transformation.* Princeton, NJ: Princeton University Press.

Harding, E. M. (1970). *The way of all women.* Boston: Shambhala Publications, Inc.

Harding, E. M. (1990). *Woman's mysteries: Ancient and modern.* Boston: Shambhala Publications, Inc.

Harris, J. (2001). *Jung and yoga: The psyche-body connection.* Toronto: Inner City Books.

Harvey, A. (2001). *The return of the mother.* New York: Tarcher/Putnam Books.

Harvey, A., & Baring, A. (1996). *The divine feminine: Exploring the feminine face of God throughout the world.* Berkeley, CA: Conari Press.

Hillel, R. (1997). *The redemption of the feminine erotic soul.* York Beach, ME: Nicolas-Hays, Inc.

Hillman, J. (1970). *The dream and the underworld.* New York: Harper and Row.

Hollis, J. (1993). *The middle passage: From misery to meaning in midlife.* Toronto: Inner City Books.

Hollis, J. (1995). *Tracking the Gods: The place of myth in modern life.* Toronto: Inner City Books.

Hollis, J. (1996). *Swamplands of the soul: New life in dismal places.* Toronto: Inner City Books.

Hollis, J. (2000). *The archetypal imagination.* College Station, TX: A & M University Press.

Hollis, J. (2001). *Creating a life: Finding your individual path.* Toronto: Inner City Books.

Hollis, J. (2007). *Why good people do bad things: Understanding our darker selves.* New York: Gotham Books.

Hollis, J. (2015, October). *The archetypal pattern of the wounded healer.* Workshop presented at the Library of the Jung Society of Washington, Washington, DC.

Hurwitz, S. (1992). *Lilith: The first Eve, historical and psychological aspects of the dark feminine.* Einsiedeln, Switzerland: Daimon Verlag.

Huynen, J. (1994). *L'enigme des Vierges noires.* Chartres: Deuxieme Ed.

Jacobi, J. (1967). *The way of individuation.* New York: Harcourt, Brace, World.

Jacoby, M. (1999). *Jungian psychotherapy and contemporary infant research: Basic patterns of emotional exchange.* New York: Routledge.

Jaffe, A. (1989). *Was C. G. Jung a mystic?* Einsiedeln, Switzerland: Daimon Verlag.

Jaffe, L. W. (1990). *Liberating the heart: Spirituality and Jungian psychology.* Toronto: Inner City Books.

John of the Cross. (1991). *The collected works of St. John of the Cross* (K. Kavanaugh, & O. Rodriguez, Trans.). Washington, DC: Institute of Carmelite Studies.

Johnson, E. (1992). *She who is: The mystery of God in feminist theological discourse.* New York: Crossroad Publishing Company.

Johnson, R. A., & Ruhl, J. M. (1998). *Balancing heaven and earth.* San Francisco: Harper San Francisco.

Jung, C. G. (1933). *Modern man in search of a soul* (W.S. Dell and C. F. Baynes, Trans.). New York: Harcourt, Brace & World.

Jung, C. G. (1953a). *C. G. Jung Letters, vol. II, 1951- 1961* (G. Adler and A. Jaffe, Eds.). Princeton, NJ: Princeton University Press.

Jung, C. G. (1953b). *The structure and dynamics of the psyche: Collected works, Vol. 8* (R. F. C. Hull, Trans.). Princeton, New Jersey: Princeton University Press.

Jung, C. G. (1954a). *The practice of psychotherapy: Essays on the psychology of the transference and other subjects: Collected works, vol. 14.* Princeton, NJ: Princeton University Press.

Jung, C. G. (1954b). *The practice of psychotherapy: Collected works, vol. 16* (R. F. C. Hull, Trans.). Princeton, NJ: Princeton University Press.

Jung, C. G. (1954c). *The development of personality: Collected works, vol. 17* (R. F. C. Hull, Trans.). Princeton, NJ: Princeton University Press.

Jung, C. G. (1955). *The symbolic life: Collected works, vol. 18.* R. F. C. Hull, trans. Princeton, New Jersey: Princeton University Press.

Jung, C. G. (1959a). *Aion: Collected works, vol. 9/2* (R. F. C. Hull, Trans.). Princeton, NJ: Princeton University Press.

Jung, C. G. (1959b). *Civilization in transition: Collected works, vol. 10.* (R. F. C. Hull, Trans.). Princeton, NJ: Princeton University Press.

Jung, C. G. (1963a). *Memories, dreams, reflections* (A. Jaffe, Trans.) New York: Vintage Books.

Jung, C. G. (1963b). *Mysterium coniunctionis: An inquiry into the separation and synthesis of psychic opposites in alchemy.* Princeton, NJ: Princeton University Press.

Jung, C. G. (1966). *Two essays on analytical psychology: Collected works, vol. 7* (R. F. C. Hull, Trans.). Princeton, NJ: Princeton University Press.

Jung, C. G. (1967a). *Alchemical studies: Collected works, vol. 13.* Princeton, NJ: Princeton University Press.

Jung, C. G. (1967b). *Symbols of transformation: Collected works, vol. 5.* (R. F. C. Hull, Trans.). Princeton, NJ: Princeton University Press.

Jung, C. G. (1968). *Psychology and alchemy: Collected works, vol. 12* (R. F. C. Hull, Trans.). Princeton, NJ: Princeton University Press.

Jung, C. G. (1969a). *Psychology and religion, west and east: Collected works, vol. 11.* Hull, R. F. C., trans. Princeton, New Jersey: Princeton University Press.

Jung, C. G. (1969b). *The archetypes and the collective unconscious: Collected works, vol. 9/1.* (R. F. C. Hull, Trans.). Princeton, NJ: Princeton University Press.

Jung, C. G. (1971). *Psychological types: Collected works, vol. 6.* (R. F. C. Hull, Trans.). Princeton, NJ: Princeton University Press.

Jung, C. G. (1973). *Letters: vol. 1, 1906–1950* (G. Adler and A. Jaffe, Eds.; R. F. C. Hull, Trans.). Princeton, NJ: Princeton University Press.

Jung, C. G. (1988). *Nietzsche's Zarathustra: Notes of the seminar given in 1934–1939.* Bollinger Series XCIX. Princeton, NJ: Princeton University Press.

Jung, C. G. (2009). *The red book* (Sonu Shamdasani, Ed.). New York: W. W. Norton & Company.

Kamerling, J. (2003). Lilth. In F. Gustafson, (Ed.), *The moonlit path: Reflection on the dark feminine* (pp. 97-110). Berwick, ME: Nicolas-Hays, Inc.

Kavanaugh, K. (1997). *Eros and the experience of God.* (Video Lecture). Washington, DC: ICS Publications.

Kavanaugh, K. (2000). *God speaks in the night.* Washington, DC: ICS Publications.

Koltuv, B. B. (1986). *The book of Lilith.* York Beach, ME: Nicolas-Hays, Inc.

Kornfield, J. (1993). *A path with heart.* New York: Bantam Books.

Kornfield, J. (2000). *After the ecstasy, the laundry.* New York: Bantam Books.

Lao, T. (2007). *Tao te ching* (Stephen Adliss, Trans.). Boston: Shambhala Publications.

Labouvie-Vief, G. (1994). *Psyche and Eros: Mind and gender in the life course.* New York: Cambridge University Press.

Lawrence, D. H. (1973). *The complete poems of D. H. Lawrence.* New York: Penguin Books.

Leonard, L. S. (1993). *Meeting the madwoman: Empowering the feminine spirit: Breaking through fear and destructive patterns to a balanced and creative life.* New York: Bantam Books.

Levine, B. H. (1991). *Your body believes every word you say.* Lower Lake, CA: Aslan Publishing.

Lopez-Pedraza, R. (2000). *Dionysus in exile: On the repression of the body and emotion.* Wilmette, IL: Chiron Publications.

Luke, H. M. (1995). *The way of woman: Awakening the perennial feminine.* New York: Bantam Doubleday Dell Publishing Group, Inc.

Luke, H. M. (1985). *Woman earth and spirit.* New York: Crossroad.

Luke, H. M. (1993). *Dark wood to white rose: Journey and transformation in Dante's Divine Comedy.* New York: Parabola.

Marlan, S. (Ed.). (1997). *Fire in the stone: The alchemy of desire.* Wilmette, IL: Chiron Publications.

Marlan, S. (2005). *The black sun: The alchemy and art of darkness.* College Station, TX: Texas A&M University Press.

Matthews, C. (2001). *Sophia goddess of wisdom: Bride of God.* Wheaton, IL: Quest Books.

Matthews, C. (1992). *Sophia goddess of wisdom: The divine feminine from black goddess to world soul.* London: Aquarian Press.

Meador, B. D. (1992). *Uncursing the dark: Treasures from the underworld.* Wilmette, IL: Chiron Publications.

Meador, B. D. (2000). *Inanna lady of largest heart: Poems of the Sumerian high priestess Enheduanna.* Austin, TX: University of Texas Press.

Meier, C.A. (Ed.). (2001). *Atom and archetype: The Pauli-Jung letters 1932–1958.* Princeton, NJ: Princeton University Press.

Meyer, M. (Trans.). (1992). *The gospel of Thomas: The hidden sayings of Jesus.* New York: Harper San Francisco.

Miller, M. (1997). *Chartres cathedral.* New York: Riverside Book Co.

Moon, B. (1997). *An encyclopedia of archetypal symbolism.* Boston: Shambhala Publications, Inc.

Mueller, L. (1996). Why we tell stories. In Mueller, L., *Alive together: New and selected poems* (pp. 150-151).

Nepo, M. (1994). *Acre of light: Living with cancer.* New York: Ithaca House.

Neumann, E. (1963). *The great mother.* Princeton, NJ: Princeton University Press.

Neumann, E. (1970). *The origins and history of consciousness.* Princeton, NJ: Princeton/Bollingen Paperback.

O'Donohue, J. (2008). *To bless the space between us: A book of blessings.* New York: Doubleday.

Oman, M. (1997). *Prayers for healing: 365 blessings, poems, and meditations from around the world.* Berkeley: Conari Press.

O'Murchu, D. (2000). *Our world in transition: Making sense of a changing world.* New York: Crossroad Publishing Company.

O'Murchu, D. (1997). *Quantum theology: Spiritual implications of the new physics.* New York: Crossroad Publishing Company.

O'Murchu, D. (2004). *Quantum theology: Spiritual implications of the new physics—Revised and updated edition with reflective questions.* New York: Crossroad Publishing Company.

O'Murchu, D. (2007). *The transformation of desire.* Maryknoll, NY: Orbis Books.

O'Murchu, D. (2008). *Ancestral grace: Meeting God in our human story.* Maryknoll, NY: Orbis Books.

O'Murchu, D. (2010). *Adult faith: Growing in wisdom and understanding.* Maryknoll, NY: Orbis Books.

O'Murchu, D. (2012). *In the beginning was the spirit: Science, religion, and indigenous spirituality.* Maryknoll, NY: Orbis Books.

O'Murchu, D. (2016). *Religious life in the 21st century.* Maryknoll, NY: Orbis Books.

Otto, R. (1923). *The idea of the holy.* London: Oxford University Press.

Pagels, E. (1979). *The gnostic gospels.* New York: Vintage Books.

Parks, F. M. (2013). Maid Maleen, an image of feminine wholeness. In Stein, M. & Corbett, L. (Eds.), *Psyche's stories: Modern Jungian interpretations of fairy tales, vol. 1* (pp. 1-13). Wilmette, IL.: Chiron Publications.

Paris, R. (1988). *Camille Claudel.* Washington, DC: National Museum of Women in the Arts.

Perera, S. B. (1981). *Descent to the goddess: A way of initiation for women.* Toronto: Inner City Books.

Pick, J. (Ed.). (1953). *A Hopkins reader.* New York: Double Day.

Powers, J. (1989). *Selected poetry of Jessica Powers* (R. Siegfried, & R. Morneau, Eds.). Kansas City, MO: Sheed and Ward.

Rahner, K. (1973). *Theological investigations X* (D. Burke, Trans.). New York: The Seabury Press.

Reeves, P. M. (1999). *Women's intuition: Unlocking the wisdom of the body.* Berkeley, CA: Conari Press.

Rilke, R. M. (1967). *Duino elegies.* (J.B. Leishman and Stephen Spender, Trans.). New York: Norton Press.

Rilke, R. M. (1982). *The selected poetry of Rainer Maria Rilke.* New York: Vintage International Books.

Rilke, R. M. (1996). *Rilke's book of hours: Love poems to God* (A. Banows, & J. Macy, Trans.). New York: Berkley Publishing.

Richo, D. (2001). *Mary within: A Jungian contemplation of her titles and powers.* New York: Crossroad Publishing Company.

Robinson, J. M. (Ed.). (1988). *The Nag Hammadi library in English* (New York: Harper San Francisco.

Rothenberg, R. (2001). *The jewel in the wound.* Wilmette, IL: Chiron Publications.

Ryley, N. (Ed.). (1998). *The forsaken garden: Four conversations on the deep meaning of environmental illness–Interviews with Laurens van der Post, Marion Woodman, Ross Woodman, and Thomas Berry.* Wheaton, IL: Quest Books.

Samuels, A., Shorter, B., & Plaut, F. (1986). *A critical dictionary of Jungian analysis.* New York: Routledge and Kegan Paul.

Sanford, J. A. (1999). *Mystical Christianity: A psychological commentary on the gospel of John.* New York: The Crossroad Publishing Company.

Sardello, R. (1992). *Facing the world with soul: The reimagination of modern life.* Hudson, NY: Lindisfarne Press.

Schaup, S. (1997). *Sophia: Aspects of the divine feminine, past and present.* York Beach, ME: Nicolas-Hays, Inc.

Sidoli, M. (2000). *When the body speaks: The archetypes in the body.* London: Routledge.

Singer, J. (1983). *The power of love to transform our lives and our world.* York Beach, ME: Nicolas-Hays, Inc.

Singer, J. (1988). *A gnostic book of hours: Keys to inner wisdom.* San Francisco: Harper.

Singer, J. (1998). *Modern woman in search of soul: A Jungian guide to the visible and invisible world.* York Beach, ME: Nicolas-Hays, Inc.

Singer, J. (1990). *Seeing through the visible world: Jung, gnosis, and chaos.* New York: Harper Collins Publishers.

Singer, J. (1999). *Knowledge of the heart.* Boston: Element Books, Ltd.

Stade, G. (2003). *The collected poems of Emily Dickinson.* New York: Barnes & Noble Books.

Starbird, M. (1998). *The goddess in the gospels.* Santa Fe, NM: Bear & Company Publishing.

Tarnas, R. (1991). *The passion of the western mind.* New York: Harmony Books.

Taylor, J. (1998). *The living labyrinth: Exploring universal themes in myths, dreams, and the symbolism of waking life.* Mahwah, NJ: Paulist Press.

Teresa of Avila. (1976). *The collected works of St. Teresa of Avila, vol. 1.* (K. Kavanaugh, & O. Rodriguez, Trans.). Washington, DC: Institute of Carmelite Studies.

Teresa of Avila. (1980). *The collected works of St. Teresa of Avila, vol. 2.* (K. Kavanaugh, & O. Rodriguez, Trans.). Washington, DC: Institute of Carmelite Studies.

Tillich, P. (1948). *The shaking of the foundations.* New York: Charles Scribner's Sons.

Turner, D. (1995). *The darkness of God: Negativity in Christian mysticism.* New York: Cambridge University Press.

Ulanov, A. B. (1971). *The feminine in Jungian psychology and in Christian theology.* Evanston, IL: Northwestern University Press.

Ulanov, A. B. (2001). *Finding space: Winnicott, God, and psychic reality.* Louisville: Westminster John Knox Press.

Ulanov, A. B. (2007). *The unshuttered heart: Opening to aliveness/deadness in the self.* Nashville, TN: Abingdon Press.

Ulanov, A. B. (2014). *Knots and their untying: Essays on psychological dilemmas.* New Orleans, LA: Spring Journal, Inc.

Underhill, E. (1961). *Mysticism.* New York: E. P. Dutton & Co.

Von Franz, M. (1972). *Problems of the feminine in fairytales.* Dallas, TX: Spring Publications, Inc.

Von Franz, M. (1980a). *Alchemy: An introduction to the symbolism and the psychology.* Toronto: Inner City Books.

Von Franz, M. (1980b). *A psychological interpretation of the golden ass of Apuleius.* Irving, TX: Spring Publications, Inc.

Von Franz, M. (1995). *Creation myths.* Boston: Shambhala Publications.

Von Franz, M. (1999a). *Archetypal dimensions of the psyche.* Boston: Shambhala Publications.

Von Franz, M. (1999b). *The cat: A tale of feminine redemption.* Toronto: Inner City Books.

Von Franz, M., & Hillman, J. (1971). *Lectures on Jung's typology: The inferior function* (Irving, TX: Spring Publications, Inc.

Wallace, E. (1990). *A queen's quest: Pilgrimage for individuation.* Santa Fe, NM: Bear Press.

Wansbrough, H. (Ed.). (1985). *The new Jerusalem bible.* New York: Bantam Doubleday Dell Publishing Group, Inc.

Welch, J. (1990). *When gods die: An introduction to St. John of the Cross.* New York: Paulist Press.

Whitmont, E. (1984). *Return of the goddess.* New York: The Crossroad Publishing Company.

Williamson, M. (2004). *The gift of change: Spiritual guidance for a radical new life.* San Francisco: Harper.

Woodman, M. (1982). *Addiction to perfection: The still unravished bride.* Toronto: Inner City Books.

Woodman, M. (1985). *The pregnant virgin.* Toronto: Inner City Books.

Woodman, M. (1992). *Leaving my father's house: A journey to conscious femininity.* Boston: Shambhala Publications.

Woodman, M. (1993). *Conscious femininity.* Toronto: Inner City Books.

Woodman, M. (1998). *The maiden king: The reunion of masculine and feminine.* New York: Henry Holt and Company.

Woodman, M., & Dickson, E. (1996). *Dancing in the flames: The dark goddess transformation of consciousness.* Boston: Shambhala Publications, Inc.

CPSIA information can be obtained
at www.ICGtesting.com
Printed in the USA
BVHW070533290220
573603BV00001B/4

9 781630 517809